We ask only to be reassured
About the noises in the cellar
And the window that should not have been opened
— T.S. Eliot

"The dark dangerous forest is still there, my friends. Beyond the space of the astronauts and the astronomers, beyond the dark, tangled regions of Freudian and Jungian psychiatry, beyond the dubious psi-realms of Dr. Rhine, beyond the areas policed by the commissars and priests and motivations-research men, far, far beyond the mad, beat, half-hysterical laughter... the utterly unknown still is and the eerie and ghostly lurk, as much wrapped in mystery as ever."
— Fritz Leiber

"As a young man I was scornful about the supernatural but as I have got older, the sharp line that divided the credible from the incredible has tended to blur; I am aware that the whole world is slightly incredible"
— Colin Wilson

"Broad daylight does not encourage the apprehension of horror."
— Guy de Maupassant

"I wish to confound all these people, to create a work of art of a supernatural realism and of a spiritualist naturalism. I wish to prove... that nothing is explained in the mysteries which surround us."
— Joris-Karl Huysmans

"Anyone who has experienced a strange episode in their life that defies all present scientific knowledge can appreciate the limits of human knowledge. There's nothing like such an event to make you keenly aware of how little we truly know and understand."
— Steven Symes

"Yet, despite all, it is a difficult thing to admit the existence of ghosts in a coldly factual world. One's very instincts rebel at the admission of such maddening possibility. For, once the initial step is made into the supernatural, there is no turning back, no knowing where the strange road leads except that it is quite unknown and quite terrible."
— Richard Matheson

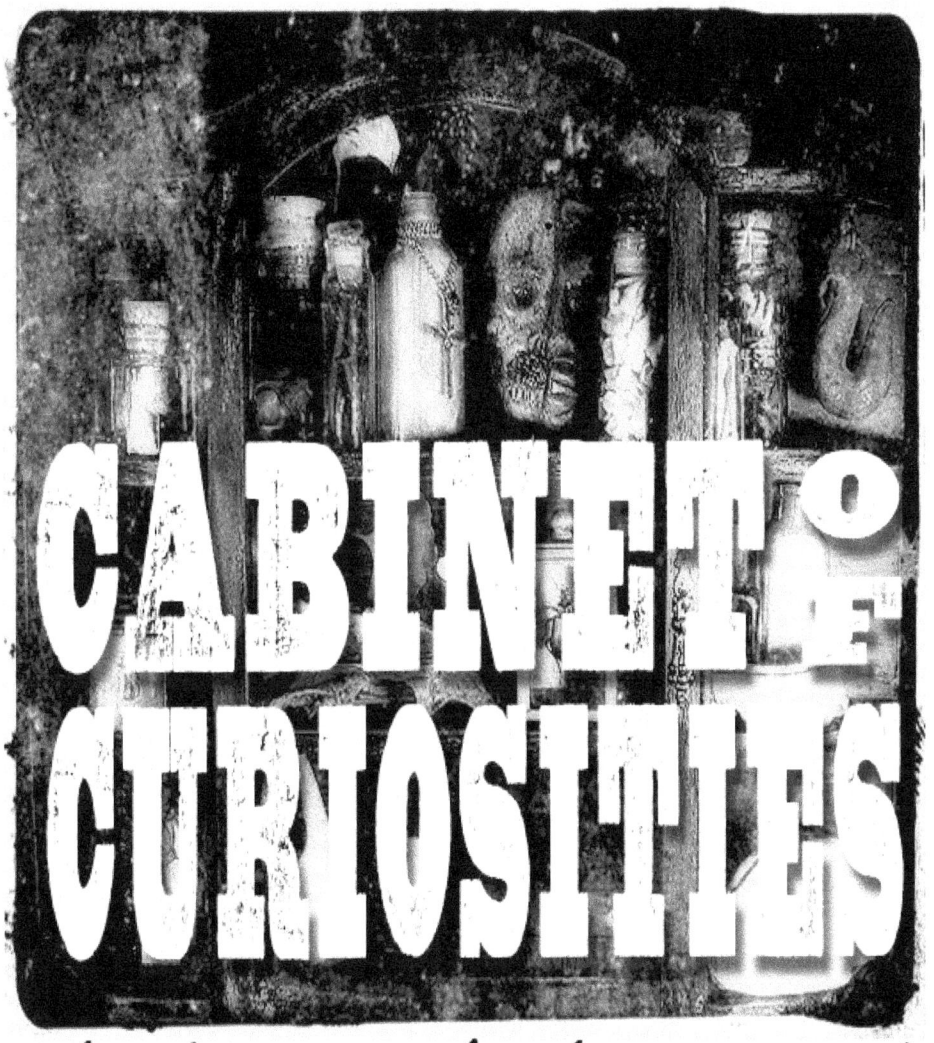

CABINET OF CURIOSITIES

The History of the Supernatural in 20 Objects

TROY TAYLOR

This book is dedicated to the women in my life who manage to keep this often runaway train from careening wildly off the tracks. You all know who you are. And to the sun and the moon and the tiny little satellite who has managed to somehow put me into her orbit.

© Copyright 2013 by Troy Taylor & Apartment 42 Productions
All Rights Reserved, including the right to copy or reproduce this book, or portions thereof, in any form, without express permission from the author and publisher

Original Cover Artwork Designed by
© Copyright 2013 by April Slaughter & Troy Taylor
Back Cover Author's Photo by Janet Morris

This Book is Published By:
Whitechapel Press
A Division of Apartment 42 Productions
Decatur, Illinois 1-888-GHOSTLY
Visit us on the internet at http: www.whitechapelpress.com

First Edition - December 2013
ISBN: 1-892523-88-4

Printed in the United States of America

INTRODUCTION

During the Renaissance, cabinets of curiosities were collections of marvels and unusual objects that symbolized concepts that were not yet clearly defined. Modern people would categorize the books, writings and artifacts found in these cabinets, which were often large rooms, instead of simple pieces of furniture, as pieces of natural history, geology, archaeology, religious or historic relics, art and sometimes outright bits of humbug, like petrified mermaid carcasses and fish with fur. But no matter what the cabinets contained, they were collections of the unexplained. Everyone loves a mystery. Man has always loved to question, to wonder and to be baffled by things that he cannot understand. Cabinets of curiosities were all the rage among European rulers, aristocrats, scientists, wealthy merchants and anyone else who could afford them. They are considered to be an ancestor of the modern museum.

By the time this book ends up in the hands of readers, I will have been writing about ghosts and the supernatural for well over twenty years. During that time, I have researched literally thousands of stories of hauntings, strange events and weird happenings and have collected a number of oddities that tell their own strange stories.

Those items led to the creation of a sort-of "cabinet of curiosities" of my own. This worn and battered old cabinet, taken from the kitchen of my great aunt's abandoned home a long time ago, has been gathering dust for years. It's a little different from the elaborate cabinets that intrigued people in centuries past. There are no fossils there, no badly preserved bodies of mysterious animals - no, my cabinet is different, although it's just as puzzling as those of long ago. My cabinet contains records and remnants of the supernatural - a curious collection of objects both literal and figurative ones that tell the story of the occult in our modern world. The record begins with the rise in interest in what lay beyond the grave in nineteenth-century America and continues to this day with some of the most perplexing and terrifying cases in recent times.

In the pages ahead, I invite you to examine the twenty objects that I present. Through the stories of these objects, you'll enter the lives of the men and women who came into contact with them, with the ghosts who were attached to them, and with the bizarre events that made these objects famous. Some items will be familiar for their importance: among them the Ouija board through which a ghost named Patience Worth dictated best-selling novels to a St. Louis housewife; the Winchester rifle that created the wealth by which a cursed widow built a haven for ghosts, and an object used in a psychical investigation that helped chronicle the most famous haunted house in history. Others will be largely unknown and might not even constitute material that most historians would call important: a spirit trumpet, a magic cabinet, a children's picture book, a ruler, a brick, a telephone, and a child's leather ball.

But each of them tells a story, and in this book, the twenty objects that I have chosen will offer a unique look at how history has been shaped by the supernatural. In turn, I'll also reveal how each of these objects marked a pivotal moment in the creation of what we see as the field of modern ghost research. Every one of them represents a vivid event, story or case in supernatural history - some of them tragic, some of them horrific and some of them simply unexplainable.

So, come and take a look inside my cabinet of curiosities. Brush the dust off the artifacts on the shelves. Just be careful when you do. If you look too closely, there's a good chance that you'll never see the bizarre world of the supernatural in the same way again.

Troy Taylor
Holidays 2013

SPIRIT TRUMPET
The Rise of the Dead in the Nineteenth Century

Historians are often fond of remarking that America has, throughout its relatively short history, been a nation of extremes. And it goes without saying that the rise of the Spiritualist movement in the nineteenth century was not America's first flirtation with the supernatural. Ghost stories have been a part of the nation's fabric since the first settlers arrived on our shores. In the latter years of the seventeenth century, witch-hunt fervor swept the colonies, leading to the tragic events that occurred in Salem, Massachusetts. The madness that arose there drained America of its lust for the supernatural for many years to come. There was no organized interest in the occult, and while many people still quietly practiced divination and folk magic, any serious scientific interest in alchemy simply disappeared.

As time marched into the latter years of the eighteenth century, Americans were preoccupied with the War for Independence, and yet tales of ghosts and hauntings took root in the popular culture. In the early 1800s, the shocking story of the Bell Witch in Tennessee spread throughout the young nation, growing and spreading largely thanks to the legendary involvement of Andrew Jackson, who later became president of the United States.

But if there was anything that directly led to the rise of Spiritualism in America, it was the public's fascination with "mesmerism" and "hypnotic trances," as well as the religious excitement that swept the nation like wildfire in the 1820s and 1830s.

Mesmerism was named for the man who developed it, Franz Anton Mesmer, who was born in Germany in 1734 and later earned a medical degree from the

University of Vienna. He theorized that a magnetic fluid surrounds or links all things and beings on earth and in the heavens, and that the "universal fluid" in the human body could be influenced to treat illnesses. Mesmer called his new method "animal magnetism" and he began to attract a huge following in Paris. In 1773, he produced his first cure when he applied magnetic plates to a patient's limbs. In 1778, he purportedly cured a blind girl, which won him even greater fame. More claims of healings followed his development of a *baquet*, a large circular tub filled with water that contained "magnetic" substances. Iron rods with magical properties from the water were applied to the patient's body in order to affect a cure.

There was sufficient controversy around these methods that an official French scientific commission, led by none other than Benjamin Franklin, was asked to investigate Mesmer's claims. According to the group, they could find no evidence of this mysterious physical force, or "magnetic fluid." Franklin chalked up the successful healings to the patients' imaginations. As a result, public interest declined and Mesmer was branded a fraud. But in 1823, a French doctor, Alexander Bertrand, became interested in Mesmer's work and a renewed interest in "animal magnetism" emerged.

While most early experiments took place in Europe, it was discovered that what were later called "hypnotic trances" were the result of the power of suggestion. Franklin had not been too far off the mark. Most of traditional science and medicine rejected "mesmerism," as it began to be called. No one thought to consider how mesmerism was affecting human minds. Those who did delve into it, though, believed they had discovered something unusual. While many patients were in a trance, they demonstrated psychic abilities that they did not ordinarily have, such as telepathy, seeing objects when their eyes were closed, clairvoyant abilities, speaking in voices not their own, and even precognition of future events.

Mesmerism arrived in America at a perfect time. During the first half of the nineteenth century, Americans were exploring new religious and spiritual ideas. Public demonstrations of mesmerism became popular in the 1830s and 1840s. There were as many as thirty different mesmerists on the lecture circuit in New England at one time. In Boston alone, at least two hundred men practiced the trade.

In one widely reported experiment of the time, a blind girl was able to "psychically discern" the contents of sealed envelopes while she was in a trance. Skeptics blasted the demonstration as a fraud. Even if the effects of mesmerism were genuine, one of their valid criticisms asked, what caused enhanced psychical abilities to occur while she was in her trance?

Nathaniel Hawthorne, one of the most noted writers of the time, was fascinated with mesmerism. In his 1851 book, *The House of Seven Gables*, a mesmerist fails to find a missing paper. He employs his ability to control a young woman until he causes her to die. Edgar Allan Poe also used mesmerism in the middle 1840s as a plot device in one of his short stories, "Mesmeric Revelation," in which a character wants to live forever. The story caused a storm of controversy, for if mesmerism could accomplish immortality, it was equal to blasphemy. Although Poe, after seeing a demonstration of mesmerism, wrote the story as fiction, there were many people who worried that such a possibility might occur. In 1837, Ralph Waldo Emerson wrote that he feared someone - possibly even himself - might be mesmerized against his will.

As with most aspects of the unexplained, Mesmerism lured in audiences by provoking their curiosity, but it also frightened them at the same time. Some called it the work of the Devil. To their credit, mesmerists quickly learned to answer their critics and detractors and corrected the misconceptions about their work.

The trance state when one was mesmerized was embraced by Spiritualists at the close of the 1840s and became an important part of the movement's growth. Although Mesmer had never shown any interest in the use of his technique for psychical purposes, mediums claimed that when they were in a state of trance, they could communicate with the spirits of the departed. At Spiritualist séances throughout the nineteenth century, it became customary for participants to join hands while the medium entered into a trance and brought forth messages from the spirit world.

The trance state dated back to ancient times, when it was widely used by oracles and shamans. It found a new home in America, where it was embraced by Spiritualist mediums who insisted that it made it possible for them to communicate with the dead. One of the first to be known as a trance medium was Mrs. W.B. Hayden of Boston. In 1852, she utilized metal disks to induce a trance state that allowed her to provide highly accurate information for her audiences about their deceased loved ones.

Ultimately, what was first called animal magnetism, then mesmerism, evolved into what we today call hypnotism. While the mesmeric movement was folded into Spiritualism, hypnosis eventually became an accepted medical technique.

Altered states of consciousness - like trances - have played an important role in the paranormal. The rapid growth of Spiritualism in the nineteenth century owed a great debt to mesmerism. The trance state that mediums used to contact the dead was a form of self-induced hypnosis that was said to greatly enhance the abilities that the medium already possessed.

There were many wide-ranging social changes in the first half of the nineteenth century, and the supernatural came to play a significant role in what Americans believed. Long-established Christian denominations now faced the threat of emerging religious sects and utopian social movements as Americans looked for alternative ways to express their spirituality.

There was also a steady stream of immigrants arriving on American shores. The new land, with its wide-open spaces, offered them unprecedented opportunity. These immigrants brought with them their own religious and cultural beliefs. In addition, many people were starting to move westward from the cities and towns that crowded the Atlantic coastline. They began seeking land in the frontiers of western New York, Ohio and beyond. By 1800, the nation's population had increased to five million - one million more than in 1790. In 1803, the Louisiana Purchase added more than 830,000 square miles to the country.

In 1825, the Erie Canal opened in western New York and provided a direct east-west water route across the state from Albany to Buffalo. This new method of transportation meant improved services, more commerce and growing cities and towns. One of the thriving communities was Rochester, which would become known, thanks to its mills, as the Flour City. It would also be the center of a region that saw great social changes, including Spiritualism, the abolitionist movement, the women's movement and the birth of new religious sects like the Mormons and the Seventh-Day Adventists.

As towns became populated, the clergy followed. Traveling preachers found fertile territory in which to win converts to evangelical Christianity in the newly settled communities. These were ministers who preached fire and brimstone, hell and damnation and the end of days. Thus was born the country's "Second Great Religious Awakening." Eventually, so many fiery preachers flocked to the region that it seemed there was no one left to convert, and western New York became known as the "burned-over region."

The mesmerists were also out and about on the lecture circuit in the 1830s and 1840s. They were immensely popular with the public, if less so with scientists. They were the period's version of the self-help movement, which in those days meant creating a completely fresh and new perspective on life. The mesmerists claimed that they could restore a deeper sense of one's balance and an understanding between living people and the unseen spirit world. Mesmerism, is its efforts to restore "health and virtue," was not unlike the religious revival sweeping America at the time.

Christianity had long taught that the way to personal betterment was through God. America's religious teachings had always raised mistrust about the extent to which people could improve themselves unless they did so through the intervention of the Holy Spirit. The revivalists offered the opportunity to be "born again" through fundamentalist Christianity, maintaining that people could take responsibility for seeking their own deliverance from sin and damnation, unlike Puritan or Calvinist beliefs of the preceding era. Of course, anything that strayed from the narrow fundamentalist belief system, such as the occult or the supernatural, was labeled the work of the Devil.

In upstate New York at this time, a young man named Joseph Smith founded a new religious faith called Mormonism, or the Church of Jesus Christ of Latter-Day Saints. Smith said that he had received his instructions from an angel named Moroni. Other new belief systems, like the Seventh-Day Adventists and the Shakers, also took root. The strict belief in the Christian God had been replaced by Transcendentalism, Unitarianism and Universalism, all liberal ways of seeking spirituality.

It was a time of religious fervor and at the same time, scientists were making new discoveries about the uses of electricity and magnetism. Mesmerism could fit comfortably with any of the new belief systems, yet it was never associated with any particular religious denomination. Mesmerists believed they could bridge the traditional divide between science and religion. Mystical illumination and ecstatic revelations were no longer dismissed as fanciful irrationalities. Mesmerism found itself welcomed by many of the new sects because it provided a scientific underpinning for spiritual beliefs. For those who were scientifically inclined, mesmerism was evidence that the abilities of the mind could go beyond the limits of the physical brain.

It wasn't long before the Spiritualist movement - using the trances and abilities of the mind espoused by believers in mesmerism - took the entire nation by storm.

According to contemporary reports, the winter of 1847-1848 was one of the worst in memory in western New York. Bitter wind, frigid temperatures and snow battered the region. On December 11, 1847, two weeks before Christmas, John and Margaret Fox and their two youngest daughters moved into a rented cottage in the village of Hydesville. The village, about twenty miles west of Rochester, consisted of a small group of homes, along with several mills and stores. It was typical of other small farming communities scattered across the countryside.

It would be in this home where the Spiritualist movement was born. Legend holds that the house was haunted before the Fox family came to live there. Those in the neighborhood often referred to it as "the spook house." The story sprang from a time between 1843 and 1844, when a couple named Bell occupied the cottage. In the last few months of their occupancy, a young local woman named

Lucretia Pulver handled the household chores. She acted as a maid of all work, cooking and cleaning for the Bells.

One day, a peddler came to the door. He brought with him a case of merchandise consisting of kitchen items, sewing supplies and other useful items for the home. He stayed with the family for several days and it has been suggested that perhaps he enjoyed a closer than was proper relationship with Mrs. Bell. It was during this time that Lucretia found herself dismissed from her position. No explanation was ever given and apparently, there were no hard feelings about her dismissal. Before she left the house, Lucretia purchased a small kitchen knife from the peddler's selection. She left him instructions to deliver the knife to her father's farm, but it never arrived.

Barely a week later, Lucretia was surprised to find that Mrs. Bell had changed her mind and was again requesting her services. Thankful to have her job back, she reported for duty the next morning. The peddler who had been staying with the family had departed and a number of things he carried in his case were now in the possession of Mrs. Bell. Lucretia assumed that Mrs. Bell must have bought the items before the peddler left for parts unknown. Nothing seemed to be out of the ordinary around the house, but that would soon change.

Shortly after returning to the house, Lucretia began to notice strange things had begun to occur. Unaccountable noises, like knocking and tapping, came from the room that the peddler had occupied. On several occasions, she also heard footsteps pacing through the house and then descending the stairs to the cellar. Not surprisingly, Lucretia began to feel nervous when she was left alone in the house. She would often send for her brother, or a friend, to come and stay with her and usually, the strange sounds would cease. However, on one occasion, they continued for hours and scared Lucretia's brother so badly that he left the place and refused to return.

One afternoon, while she was in the cellar fetching potatoes for the evening meal, Lucretia stumbled and fell over a patch of freshly turned dirt. Mr. Bell explained that the mound of dirt had been dumped there to cover up rat holes.

A short time later, the Bells moved out and the Weakman family moved in, along with a relative, a Mrs. Lafe. Their stay would prove to be a short one. One day, Mrs. Lafe entered the kitchen and as she closed the door behind her, she spotted the apparition of a man in a black frock coat standing across the room. She screamed in terror and the figure vanished. Soon, they all began to hear rappings and footsteps in the house. The family would sometimes come during the daylight hours, but mostly they were heard at night, bothering everyone as they tried to sleep. Finally, the odd happenings proved to be too much for them and they abandoned the place.

Then, in December 1848, the Fox family moved into the house. John Fox was a blacksmith. He and his wife, Margaret, were both past fifty. The two children that lived with them, Maggie, fourteen, and Kate, twelve, were pretty girls with dark hair and eyes. The other Fox children were older and lived on their own. One son, John, was a blacksmith and farmer, like his father. Another son, David, resided nearby with his family. Of the three elder daughters, one of them, Leah, was a piano teacher who lived in Rochester, the nearest large city in western New York. The Foxes were a close family. Mrs. Fox was a friendly and caring woman who was well-liked by those who knew her. Both the elder Foxes attended the local Methodist church and prayed daily. Their lives were typical of struggling rural Americans in the first half of the nineteenth century.

When the family moved into the Hydesville cottage, their stay was meant to be only temporary. John Fox had purchased some land nearby where he planned to build a home. He moved his family into the cottage until the new house could be completed. Their stay would turn out to be an eventful one.

Within days of moving in, the noises began. Banging and rattling sounds pounded loudly each night, jolting them all from their sleep. At first, John Fox thought they were merely the sounds of an unfamiliar dwelling, amplified by active imaginations. Soon, however, things took a sinister turn. Kate woke up screaming one night, saying that a cold hand had touched her on the face. Margaret insisted that rough, invisible fists had pulled the blankets from her bed. Mrs. Fox swore that she had heard disembodied footsteps walking through the house and then going down the wooden steps into the dank cellar.

Fox was perplexed. He tried walking about the house, searching for squeaks in the floorboards and along the walls. He tested the windows and doors to see if vibrations in the frames might account for the sounds. He could find no explanation for the weird noises. Mrs. Fox admitted that she was upset by the inexplicable sounds. She concluded that some "unhappy restless spirit" was haunting the place.

On the evening of March 31, John Fox began his almost nightly ritual of investigating the house for the source of the sounds. The tapping had begun with the setting of the sun and although he searched the place over and over again, he was no closer to a solution. Then, Kate began to realize that whenever her father knocked on a wall or doorframe, the same number of knocks would come in reply. It was as if someone, or something, was trying to communicate with them.

Finding her nerve, Kate spoke up, addressing the unseen presence by the nickname that she and her sister had given it. "Here, Mr. Splitfoot," she called out, "Do as I do!"

She clapped her hands two times and seconds later, two knocks came in reply, seemingly from inside of the wall. Maggie then rapped on the table and the precise number of knocks came again. The activity caught the attention of the rest of the family. Mrs. Fox tried asking questions, such as the number of children she had borne. Seven raps came back. How many were still living? Six raps. Their ages? The correct number of raps came back. Each reply was eerily accurate.

Unsure of what to do, John Fox summoned several neighbors to the house to observe the phenomenon. The first was Mary Redfield, who was dismissive about the presence of a spirit. She assumed the girls were playing a prank. It was the night before April Fools Day, after all. She soon changed her mind and became frightened after she questioned the spirit and received correct answers.

One neighbor, and a former tenant in the house, William Duesler, decided to try and communicate with the source of the sounds in a more scientific manner. He assigned numbers to letters of the alphabet so that the spirit could reply not only to questions involving numbers but communicate in entire sentences. He also was able to determine the number of knocks that could be interpreted as "yes" and "no." In such a manner, he was able to determine the identity of the creator of the disturbances. The secret of the haunting came out before an assembled group of witnesses. The presence claimed that it was the spirit of a peddler who had been murdered and robbed in the house years before.

As it happened, one of the neighbors who had assembled that night was Lucretia Pulver, the Bells' former maid. She came forward with her story of finding the mound of dirt in the cellar. Things now took on a distinctly sinister tone. John Fox and William Duesler went to the area of the cellar that Lucretia described and began to dig. They gave up after they came to water. The digging would have to wait until conditions were better. When they tried again, a few months later, they dug to a depth of five feet before hitting a plank. Underneath was charcoal and quicklime, and under that was what appeared to be a small piece of bone with a few strands of hair still clinging to it. A local doctor identified the bone as a piece of a human skull. That was enough to convince the Fox family that the presence in the house was indeed the ghost of the luckless peddler.

As word of the Hydesville rappings spread, Kate and Maggie were both purported to have mediumistic powers. By November 1849, the girls were giving public performances of their skills and the Spiritualist movement was born. The mania to communicate with the dead swept the country and the Fox sisters became famous.

Over the years, the credibility of the Fox family was often called into question. As no real evidence existed to say that a peddler was killed in the house, many accused the family of making up the entire story to support their claims of the girls' supernatural powers. It may come as no surprise to the reader that the Spiritualist movement was riddled with fraud, but was the story of the murdered peddler merely a ruse to give credence to the powers of the Fox sisters?

It's possible that Maggie and Kate, had they not died years before, would have been vindicated in 1904. By that time, their former home had been deserted for some years. A group of children were playing in the abandoned house one day when the east wall of the cellar collapsed, nearly killing one of them. A man who came to their aid quickly realized the reason for the wall's collapse. It appeared to be a false partition that had been hastily and poorly constructed. Between the false brick wall and the genuine wall of the cellar were crumbling human bones and a rusted tin trunk like the ones carried by peddlers decades before.

Dead men, as they say, really do tell tales.

Soon, news of the spirit rappings attracted so much attention that hordes of uninvited visitors began showing up at the Fox home. Many of them demanded entry, numbering up to five hundred people in a single day. John Fox complained, "It caused a great deal of trouble and anxiety. I am not a believer in haunted houses or supernatural appearances." Still, Fox could not account for the noises, which not only grew worse, but were also transformed into other startling manifestations. In addition to the strange rappings, other inexplicable events began to occur, including slamming doors, shaking beds, the ghostly sounds of a struggle, and what sounded like someone being dragged down the cellar stairs. All of this caused the neighbors to gossip about the family even more. By early April, raps were heard during the day as well as at night.

The startling revelations spread quickly beyond Hydesville and attracted curiosity from both believers and skeptics. This was no mere ghost story. It seemed that the Fox sisters and an unseen entity had established a communication network that was unlike anything ever heard of before. The story touched a nerve among a population that was eager to look beyond the physical limits of everyday existence and into the mystery of death.

The local newspaper, the *Western Argus*, quickly reported the story and it wasn't long before an enterprising writer named E.E. Lewis published a pamphlet called *Report of the Mysterious Noises*. Another local writer published a booklet about the Weakman family's "unpleasant experiences" in the house. Mrs. Fox contributed her own written statement about the events: "I am not a believer in haunted houses or supernatural appearances. I am very sorry there has been so much excitement about it. It has been a great deal of trouble to us.

I cannot account for the noises; all I know is that they have been heard repeatedly as I have stated."

With their apparent ability to communicate with the spirit inhabiting their house, the young Fox sisters had tapped into the public's enthusiasm for the supernatural. Within a matter of months, what began in Hydesville spread to surrounding communities, and from there, via newspaper reports, to the large cities. There was no way to explain why this particular event so vividly captured the public's imagination. It was as if people were fascinated by the idea that two seemingly ordinary little girls could be a conduit to communication with the spirit world.

As the rappings in the Hydesville house continued, it was decided that Kate and Maggie should be sent to stay with their older sister, Leah Fish, who lived in Rochester. This may have had the opposite effect to that intended by the girls' parents, for the rapping sounds were soon to follow them to Rochester. There, in this much larger town, the Fox sisters attracted even more attention. The girls were split up, with Kate going to Auburn, New York, to live with one of her brothers. Margaret, however, was soon the center of a devoted "spirit circle," which allowed participants to come together to receive spirit communications from their dead loved ones. The circle worked out a more manageable code to communicate with the spirits: one rap indicated "no," two raps meant that the spirit was unable to answer a question, and three raps meant "yes."

Many residents of Rochester made it a nightly occurrence to gather at Leah Fish's home to witness the wonderful revelations that came to Maggie via the "rapping telegraph." It was at this time that the financial possibilities of Maggie's talents became apparent to her elder sister. Leah was twenty-three years older than Maggie. Her marriage had ended and she eked out a precarious existence for herself and her daughter by teaching music to the children of Rochester's wealthy citizens. Then the sensational news broke of Maggie and Kate's phenomenal abilities and she lost some of her students. It's not surprising that she seized on her sisters' talents as a way out of her dire circumstances. With Rochester divided between acceptance and denunciation, Leah cleverly arranged a public lecture and demonstration. The event was to be held at Corinthian Hall, the city's largest auditorium. The admission was the for the time steep price of one dollar per person.

If skeptics expected to witness a public exposure of fraud in return for their dollar, they were undoubtedly disappointed. A committee of leading citizens reported it was unable to give a natural explanation for the rappings, which each of them had heard. Disappointed, the debunkers formed a second committee. That group also declared that it had been unable to detect any trickery. A doctor had even listened to Maggie's chest and throat with a stethoscope in order to rule out ventriloquism, all to no effect.

Public opinion in Rochester soon became heated. A third committee was formed and one of its members swore publicly that if he could not discover how the raps were made, he would throw himself over Genesee Falls. Hopefully, this man's friends were able to dissuade him from such a rash course of action because the third committee had no more luck than the previous two. Though some of its members were privately certain that spirits did not cause the raps, the third committee, like the others, was forced to admit that it couldn't tell how the sounds were being accomplished. The public was becoming frenzied. Were they being deceived by a pair of little girls? Was the Devil somehow involved? On one occasion, the audience in Corinthian Hall became enraged during one of the sisters' demonstrations. Amid angry shouts and threats, a squad of police arrived to break up the meeting and was forced to escort Maggie and Leah home in order to protect them from the indignant mob.

Despite the fact that the majority of the spectators on this particular night proved they had little use for the spirit world, this meeting in Rochester was only the first ripple in a flood that soon spread far beyond the city.

Kate soon rejoined her sister and the two girls quickly became the talk of Rochester. Their fame spread, as they received publicity from throughout the state. While Kate had lived in Auburn, she had not been idle. She had also conducted séances there and had her own believers flocking to join her spirit circle. It wasn't long before news of their demonstrations was being reported in other large cities. The girls were becoming nationally known.

Kate and Maggie Fox went on to lengthy careers as professional mediums. After their initial rise to stardom in public and Spiritualist circles, the sisters began to appear in a variety of venues. The publicity surrounding them was intense. Some newspapers hailed them as frauds and others as sensations. Regardless, people flocked to see them in massive numbers, all of them gladly paying for the privilege. They toured the country, becoming hugely popular, and their séances became more elaborate, with objects moving about, spirits appearing and tables levitating. They also gave private demonstrations for those customers who could afford them.

The Age of Spiritualism had begun and was already generating money. Skeptics, to their chagrin, were powerless to curb the enthusiasm of the hundreds of thousands of people who sought contact with the spirit world. There was a sudden demand for spirit mediums, and although the Fox sisters were there first, they soon had competition that would force them to vie for a place in an increasingly crowded market. Other mediums were breaking into the scene for their share of the limelight.

The skeptics and detractors had actually done the Fox sisters a favor. Since the girls could not easily be exposed as frauds, most people concluded that they must be genuine. It also didn't hurt that Maggie and Kate were young and attractive. The sisters were embraced by such celebrities as P.T. Barnum, poet and journalist William Cullen Bryant, Harriet Beecher Stowe and newspaper editor Horace Greeley, who invited the girls to stay at his mansion. Greeley and his wife had lost four of their five children, and when he met the girls, he was still grieving over the recent death of his son. The possibility that the dead might be still accessible to the living was of great interest to him. After he witnessed the "rapping phenomena" several times, under what he described as "test conditions," he pronounced himself perplexed by what he saw. He wasted no time in writing an editorial in the *New York Tribune* titled "The Mysterious Rappings." Greeley said that he believed the raps were genuine, if inexplicable, but he initially had doubts that spirits were responsible. He later changed his mind and there is no question that Greeley's support for the Fox sisters did a great deal to boost their fame and credibility, as well as that of the entire Spiritualist movement.

P.T. Barnum, that sensational showman, read news accounts of the Fox sisters' powers and he offered to feature them at his American Museum, Barnum's home-grown American version of a cabinet of curiosities. The building was a marble showcase on Lower Broadway in New York City, decorated with blazing flags and packed with more than 600,000 living and dead curiosities --- from stuffed animals to fortune-tellers, to three-legged men and bearded ladies.

The pretty Fox sisters became quite an attraction. They were shy, barely educated and simply dressed in neat dark frocks with white collars. Barnum was sure that paying customers would clamor to sit down with the girls who talked to the dead and he was right. Regular admission to the American Museum was twenty-five cents but to converse with ghosts, people might pay a dollar --- or perhaps even more.

One of those who came to see Maggie Fox was novelist James Fenimore Cooper, author of *The Last of the Mohicans*. He had heard much about the girls and wanted to see them for himself. He also had questions that he wanted to ask about a deceased relative. When he left the museum, Cooper told his companions that every answer that Maggie had given him had been correct. He had been thinking about his sister who, fifty years ago that month, had been killed in a riding accident. Cooper decided not to return to see the girls again. He was spooked and was not afraid to admit it.

On January 6, 1853, only two months before Franklin Pierce was to be inaugurated as America's fourteenth president, tragedy struck him and his wife, Jane. The Pierces were traveling by train with their only child, eleven-year-old

Benjamin, when the car they were in became uncoupled and derailed. The train tumbled, split apart and crashed down a rocky ledge. President-elect and Mrs. Pierce suffered only minor injuries. Young Benjamin Pierce was the only fatality. His head was struck by a large rock, crushing his skull while his parents helplessly watched.

For the frail Jane Pierce, witnessing her son's death was so traumatic that she never recovered emotionally. She was inconsolable for weeks and so paralyzed by grief that she was unable to attend her husband's inauguration in March 1853. Benjamin's death cast a pall over the couple's life and over the presidency. Jane became one of the most tragic figures to ever occupy the White House. Those who knew the pretty young woman scarcely recognized the pallid, sad shadow that she became. Her life had effectively ended on the day of the railroad accident.

She remained in solitude in the White House family quarters, where she wrote lengthy letters to her dead son, whom she never stopped mourning. Servants said that they would hear her call to Benjamin, while at other times she was heard playing with her three departed children - Benjamin, a first-born son who died as an infant and a second son who died at age four.

If Jane was unbalanced, her religious beliefs could easily be blamed. She had been raised in a strict family, awash in Calvinist beliefs. Not surprisingly, she arrived at the erroneous assumption that Benjamin's fate was divine punishment for her husband's political ambitions. Franklin Pierce, himself pierced with guilt, also concluded that his son's death was God's judgment against him.

Jane Pierce ached for contact with her son's spirit. She was familiar with the Fox sisters, who were receiving national publicity as Spiritualism swept the nation. The two young mediums were invited to a séance at the White House, where they would attempt to receive spirit raps from Benjamin in the next world. Exactly what occurred during the séance is unknown, for no records exist to say what, if any, messages were given to Mrs. Pierce. The sisters never revealed any details about their White House experience, but rumors circulated that it was successful.

Even though most major American newspapers branded Spiritualism a "swindle," their criticism was largely ignored as people enthusiastically sought out mediums to contact the spirit world. Skeptics continually ranted against Spiritualism, but a huge number of Americans weren't listening. What they preferred to hear were hopeful messages from parents, aunts, uncles, cousins and children in the next world that death was not the end, that they would someday be reunited.

Notwithstanding the genuine problem of fraud and trickery in the Spiritualist movement - and there was plenty - people were anxious for a sign from a departed loved one or some message from beyond the veil. A significant change in the American attitude about death was taking place, for Spiritualism was encouraging a new mind-set. It was also polarizing public opinion. There were millions of adherents and believers who had little or no doubt that the Fox sisters were in contact with the other side. On the other hand, many were quick to debunk even the possibility of communication between the living and the dead. Traditional members of the clergy promptly denounced Spiritualism as a manifestation of evil, not unlike the first spirit raps that were heard by Mrs. Fox, and named "Mr. Splitfoot," a religious allusion to the Satan's cloven hooves, since from the Foxes' Methodist perspective, the rappings were considered evil. Conversely, others interpreted the spirit raps heard at séances as evidence of the existence of God. The bottom line was that Spiritualism could be viewed in different ways: to some it was a "devil's tool," to others it was the herald of the new age, while for many there was great uncertainty about the source and meaning of spirit raps.

There were a sufficient number of the curious at the beginning of the Spiritualist craze determined to find an answer, no matter what. Not everyone was as convinced by the sisters as Greeley, Cooper and the Pierces had been. The Fox sisters were routinely condemned by skeptics as fakes. It was claimed they produced their phenomena in a variety of ways ranging from cracking their toe, knee and ankle joints to ventriloquism to assorted mechanical devices. Despite this, no trickery was ever discovered. A number of committees and forums were created to test the powers of the sisters. Most involved posing questions to the spirits and while the replies were often inconsistent, they were accurate enough to make an impression. One test involved the girls being bound tightly about the ankles so that they could not move their feet. Even trussed up, they still managed to produce eerie rapping sounds. A committee of women checked the girls' undergarments to ensure that nothing was hidden there to produce the sounds. They found nothing. Despite the hostility shown to the sisters by the committees, most were forced to admit that they were unable to detect any fraud.

In spite of this, many of the accounts of the sisters' activities have been questionable at best. Leah, who acted in the capacity as her sisters' manager, was often accused of trying to glean personal information from the sitters at séances that would help the "spirits" give out correct answers. Maggie and Kate excelled at calling in the spirits of the famous dead. The results of this were not always impressive. When one sitter noted that Benjamin Franklin's spirit seemed to be surprisingly ungrammatical, Maggie Fox stomped away from the séance table with the reply of, "You know I never understood grammar!" As dubious as the séances may have been, though, many were convinced that the girls were genuine and business boomed.

In March 1850, yet another committee was formed to investigate the sisters. It was far from the first, but it was the first that actually managed to form an opinion as to how the girls were "creating" the rapping phenomena. The three committee members, all professors of medicine, took their task very seriously. In addition to conducting the usual examinations, the three of them sat on the floor in a soundproof room for an hour while firmly holding onto Maggie's legs. It was a rather scandalous way for three distinguished gentlemen to pass the time with a young girl in those days, but they tackled the task with great fervor. According to their report, they were rewarded for their effort. It was noted that the spirits only chose to make themselves heard when one of the investigators was forced to relax his hands a little bit from fatigue. The committee stated that, in the opinion of the investigators, Maggie's knee joints were what made the spirit rappings. It was suggested that she had the ability to snap her knees in much the same way that some people can crack their knuckles. She accomplished this, the investigators claimed, without any visible motion.

Shortly after the committee report became public, the sisters especially Leah issued immediate denials. She asserted that there had been few rappings heard during the investigation because the "friendly spirits had retired when they witnessed the harsh proceedings of the persecutors." Leah's defensiveness was understandable, since she stood to lose her share of what had become a thriving business, but what was more remarkable was the way that many prominent people sprang to Maggie's defense. The accusations were untrue, they insisted, simply because they could not be true! Everyone knew that spirits existed, so why in the world would Maggie use her knee joints to imitate their rappings?

One of the members of the controversial committee had been Dr. Charles Alfred Lee. He became so disturbed by the fact that the committee's findings were being ignored, and the Fox sisters were more in demand than ever, that he decided to do something about it. Lee conducted a search among his friends and patients until he found a man who was able to crack his joints and make noises that were even louder, and harder to detect, than Maggie's were. Then, under the sponsorship of the University of Buffalo, he set out to put an end to the nonsense of spirit rappings once and for all. Accompanied by the man with noisy joints, Lee went on a lecture tour of upper New York State, stopping to give demonstrations and to show how the Fox sisters were frauds. Unfortunately for Lee, he fell into the trap that has ensnared so many other debunkers over the years: Just because he could duplicate what was being done by the Spiritualists did not mean the original phenomena were not genuine.

Dr. Lee soon came to the realization that his lectures were having the opposite effect from what he had intended. Instead of being warned away from the tricks of false mediums, many of those in Lee's audience became converted to Spiritualism instead. The Fox sisters had apparently aroused a determination to believe that simply could not be undermined.

In 1853, the sisters demonstrated what was described as "their most powerful early manifestations." It consisted of a table levitating with Nathaniel P. Tallmadge, a U.S. Senator from New York, seated on top of it. Tallmadge also claimed that he'd received a spirit message from another notable political figure, the late John C. Calhoun, Andrew Jackson's vice president.

In 1854, it appeared that the sisters' popularity was beginning to wane. For one thing, the public wanted more exciting spirit demonstrations that mere rappings and the girls were facing competition from many other mediums, even as the skeptics continued their attacks on them. In 1857, the *Boston Courier* arranged for a committee of four Harvard professors to examine a number of mediums. Among those who accepted the invitation were Kate and Leah Fox. The group of skeptical academics was difficult to please. The committee promised to issue a report of its findings, but it never did.

Later in their lives, Kate and Maggie fell on hard times, after years of séances, public appearances, tours, tests, and scrutiny, much of it antagonistic. Those who knew the sisters felt they had been physically and emotionally drained by their grueling schedule. They simply were not sophisticated enough to understand when they were young that they were being exploited by their older sister, their promoters and their desperate audiences. Nor did they fully comprehend the depth of the hostility of the religious and scientific controversy that surrounded Spiritualism. They were the first to venture professionally into the new movement, and they paid the price for it.

Maggie abandoned mediumship for love. In Philadelphia, she met and fell in love with famed Arctic explorer Elisha Kent Kane. He was the dashing son of an aristocratic family, who did not deem Maggie worthy of marrying into their line. The couple exchanged vows and rings in the company of friends but were never legally wed. Unfortunately, the affair ended in tragedy when Kane died of heart disease at age thirty-seven in 1857. Kane's celebrity was so great that his funeral was the largest in American history, until that of Abraham Lincoln, a half-decade later. Maggie was left broken-hearted and almost penniless. She had abandoned mediumship but now had to take it up again. She considered herself a widow and began calling herself Margaretta her given name Kane, She also began drinking and her health and her mental state began to decline.

Leah had also begun practicing as a medium. She married for a third time in 1858 to Daniel Underhill, a successful insurance man. Like Maggie, she withdrew from Spiritualism for a time.

Kate, however, continued her career. In 1861, she went to work as a medium for wealthy New York banker Charles Livermore. His wife, Estelle, had died the previous year. Over the next five years, Kate provided the banker with close to four hundred séances in his home. There were many witnesses to the sittings and written documentation was kept. Eventually, at the forty-third sitting, the spirit of Estelle Livermore "materialized" and was seen surrounded by what was described as a "psychic light." The spirit communicated to Kate via rappings and automatic writing. According to accounts, Estelle and another spirit, calling himself Benjamin Franklin, wrote on cards that were placed before Livermore. While Estelle was writing, Kate's hands were held tightly by one of the sitters at the séance table. Witnesses claimed that the script on the card was a perfect reproduction of Estelle's earthly handwriting.

Finally, during the three hundred and thirty-eighth séance, Estelle made it known that she would no longer materialize. True to this communication, Livermore never saw his late wife's spirit again. Because he was grateful to Kate for the comfort that she had brought him in his grief, he paid for her journey to England in 1871 so that she could continue her work there as a medium.

In England, her career thrived. She often gave sittings for well-known figures of the day. Kate also made herself available for testing by British scientists like Sir William Crookes, one of the greatest physicists of his time, and one of the first advocates for serious inquiry into the paranormal. She shared a number of séances with the famed mediums of the era, including Daniel Dunglas Home and Agnes Guppy-Volckman.

Kate remained in England and the following year, she married Henry Jencken, a barrister, with whom she had two sons. The first, Ferdinand, was born in 1873 and was reportedly a medium by the time he was three years old. It was said that spirits took over his body and caused an "unearthly glow" to emanate from his eyes. Her reputation as a medium earned Kate a visit to Russia in 1883, where she demonstrated her gifts for Czar Alexander III.

There was a lesson to be learned by Kate's rise to stardom in Europe and by her earlier employment by men like Charles Livermore. It was a lesson that was overlooked by many scientists, clergy, intellectuals and rational thinkers in their zeal to debunk and expose Spiritualism as a fraud. The fact was that millions of people, just like Livermore and Jane Pierce, regardless of their social or economic status, were seeking a way to cope with death and the grief that followed. Spiritualism, for all its flaws, fakes and frauds, offered a comforting connection between this world and the afterlife. The spirit world offered hope that death was not the end and that we would be reunited with our loved ones in the next world. Many scientists, skeptics and rationalists never quite grasped the value of Spiritualism and the need that it fulfilled for so many people. Nor could they understand that their cold logic failed to offer anything that could ease the fear and mystery of death.

Like it or not, Spiritualism in the nineteenth century produced a critical shift in the way that Americans thought about life and death. All mediums were not proven to be fraudulent and many who investigated them, including some of the most learned men of the time, concluded that there was evidence to make a case for communication with discarnate spirits.

For both the dying and the bereaved, Spiritualism offered something more tangible than unyielding and often impersonal religious dogma, which is why it attracted people from every religious denomination across America. Although fundamentalist clergy strongly disapproved of it, many people found that the message and hope of Spiritualism was very similar to Christian teachings. In many places in the New Testament, the Bible spoke of eternal life, the same belief that the Spiritualists espoused about the afterlife. However, traditional Christianity would continue to preach against Spiritualists, reminding the faithful that the Old Testament condemned any association with mediums, fortune-tellers, necromancers and the like.

Americans in the nineteenth century had a much closer contact with death than their present-day descendants. More people died at home, and were typically laid out in the parlor, which is why the term funeral parlor was used when ceremonies surrounding death were moved out of the home. The parlors once found in homes began to be called the living room to erase the memory of what the rooms were once used for. Life expectancy in the nineteenth century was much shorter than it is today. Infections, epidemics and unsophisticated medical treatments claimed many lives. Families had large numbers of children partly because high infant mortality rates, accidents and childhood diseases claimed the lives of so many infants and toddlers.

When the Fox sisters were growing up, death was not an unusual topic, even in public schools. Schoolbooks, songs and poems featured sentimental accounts of dying children. By today's standards, they seem morbid and inappropriate for young children, but death was ever-present in the nineteenth century and making sure children were prepared for it, even at an early age, was considered both practical and responsible on the part of parents, schools and churches. When the Civil War came along, Americans saw wholesale slaughter in numbers that could never have been imagined before. With all of this death it was no surprise that Spiritualism was instantly popular. It added a measure of comfort and offered hope of what awaited us when we left our physical bodies.

In 1876, Maggie Fox visited England for a time and then returned home to the United States. She was still a medium, albeit a reluctant one, forced to continue practicing because of her dire economic situation. Those who knew her recalled that she lived in poverty during her last years.

Then, the lives of the Fox Sisters took another unhappy turn. While the reasons remain unclear, the three of them became embroiled in quarrels and disputes with one another that were apparently instigated by Maggie. Their later years were mired in public controversy and personal difficulties, made worse by alcohol and a lack of funds. Leah was the only one of the Fox sisters who had ever really prospered financially from the talents of her younger siblings..

In spite of this, the Fox sisters remained known in the Spiritualist community. In 1884, Maggie appeared before the Seybert Commission in Philadelphia. The commission was founded by a local Spiritualist named Henry Seybert, who donated $60,000 to the University of Pennsylvania for an investigation of Spiritualism. Among the psychic phenomena that the commission studied were slate writing, spirit materialization, spirit photography, spirit rapping, telekinesis and "direct voice" communication.

When Maggie demonstrated the rapping noises that she and her sisters were famous for, she did so while standing on four glass tumblers. Commission members were unable to arrive at any definitive conclusions about the nature of the rappings. One member, Horace Howard Furness, stated that he believed the rappings were being created outside of her body and yet, overall, suggested that they might not be supernatural. The noises could have been made by voluntary muscular action, the commission said.

The Seybert Commission's findings were largely negative about Spiritualism. The results outraged the community and some of their frustration might have been legitimate. For one thing, out of the eleven members of the commission, there was only one Spiritualist among them, Thomas Hazard, a close friend of Henry Seybert. Hazard had been picked by Seybert to determine the best means of testing mediums but his ideas were ignored. He lodged a formal protest about the techniques that the commission members used to investigate Spiritualism, but no one listened.

In May 1887, the Seybert Commission issued a preliminary report about the tests that was substantially unfavorable about the entire subject of Spiritualist phenomena. The findings of the commission, legitimate or not, were damaging to Spiritualism, especially in the eyes of many scientists. Several years later, a commentary written by Frank Podmore acknowledged that the intentions of Howard Seybert were never fairly carried out. This was typical of how psychical phenomena were often treated by the orthodox scientific community. Medical doctors were among the most hostile to Spiritualism, apparently fearing competition from mediums, some of whom employed spirit contact or clairvoyance to diagnose and treat illnesses. It was all "humbug," said the scientists, skeptics and debunkers of the nineteenth century - an opinion still shared by most in those categories today.

By 1885, Spiritualism was on the decline and investigations of fraud began to increase. This year brought further tragedy to the Fox sisters. Maggie performed before a commission in New York to prove her skills, a test that she failed miserably, and Kate's husband died from a stroke. She returned to New York where, in early 1888, she was arrested for drunkenness and "idleness." On Leah's instigation, welfare workers took custody of her sons. Maggie, in a moment of kindness for a sister with whom she had been feuding, was unable to get custody of the boys herself, but she did manage to get them into the custody of an uncle who lived in England.

In 1888, Spiritualism was dealt a savage blow that sent it reeling. On October 21, Maggie took part in a lecture and demonstration that would become an infamous event in the history of the Spiritualist movement. On this night, at the New York Academy of Music, she denounced Spiritualism as a complete and total sham. The years of alcohol abuse, loneliness and grief had taken their toll on her and she weighed the idea of committing suicide before choosing confession instead. She walked out on stage to announce that she and Kate had created the strange rappings heard in their Hydesville home by simply cracking their toes. She also stated that Leah had forced them into performing as mediums for the public. "I have seen so much miserable deception," she reportedly said. "That is why I am willing to state that Spiritualism is a fraud of the worst description... It is the greatest sorrow of my life. I began the deception when I was too young to know right from wrong."

In its coverage of the shocking event, the *New York Herald* described the audience's reaction to Maggie's public confession:

There was dead silence; everybody in the hall knew they were looking upon the woman who is principally responsible for Spiritualism. She stood upon a little pine table with nothing on her feet but stockings. As she remained motionless, loud distinct rappings were heard, now in the flies, now behind the scenes, now in the gallery.

It was believed that while Maggie was causing the raps, it was the acoustical properties of the room that was giving the audience the illusion that the sounds were coming from different directions.

While the critics laughed and cried, "I told you so," devoted Spiritualists denounced Maggie's confession as the ravings of a sad and tired drunk. Kate, who did not speak at the public appearance, later stated that she did not agree with her sister and she continued to perform as a medium. It was also publicly argued by various individuals and groups that Maggie had been forced into a false confession, either by churches or because she was bribed by the newspapers. It was also pointed out, a little more reasonably, that the existence of one fraudulent medium did not prove that all others were not genuine. Some even claimed that Maggie did not know her own powers and was a true medium, despite what she may have thought about herself.

After Maggie had stepped in to help Kate with her children, the two sisters mended fences and began battling with Leah. Tensions were running high and each sister blamed the other for her problems - and there were plenty of problems. Maggie and Kate were nearly penniless alcoholics and had great resentment against Leah, perhaps for good reason. Leah had profited nicely from her career, usually at the expense of her sisters. It had been Leah who had accused Kate of being an unfit mother and had her children taken away. The result of all of this anger was an alleged plan between Maggie and Kate to ruin Leah - a plan that became even darker when Kate, possibly to ruin Leah's reputation, decided to join Maggie and support her confession.

The confessions were the news that the debunkers had long been waiting for. Many of them were elated that the sisters claimed that the rappings were their own creation, and not the work of the supernatural.

But while the sisters' admissions were certainly a blow to the credibility of Spiritualism, they were too little and too late to destroy a movement that had captivated the country for the forty years. Spiritualism was not dead, much to the frustration of its enemies. The Spiritualists simply rallied their forces and offered explanations for Maggie's behavior, ranging from alcohol to bribes.

The convoluted story became stranger in 1889, when Maggie recanted her confession. She explained that financial pressures were responsible for her temporary disavowal of Spiritualism. She also implied that influence from certain groups who were hostile to the subject, likely churches, forced her into the erroneous confession. The obvious implication was that Maggie and Kate were paid to say that the spirit rappings were a hoax. Now, in her retraction, she said the opposite. Some historians have suggested that the sisters had been promised a sum of money to renounce Spiritualism but when they were never paid, they were forced to return to being mediums to eke out a meager living.

The confession and the subsequent retraction did nothing for Maggie's career. The public was angry, indignant and confused. By that time, both Maggie and Kate were plagued by poverty, alcoholism, loneliness and a variety of serious physical and emotional problems, so the turmoil that surrounded them probably didn't matter as much as it once might have. The publisher Isaac Funk, who knew the sisters, sadly remarked about Maggie, "For five dollars she would have denied her mother, and would have sworn to anything."

Leah, on the other hand, lived well until the end of her life. She was the first of the sisters to die, in 1890. Neither Maggie nor Kate attended the funeral. Maggie and Kate both died tragically, having been largely abandoned by those whose fortunes they had created with the birth of the Spiritualist movement. Kate drank herself to death in July 1892 at the age of only fifty-six. Her body was discovered by one of her sons.

Maggie was fifty-nine when she died in March 1893. She spent her final days bedridden in a friend's cramped tenement apartment in Brooklyn. She was cared for by another Brooklynite, Dr. Ida Mellen, who happened to be one of the world's most respected authorities on the ailments of fish. Dr. Mellen was chief aquarist at the New York Aquarium and the *Brooklyn Daily Eagle* reported that she was an expert at caring for all manner of creatures, including penguins and alligators, as well as fish. The doctor was not a Spiritualist, which makes her observations about Maggie's last minutes all the more curious. Dr. Mellen said that during Maggie's last hours of life, there was a series of loud raps in the room. The tiny apartment contained no hiding places, not even a closet. In addition, Maggie was nearly paralyzed; she could move neither her arms nor legs. When the doctor asked about the noises, Maggie replied in a quiet, labored voice, "It was my friends watching over me." A few minutes later, she died.

In 1916, the Fox cottage in Hydesville was moved to Lily Dale, a small community in western New York where Spiritualists had formed a gathering place and headquarters. In 1955, the house burned to the ground. A replica was built thirteen years later as a tourist attraction. Nothing remains of the original house today, save the legends. In Hydesville, there is a marker at the former site of the house that notes that it was where Spiritualism was born.

The one thing that must be remembered in the story of the Fox sisters is how Spiritualism became a huge movement in America that attracted millions of believers, all the way to the White House, and that its significance moved far beyond whether or not the sisters were genuine mediums. However, if they were frauds, no one has explained how they so successfully perpetrated a hoax for so many years. Could the rappings have been carried out by trickery? Of course, that was a possibility. But many questions remain unanswered so that no one can say with any certainty what actually occurred in those theaters, opera hours, meeting halls and private residences where the sisters performed. Perhaps the girls really did contact the spirits of the dead. Or perhaps they manifested psychic abilities, like psychokinesis, that allowed them to make sounds and move objects, meaning the rappings had nothing to do with spirits at all.

In the end, it may not matter. From a historical perspective, one has to be amazed that two young, unsophisticated girls from a rural community caused a stir that captured the attention of millions of Americans for more than half a century. Spiritualism became a significant force that spurred science, psychology and theology to think in new ways. While it challenged long-held beliefs, it motivated millions to question the very nature of life and death. It also proved to be a solace to thousands of grieving people, especially after the Civil War. The movement that the sisters began grew to be much larger than just two women. Their confessions and recantations came too late to stop Spiritualism and the surge of interest that it created in the supernatural that continues to this day. The bottom line was that Spiritualism represented great change, which was a threat to many, but it offered great promise to others.

As mentioned previously, America has always been a nation of extremes. It's a place of strong passions and great enthusiasms, both good and bad. Those passions have ranged from the vicious hysteria of the lynch mob to the ecstasies of the religious revival meeting and everything in between. Nowhere is this great passion as evident as it is in the history of Spiritualism. The movement swept the country in the days before radio, television and mass communication. People became obsessed with the alleged ability to communicate with the dead and even the most conservative and uneducated became part of the new movement.

However, it did not spread without opposition. Most of the attacks against Spiritualism in the early days came from the fundamentalist Christians. These conservative religious groups held the opinion that communion with the spirits was possible, but it was evil and dangerous to the welfare of one's soul. Many church leaders saw Spiritualism as a grievous threat to organized religion, but interestingly, Spiritualism was never meant to turn into a faith or religious movement. It was little more than a popular past time at first and the idea of communicating with the spirits was an amusing way to spend a long winter evening. There were a couple of factors that worked independently to cause Spiritualism to be inflated in importance and to be accepted as an actual religious faith. One of these was the rise of the Apostolic Church in America, which also got its start in New York. The idea of speaking in tongues and being taken over by the Holy Spirit appealed to many and the Pentecostal faith and its many offshoots is still going strong today. Despite the fact that many ministers condemned Spiritualism as the "work of the Devil," it was not a far stretch for many to accept the possibility of strange events surrounding spirit communication and religious fervor at the same time.

Scientific realists had their own beliefs. They believed that spirit communication was impossible and that all Spiritualists must be frauds or candidates for the asylum. A great many Americans espoused this point of view as well. Many of them were doggedly determined to defeat the pro-Spiritualism forces and these opponents of Spiritualism were often as energetic as its advocates. In addition to scathing denunciations in the press, books were published, public prayer meetings were held and lecture tours were organized so that the opponents could express their views. Lecture tours were popular forms of entertainment in those days and speakers on controversial subjects often attracted large audiences.

The opposition to the movement would cause some damage in the years before the Civil War. In fact, Spiritualism saw a period of decline between 1856 and 1860. In the years of the war itself, the country had too much on its mind to pay much more than a passing attention to Spiritualism. In the post-war period, though, it would be the death and destruction during the fighting that made the movement stronger than ever. Thanks to the huge number of bereaved wives, parents and loved ones, Spiritualism offered the hope of direct communication with those who had died. Soon, an even greater number of people from all economic levels began flocking to mediums and séances around the country.

The movement had already seized the attention of Americans. Within only a few years, there were an estimated two million Spiritualists across the country, with the movement showing no signs of slowing down. People from every level of society believed in contact with the spirits, from the lowliest tenement dwellers to the occupants of the White House.

In 1848, when Maggie and Kate Fox first reported the spirit rappings, the president of the United States was James Polk. There's no record that he had any interest in Spiritualism, but he did experience a premonition of his death in 1849. He died that June and was followed in office by Zachary Taylor, who had become a hero during the Mexican War. After a hot day during the Fourth of July event in 1850, President Taylor became ill after eating a bowl of cherries and milk. He had had a foreboding that he would not survive. He lingered for several days and then died on July 9 - just as he had predicted. He was followed in office by Millard Fillmore, who hailed from western New York, the same region that gave birth to Spiritualism.

The 1850s were a time of some of the greatest of America's literary figures. Almost all of them expressed curiosity - or disdain - for the growing Spiritualist craze, but they did not reject supernatural or psychic events.

Ralph Waldo Emerson was a transcendentalist who believed in the afterlife. Henry Wadsworth Longfellow shared his views. Henry David Thoreau, also a transcendentalist, expressed interest in reincarnation. William Cullen Bryant took part in séances and so did Nathaniel Hawthorne, who then rejected Spiritualism, but created a Spiritualist character for his 1852 novel, *The Blithedale Romance*. However, throughout his life, he acknowledged that he had witnessed apparitions. In one incident, Hawthorne, who often went to the Boston

Athenaeum, a research library in the city, always noticed an elderly minister there reading. One evening, Hawthorne saw the gentleman in his usual chair. He was stunned to learn that the man had died before he saw him. Hawthorne concluded that he had seen the man's ghost, which continued to appear for several more weeks.

Herman Melville, author of the 1851 book Moby Dick, was a believer in the afterlife. Walt Whitman understood phrenology an occult "science" based on the measurements of the skull well enough to make allusions to it in his poetry. It was in 1851 that James Fenimore Cooper, a supporter of the Fox sisters, died. Later in the century, Henry James included Spiritualists in his books and the creator of Sherlock Holmes, Sir Arthur Conan Doyle, became one of the greatest proponents of Spiritualism in history.

The popular English poet, Elizabeth Barrett Browning, was drawn to Spiritualism. She joined in séances conducted by the famed medium Daniel Dunglas Home. However, her husband, Robert Browning despised Home and publicly mocked Spiritualism as a fraud, hoping in some small way to injure the reputation of the medium. Novelist William Thackeray, whose works included *Vanity Fair*, attended séances given by the Fox sisters and D.D. Home, but admitted his reaction to Spiritualism was "mixed" at best.

In 1852, the best-selling author Harriet Beecher Stowe published one of the most influential books of all time, *Uncle Tom's Cabin*. It was responsible for converting many people from the northern states to the abolitionist cause. Stowe was seriously interested in the new Spiritualist movement and attended séances, as did noted abolitionist and newspaper publisher William Lloyd Garrison, whose interests also included mesmerism and phrenology.

Poet Emily Dickinson mentioned the spirit world in her writings, and author Louisa May Alcott discovered that supernatural events did not occur only at séances. Alcott, who later wrote the classic novel *Little Women*, was only twenty-five years old in 1858 and lived at her family's home in Concord, Massachusetts. Despite the great interest in Spiritualism, she remained uninvolved. But she found out that one did not need to be a Spiritualist to have an experience with the spirit world. At the time, her younger sister, Beth, was desperately ill with scarlet fever and her condition was growing worse. Louisa and her mother remained at Beth's bedside as her health declined. They knew that Beth was dying. Louisa wrote the following in her diary on March 14, 1858:

My dear Beth died at three this morning, after two years of patient pain. Saturday, she slept, and at midnight became unconscious, quietly breathing her life away until three; then with one last look of the beautiful eyes, she was gone.

A curious thing happened, and I will tell it here, for Dr. G said it was fact. A few moments after the last breath came, as Mother and I sat silently watching the shadow fall on the dear little face, I saw a light mist rise from the body and float up and vanish in the air. Mother's eyes followed mine, and when I said, "What did you see?" she described the same mist. Dr. G said it was the life departing visibly.

Did Louisa and her mother actually see Beth's spirit as it left her body? It seemed so. What is equally amazing about this excerpt from her diary is the doctor's reply to her about what she had seen - that he had witnessed this phenomenon on other occasions. The Alcotts' experience also suggested that what they had witnessed was more than a belief; it was a genuine paranormal event.

It was around this time, in 1852, that the terms Spiritualism and Spiritualist came into popular use. Before that, no one was really sure what to call the strange and inexplicable ghostly events. Suddenly, the Fox sisters were not the only mediums of note, although they were still the best known in those days. Mediums, séances and spirit circles could be found in most communities, large and small, throughout the country. New York City reported hundreds of known mediums and no less than 40,000 serious believers in "spirit rapping." Even a small town like Auburn, New York, not far from where the Fox sisters grew up, had dozens of mediums by the 1850s. Across the country, especially in the Northeast and New England, the number of mediums exploded. Philadelphia claimed fifty to sixty private spirit circles and a large number of mediums. In Ohio, there were over two hundred spirit circles reported. In 1854, Illinois Senator James Shields presented the U.S. Congress with a petition containing fifteen thousand signatures, calling on the federal government "to investigate communications from the dead." U.S. Senator Nathaniel P. Tallmadge and Ohio Congressman Joshua Giddings were among the politicians who practiced Spiritualism.

Even if the Fox sisters had faked their spirit communications, they'd been very influential. By 1855, the New England Spiritualist Association estimated some two million believers across America.

As the popularity of the movement continued to spread, there were a number of publications, both supportive of and opposed to Spiritualism, being printed across the country. By 1851, New Yorkers had a new daily newspaper - the *New York Times*. It immediately took a strong anti-Spiritualism stance, but if Spiritualism caught your fancy, there were dozens of publications devoted to the movement that were readily available in towns and cities across the country.

The *New York Tribune*, whose publisher Horace Greeley welcomed the Fox sisters into his home, was always the city's "radical newspaper." It was supportive of the rise of the movement and Greeley and his wife became converts after the death of their son in 1849.

In Washington D.C., a newspaper called the *National Intelligencer* was so opposed to Spiritualism that in April 1853, it branded the movement a "pestilence" and stated that it was a production of "delusions." It accused Spiritualism of "distracting the minds of the nervous, feeble-witted and the timid into actual insanity." The editors went on to demand laws to prohibit séances.

The popular magazine *Harper's Weekly* also strongly objected to Spiritualism, suggesting that spirit circles, like "gambling dens and other places of ill-fame," should be closed down.

But the several million Americans who were adherents to Spiritualism had no lack of their own publications to choose from as an antidote to the skeptical press and the newspapers and magazines put out by the Catholic Church and the fundamentalist Christians. These groups had an antipathy against Spiritualism based on religious grounds - and because of the threat they believed the new movement posed for organized religion.

For Spiritualists, there were literally, starting in the 1850s and through the 1890s, hundreds of magazines, pamphlets, and newspapers devoted to the movement that came and went. Among the most successful were *Messenger of Light, Banner of Light, The Spirit World, Spiritual Philosopher* and, perhaps best known, the long-running *Spiritual Telegraph*, which started publication in 1852. There were also many books published on the subject throughout the second half of the nineteenth century. By the early 1870s, annual sales of books about Spiritualism totaled over 50,000 copies, with another 50,000 pamphlets devoted to the subject sold each year.

For both sides of the debate, it was a boisterous time. There was debate about whether Spiritualism should be defined as a religion, as many believers considered it. Some called it a "scientific religion" while others thought of it as a "quasi-religious" movement. But there were practical reasons for Spiritualists to want their beliefs under an umbrella of religion. Several states were passing laws against "fortune-tellers and conjurers," as a way to limit the rights of Spiritualists. If they could claim protection as a religious denomination, they would have a weapon to use against hostile government authorities that were trying to legislate the movement out of existence.

The growth of Spiritualism had not gone unnoticed by those that opposed it. In Alabama, for example, a law was passed to impose a $500 fine on anyone who gave a public display of mediumship. Other states followed suit, limiting or banning displays by mediums. Fortunately for Henry Gordon, New York City did not take such a harsh stand when he allegedly became the first American medium to perform levitation, lifting himself off the ground in full view of an audience in 1852.

But despite the critics and the skeptics, it was astonishing to see the speed with which interest in Spiritualism spread across America. Much to the surprise of the critics, it was not just the so-called superstitious and uneducated who were drawn to the movement. Increasingly, many educated, wealthy and prominent people could be found at séances. When the first large scale Spiritualist society was founded in 1854, its organizers included a former U.S. senator, four judges, two military officers and several successful businessmen.

There has never been another cultural phenomenon that affected so many people or stimulated as much interest as Spiritualism did in the decade before the Civil War or, for that matter, in the subsequent decades that followed it. Yet, nearly every recent traditional history book or biography about this period either chooses to ignore Spiritualism entirely, or makes a passing reference to it, dismissing it as a short-lived fad. To the contrary, in its time, Spiritualism became so popular that even many non-believers felt that it might become "the religion of America." But Spiritualism never assumed the rigid structure of ordinary religious denominations. It was accessible to everyone, and while that openness appealed to many, ironically, its lack of organization may have been the movement's greatest weakness.

It quickly became apparent that the movement was riddled with trickery and fraud. Still, people of all walks of life sought out mediums and séances in the hope of communication with the next world. However, there were those who remained incredulous that so many could believe such claims. The country was experiencing unprecedented growth and mobility, and Spiritualism appeared to reflect the changes that America was going through. It was an age of religious and social agitation and excitement, coupled with new marvels in science and technology.

In 1859, barely a decade after the Fox sisters became public figures, Charles Darwin published his controversial book *Origin of Species*. The impact of his theory of evolution was stunning. Some said that by accepting Darwin's theory, it meant that you were replacing a God in whose image man was created with the anatomical results of natural selection and an ape for an ancestor. In this heady mixture, Spiritualism threatened to redefine man's very nature, abilities and purpose. For if people really did possess "other abilities," then the current concept of mankind, religion and perhaps even God, would have to be changed, or at least re-examined. Spiritualism became a starting point for a great many people in search of answers to some of the great mysteries of life and death.

For many bereaved people, Spiritualism was a godsend. The early and middle nineteenth century was a time of short life expectancy and high child mortality rates. Two out of every ten babies did not live to see their first birthday. It was not unusual for mothers to die during childbirth. Simply living to adulthood was an achievement and even then, a great many people did not live beyond their forties. Medical treatment was limited, painful and often deadly. There were no therapists to help the grieving deal with death. Whether they knew it or not, mediums were suddenly placed in the role of grief counselors. Spirit contact meant comfort, no matter what the church, the press and the scientists said about it. Attending séances became more than mere entertainment. For many, it became a necessity.

Séances were usually held in the home of the medium or that of one of the sitters. To begin, the lights were normally turned down very low or extinguished altogether. The reason for this, Spiritualists believed, was that spirit forms were more easily seen in the darkness. Often they manifested as luminous apparitions or would cause objects to move about in ways that would only be done if whatever was causing things to move could remain unseen. Debunkers and skeptics, of course, offered another reason for this: that darkened conditions hid the deceptive practice of fraud.

The sitters were normally divided by gender and those who were skeptical were generally excluded. A circular arrangement of chairs worked best, normally around a large table. Their hands were placed flat on the table, sometimes clasped together or with their outspread fingers touching.

There were a number of unwritten rules for séances. Usually, no more than two or three were held in a week and they were to last for no more than two hours unless the spirits asked for an extension. Sitters were not allowed to touch the medium or any of the manifested spirits, unless the spirits touched them first. This could cause the medium to snap out of her trance, which was considered to be dangerous on the grounds that a sudden return to consciousness could result in the medium becoming ill, insane or even dying.

The phenomena reported at the séances varied greatly. Sitters often recognized the arrival of the spirits by a rush of cold air in the room, followed by rapping and tapping, knocking and perhaps strange lights, sounds and voices. The phenomena would often intensify as the evening progressed. Simple noises and lights were often followed by elaborate messages from the beyond, usually coming directly through the medium.

In the most dramatic cases, some mediums who claimed to be adept at spirit summoning, were able to cause ghosts to appear in the midst of the sitters. In some of the most famous cases, like that of teenage medium Florence Cook, spirits materialized who could touch, shake hands and even embrace the sitters.

Another vital ingredient for a successful séance was appropriate music. Most sittings opened with the sitters joining in singing hymns, and on many reported occasions, the spirits joined in. Sometimes, the spirits were even said to play melodies on trumpets, horns and tambourines left lying about the séance room. In many cases, the voices of the spirits chimed out from metal cones called "spirit trumpets," the first on our list of supernatural objects.

The furnishings of the séance room were normally simple, everyday objects that could be found in any home. Small tables were used for tilting and tapping by the spirits and sitters were normally provided with basic wooden chairs.

Many physical mediums also made use of what were called "spirit cabinets," an enclosure where the medium could be segregated from the sitters while entering the trance state. Many of the cabinets were actual wood enclosures, although it was more common for a corner of the room to be hung with a curtain and closed off from view. The cabinet became the physical medium's work space and its purpose was to "attract and conserve spiritual forces." Paranormal researcher Hereward Carrington referred to a spirit cabinet as a "spiritual storage battery."

Although spirit cabinets later became standard equipment for mediums, it was first introduced into the American Spiritualist movement by the Davenport brothers in the middle 1850s. None of the earlier mediums in the movement, including Spiritualism's founders, the Fox sisters, ever used such a device. The idea behind the cabinet was to be able to section off the medium from the sitters so that they would be out of direct view when producing strange phenomena. This would prove to be astounding to audiences, as the mediums were generally bound hand and foot in the cabinet while seemingly impossible phenomena manifested around them.

For fraudulent mediums, the spirit cabinet was a great gift. With only a limited amount of skill as an escape artist, the medium could amaze his sitters while hidden away behind curtains and wooden doors. Ropes could be easily shed and then an assortment of "spirit phenomena" could be produced. In most cases, the sitters would be invited to inspect the cabinet ahead of time so that they would be satisfied that no secret entrances or trap doors were present. Secret entrances were usually located elsewhere in the room and accomplices playing the role of spirits would simply slip through and move about in the darkness, lightly touching the participants, whispering and producing any other effects that seemed suitable.

The medium would then enter the cabinet and be seated in a chair, where they would often be tied up to prevent fraud. After slipping their bonds, the

Princess Margaret of Orleans for an apport of a cactus. Twenty of them promptly fell from the ceiling. Debunkers made earnest efforts to determine how she produced these phenomena. In 1869, when she was studied by an investigative committee, one member noticed that the bottoms of flower apports looked like they had been burned. When asked about it, Agnes replied that electricity from the spirit world was to blame. Whether that was true or not could not be determined, but one fact is known: all of Agnes Guppy-Volckman's apports materialized in well-lighted rooms!

How some of the apports that purportedly appeared is still subject to debate today, but in the early years of Spiritualism apports were supposedly proof that the spirit world was at work. Accusations of fraud relentlessly followed physical mediums. The fact was that when experiments were attempted under more or less controlled conditions, their deceptions were overwhelmingly uncovered. So many deceptive mediums were exposed that the credibility of all of them was called into question. In the latter years of the nineteenth century, far fewer mediums employed apports, until there were barely any.

Perhaps more important to the question of apports was not so much how, but why? Exciting as it must have been to see objects appear, seemingly out of nowhere, how did these demonstrations elevate spirituality? Did a trumpet floating through the air in a darkened room, mysterious music playing, bells ringing or even a levitating medium really add to one's spiritual growth? Or were the critics correct, and it was just good theater? Was there anything to be learned otherwise? Even if psychic powers were genuine, what lessons could be learned from flying tambourines?

Critics complained that if the spirit world had any real wisdom to impart, very little of it was being communicated at most séances. In addition, some claimed, if the discarnate communication was genuine, then how were men who never had schooling beyond third grade suddenly in possession of the "wisdom of the ages" now that they were on the other side? Time and time again, throughout the history of Spiritualism, debunkers found fault with messages from departed loved ones that seemed rather trivial and mundane. Even when the message contained information known only to the recipient, it was rarely profound or revelatory. Spirit messages were more like letters or telegrams; often they were simply greetings or assurances to loved ones left behind.

In the 1850s, it was not unusual to be invited to someone's house for tea and "table tipping," one of the most popular home circle entertainments of the day. Those who participated in this type of séance were asked to place their hands on a small table and then wait until the table moved, turned or tilted of its own volition. Not unlike spirit rapping, messages were tilted in code that corresponded phenomena would begin. There were several ways for mediums to collect their materials for the hoax. Often, "spirit forms" would appear and they would usually be made up of soft cloth or chiffon, which was very compressible. It could be easily secreted in the medium's clothing and when unwrapped or draped over the medium for a full materialization would appear ghostly in the dim light. If the medium allowed himself or herself to be searched prior to the séance, the materials could also be smuggled in by the "cabinet attendant," who acted as the medium's bodyguard. Spiritualists said that this person was present to protect malicious intruders from touching the medium's ectoplasm which could cause injury or death but in reality, they were merely accomplices in the fraud.

The medium would be dressed completely in black and when they emerged from the cabinet with the "ghostly" cloth, it would appear to be moving on its own. The ball of material would be slowly unwound and in the near total darkness, would be eerily convincing. The medium could also drape his body in the material and then, while standing in front of the cabinet and moving the black curtains back and forth, he could create the illusion that the spirit form was moving sideways and up and down. Combined with music and chilling dramatics, it is no wonder that so many were convinced of the reality of the spirit cabinet séances.

As you can see, with the rise in popularity of physical mediumship as a way to demonstrate spirit contact, mediums became forced to put on quite a show at their séances. Objects flew about, music played and spirits materialized, always to the delight of the participants. Another phenomenon was a physical manifestation called an "apport." An apport was any object that a medium could make appear. It might be a piece of jewelry, a vase, flowers, fruit, or even a small animal. One favorite apport was a dove. At one spirit circle in Boston, no less than eleven people confirmed that a white dove inexplicably appeared in a closed room.

For believers, it was all wondrous work attributable to the spirit world. To skeptics, séances were nothing more than the product of trickery and deception, just like that employed by stage magicians. As séance participants grew more sophisticated, many of the apports were uncovered as fabrications that were perpetrated by fraudulent mediums. But not every medium was exposed as a charlatan; sometimes their demonstrations of psychic abilities were beyond the ability of the most hardened debunkers to explain.

One of those who baffled the skeptics was Agnes Guppy-Volckman, who hailed from London but was well known to American Spiritualists as well. At her séances, music would play and apports such as fruit or flowers would fall onto the table. Other times, a dog, cat or butterflies would materialize. When dazzling the French court of Napoleon III with one of her séances, Agnes was asked by to the alphabet. Séance participants would often communicate directly to the table by asking questions that it answered through turns and tips.

Although the process of table tipping dated back to the days of ancient Rome, it became enormously popular in America during the early days of Spiritualism. Spiritualists explained that table tipping worked as a result of a form of psychic energy that emitted from each and every object in the world. Mediums were supposed to be especially sensitive to this energy.

But table tipping was just as controversial as any other alleged psychic power. In churches, ministers railed against it as demonic and a number of physicians warned of the danger to one's sanity from participating in supernatural activities.

In 1853, famed British scientist Michael Faraday rejected Spiritualist explanations and announced his tests had produced the theory that table tipping had nothing to do with ghosts. The table moved thanks to the séance participants and their own "unconscious muscular action." While many scientists agreed with Faraday, table tipping had its defenders who insisted that the movements were generated by spirit forces or some kind of psychic energy.

There was also a phenomenon known as "automatic writing," a type of mediumship that became very popular in the nineteenth century. As interest in Spiritualism grew and more people became involved in it, the tiresome and time-consuming method of knocking and rapping fell out of fashion and mediums began to produce messages through automatic writing. This was essentially writing that was done in an altered state of consciousness and was attributed to spirits of the dead. It was believed by some that the spirits literally manipulated the writing utensil in the hands of the medium to communicate, as the writer was often unaware of what was being written and would often scrawl out text in handwriting that was markedly different from her own. Others believed that perhaps the spirits communicated by forming messages in the mind of the medium, which were reproduced on the page.

Through automatic writing, mediums claimed to produce messages from famous persons in history, deceased authors and even classical music composers. In the 1850s, John Worth Edmonds, a judge on the New York Supreme Court, became interested in Spiritualism after the death of his wife. After a séance with the Fox sisters, he became intrigued with the movement and publicly acknowledged his support of it, despite the potential damage to his legal career. He became most interested in spirit communications and began encouraging a medium friend, Dr. George T. Baxter, to try and contact famous and literary figures that had passed over. In no time, Edmonds and his small circle of Spiritualists were receiving discourses from Francis Bacon and Emanuel

Swedenborg, or as the Swedish seer insisted on spelling his name when communicating with the judge -- "Sweedonborg."

The material produced by these sessions sounded nothing like the earthly work done by either man. It was described as being pompous, artificial, slightly condescending in tone and often sounded as though the entire personality of the author had been eliminated. As William James stated: "One curious thing about trance utterances is their generic similarity in different individuals ... It seems exactly as if one author composed more than half of the trance utterances, no matter by whom they are uttered."

Other forms of automatic writing went beyond mere messages and included drawings, paintings, and even musical pieces that were allegedly inspired by the dead. In some cases, mediums or individuals with little or no artistic training would suddenly feel compelled to paint or draw in distinctive, professional styles. They felt guided by a spirit, as if another hand was guiding their own.

If séances participants wanted physical manifestations of spirit contact, there was also what was called "slate writing." It became another favorite form of psychical phenomena. The technique consisted of the medium and the attendee seated opposite each other at a table small enough that each could hold a corner or edge of a small chalkboard slate. The slate was then pressed tightly against the underside of the table. Between the slate and the table, a small piece of chalk had been placed. If a scratching noise was heard a short time later, it presumably meant that the spirit was writing something on the slate. When the process was completed, raps were heard, the slate was turned over and there would be a message on it - supposedly written by the spirits.

Although slate writing was often criticized, it remained popular throughout the nineteenth century. There is no question that it was susceptible to fraud, which was proven by scores of magicians in the early 1900s. Even so, there were an estimated two thousand "writing mediums" all over America who claimed they wrote down, under spirit control, messages communicated to them from the other side.

One American medium named Henry Slade became particularly known for his slate-writing abilities. After working as a medium in the United States for fifteen years, he went to perform in St. Petersburg, Russia. Among those who observed him was Helena Petrovna Blavatsky, the founder of the mystical Theosophical Society in 1875. She was impressed with Slade and called him a genius. She described his technique of using "double slates, sometimes tied and sealed together, while they either lay upon the table in full view of all...or held in a ...hand, without the medium touching it."

Then, at the peak of his popularity, Slade became embroiled in allegations of fraud when debunkers found a previously written message on what was supposed to be a blank slate. In London, he faced criminal charges after a similar deception was discovered. He was found guilty, but the verdict was overturned on a technicality, and he wasted no time in getting out of England.

In 1885, Slade was tested by the Seybert Commission in Philadelphia and they declared him a fraud. The accusations of trickery claimed that Slade prepared the writing on his slates in advance. The writing was simply a generalized message that offered no evidence of being produced by spirit phenomena. By the early part of the twentieth century, slate writing was thoroughly discredited and was rarely seen again.

Another form of spirit communication became a lasting favorite. In 1853, French Spiritualists came up with a writing device called a "planchette," or little plank. It eventually evolved into a heart-shaped piece of wood with three small wheels on the bottom of it. The point of the heart held a small, downward-facing pencil. The idea was for the medium to place his or her hand on the planchette and then the pencil would write out messages from the spirit that was controlling the medium. When the planchette became available in American in 1868, thousands were sold. It was the forerunner of the immensely popular Ouija board. To what extent the messages obtained are from spirits or from unconscious activity by the person holding the planchette is still debated today.

Direct voice phenomena, like automatic writing, was supposedly produced by the spirits without the intervention of the medium. One favorite test of the debunkers was to have a medium fill her mouth with water while the discarnate entity spoke. Assuming there were no confederates creating a second voice, this was one way of determining whether or not the medium was engaged in trickery. In some cases, two distinct voices were heard, one presumed to come from the medium and one from the spirit. Several mediums confounded skeptics with "direct voice" phenomena, particularly in the days before recordings.

One of the strangest of all of the manifestations produced by physical mediums was "ectoplasm," an odd and elusive substance that was reported to be totally repulsive. It was a seemingly lifelike substance, solid or vaporous in nature, which allegedly exuded from the bodies of mediums and could be transformed into materialized limbs, faces and even the entire bodies of spirits. Ectoplasm often appeared to be milky white in color and smelled like ozone, according to most reports. Coined by a French scientist named Charles Richet in 1894, the term ectoplasm came from the Greek words of "ekto" and "plasma," meaning "exteriorized substance." There were countless witnesses to the peculiar substance emanating from mediums during séances, but no one was certain about what its function truly was. According to one Spiritualist theory, it may have been the physical manifestation of some kind of essential energy that was then absorbed back into the medium's body.

The emanations were reportedly warm to the touch and often were reported as thick, clotted, mucus-like substances. They could be rubbery and dough-like and emerged from a body orifice, such as the mouth, ears or nose but could also come from the eyes, navel, nipples and even the vagina. Ectoplasm was also reported to disappear when exposed to light and would snap back violently. Touching the ectoplasm, or exposing it to light, was said to be able to cause injury to the medium. This was one of the reasons that mediums insisted that séances should take place in near darkness and that sitters should not approach the mediums or the emanations that had formed.

Critics asserted that the reason for darkness and the avoidance of exposing ectoplasm to investigation was simple: fraud. Analysis that had been carried out on samples of the substance yielded few clues. Most critics claimed that it was chewed paper, gauze or fabric, which had likely been regurgitated. One investigator stated that the ectoplasm that he studied was nothing more than "butter muslin." He added: "I did see some produced in a séance once. It smelt appallingly of body odor, which wasn't surprising, considering where it was kept."

Investigator and magician Harry Houdini found most of the ectoplasm that he collected to be obvious trickery. He had seen mediums who used rubber bladders to blow ectoplasm from their mouths and had found others using cotton rubbed with goose grease and still others using strips of cloth that had been fashioned into odd shapes and veils. It was also easy, as Houdini knew from his own act, for the mediums to swallow all sorts of substances and then regurgitate them at will. Houdini had done the same trick with keys, needles and thread.

Most investigators came to the conclusion that séance attendees were amazed by ectoplasm due to the power of suggestion. Strange and bizarre substances that appeared in the midst of a sitting would seem incredibly dramatic in a dimly lit séance chamber. Once the lights came up, the ghostly emanations would have vanished. Who wouldn't be amazed?

Believers were absolutely convinced of the reality of the stuff and skeptics dismissed it as humbug. Who was right? It's hard to say, but Houdini once wrote: "Nothing has crossed my path to make me think that the Great Almighty will allow emanations from the human body of such horrible, revolting, vicious shapes, which like 'genie from the bronze bottle' ring bells, move handkerchiefs, wobble tables and do other flapdoodle stunts." The fad eventually faded away.

And as time marched on, many hoped that Spiritualism would do the same. Much like today, when fads come and go quickly, earlier generations of Americans eventually grew bored with demonstrations of the same psychic phenomena. This was the reason that mediums found it necessary to progress from spirit rapping to the more elaborate séances that including automatic writing, trance speaking, levitations and spirit manifestations. By the end of the 1850s, Spiritualism was starting to lose some of its appeal and seemed to be - many hoped - finally fading away. But national politics and war would soon intervene and would bring even greater interest in the Spiritualist movement.

From the beginning of Spiritualism, most of the adherents to the cause had aligned themselves with the abolitionist anti-slavery movement, as they had done with other social reform movements, including women's rights. By the 1850s, the nation was moving in an incredibly divisive direction over the institution of slavery. Slavery in America was a way of life that no one could truly defend and yet the Southern economy had been built upon the backs of slaves. While the North became industrialized, the South remained stagnant, entrenched in its farms and plantations. Throughout the first half of the nineteenth century, abolitionists in the North had become increasingly influential. In 1831, William Lloyd Garrison began publishing *The Liberator*, a radical abolitionist newspaper, in Boston. Garrison, in addition to his interest in Spiritualism, was unequaled in his passionate condemnation of the horrors of slavery.

Then there was the amazing impact of Spiritualist Harriet Beecher Stowe's novel *Uncle Tom's Cabin*. It sold more than 300,000 copies in 1852, the year it was published, and another 1.5 million unauthorized copies were also in print. Its portrayal of the evils of slavery was so effective that it touched the hearts - and enraged the passions-- of millions of Northerners. The book had more power than Stowe, or any of the abolitionists, could have imagined. Some years after the start of the Civil War, President Abraham Lincoln met Mrs. Stowe for the first time. He smiled kindly as he shook her hand and then sighed softly, "So, you're the little lady who started this war."

In October 1859, a militant abolitionist named John Brown and a band of followers staged a raid on the federal arsenal at Harper's Ferry, Virginia. Their plan was to arm the slaves of the South and start a bloody insurgency. But Brown's plan failed and he was hanged in December. In the North, he became a martyr to the abolitionist cause. On the gallows, Brown prophesized that slavery would only be eradicated by bloodshed. Sadly, his prediction was soon proven correct.

Several mediums also reported that they had experienced ominous visions of a terrible war ahead. Increasingly, there was talk of secession in the South. Southerners insisted that they needed slavery for their economy to survive. In the North, the abolitionists were equally intent on ending the "evil institution." It appeared that no compromise could be reached and there were grave doubts that the Union could be preserved. The nation was in danger of coming apart.

In November 1860, Abraham Lincoln was elected as the sixteenth president of the United States. The victory that did not sit well in the Southern states, even though he had pledged not to intervene in states where slavery already existed. But there was such anger at Lincoln - and at a Union that was seen as meddling in the rights of the individual states - that South Carolina took the step that all had feared. In the autumn of 1860, it became the first state to secede from the United States. Other Southern states quickly followed. By February 1861, the Confederate States of America formed and Jefferson Davis was named as its president. In April 1861, the Confederate artillery fired on Fort Sumter, a federal fortress in Charleston harbor. The Civil War had finally begun.

Although it has been largely ignored by traditional historians and biographers, there is no other president in our history that is more closely connected to the paranormal than Abraham Lincoln. Poet Walt Whitman, who witnessed the horrors of war first-hand, once wrote to describe Lincoln, "More than any other man in history, the foundation of his character was mystic." It cannot be disputed - no matter how many have tried - that Spiritualism, precognitive dreams, visions, premonitions and clairvoyance all played important roles in Lincoln's life.

On the night that he won the election, he later described a prophetic dream of seeing his face appear two times in a mirror. One face looked healthy and the other was worn and weary. He believed it to mean that he would be elected two times to the presidency, but would not survive his second term. Shortly before he was assassinated, he recounted a dream about being in the White House and seeing a funeral catafalque in the East Room. In the dream, he asked someone who it was who had died and was told that it was the president. Lincoln was killed soon after and his body was laid to rest in the East Room, just like in his dream.

The Civil War took a terrible toll on Lincoln but there is no doubt that the most crippling blow that he suffered in the White House was the death of his eleven-year-old son, Willie, in 1862. Lincoln and his wife, Mary, an emotionally unstable woman during the best of times, grieved deeply over Willie's death. Lincoln was sick at heart over Willie's death and it was probably the most intense personal crisis in his life. Some historians have even called it the greatest blow he ever suffered. Even Confederate President Jefferson Davis sent a letter to Washington to express his condolences over the boy's death.

Death came for Willie on the afternoon of February 20, 1862. Lincoln covered his face and wept in the same manner that he had for his mother many years before. He looked at Willie for a long time, refusing to leave his bedside.

Mary Lincoln collapsed in convulsions of sobbing and her closest confidante, her black seamstress Lizzie Keckley, led her away to comfort her. The talented

Mrs. Keckley, a former slave who previously worked for Mrs. Jefferson Davis, had become an almost constant companion of Mrs. Lincoln after completing her ball gown for the inauguration. She was one of the few people who possessed the patience and strength needed to deal with the high-strung First Lady. Mary trusted her implicitly. Keckley listened to Mary, sympathized with her and advised her as best she could. She would soon influence Mary greatly when it came to her beliefs in Spiritualism.

After Willie's death, it was Lizzie who washed the boy's body and dressed him in a plain brown suit of clothes for the funeral. She herself had lost her only son and understood Mary's pain at the loss of Willie.

President Lincoln was unable to stomach his own loss. He managed to stand after Mary was led away by Lizzie Keckley and stumbled into John Nicolay's office to share the horrible news. Then, sobbing, he walked to Tad's room. He sat down with the boy and tried to tell him that Willie would not be able to play with him anymore; that his brother had died. Tad refused to believe it for a time and then he too began to cry.

It was a tragic time in the White House and according to the tradition of the day, the mirrors in the house were covered and the mansion was draped in black. The Lincolns hardly stirred from their rooms. If not for their friends and Lincoln's most trusted staff, the White House would have come to a standstill.

On February 24, a minister conducted the funeral in the East Room, while Willie lay in a metal coffin in the nearby Green Room. It was said that the boy appeared to be sleeping as his friends and family passed slowly by him, their faces twisted in grief. Lincoln stood with his eldest son Robert by his side but Mary did not attend the funeral. She was in such a state of shock that she was unable to leave her room. Most of official Washington was there. Members of Lincoln's cabinet wept openly. General George McClellan was so moved by the president's suffering that he later sent Lincoln a compassionate note expressing his sorrow and thanking him for standing by him during failure after failure on the military front. When the service was concluded, the pallbearers and a group of children from Willie's Sunday school class carried the coffin outside and to the waiting hearse.

Willie was placed in a tomb at Oak Hill Cemetery in Georgetown but Lincoln wasn't able to leave his son unattended there for long. Word spread that Lincoln returned to the tomb on two occasions and had Willie's coffin opened. The undertaker had embalmed Willie so perfectly that he appeared to be merely asleep. The president claimed each time that he opened the casket that he wanted to look upon his boy's face just one last time.

After the funeral, Lincoln tried to go on with his work, but his spirit had been crushed by Willie's death. One week after the funeral, he closed himself up in his office all day and wept. It has often been said that Lincoln was on the verge of suicide at this point, but no one can say for sure. He did withdraw even further into himself though and he began to look more closely at the spiritual matters that had interested him for so long.

Lincoln had great difficulty moving on after Willie's death. He treasured small items and drawings given to him by Willie, sometimes arranging them on his desk while he worked. His friends stated that Lincoln would often watch the door while he worked, as if expecting the boy to run through it and give his father a hug, as he often did in life. Lincoln began to speak of how Willie's spirit remained with him and how his presence was often felt in his home and office.

Lincoln may not have publicly acknowledged his belief in Spiritualism, but after Willie's death, Mary embraced it openly. As time wore on, Mary remained unstable. Her mood swings, headaches and explosive temper were worse than ever. Perhaps the only thing that really provided her with any comfort at all was her embrace of Spiritualism. By the summer of 1862, Mary was meeting with a number of different Spiritualist mediums and invited many to the White House, as each claimed to be able to "lift the thin veil" and allow her to communicate with Willie.

Through Lizzie Keckley, Mary made the acquaintance of a Miss Bonpoint, a journalist who was writing about Spiritualism in the papers. It was she who introduced Mary to the Lauries, a husband and wife medium team that lived in Georgetown. Cranston Laurie was chief statistician for the Post Office Department. His wife, Margaret Ann, was credited with having strong mediumistic ability. After that, the black presidential carriage was often seen outside of the Lauries' brownstone. Later that year, Mary met the woman who became her closest Spiritualist companion, Nettie Colburn Maynard, a medium that President Lincoln also met with. Many are familiar with a tale told about a séance attended by Nettie Maynard in 1863 where a grand piano levitated. A medium was playing the instrument when it began to rise off the floor. Lincoln and railroad lobbyist Colonel Simon Kase were both present and it is said that both men climbed onto the piano, only to have it jump and shake so hard that they climbed down. It is recorded that Lincoln would later refer to the levitation as proof of an "invisible power."

Rumors spread that Lincoln consulted with mediums and clairvoyants to obtain information about future events in the war. He found that sometimes they gave him information about Confederate troop movements --- information that sometimes matched his own precognitive visions. There is much written about Lincoln and the Washington Spiritualists of the day in the accounts and diaries written by friends and acquaintances. One such acquaintance would even claim that Lincoln's plans for the Emancipation Proclamation, which freed the slaves, came to him from the spirit of Daniel Webster and other abolitionists of the spirit world.

Most of the information about Lincoln and his interest in Spiritualism came from the aforementioned Nettie Colburn Maynard, who published a manuscript on the subject in 1891. In the 1850s, a teenaged Nettie became aware of her mediumistic abilities when she discovered that she could induce spirit rappings, or knocking sounds purported to be communications from the other side. Her ability manifested itself during the 1856 James Buchanan and John C. Fremont presidential election, in which Nettie's father, a staunch Fremont supporter, found out how accurate his daughter's talents could be. Too young and inexperienced to comprehend the political differences between the two candidates, she was nevertheless "seized by a power that I could not control" on the day before the election. Grabbing a piece of paper, Nettie scrawled the word "Buchanan" on it and as she did "loud raps came upon the table." Her startled father asked if this meant that Buchanan would win the election. Nettie said that it did and the next day, her prediction proved to be accurate. Her father became convinced that she could help others with her talents.

With her father's approval and support, Nettie went on to become a "spirit lecturer," mainly in New England towns and villages. When the Civil War began in April 1861, despite Northern boasts of a quick victory, she predicted otherwise. "Our spirit friends," she said, "reply ... it would continue four years and require five practically to end it."

Nettie moved to Washington during the years of the war and took up residence in the home of a friend, Mrs. Anna Crosby, whose father had been Robert Mills, the architect who had designed the capitol building. While living in the Crosby home, Nettie met a number of prominent people, including General Simon Cameron and Joshua Speed, Lincoln's former law partner and one of his closest friends. She gave private and public séances for many of these people, and through Spiritualist circles, became acquainted with Mary Lincoln.

According to Nettie, she first met President Lincoln on February 5, 1863, during a séance in Georgetown that he was not scheduled to attend. The medium would later claim that her "spirit guide" told her that "the long brave," as she called Lincoln, would be in attendance. The host of the party declared that this was unlikely to happen, as Lincoln rarely attended séances away from the White House. To his surprise, though, the president did come and the host exclaimed upon seeing him that he had been expected. Lincoln was reportedly shocked and stated that he had not been planning to come, but only accompanied Mary that night on a whim.

During the séance, Lincoln was allegedly contacted by an "old Dr. Bramford," who is said to have given him information about the state of the war and the demoralized condition of the Union troops. It was suggested that Lincoln visit the troops on the battlefield and that this would give them courage. In April, Lincoln paid the Army of the Potomac a lengthy visit, arriving at Aquia Creek in Stafford County, Virginia, where an exchange of cannon fire between Union gunboats and Confederate shore batteries were to take place between May 29 and June 1, 1861. From there, he traveled by train to Falmouth where General Joseph Hooker's men were camped. From there, Lincoln could see with a spy glass across the Rappahannock to Fredericksburg, where Robert E. Lee's Army of Virginia waited, less than a half mile away. A short time later, the overconfident Hooker led his troops to one of the costliest defeats of the war. In the midst of this disaster, though, his men followed him bravely into battle. It was believed that their courage had been restored by the visit from President Lincoln.

Nettie Maynard later recalled that after the advice given by Dr. Bramford, the spirit and the president continued to speak about the state of affairs in regards to the war. The spirit also told Lincoln that "he would be re-nominated and re-elected to the Presidency." This was more unusual than most modern readers might believe because, at that point in history, no president had ever been elected to a second term.

It was during this very séance that the famous incident with the levitating piano took place. The medium said to have performed this wonder was Isabella "Belle" Miller, the daughter of Spiritualists Cranston and Margaret Ann Laurie, and herself a prominent Washington Spiritualist. Belle had married Lincoln's friend, James J. Miller, in 1862. Mrs. Miller was playing the piano during one of Lincoln's visits to her parents' home when, and under her influence, the instrument "rose and fell," keeping time to her touch in a regular manner. One of those present suggested that, as an added test of the invisible power causing the instrument to move, Belle should place her hand on the piano and stand at an arm's length from it. This would show that she was in no way connected to it except as an agent of the mysterious power. President Lincoln then placed his hand underneath the piano, at the end that was closest to Mrs. Miller, who placed her hand upon his. In this position, the piano rose and fell a number of times, seemingly at their bidding. Lincoln even changed places to stand on the other side of the piano, but the same thing continued to happen.

The president was reported to have grinned at the display and said that he believed he could hold the instrument to the floor. He climbed up onto it, sitting with his long legs dangling over the side, as did Congressman Daniel E. Somes of Maine, Colonel Simon Kase, and an unnamed Federal Army major. The piano, ignoring the enormous weight now upon it, continued to wobble up and down until the sitters were obliged to "vacate the premises."

The audience was, by this time, satisfied to the fact that no mechanical means had been used to move the instrument and Lincoln himself declared that he was sure the motion was caused by some "invisible power."

Somes spoke up, "Mr. President, when I have related to my acquaintances that which I have experienced tonight, they will say, with a knowing look and a wise demeanor, 'you were psychologized and as a matter of fact, you did not see what you in reality did see.'"

"You should bring that person here," Lincoln quietly replied, "and when the piano seems to rise, have him slip his foot under the leg and be convinced by the weight of the evidence resting upon his understanding."

His sly comment brought a wave of laughter to the room but when the chuckles died down, the president wearily sank into an armchair, "the old, tired, anxious look returning to his face."

Nettie Maynard held a number of séances with the Lincolns during the latter days of February and early March 1863. They all took place by appointment and after the close of each session, Mary made another appointment to come at a certain hour of another day, usually around the time that the president took his lunch in the afternoon.

On one occasion, Nettie was summoned to a séance by Mr. Somes, who told her that the meeting was of such a private nature that he was not at liberty to say more. Somes picked her up in a carriage that evening and informed her that her destination was the White House. He explained that while at the War Department that afternoon, he had met President Lincoln coming from Secretary Edwin Stanton's office. Somes spoke to him briefly and Lincoln asked him if he knew whether or not Nettie was in the city and if so, would it be possible for her to visit the White House that night. When Somes told him that Nettie was indeed in Washington, Lincoln asked that she come that evening, but that the matter should be kept confidential.

By the time that Somes had finished explaining what had occurred, the carriage had arrived at the White House. A waiting servant ushered them inside and they were hurried up to the president's office, where Lincoln and two other men were waiting. The president sent the servant out of the room and a few moments later, Mary entered the chamber. Lincoln told Nettie that he wished for her to give the visitors an opportunity to witness something of her "rare gift" and he added that "you need not be afraid, as these friends have seen something of this before."

Nettie described the men as being military officers, although their coats had been buttoned to conceal any insignia or mark of rank. One of the men was tall and heavily built, with auburn hair and dark eyes. He had thick side whiskers and carried himself like a soldier. The other man was of average height and she had the impression that he was of a lesser rank than his companion. He had light brown hair and blue eyes and was deferential towards his companion.

The group sat quietly for a few moments and then Nettie entered a trance. One hour later, she became conscious of her surroundings and was standing at a table upon which was a large map of the Southern states. She held a pencil in her hand and Lincoln and the two men were standing close to her, bending over the map. The younger man was looking curiously and intently at her.

"It is astonishing," Mr. Lincoln was saying to the larger of the soldiers, "how every line she has drawn conforms to the plan agreed upon."

"Yes," answered the other man. "It is astonishing."

Looking up, both of the men saw that she was awake and they instantly stepped back. Lincoln took the pencil from Nettie's hand and eased her into a nearby chair. Mary Lincoln soon appeared at her side to offer some comfort.

"Was everything satisfactory?" Somes asked the assembled men.

"Perfectly," Lincoln replied. "Miss Nettie does not seem to require eyes to do anything."

Shortly after, the conversation turned to more mundane matters and after a brief time, the military men took their leave and then it came the president's time to depart. He carefully shook Nettie's hand and said to her in a low voice: "It is best not to mention this meeting at the present."

This was the last time that the private séance was ever mentioned and Nettie never learned the identity of the two men who were with President Lincoln that night --- or just what the spirits may have revealed with the map of the Confederacy.

According to accounts, Nettie Maynard's contact with the next world was said to have brought relief to Lincoln on more than one occasion. She was at the White House to visit Mrs. Lincoln in May 1863, around the time that the battle of Chancellorsville was being fought. Nettie was brought into Mary's bedroom and found the First Lady in her dressing gown. Her hair was loose and she was pacing back and forth in a distracted manner. "Oh Miss Nettie," Mary cried, "such dreadful news; they are fighting at the front; such terrible slaughter; and all our generals are killed and our army is in full retreat; such is the latest news. Oh, I am glad you have come. Will you sit down a few moments and see if you can get anything from the beyond?"

As no news of the battle had yet reached the public, Nettie was surprised by what she heard. She put her things aside and sat down with Mary to let her "spirit guide" take control of her. In a few moments, she was able to reassure Mary that her fears were groundless. A great battle was being fought but the Union forces were holding their own and while many thousands had been killed, none of the generals, as she had been informed, were slain or injured. She would, Nettie assured her, receive better news by nightfall.

This calmed Mary somewhat but when President Lincoln entered the room a short time later, it was obvious that he was still anxiously worrying about what was occurring at the front lines. He greeted Nettie with little enthusiasm but Mary insisted that he listen to what the medium had to say. Lincoln listened attentively to what had been passed on from Nettie's "spirit guide," recounting the true conditions at the front and assuring him of the good news that he would receive before nightfall. The battle would be costly, the spirits said, but not disastrous, and though not decisive in any way, it would not be a loss to the Union cause. Lincoln brightened visibly under the assurances that he was given and he later learned that Nettie's information had been correct. Chancellorsville resulted in the loss of many lives and effectively ended the career of General Hooker but no real ground was lost by the Union. Hooker had marched into a Confederate-controlled area and his outnumbered army was sent into retreat but regrouped to fight another day.

Perhaps the most notorious White House séance attendee, who also had an encounter with Nettie Maynard, was General Daniel Sickles. The colorful and controversial politician and Civil War officer spent nearly three months in Washington in the summer of 1862 and became well acquainted with the Lincolns. Sickles was an unusual man and as an antebellum New York politician, was involved in a number of public scandals, most notably the killing of his wife's lover, Philip Barton Key, son of Francis Scott Key. Sickles was acquitted with the first use of temporary insanity as a legal defense in American history. He became one of the most prominent political generals of the Civil War and at the battle of Gettysburg he insubordinately moved his troops to a position in which it was virtually destroyed. His combat career ended at Gettysburg when he lost a leg to cannon fire.

Sickles was interested in Spiritualism before the war. In fact, on the night of February 24, 1859, when he learned that his wife was cheating on him with the handsome widower Phillip Barton Key, he and his wife had given a dinner party at their Washington home that was enlivened by the presence of the Scottish wife of *New York Herald* editor James Gordon Bennett, an ardent Spiritualist. Mrs. Bennett had attended many séances in Washington and spoke openly of them.

A few years later, during the summer after Willie Lincoln's death, Sickles often joined Mary Lincoln at séances in the city. He returned to Washington after losing his leg at Gettysburg and continued the regular visitations. In fact, in early 1864, Sickles concocted a ruse to test the mediumistic powers of Mary's young medium, Nettie Maynard. Mary agreed to go along with the ruse, perhaps to teach a lesson to the arrogant general.

Nettie had recently returned to Washington after a brief absence and was living at the home of Mr. and Mrs. Somes. Nettie soon called at the White House, to pay her respects to the president and Mrs. Lincoln, and was warmly received. Lincoln expressed the hope that she had come to Washington to spend the rest of the winter.

A few days later, Nettie and the Mr. and Mrs. Somes were invited back to meet a friend - Daniel Sickles in a disguise. Mrs. Lincoln, in her invitation to Nettie, mentioned her desire to see if Nettie's "spirit guide" would be able to tell her who the friend was.

The party arrived at half past eight and was welcomed by the First Lady, who introduced them to a distinguished, soldierly gentleman, who was wrapped in a long cloak. Mrs. Lincoln did not call him by name, apologizing for not doing so, and explaining that she wanted to see if her spirit friends could recognize him. She promised to present him afterward. Mr. Somes recognized Sickles immediately, but gave no hint of the general's identity.

President Lincoln had a late-night cabinet meeting and after joining the group, asked that the proceedings be brief. Silence fell on the group and Nettie entered into a trance. The spirits that spoke through her turned all of their attentions on Lincoln. Their remarks related to the condition of free black people in Washington, declaring that their condition was deplorable. They were half fed and half clothed and that the manner of their existence should be an embarrassment to the country. The spirits called on Lincoln to form a special committee to investigate the condition of these people, and to organize a bureau to control and regulate the affairs of the freedmen. The bureau was eventually formed in March 1865.

It was only after this communication that the spirit, through Nettie, turned to Sickles and referred to him as "General" and praised him for the "noble sacrifice" of his leg at Gettysburg. A few moments later, another presence took control of Nettie - her usual "spirit guide," an Indian maiden - and she turned to Sickles and addressed him as "Crooked Knife," her Native American name for him. That was close enough to "Sickles" for a sickle had a crooked blade that everyone present was satisfied.

After Lincoln hurried off to his meeting and Nettie awoke from her trance, Mary Lincoln made the promised presentation of General Sickles, who put aside his cloak, revealing his uniform and concealed crutch. Sickles had no choice but to confess that he was impressed with Mary's young medium.

President Lincoln was eventually killed at Ford's Theater one night by a deranged actor named John Wilkes Booth. Just as he had seen in his dream,

Lincoln's casket was placed on display on a platform in the East Room of the White House, watched over by soldiers. Then after lying in state for crowds of mourners, a special train took his body home for burial in Springfield, Illinois. Along the route of the sorrowful journey, the train made its way through towns and cities where millions turned out to pay their last respects to the fallen president. The nation had been plunged into a deep and unprecedented grief.

Mary Lincoln went on to become one of the most misunderstood and maligned figures in American history. Most of the later biographies of her life, if they refer to her interest in Spiritualism at all, regard it as a reflection of her emotional problems. At the same time, her husband's interest in one of the greatest American cultural movements of all time is ignored almost entirely.

But Mary's many problems - and her fascination with Spiritualism that was shared by millions of people - deserves more sympathy than she has been given. Like Jane Pierce, the wife of her husband's predecessor in office, Mrs. Lincoln had experienced the untimely deaths of two of her children, Eddie and Willie. By the end of the Civil War, notwithstanding whatever mental issues she may have suffered from, she was a bereaved mother and a disconsolate widow. While still aching from the loss of Willie, Mary suffered another staggering loss when her husband was assassinated. Still, her faith in her ability to make contact with the spirit world remained intact and she continued to practice Spiritualism throughout the rest of her life.

Just as she had been desperate to hear from Willie at séances, she also ached for a message from her departed husband, a sign to skeptics that she had become "unhinged." In fact, people believed that Mary had lost her mind when, in reality, she had retreated into the only refuge that she knew that ease her loneliness and grief - Spiritualism. Like millions of others who had lost loved ones during the war, Mary embraced Spiritualism to cope with her pain. Before the war, the movement had started to fade in popularity, but after the devastation felt by untold wives, mothers, children and loved ones, the hope of communication with the dead was greater than it had been before.

For Mary Lincoln, her grief was exacerbated by the result of another personal tragedy in 1871 when Thomas, or "Tad," as he was known, fell ill with tuberculosis and died at age eighteen. Tad had been his mother's constant companion since his father had been killed. Mary bitterly wrote, "Ill luck presided over my birth and has been a faithful attendant ever since."

Mary found some sanctuary in her beliefs, residing in a "Spiritualist commune" for a time, so that she could develop her ability to see spirit faces and to attempt contact with her late husband. Mary later traveled to Boston, where, using an alias and a heavy veil to avoid being recognized, she attended a séance and reported contact with Lincoln's spirit, claiming to have felt his hands on her shoulders. She also visited a Spiritualist photographer, who claimed that he could capture the images of the spirits on film.

Sadly, photography was still in its early days in the 1870s and few were sufficiently to recognize a fraud. Many people believed that if a camera could capture an image of a person, it could also capture the image of a ghost. Thanks to this, spirit photography became a popular fascination during the latter half of the nineteenth century. The concept was quite simple: the spirit photographer claimed that he could take a picture of a live subject and when the plate was developed, the apparition of a deceased loved one would appear in the print. Typically, the spirit appeared ethereal and filmy so that it projected an otherworldly quality in the final image.

Mrs. Lincoln yearned for her husband to manifest in one of these photographs and so, under the assumed name "Mrs. Tundall," she visited William Mumler, the best-known spirit photographer of the time. From 1861 on, Mumler had maintained a profitable business producing photographs that showed shadowy likenesses of deceased loved ones lurking behind his customers. Wearing her widow's black, Mary sat, her hands folded, her round face older, more tired and heavier than only a few years before, while Mumler placed photo plates into his camera and asked her to stay motionless so that he could expose the picture he was taking of her.

When the plate was developed, Mrs. Lincoln was not disappointed. Behind her she could make out the hazy, nearly transparent image of Abraham Lincoln with his hand on her shoulder. He was bathed in a cloudlike fog and his body appeared as a white form. Many suspected an obvious double exposure, although Mumler had many supporters who vouched for his honesty. Mrs. Lincoln was certain that Mumler did not recognize her - and that the photograph was genuine. The spirit photograph of Mary Lincoln, with her late husband looming behind her, became Mumler's most famous image. Was it genuine? There is no clear answer to that question - but it should be noted that Mumler was later arrested and charged with fraud for some of the other photographs that he produced.

Mary Lincoln's last years were spent in misery and depression. She died in Springfield, Illinois, on July 16, 1882. She was buried wearing her wedding ring, which was inscribed with the words Love is Eternal.

At the end of the Civil War, interest in Spiritualism increased among the bereaved who had lost loved ones in the fighting and yearned to speak with them again. Nearly every family in the nation, North and South, had been touched by the unwelcome presence of death and was paralyzed with grief. The scale of the carnage was almost unimaginable. The war had left more than 600,000 men and boys dead, and nearly another million wounded.

As a result, many turned to Spiritualist mediums in hope of hearing from their departed husbands, sons, brothers, and friends. Physical mediums entered the spotlight in a way that they had never done before, and mental, or speaking mediums, began to pass along scores of messages from the spirits.

The Golden Age of Spiritualism had arrived and America would never be the same.

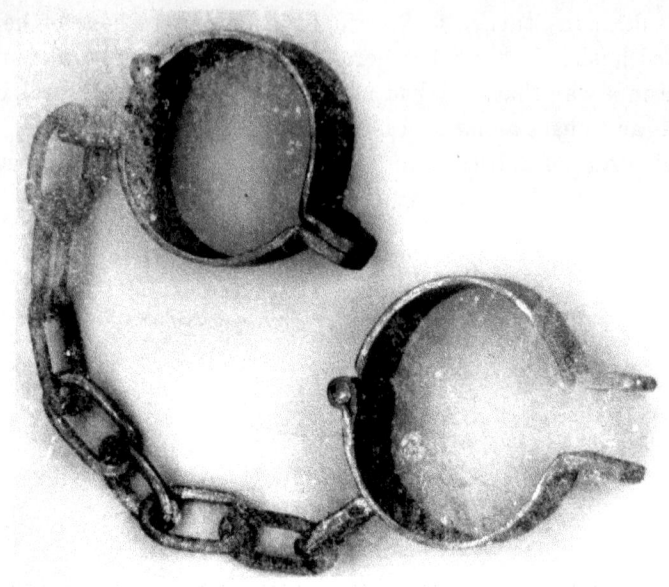

SHACKLES AND CHAINS
The Legend of Delphine Lalaurie

Slavery was one of the greatest horrors in American history. Men, women and children were held in bondage and forced to work like animals, all because of the color of their skin. It was the "peculiar institution," as it was known in some places during the first half of the nineteenth century, which gave birth to one of the greatest ghostly legends of all time. It's a tale that has its roots in the French Quarter of New Orleans, but it managed to spread across the country and serves as a perfect example of how stories become legend.

There are many elements of the story of Delphine Lalaurie that are nothing but myth, but sometimes truth is stranger than fiction - and much more horrible.

It was April 1834 when the horrors of the Lalaurie mansion were first revealed.

A ribbon of smoke curled out of a lower window of the brick, stucco-covered house that stood at the corner of Royal and Hospital Streets in New Orleans' French Quarter. No one knows who saw the fire first, or who raised the alarm, but there were many people on the busy streets that evening. There were few who did not know of the occupants of the largest and finest home in the neighborhood.

The mansion was the tallest on the street, looking out as far as the Mississippi River and Jackson Square, and back over the city's roofs, toward Congo Square, where the black residents of the city held their voodoo ceremonies. It was built in the era of Napoleon, which was obvious in the design of the iron grillwork that closed the entrance, in the black and white marble floor of the vestibule, and in the richly carved wood of the front door. Inside, the mahogany-railed staircase curved upward two stories. On the second floor were three large drawing rooms, opening one into another by ornamental sliding doors. Glancing out of the high, wide windows, set between fluted Corinthian pilasters, one would see the old slave wing at the back of the house and the paved courtyard that stretched out in front of it.

The drawing rooms were spacious and the doors that led into them and the great sliding doors between were decorated with panels that were beautifully carved with flowers and human faces. Around the walls of the rooms was a frieze with artwork that represented angels with folded wings holding palm branches and trumpets. The high ceilings and framework of the doors were beautifully carved with stars and raised garlands of flowers. The large fireplaces were graced with black marble mantelpieces and hung, glimmering chandeliers hung from the ceilings. These rooms showcased rich furniture of the period, the lounges and couches, carefully turned wooden chairs, colorful glass lamps, crystal sconces and heavy carpets that were imported from France and the Far East.

The house has not been the first to be located on that site. For many years, the location was known as the Remairie place. During the colonial history of New Orleans, Jean and Henri Remairie had lived there. Later, another house was built and the property passed into the hands of Barthelemy Louis de Macarty, the descendant of an Irishman who had acquired a title from the French government. One of the Macarty children was a daughter named Marie Delphine who inherited the property after her father's death. Delphine married twice before she was wed to Dr. Leonard Louis Nicolas Lalaurie in 1828. She and her husband redecorated the mansion, which was considered to be a showplace of the Vieux Carre for six years.

The parties and balls held at the Lalaurie mansion became the stuff of legend. The dinners were unmatched in their refinement and Madame Lalaurie became the most famous woman in the city. Noted for her grace and beauty, she charmed the men and befriended the women. An invitation to her wonderful home was something to be both desired and envied. She was an excellent hostess, and nearly all of her guests took note of her genuine kindness. Her home and her manner were considered to be beyond reproach and the Lalauries were among the most admired families in the city.

But all of that changed on the day of the fire...

On the afternoon of April 10, a blaze broke out in the Lalaurie house. It would later be alleged that the fire was started by the cook, a slave who preferred burning to death to spending another day in the kitchen of her mistress. The fire swept up the walls of the kitchen and the second floor began to burn. Smoke and flames poured from the windows on one side of the house, quickly drawing a crowd. Shouts were heard up and down the street and word reached the volunteer fire department, which was soon on hand with buckets of water. Bystanders began crowding into the house, trying to offer assistance.

During the excitement of the fire, Delphine Lalaurie remained calm. Throughout the chaos, she directed the volunteers who carried out the expensive paintings and smaller pieces of furniture. She was intent on saving the house but would not allow panic to overcome her.

A neighbor asked if any of the slaves were in danger from the fire but he was interrupted by Delphine, who told him not to interfere in her family's business. The man was startled by this response and appealed to Judge Jean-Francoise Canonge, a friend and local official who was also present, asking him to help search the house. They began searching for the rest of the servants and were joined by a man named Fernandez and several of the firefighters. They made an attempt to reach the upper floor of the house, but found locked doors barring the way. Finally, they discovered a locked wooden door with iron hinges that led to the attic. They pounded and pulled at the door, but it refused to budge. They could not get into the attic without a key and only the master of the house was likely to have it. One of the men went downstairs to search for Dr. Lalaurie but he refused to open the door or hand over the keys. Angry, the three men broke the door down and climbed the narrow staircase to the attic.

What they saw there would change their lives and the history of New Orleans forever. It would also create a legend out of a woman whose name, more than 175 years later, conjures up the image of evil incarnate.

Marie Delphine Macarty was born into a wealthy New Orleans family in about 1775. Her family boasted a mayor, a governor, three chevaliers of the French crown, Irish nobility, several slave traders and some of the most prominent members of the burgeoning colony. They could trace their roots back to the very founding of the city, a city that - although many hated to admit it - had largely been created by thieves, cutthroats and whores.

New Orleans began, on a swampy piece of river land, as little more than a land swindle in the 1700s. It was French territory, but in those days the French were broke. They were approached by a Scottish man named John Law who offered them a deal. For a small investment, he could ensure that the French would colonize the lower Mississippi River valley and take advantage of the natural resources of the region. All that he asked for was some start-up money and a monopoly on all trade in the region. When it was eventually realized that Law's plan was a confidence scheme to bilk investors out of their money, the settlers in the area decided to ignore this and stay on in La Nouvelle Orleans, which was established in 1718.

The development of the city was slow, mostly due to constant flooding, overwhelming heat, mosquitoes and crocodiles, but the settlers were a hearty bunch and endured great hardship. Meanwhile, John Law was still trying to obtain money from his investors, which required him to have 6,000 colonists living in Louisiana by 1727. The biggest problem was the shortage of women - which was solved by emptying the Paris jails of its prostitutes. They were shipped over to the New World and became wives of the settlers, who were starved for female companionship. These men couldn't afford to be choosy. Most of them had been thieves, vagabonds, deserters and smugglers who had come to Louisiana to avoid their own stint in prison. Mixed among them were French businessmen and aristocrats, some of whom had also ended up on the wrong side of the law for one reason or another.

New Orleans lacked schools and medical care, problems which were solved by the arrival of Ursuline nuns in 1727. They opened a school, cared for orphans and established the first hospital in the colony. They also provided a safe haven for the "casket girls," young middle-class women who came in answer to the call for suitable wives. They received their nickname for the government-issued casket-shaped chests that contained the clothing and linens that they brought with them. The first of the "casket girls" arrived in 1728, and they continued to come until 1751, marrying single male colonists who had been unable to snag one of the "professional" girls sent over from the Paris jails a few years before. Not surprisingly, in the years to come, upper-crust society families always insisted they could trace their lineage in New Orleans back to these women - and never to the prostitutes who had come to New Orleans to avoid their time in jail.

The city began to change, but there were still many problems, not the least of which were squalid conditions, violence, bloodshed and Indian attacks. The political disorder at the time, in addition to the financial problems, forced France to abandon the colony and ownership of Louisiana passed to Spain. This marked a period of anger and unrest for the people of New Orleans. They saw the Spanish as oppressors and even tried to overthrow the Spanish governor in 1768. The revolution was doomed from the start and eventually the people endured Spanish rule for several decades.

In March of 1788, New Orleans was almost completely devastated by a fire, which destroyed the congested French community of poorly constructed wooden homes and buildings. The Spanish rebuilt, creating the Vieux Carre French Quarter that we know today, using brick, plaster, heavy arches and tile roofs. The buildings were erected flush against the sidewalks, balconies hung over the streets and shaded courtyards were placed between and behind the stately homes, hiding banana trees, gardens and fountains. A new cathedral was built, along with a new hospital and government building, all of which still stand today around Jackson Square.

The first hope that the city might again be governed by France came in the 1790s when news of the French Revolution reached New Orleans. The Spanish remained in power until 1800, when Louisiana was secretly returned to France, only to be sold to the new United States in 1804. The transfer of the Louisiana Territory, including New Orleans, took place on the balcony of the Cabildo, the city's government building overlooking the square. New Orleans officially became an American city - an event met with great disdain by the people of New Orleans who considered Americans barbaric frontiersmen with none of the social skills of New Orleans' cultured class. Snubbed by the French families, the newly arriving Americans created a society of their own outside of the French Quarter. Thanks to frequent altercations, a "neutral ground" had to be created between the French and American sections. It's known as Canal Street today.

By 1810, with a mixture of French and Spanish-speaking upper class families, Americans, slaves and free people of color, New Orleans was established as the largest city in the South and the fifth-largest city in America. The city had truly come into its own, a fact proven when steamboats began arriving, ushering in a new period of prosperity. The aristocrats filled their lavish homes with the finest Persian rugs, crystal chandeliers, and the best French wines that money could buy.

A few years later, in late 1814, New Orleans was nearly invaded by British troops during the last days of the War of 1812. The attack was repelled under the command of General Andrew Jackson, who led an assault by a contingent of pirates and a ragtag army of slaves, workmen, and frontiersmen. The makeshift army trounced the experienced British troops and forced their surrender, later to discover that a peace treaty had been signed in Europe several days before the battle. Nevertheless, the people of New Orleans were so grateful to Andrew Jackson that the public square was named in his honor.

The people of New Orleans also did battle with frequent outbreaks of disease in the early half of the 1800s. Located below sea level in a hot and humid climate, it was infested with mosquitoes and unclean conditions, often caused by river flooding. The land was so wet that the dead had to be entombed above ground. These conditions often caused epidemics to ravage the population. Throughout the first three decades of the 1800s, the city was struck with both cholera and yellow fever epidemics, killing thousands of people. Cholera was spread by dirty drinking water and yellow fever was spread by mosquitoes, which bred in the cisterns that supplied water to households. No one understood how infection was spread at the time, which only led to more death. Seeking a cure, days of prayer were organized and cannons were fired each day to break up clouds over the city, which some believed were responsible for the disease.

New Orleans was not a place for the weak or the sickly. A stout heart was required on order to survive. This was the era during which Delphine Macarty spent her early years. Her family was seldom touched by the unclean conditions and the crime that plagued most of the city. They were among the elite of New Orleans, a wealthy Creole family that lived in as much splendor as the time and location allowed.

The Creole families were the city's preeminent culture. They traced themselves back to the late 1820s, rarely admitting that their families had been present when the colony was originally founded. In those days, John Law's company needed settlers to get the colony off the ground. It accepted just about any able-bodied volunteer, but because Louisiana was seen as a lawless and distant frontier, it was soon realized that no decent folk wanted any part of it. Because of this, the eager "volunteers" usually came from France's debtor prisons and houses of correction. This meant most of the original settlers were convicts and prostitutes.

In 1720, an agent of France named Phillipe, Duc d'Orleans put a stop to the practice of flushing out the unsavory elements of the French prisons and sending them to New Orleans. Of course, this was the reason why, among upscale residents of the city, it became rare to find anyone who claimed an ancestor in New Orleans prior to the middle 1720s.

The Creoles were seen as New Orleans' original city leaders. But "Creole" could be a confusing title since two distinctly separate groups claimed it. White families used the title Creole as a way to describe themselves as people of European colonial ancestry. They were the descendants of the aristocratic families who traced their roots to the French and Spanish colonists. The other group who claimed the title of Creole was the light-skinned, part-African Catholics, once referred to as "mulattoes," "quadroons" and "octoroons," depending on their degree of black ancestry. Many of them had the same surnames as the white Creoles and often traced their lineage back to the same ancestors. They were of a higher class, so to speak, than the average black residents of New Orleans, but not on the same level as the white families, because of their black ancestry. Regardless, both groups used the title to set themselves apart socially from the other residents of New Orleans.

Delphine Macarty came from one of these wealthy Creole families. If there had been any hint of her dark future in her early years, her family would have kept it well hidden. Likewise, if she had been abused in some way that would have affected her mental state, it would have been a closely held secret. There is nothing written about her childhood that would lead anyone to believe that she would become a monster, but somehow, she did.

Delphine's father Louis Barthelemy de Macarty he changed his surname from McCarty after emigrating to America married Marie Jeanne Lovable. The union produced two sons, Jean Baptiste Francois and Barthelemy Louis, and an uncommonly beautiful daughter, Marie Delphine. There is little known about her early years, only that she was a beautiful child. Accounts of her charm and beauty followed her throughout her entire life.

Delphine grew up in a typically wealthy Creole home. The family owned a plantation north of the city and a house in the Vieux Carre. She was a happy, sociable girl and neighbors spoke of her visits to their homes. The Macarty plantation was a popular spot for parties and for visiting dignitaries, which would have given her plenty of practice when refining her manners and charm. As the daughter of a well-bred family, she would have been taught to read and write, but the bulk of her education was likely in music, art and etiquette. She would have learned what she needed to know about running a household from her mother.

In that era, Creole girls were introduced into society at the age of fifteen and usually married by the time they were sixteen or seventeen. For some unknown reason, Delphine was not married until she was about 24. It may be that her marriage was not late at all, and that records were poorly kept and her birth date is wrong - or it could be a sign of a greater problem. Perhaps, in spite of her beauty, Delphine was seen as a "difficult" young woman, one for which a suitable husband was hard to find. No one knows for sure, but her first husband turned out to be a controversial and prominent figure in the Spanish government that ruled Louisiana at that time.

Her first husband was Don Ramon Lopez y Angulo, the intendant or consul general of Louisiana for the Spanish government, who had taken office on January 1, 1800. Likely introduced by her aunt, Celeste Miro - wife of Governor Esteban Rodriguez Miro - Delphine married Don Ramon on June 11, 1800. They were wed in the St. Louis Cathedral with her parents as witnesses.

Little is known about their marriage. However, there are quite a number of Lopez y Angulo's letters in the St. Vrain Collection of the Missouri History Museum's archives. Most of them are correspondence between him and Charles de Hault Delassus, the last Spanish lieutenant governor of Upper Louisiana. Based on the letters, Lopez y Angulo was constantly worried about money and pushed to have the slave trade opened back up in the Louisiana Territory. He was concerned about the lack of manpower to keep the crops, and the money, moving into governmental accounts. His request was denied and his frustration about the lack of funds is evident in subsequent letters. He seemed to be a man who was deeply invested in his job, but Louisiana historian Arthur Preston Whitaker discovered the opposite. He wrote that his papers were in "utter confusion" when he left his position in 1801, due mostly to his lack of interest in his work.

Don Ramon was a pensioner of the royal and distinguished order of Charles III. He had married Delphine without the permission of the king of Spain, which was against government protocol, but was something that had been done by other Spanish officers in Louisiana before him. Even so, why he would have done this is unknown. It could have been that he was so taken with Delphine that he could not resist her, but more likely, her family's finances and power were too good to pass up. His actual reasons will never be known, but he paid a heavy price for his rash decision.

For violating the law, he was stripped of his office in 1801 and ordered to return to the Spanish court. He pleaded extenuating circumstances and pointed out that other officers, including Governor Miro Delphine's uncle had committed the same offense, but it was to no avail. The bishop of Louisiana attempted to intercede on his behalf, but it didn't help. For some reason, Don Ramon had earned the anger of the king. He was exiled to San Sebastian on the northern coast of Spain.

Don Ramon surrendered his office to Don Juan Ventura Morales and prepared to depart for Spain, but before he could leave, his successor noticed serious problems with the accounts and brought an accusation against him before the Spanish ministry. Don Ramon filed his own complaints against Morales and the case became mired in legal delays and litigation. In the midst of it all, Don Ramon once again asked the court to suspend its decision against him. As it happened, Spain had ceded Louisiana back to France in 1800, but still held a strong presence in the area. Simply put, they were still managing things for the French, which kept the Lopez y Angulo and Morales complaints swirling about in the court system for almost three years. Eventually, Don Ramon returned to Spain to fight his legal battle, bringing Delphine with him.

On March 26, 1804, Don Ramon was pardoned by the Spanish government for marrying Delphine without permission of the court. The case brought against him by Morales was thrown out and he was again given a government position in New Orleans. Legend has it that Delphine was the one who managed to sway the Spanish court in her husband's favor. She allegedly obtained an audience with the queen, who was so taken with Delphine's beauty and charm that she granted her petition.

What happened for certain is unknown, but we do know that Don Ramon died during the return trip to Louisiana. During a stop in Havana, Cuba a common port on the way from Europe to New Orleans , he passed away, leaving behind a pregnant Delphine. She gave birth to a daughter either in Havana, or on board the ship; the records are unclear.

The girl was named Marie Francoise de Boya de Lopez y Angulo. She was nicknamed "Borquita." The girl, noted for her beauty, was educated in Europe and eventually married into the Forstall family, one of the most prominent families in New Orleans and Louisiana history.

In 1808, Delphine, now probably thirty-two and with an eight-year-old daughter, married a man named Jean Pierre Paulin Blanque, who had come to New Orleans in 1803. He was reputed to be an important man in New Orleans business and politics. Stories say he was strikingly handsome, with dark hair and eyes. After the marriage, the family moved into a new home at 409 Royal Street.

Over the course of the next eight years, the couple had four children: Marie Louise Jeanne born 1810 ; Louise Marie Laure born 1811 ; Jean Pierre Paulin born 1815 ; and Marie Louise Pauline born 1816 . Borquita, Delphine's daughter from her previous marriage, also lived in the household until she herself was married. On the surface, Delphine and her family appeared to be living the respectable, comfortable life of a wealthy Creole family - but where Jean Blanque got his money was a bit of a mystery.

In his book, *Old New Orleans*, Arthur Cisby wrote:

Jean Blanque, once a well-known figure in old New Orleans. Merchant, lawyer, banker, legislator and - this was told in whispers - the "man higher up" in certain transactions relative to the importation of "black ivory" and goods upon which customs duties were not collected. M. Blanque earned this distinction during the hectic days before the Battle of New Orleans was fought, when slave smuggling activities of a swaggering company of Baratarians under the leadership of Pierre and Jean Lafitte, sometimes designated as pirates, were at their height.

The Baratarians were pirates who operated out of Louisiana's Barataria Bay, south of New Orleans on the Gulf of Mexico. According to history, mixed wildly with rumor, Blanque was engaged in the slave smuggling business in New Orleans. Slavery importation had been outlawed in the United States in 1808, but New Orleans was exempted from this law until 1812. In spite of this, many continued bringing in slaves illegally. Blanque's name appeared more than 350 times in the slave schedules, buying and selling slaves. It was also widely known that he owned ships that were used for smuggling and privateering.

He was on the New Orleans City Council, but his main claim to fame seems to have been that the pirate Jean Lafitte wrote to him for assistance when Lafitte was negotiating with the American military to help them during the Battle of New Orleans. The implication is that Lafitte and Blanque knew one another very well and likely had engaged in quite a bit of business together already.

In his book *The Pirates Lafitte*, author William C. Davis wrote of Jean Blanque as one of the "few less scrupulous New Orleans merchants... ffiwhoffl engaged sailors who plied both side of the laws." In 1806, he had been taken to federal court for purchasing 27,000 pounds of illegally obtained coffee. Many merchants took advantage of the low prices and variety of goods offered by the pirates, but Blanque attracted so much attention with his purchases that he wound up in court.

Blanque was not merely a crooked businessman and friend to pirates. He had come to Louisiana as a French public servant with Louisiana's last French governor, Pierre Clement de Laussat. In 1804, he had attended the meetings with William C. Clairborne and General James Wilkinson that transferred the Louisiana Territory to the United States, so he must have been a man of some influence. Laussat used Blanque's commercial house for financial transactions for the French government, which gave Blanque a hefty commission for every transaction. As New Orleans grew, so did Blanque's role in a variety of offices and organizations. He was named as one of the officers of the new Masonic lodge in 1812 and was instrumental in gaining American protection for the city when a British invasion threatened during the War of 1812.

After the war, less was written about Blanque but it's likely that he continued his questionable business practices, buying and selling smuggled merchandise and slaves. Then, in 1818, Blanque either died or disappeared; no one seems to know which occurred, but he was gone, leaving Delphine with four children to raise on her own. There is no documentation of his date of death and no notice in the newspapers of the era. If he ran due to his various problems with the law, there is no mention of it. His death was never mentioned, but according to legal papers filed in July 1819, Delphine was back to using her maiden name of Macarty.

There is no question that Delphine thrived during her marriage to the volatile and rather mysterious Jean Blanque. She lived in a grand home and had more money than she could possibly spend. Whether she knew about his illegal activities or not is unknown, but in all likeliness, she did. She had grown accustomed to a way of a life that was as grand - or perhaps was even grander - than the comfortable life she had known as a child and her newfound freedom as a second-time widow allowed her to become a well-known fixture in the city's Creole society.

On January 12, 1828, Delphine married Dr. Leonard Louis Nicolas Lalaurie, who had arrived in New Orleans from France in February 1825. Lalaurie's birth date is unknown, but it falls somewhere between 1771 and 1800. It is alleged that he was somewhat younger than his new wife. He was born in Villeneuve-sur-Lot in Aquitaine and after attending medical school, he eventually graduated from dental school in Toulouse. After he finished school, he prepared to emigrate to Louisiana.

Although not much is known about Dr. Lalaurie's personality, there are dozens of letters between him and his father that are still housed with the Missouri Historical Society. His father, Francois Jean Lalaurie wrote to his son about every two weeks. There are also a number of letters between him and his sisters, Victoire, Rosalie and Helene, and he seems to have had a warm and loving relationship with them. There is no indication that he was anything other than a kind, personable young man, although a rather poor medical student.

Lalaurie kept a detailed record of his journey across the Atlantic to America. He departed on December 8, 1824 and arrived in New Orleans on February 13, 1825. About a month after his arrival, he sought to establish a medical practice in the city, which was a little odd since he had only fully completed his studies at dental school. In a newspaper advertisement, he stated that he had graduated from an accredited French medical school and while this was not entirely a lie, it definitely shaded the extent of his degree. The practice of medicine was almost unregulated in those days, though, so it wasn't unusual for doctors who studied in one field of medicine to randomly switch to another, as Dr. Lalaurie did. Even so, a switch from dentistry to surgery seems to be a quite a leap.

Dr. Lalaurie and Delphine became acquainted at some point in 1827 and were married early the next year. Their son, Jean Louis was born later in 1828.

The Lalauries moved into the mansion at 1140 Royal Street in 1832, four years into their marriage. The house, a beautiful two-story Creole-style building had several balconies that allowed air to circulate through the house and a shaded courtyard that was paved with bricks. The house had been built in 1831 and was one of the finest in the Vieux Carre. The Lalauries lavishly decorated their new home, filling it with rich furniture and fine art. The couple threw lavish parties which often saw them featured in the society pages of the day.

Delphine was a queen of Creole society, a woman to be admired and envied. For years, she had been handling her own business affairs and was respected for her intelligence and style. Her daughters were among the finest-dressed girls in New Orleans. Those who received her attentions at her wonderful gatherings could not stop talking about her. Guests in her home were pampered as their hostess bustled about the house, seeing to their every need. They dined on European china, danced on Oriental carpets and rested on furnishings upholstered in fine fabrics that had been imported at great expense. One of the things that nearly all of her guests recalled about her was her extraordinary kindness.

But this was the side of Delphine that her friends and admirers were allowed to see. There was another, darker, side. Beneath her beautiful and refined exterior was a cruel, cold-blooded and possibly insane woman that some only suspected, but others - namely the slaves who attended to her house -- knew as fact.

There is no record to say that Dr. Lalaurie ever established a medical practice in New Orleans. However, there are a number of receipts and written requests for Lalaurie's services kept in historical archives. One acquaintance wrote to Lalaurie for assistance with a sick slave and Lalaurie billed him for a potion. It should be noted that slaves were often the test subjects for a variety of untried medical potions and remedies. This was not illegal, and was not even considered unethical. Another client asked for a tooth to be removed and Lalaurie later billed him for treatment. He was apparently working from home, which was not uncommon at the time.

Curiously, Dr. Lalaurie is mostly left out of the accounts of the atrocities that were discovered in his home in 1834. He is occasionally mentioned as one of the perpetrators, but is mostly seen as a background figure, hidden in the shadow of his wife's overpowering evil. This is strange, considering that in some erroneous accounts of the horror, medical experiments are mentioned. Since he was a doctor, who would have been more likely to conduct such experiments? He should have been the likely suspect, but he never was. Perhaps this is because - in all of the true, historical accounts of the terrible events - no medical experiments were ever mentioned. It is my personal belief that Dr. Lalaurie was truly an unwilling conspirator in the events that occurred both before and after April 1834.

The Lalauries continued their privileged life during 1832, but then a strange incident took place on October 26, 1832. On that date, the Lalauries petitioned the court to free a slave they owned named Devince, who was described as "a Creole of Louisiana of about 40 or 45 years of age." The petition would be granted in August 1833. Eight months later, Delphine and her husband would be revealed as the torturers, and possibly murderers, of slaves.

What could have happened to cause them to free one of them? While the record remains unclear, I have an idea, primarily based on what happened soon after.

On November 16, 1832 - less than one month after the court petition - a summons was issued to Dr. Lalaurie, who was residing in Plaquemines Parish at the time. In the summons, Delphine petitioned for separation from her husband. She cited that "through a series of ill treatment from the said Louis Lalaurie that indeed the said Lalaurie acted toward her a long time since in such a manner as to render their living together insupportable." Delphine swore that Lalaurie beat and mistreated her on October 26, 1832. She asked to be allowed to separate from him and for the court to let her remain at the house on Royal Street. Judge Joshua Lawn signed an order that allowed her to sue her husband for legal separation.

It remains a mystery as to what happened that day, but it was serious enough to convince Delphine to separate from her husband, which was an uncommon occurrence in those days. Note the date of the alleged beating - October 26. This is the same day that the Lalauries were recorded as petitioning the court for the freedom of the slave Devince. What happened? Anyone who can say for sure is long dead, but based on what happened later, I have a theory. I believe that Dr. Lalaurie did in fact beat his wife that day - as a response to her brutal treatment of the Devince. I believe that he put a stop to her attack on the man and went as far as to strike her to prevent her from doing serious harm to him. Lalaurie was so shocked by her actions - and perhaps by his own - that he abandoned his wife and moved out of the house. At some point, however, he had a change of heart. It may have been his wife's legal summons, or perhaps something else, but he soon returned. Delphine never went forward with the case against her husband. I believe that the freeing of Devince was likely the price that Delphine had to pay to ensure her husband's silence about her cruelty; or perhaps Dr. Lalaurie freed the man out of guilt for allowing the cruelty to occur in the first place. Once again, we will never know for sure, but there is no question that the mistreatment of slaves was a serious offense in New Orleans in those days.

As early as 1727, New Orleans had set itself apart from other Southern cities by adopting the "Code Noir" - a set of rules for the proper treatment of slaves. The so-called Black Codes were created to ensure the proper behavior of slaves. They also offered the first protections for slaves from the tyranny, neglect, oppression or cruelty of their masters. The codes and laws were taken seriously because, in addition to thousands of slaves, New Orleans was also home to scores of free blacks, or "free persons of color," as they were referred to at the time. Free blacks in New Orleans were allowed to own property and seek justice in the courts, rights that were not given to them in any other American city. The mistreatment of slaves was a serious offense in New Orleans, as the Lalauries would soon discover.

Those who attended the grand parties at the Lalaurie house often spoke of the quiet gracefulness of the house slaves. Nearly as elegant as the guests, these men and women went about their work with silent skill. They moved about the house like shadows, rarely speaking and never raising their eyes. There were those who wondered about them, and perhaps this is how the rumors began to circulate. It is more likely, however, that no one spoke of Delphine's cruelty until after the incident in 1833. Years later, people whispered of the brutality that they never suspected and the terrible treatment that they had somehow missed. Delphine kept her cook chained to the fireplace in the kitchen, the stories said, forcing her to prepare the sumptuous dinners that they had enjoyed. There were also tales that were much worse - stories that went far beyond mere cruelty.

It was a neighbor on Royal Street, a man named Montreuil, who first began to suspect something was not quite right in the Lalaurie house. There were whispered conversations about how the Lalaurie slaves seemed to come and go quite often. Parlor maids would be replaced with no explanation or the stable boy would suddenly disappear, never to be seen again. He made a report to the authorities but, even though he was friends with a number of prominent people, nothing was done about it.

Then, in late 1833, another neighbor heard a scream and witnessed Delphine chasing a young black girl across her courtyard with a whip. The neighbor watched the girl being pursued from floor to floor on the exterior staircase until they at last appeared on the rooftop. The child ran down the steeply pitched roof and then vanished. Moments later, the neighbor heard a horrible thud as the small body struck the flagstones below. Late that night, the woman claimed that she saw one of Delphine's slaves carry a bundle into the courtyard and bury it. She believed that it was the body of the young girl, but it was never proven. She told her story to the police, and this time action was taken.

The Lalaurie slaves were impounded and sold at auction. Unfortunately for them, Delphine coaxed some relatives into buying them and then selling them back to her in secret. She explained to her friends that the entire incident had been a horrible accident. Some believed her, but many others did not and the Lalaurie's social standing began to slowly decline.

The stories spread about the mistreatment of the Lalaurie slaves and uneasy whispering began among Delphine's former friends. Party invitations were declined, dinner invitations were ignored, and the family was soon politely avoided by other members of Creole society. Finally, in April of 1834, all of the suspicions about Delphine Lalaurie were realized at last.

On April 10, a fire broke out in the Lalaurie house. It started in the kitchen, accounts state, and then spread to the upper floors. As smoke billowed out the windows overlooking the street, it got the attention of passersby and neighbors who hurried to the house to lend assistance. Legend says that the fire was purposely started by the cook, who was kept chained in the kitchen. She allegedly stated that she would rather burn to death than endure any more of the abuse she had suffered at the hands of Madame Lalaurie.

An alarm was sounded to the volunteer fire department, members of which were soon on the scene to douse the blaze with water and to help remove people and household items from the mansion. Locals crowded into the house, some to help, others motivated by sheer curiosity. Many rushed about the scene, shouting and adding to the growing chaos. Delphine remained calm in the midst of it all, directing volunteers and steering firefighters toward the worst of the flames. She was intent on saving the house, and everyone who recalled that day stated that she never panicked or raised her voice.

Montreuil, the neighbor who had first aroused suspicions about Delphine and her treatment of her servants, was among those who assisted during the fire. He demanded to know if any of the household slaves were in danger and was allegedly told not to interfere in family business. Montreuil then appealed to his friend, Judge Jean-Francoise Canonge, and they began searching the house. They were accompanied by a man named Fernandez and many of the firefighters. Several of the servants were found as they climbed the stairs to the upper floors and sent out of the house.

According to a statement that was later given by Judge Canonge, a man named Felix Lefebvre had approached him in the house and told him that he had looked through a broken pane of glass and saw several slaves confined in a locked room. A man named Deponent, along with several others, went with Lefebvre and broke into the room. They found two slaves inside, both women. One of them had a heavy metal collar around her neck and chains attached to her feet. She directed the men to another nearby room where they found a third female slave stretched out on a bed. She was an old woman with a deep wound on her head. She was too weak to get out of bed on her own, and when the men helped her up, she was unable to walk. Deponent had several of the men hoist the mattress with her lying on it to carry her out of the house.

Meanwhile, Montreuil and Judge Canonge had finally reached the upper floor through the smoke to discover a wooden door that led to the attic. It was locked. According to the *New Orleans Courier* of April 11, 1834, Judge Canonge sought out Dr. Lalaurie, who was also present in the house. He is said to have asked him politely to open the attic door so that they could check for the presence of slaves, but the judge received a rude reply: "There are those who would be better employed if they would attend to their own affairs instead of officiously intermeddling with the concerns of others."

It's hard to know what to make of this statement by Dr. Lalaurie, and of his refusal to open the attic door. It is possible that he felt the attic was in no danger from the fire and didn't want the men poking around up there - since he undoubtedly knew what they would find. His statement was surely meant in reference to his neighbor, Montreuil, who had already caused problems for the family over the treatment of their slaves. He had tried to protect his wife or more likely, the family's reputation during the incident with the slave Devince by freeing the man so that the story would not become public. The couple had recently suffered embarrassment at having their slaves impounded, and discovery of what was hidden in the attic would leave the family devastated.

Perhaps Dr. Lalaurie felt his refusal to open the door would be enough to turn the men away, but he had not counted on the persistence of Montreuil and Judge Canonge. The judge ordered the firefighters to break open the door and they forced themselves into the attic.

What greeted them behind the door shocked and dismayed the men. According to the *New Orleans Bee* of April 11, 1834, "Seven slaves, more or less horribly mutilated, were seen suspended by the neck, with their limbs apparently stretched and torn from one extremity to the other. These slaves had been confined by the woman Lalaurie for several months in the situation from which they had thus providentially been rescued, and had been merely kept in existence to prolong their suffering and to make them taste all that the most refined cruelty could inflict."

The *New Orleans Courier* added, "A most appalling sight was presented in the shape of several wretched negroes emerging from the fire, their bodies covered with scars and loaded with chains. Amongst them was a female slave, upwards of 60 years of age who could not move... We saw one of the miserable beings. The sight was so horrible that we could scarce not look at it. The most savage heart could not have witnessed the spectacle unmoved. He had a large hole in his head. His body was covered from head to foot with scars and filled with worms. The sight inspired us with such horror that even in the moment of writing this article we shudder from its effects. Those who have seen the others represent them to be in similar condition."

In some modern accounts of the discovery behind the locked attic door, detailed descriptions of all sorts of perverse tortures and experiments have appeared. Tales have been told of makeshift operating tables, slaves locked in cages, bodies cut open and holes that had been cut into human skulls in order for the victim's brains to be stirred. In most cases, the *New Orleans Bee* is cited as the source for this horror, but a check of the actual newspaper accounts proves this to be untrue. All of the stories and eyewitness accounts of the time confirm the discovery of the badly treated slaves in the house, as well as the horrific condition of the slaves kept in the attic. The story of the hole cut in the man's head "so that his brains could be stirred" undoubtedly came from the *Courier's* mention of the man with the hole in his head. This was actually referring to a deep wound, not an actual hole. Even so, he had been left in the attic with his wounds untreated for so long that he had become infested with maggots. Later sources from the late nineteenth and early twentieth centuries, including some written by New Orleans natives who knew the case, also failed to mention anything other than the emaciated slaves who had wounds that were consistent with a long period of incarceration and abuse. This doesn't make things any better. The slaves suffered horribly at the hands of a cruel and malicious master. Lurid tales of medical experiments take away from the fact that this was a horrible, vile situation.

The first mention that I located of the terrible experiments, which have since become a staple in the re-telling of the Lalaurie story, is in 1946. In *Ghost Stories of Old New Orleans*, author Jeanne deLavigne claims that the first men who entered the attic found:

...powerful male slaves, stark naked, chained to the wall, their eyes gouged out, their fingernails pulled out by the roots; others had their joints skinned and festering, great holes in their buttocks where their flesh had been sliced away, their ears hanging by shreds, their lips sewed together, their tongues drawn out and sewed to their chins, severed hands stitched to their bellies, legs pulled joint to joint. Female slaves there were, their mouths and ears crammed with ashes and chicken offal and bound tightly; others had been smeared with honey and were a mass of black ants. Intestines were pulled out and knotted around naked waists. There were holes in skulls, where a rough stick had been inserted to stir the brains. Some of the creatures were dead; some were unconscious; and a few were still breathing, suffering agonies beyond power to describe.

It's certainly a terrifying scene - but there's not a shred of truth to it. The horrifying account from the book was picked up, told, and re-told by various authors over the years. It's been repeated time and time again and still is on the lesser ghost tours in New Orleans today , often by people who should have known better. What Delphine Lalaurie did to her slaves was horrible enough, but apparently, by the 1940s, just mistreating and abusing slaves was not bad enough. To make the story even more frightening, it had to be taken one step further. Looking back on this story today, we can see what Delphine did in the house on Royal Street was the work of a sadist and a sociopath - and more than ample reason for the house to gain a reputation for being haunted.

As the mutilated slaves were carried and led out of the house, the crowd outside grew. Only one of two friends remained beside Madame Lalaurie. By this time, Dr. Lalaurie was gone. There are no further mentions of him in the accounts of what happened next at the house, but we do know that he and his wife were separated after the fire. This time, it was for good. Delphine managed to get someone to lock the doors and to seal the wooden gates that led from the street into the courtyard. This effectively sealed the Lalaurie household off from the crowd outside, which was milling about, waiting to see if any arrests were going to be made over the cruel treatment of the slaves. Nothing happened over the course of the several hours that followed. The fire was out by this time and little damage had been done to the house.

Word spread of the atrocity discovered in the Lalaurie home and people spoke again of the little girl who had allegedly been killed, the slaves that had been taken away from the Lalaurie family, and the rumors of the slaves that went missing and were never seen again. According to reports in the *New Orleans Gazette*, "at least 2,000 people" came to the courthouse to see the slaves that had been taken from the mansion. The slaves received food and medical care and were prodded with questions about their captivity and abuse. A long wooden table was filled with instruments of torture that had been brought from the attic. They included whips, chains, shackles, and knives - some of which were said to be crusted with dried blood.

One of the statements given came from a female slave who testified that Madame Lalaurie would sometimes beat and torture her captives while parties were going on below. She would come into the locked room, still clad in her ball gown, and lash the slaves as they cowered on the floor. After a few lashes, she would appear to be satisfied and would leave. One of the women also testified that Delphine once beat her own daughter for bringing food to the starving slaves.

Passionate words swept through New Orleans as curious crowds came to gape at the starving and brutalized slaves. As the wounded creatures gulped down the food that was given to them, Judge Canonge, Montreuil, Fernandez and Felix Lefebvre all made formal statements to the authorities about their discovery of the locked chamber.

In the meantime, the mob was still waiting outside the gates to the house on Royal Street. They expected to see arrests made and for the authorities to demand entry to the house. Hours passed and the police did not arrive. The mob continued to grow. More and more people came, and as each hour passed, they grew more restless and belligerent. Soon, threats were being shouted at the shuttered windows and calls for vengeance were heard from the street.

Suddenly, late in the afternoon, the gates to the high-walled courtyard burst open and a carriage roared out. It plowed directly into the mob and men scattered before the hooves of the horses. The coach pushed through the crowd and disappeared from sight, racing down Hospital Street toward the Bayou Road. It happened so quickly that everyone was taken by surprise. Someone cried out that the carriage had only been a decoy -- that Madame Lalaurie was actually escaping through a rear door. While some went to look, others swore that she had been in the carriage alone. Dr. Lalaurie was nowhere to be found. Delphine's children it was rumored afterward had been forced to escape the house by climbing over a balcony and into a house next door.

But it was Delphine who the angry mob sought and she had easily escaped their clutches. The carriage drove furiously along the Bayou Road and it is said that a sailing vessel waited for her there and left at once for Mandeville. Another story claimed that she remained in hiding in New Orleans for several days and only left the city when she realized that public opinion was hopelessly against her. No one knows which of these stories is true, but we do know that she was in Mandeville nearly ten days later because she signed a power of attorney there that would allow an agent in New Orleans to handle her business affairs on her behalf.

The seething mob that remained behind on Royal Street continued to grow. Delphine's flight had enraged the crowd and they decided to take their anger out on the mansion she had left behind. The *New Orleans Courier* reported that "doors and windows were broken open, the crowd rushed in, and the work of destruction began."

Feather beds were ripped open and thrown out into the street while curtains were pulled down from the windows and pictures torn from the walls. Men carried pianos, tables, sofas and chairs and hurled them out the windows to see them splinter on the streets below. After destroying nearly every belonging left in the house, the mob, still unsatisfied, began to tear apart the house itself. The mahogany railings were ripped away from the staircase, glass was broken, and doors were torn from their hinges.

The *New Orleans Bee* of April 12, 1834 stated, "It was found necessary for the purpose of restoring order, for the sheriff and his officers to repair to the place of the riot and to interpose the authority of the state, which we are pleased to notice proved effectual, with the occurrence of any of those acts of violence, which are common on similar occasions... Nearly the whole of the edifice is demolished and scarcely anything remains but the walls, which the popular vengeance have ornamented with various writings expressive of their indignation and the justness of their punishment."

It was later suggested that the house be torn down, but cooler heads prevailed. Instead, the house was closed and sealed. It remained that way for several years, silent, uninhabited and abandoned. Or was it?

After her flight from New Orleans, Delphine set up residence in Paris. The ghastly discovery in the attic had been enough to drive the family, despite their wealth and social standing, out of the country. Her husband did not flee to Paris with her. His reputation had been destroyed and Delphine ensured that it would be further tarnished early in her exile. Her son, Paulin, wrote a letter to his brother-in-law, Auguste Delassus, in which he spoke of the bad treatment that his mother received at her husband's hands. He said Dr. Lalaurie had also been present when others had treated Delphine badly and had done nothing to defend her.

I'm sure that this was the way that Delphine saw things, and the way that she passed it on to her impressionable son. She was the abused one. Her husband had done nothing to defend her when she was attacked for beating her slaves, which she felt she had every right to do since they were her property. Lalaurie had then abandoned her, unable to deal with her cruelty and sadistic nature, which Delphine saw as the ultimate betrayal. As far as is known, Dr. Lalaurie never saw his wife again.

He nearly vanished from history, only emerging in 1842 when he wrote a letter from Cuba to Auguste Delassus, who was his son-in-law through marriage. The two men had been friends years before and Lalaurie called on that friendship to ask that some of his possessions be sent to him in Havana. Those possessions included a case of books, some diplomas and treasured Masonic materials that had been left in safe-keeping with Delassus years before. No record exists of the shipment or of further correspondence between the two men, although based on the letters, it is evident that they had been writing back and forth for some time. As Delassus had not abandoned Lalaurie, one has to wonder what he thought of Delphine, the mother of his wife, and the attempts that had been made to discredit Dr. Lalaurie in his eyes.

Lalaurie died in Cuba, but no record of his date of death has ever been found. He remained exiled on the island for the remainder of his life, his professional reputation in tatters and his name all but destroyed. While never tortured, beaten or killed by her hand, Dr. Leonard Louis Nicolas Lalaurie was nevertheless a victim of the sadistic cruelty of Delphine Lalaurie.

Delphine settled comfortably into her Paris life. When she arrived, she was accompanied by her six-year-old son, Jean Louis and three of her adult children by Jean Blanque: her daughters Marie Louise Pauline and Louise Marie Laure and her son, Paulin.

Despite some stories, she was never in hiding while living in Paris. She could not be prosecuted for any of the crimes she had committed in New Orleans, so her whereabouts were no secret. Her daughter Jeanne, who was married to Auguste Delassus, visited her mother in Paris in the late 1830s with her husband and children. Delphine had given power of attorney to Delassus before fleeing New Orleans, but eventually Jeanne and Auguste separated. He moved to Missouri and his wife joined her mother in France. Auguste continued corresponding with his mother-in-law for some years, notably asking about her finances and mental health, and continued to handle her business affairs until her son Jean Louis came of age.

Delphine thrived in Paris, conducting her business in Louisiana from France. She paid her taxes and financed the repair of a residence in New Orleans' Marigny District that was later rented out. She would later return to New Orleans and live in this house until her death.

In the early 1840s, letters written by Delphine began taking on a different tone than ones written just a few years before. One correspondence exchanged with Auguste Delassus made repeated inquiries about money and made several frantic references to his failure to write back to her as quickly as she would have liked. Delphine's son Paulin wrote to Delassus that his mother seemed to be using her concerns about the state of her finances in Louisiana as a reason to return to New Orleans. Her children were appalled that she would even consider such an action, but they were unable to talk her out of it.

Unsuccessful in convincing her to stay in France, most of the children returned with her to New Orleans. Jeanne had come to Paris after her marriage had ended and she returned to America with Delphine, as did Paulin and his sister, Pauline. Louise Marie Laure stayed in France for some time after her family departed, but by late 1842, she had also returned to New Orleans. Only Jean Louis maintained residences in both Paris and New Orleans, traveling back and forth as he endeavored to handle his mother's business affairs. He took care of family business until his death in 1883 at the age of fifty-five.

Delphine's oldest daughter Borquita lived in New Orleans her entire life. There is no evidence that she ever visited her mother in Paris, or any record that she had any contact with her at all. What relationship they may have maintained, and whether or not the atrocities at the house on Royal Street had any effect on her life, is unknown.

Just as a number of erroneous stories about what happened to Delphine after she left New Orleans made the rounds, there were a number of tales that were told about her death. When she fled the city, some claimed that she spent the rest of her life in the forest along the north shore of Lake Pontchartrain. According to the author George W. Cable, Madame Lalaurie made her way to Mobile and then went on to Paris. He went on to say that her reputation preceded her to France and when she was confronted and recognized in Paris, she spent her days "skulking about in the provinces under assumed names."

Several different accounts of the death of Delphine Lalaurie have also been recorded. One claimed that she was killed by a wild boar while hunting in France. Another story, which appeared in the *Daily Picayune* in March 1892 insisted that she died among family and friends in Paris. Others claimed that she secretly returned to New Orleans and died there. In the early 1900s, Eugene Backes, who served as sexton to St. Louis Cemetery 1 until 1924, was said to have discovered an old, cracked, copper plate in Alley 4 of the cemetery. The inscription on the plate read: "Madame Lalaurie, née Marie Delphine Macarty, décédée à Paris, le 7 Décembre, 1842, à l'âge de 68 ans." No record of any burial has ever been found, however, further adding to the mystery.

More recently, other information has revealed that Delphine was alive for a number of years after 1842, which was, incidentally, the year that she returned to New Orleans from Paris. According to court papers, Delphine was apparently still alive in 1850, the year that her brother L.B. Macarty's estate was settled. His will directed that property that he had given in his lifetime to his daughter, Marie Louise Macarty, be counted as her one fourth share of the estate. Inheritance laws at that time directed that children would receive a one-fourth share of their parent's estate, no matter what a will might say. By designating the previously given property as Marie's share and leaving her nothing of his current estate, Macarty was essentially cutting his daughter out of his will in favor of another heir, which was Delphine. Macarty's executors appraised the property left to Marie at $28,100 and took a commission from that. Delphine, Macarty's sole heir under the terms of the will, challenged the executors in court, arguing that the property left to her was never part of the estate and they should not get a commission from it. Delphine not only got her brother's entire estate, but she cleverly managed to cut the executors out of their commission. This seems to show that she was not only alive, but was still in command of her business dealings in 1850.

The next appearance of Delphine Lalaurie in any documents seems to be after her death. A newspaper advertisement appeared in the *New Orleans Times* in 1858 about the sale of "parcels" to settle her estate. However, no burial notice appeared in the newspapers at that time - or at any other time. Based on how long it normally took to settle an estate in those days, Delphine probably died between 1855 and 1858, but no one knows for sure. There is also a question about where she was interred. She could have been buried in any of the Macarty family crypts, those of the Forstall family, or even in some anonymous tomb. Nothing exists to say either way. The copper plaque with a mysterious death date offers only a tenuous connection to St. Louis Cemetery 1, but even that has been disputed.

What became of one of New Orleans' most infamous women? No one will ever know for sure. Those who can answer that question are now long dead. Whatever became of her is a mystery - much like the one that still surrounds her once-grand home on Royal Street.

The haunted history of the Lalaurie mansion is perhaps one of the best-known ghost stories in a city famous for its ghosts. For generations, it has been considered the most haunted house in the French Quarter and in many early writings, it was referred to simply as "the haunted house." The name of the mansion was seldom mentioned, and yet everyone seemed well aware as to what house the writer was referring to. Horrible things happened in this house -- horrible enough to earn the house a reputation that still lingers almost two centuries later.

The stories of a haunting at 1140 Royal Street began almost as soon as the Lalaurie carriage fled the scene. According to legend, firemen, police officers and scavengers heard scratching and moaning sounds coming from the house for several days after the fire, but they were unable to find anyone - living or dead. No bodies were found in the ruined portions of the house. Stories later circulated about "Madame Lalaurie's graveyard" being found on the property, and of bodies being found beneath the floorboards in the 1970s, but no record of remains being discovered exists today. One has to wonder what became of the servants who vanished and were never seen again, or what became of the body of the little girl that a neighbor reportedly saw being buried in the courtyard. Were these disappearances merely part of the Lalaurie legend, or was there truth to the stories?

Ghastly tales circulated about the house. It remained vacant for a few years after its sacking by the mob, falling into a state of ruin and decay. Many people claimed to hear screams coming from the empty house at night and saw the apparitions of slaves walking about on the balconies and in the yards. Some stories even claimed that vagrants who had gone into the house seeking shelter were never heard from again.

The house was still owned by the Lalaurie family, and managed by Auguste Delassus, until 1837, when it was sold through the city. It was then rebuilt in its current, three-story configuration. When the Lalauries lived in the house, it was a typical two-story Creole home. While it is the same house that occupies the lot today, it was extensively renovated and is now in the style of 1840s New Orleans.

The man who purchased and remodeled the mansion only kept it for three months. He told his family and friends that he abandoned the place because he was plagued by strange noises, cries, and groans in the night. He tried leasing the house to a barbershop and to a store that rented the basement for a short time, but none of the tenants stayed for long. He tried to rent rooms out, but nobody remained for more than a few days. Finally, he gave up and the house was abandoned.

Following the Civil War, Reconstruction turned the empty Lalaurie mansion into an integrated high school for "girls of the Lower District," but in 1874 the White League forced the black children to leave the school. League members actually lined the girls up and questioned them about their family backgrounds, trying to find out which ones were colored, and which were not. In a city as racially diverse as New Orleans, many had both white and black ancestors. To racists, even having a black ancestor several generations removed was enough to brand someone as "colored." Those girls were forcibly removed from the school.

Soon after the school was closed, the house was listed as a leaf tobacco business owned by Joseph Barnes. In addition, the 1938 *New Orleans City Guide* stated that the building was used as a gambling house in the 1870s. According to the guide, "Stories were told and retold of the strange lights and shadow objects that were seen flitting about in different apartments, their forms draped with sheets, skeleton heads protruding. Hoarse voices like unto those supposed to come only from the charnel house floated out on the fog-laden air on dismal and rainy nights, with the ominous sound of clanking chains coming from the servants' quarters, where foul crimes are said to have been committed." Needless to say, it's rather hard to take this over-wrought account too seriously, but it does lend credence to the fact that stories were still circulating about Delphine and her victims many years after the discovery of her abused slaves.

In 1876, the *Daily Picayune* published an article about the house being up for auction. The building was described as "admirably adapted for a large boarding school, asylum, first class boarding house or spacious summer residence. The building is leased for the summer, renting at a rate of $150 per month."

In 1878, the New Orleans schools were officially segregated and the house, once a school where all of the "colored" children were forced to leave, became a school for black children only. This lasted for only one year.

In 1882, the mansion once again became a center for New Orleans society when an English teacher turned it into a "conservatory of music and a fashionable dancing school." All went well for some time, as the teacher was well known and attracted students from the finest of the local families, but things came to a terrible conclusion. A local newspaper apparently printed an accusation against the teacher, claiming some improprieties with female students just before a grand social event was to take place at the school. Students and guests shunned the place and the school closed the following day.

A few years later, more strange events plagued the house and it became the center for rumors regarding the death of Joseph Edward Vigne, the eccentric member of a wealthy New Orleans family. Vigne lived secretly in the house from around 1889 until his death in 1892. He was found dead on a tattered cot, apparently living in filth, while hidden away in the surrounding rooms was a collection of antiques and treasure. A bag containing several hundred dollars was discovered near his body and another search found several thousand dollars hidden in his mattress. For some time after, rumors of a lost treasure circulated about the mansion, but few dared to go in search of it.

In June 1893, an article ran in the *Times Democrat* that stated, "F. Greco purchased the haunted house at Hospital and Royal ... yesterday he posted large flowing placards upon the walls of the building announcing in both Italian and English, 'The Haunted House.' There is an end to everything, so there is with ghosts. Come and be convinced. Admission ten cents." This was apparently New Orleans very first ghost tour! How long this "attraction" ran is unknown, but by late in the decade, the house was empty once more.

Starting in the 1890s, the house changed hands five times in the next two decades. Author Henry C. Castellanos disdainfully noted in 1895, "A year or two ago, it was the receptacle of the scum of Italian immigrants, and the fumes of the malodorous filth which emanated from its interior proclaimed what it really was." While Castellanos was as biased toward Italians as many in New Orleans were at the time, this was a period of great immigration to America and many Italian immigrants flocked to the city. By 1890, there were more than 15,000 of them living there, mostly in the crumbling French Quarter, which by then had fallen out of favor with most Creole families. Outside of New York, New Orleans saw more Italian immigrants than anywhere in America. The majority of them came from Sicily.

Landlords quickly bought up old and abandoned buildings to convert into cheap housing for this new wave of renters. The Lalaurie mansion, with its more than forty rooms, became just such a house. For many of the tenants, though, even cheap rent was not enough to keep them there.

It was during this time that the first accounts surfaced of bodies being found under the floors of the house. As workmen came in to repair the old wooden floors, human skeletons were found lying beneath. According to author Jeanne deLavigne who we have already discovered is not totally reliable , "It all simmered down to one conclusion - they were bodies of Lalaurie slaves, buried thus in order that their manner of death should not become known." Was there any truth to this story, or was it just one more of the author's fanciful additions to the legend? There is no documentation of such a discovery in newspaper articles or police reports, but can we be absolutely sure that a slumlord and his cheaply paid workmen would have reported such a find? Isn't it entirely possible that the owner of the ramshackle old house could have simply ordered the men to just cover up what they found so that he could quickly rent out the rooms?

We may never know, but what we do know is that during the time when the mansion was a tenement house, a number of strange events were reported. Among them was an encounter between an occupant and a naked black man in chains who attacked him. The black man abruptly vanished. Others claimed to have pets butchered in the house; children were attacked by a phantom with a whip; strange figures appeared wrapped in shrouds; and of course, there were the ever-present sounds of screams, groans and cries that would reverberate through the house at night. The sounds, they said, came from the locked and abandoned room where the slaves had been discovered during the fire.

One young mother claimed to be terrified one night when she looked over to where her baby was sleeping and saw a dark-haired woman in elegant evening clothes bending over her sleeping infant. The ghostly woman was said to have been Delphine Lalaurie herself. When the mother let out a bloodcurdling cry, the apparition vanished.

It was never easy to keep tenants in the house and finally, after word spread of the strange goings-on there, the mansion was deserted. By 1922, it was vacant once again.

The house was renovated and sold in 1923 to William Warrington, who established the Warrington House, a refuge for wayward boys. For the next nine years, the house opened its doors to a succession of "madcap" young men, as Warrington blithely called them, who were released from jails and prisons and put into Warrington's care.

In 1932, the mansion was sold to the Grand Consistory of Louisiana, an organization like the Freemasons, who kept the place for the next decade. They sold the house in 1942.

In 1943, in the midst of World War II, the mansion saw a new group of tenants. According to an Associated Press story from June 1943, "The sheet waving, bone rattling crew that has occupied New Orleans' most widely known haunted house for the last 111 years has been dispossessed to make way for war workers. Despite the kindness which this city - and the entire South - has always shown to its ghosts and 'ha'nts,' no investigation by the rental division of the OPA is anticipated. With the city's normal half-million population augmented by 50,000 war workers and an additional 12,000 workers anticipated to man now-building aircraft plants, the ghosts will have to shift for themselves."

As it was during the great immigration wave of the 1890s, New Orleans saw itself bombarded with new and temporary arrivals during the war years, all of them were looking for places to live. With so many empty buildings in the French Quarter, government services took over the old Lalaurie mansion and converted it into apartments for the workers. Their tenancy lasted until the end of the war, when the house was put back on the market.

There is no record of any supernatural activity occurring in the house at this time, but the story stayed fresh in the minds of locals, which leads many to believe that tales were still being told. In 1945, the first floor of the house was turned into a tavern, which the proprietor called the "Haunted Saloon." Taking advantage of the house's eerie history, he kept a record of the strange things that were experienced there by the staff and patrons.

After the bar closed, the space became a furniture store. It did not fare well. The owner first suspected vandals when all of his merchandise was found ruined on several occasions, covered in some sort of dark, stinking liquid. He finally waited one night with a shotgun, hoping the vandals would return. When dawn came, the furniture was ruined again, even though he knew that no one had entered the building. Exasperated and frightened, he closed the place down.

The house was apparently empty for most of the early 1960s. An article that appeared in the *Times-Picayune* in 1964 reported that a preservation group, the Vieux Carre Commission, was trying to stop the deterioration and partial demolition of the former Lalaurie house. Evidently, people had been looting the abandoned house and stealing anything of value out of it that could be taken. The preservation group noted that "the building has been stripped of the floor boards in the upper balcony," among other things.

As it turned out, the house was saved, although in 1969, it became an apartment building again. It had been divided into about twenty apartments for war workers in 1943 and they were now being rented out again - with ghostly results. Zella Funck, an artist who lived in one of the apartments, stated that the poltergeists in her place were "...playful. They're not around every day, but they do surprise visitors." She stated that one of the ghosts that she had seen was that of a handsome man in old-fashioned clothing, which may have been Dr. Lalaurie.

Another tenant, a Mrs. Richards, reported numerous incidents in her apartment, such as water faucets and showers turning on by themselves, and locked doors becoming unlocked.

In 2000, the mansion was purchased by a New Orleans doctor, who decided to restore the house to its original state although it was actually the second incarnation of the house. He restored it with a living area in the front portion and five luxury apartments to the rear. He had no paranormal experiences while living in the house and there are many this author included who believe that the haunting had started to diminish by the late 1970s.

In 2007, actor Nicolas Cage bought the Lalaurie mansion through his Hancock Park Real Estate Company. Rumor had it that Cage was living in the front section of the house and renting out the back gallery, where the slaves quarters were once located. Cage was spending a lot of time in New Orleans in those days and even had a tomb built for himself at St. Louis Cemetery 1. If he was living in the mansion, however, his tenancy was short-lived. In 2008, the house was back on the market listed at $3.5 million. A year later, the bank foreclosed on the home along with two other haunted houses in New Orleans that Cage had acquired. It was purchased by the Regions Financial Corporation in November 2009.

As of this writing, the house was still on the market and available for purchase.

Would it be the perfect property for a wealthy person who was looking for a haunted house? Perhaps not. While the mansion is beautiful, with a rich and horrific history, I doubt very much that it is still haunted. While the place certainly deserves the long account of haunted happenings that occurred over the years, it's been quiet now since the late 1970s. I believe that the haunting has faded with time, like a powerful battery that eventually loses its charge.

Yes, there were plenty of people who believed that they encountered ghosts at the Lalaurie mansion, but not in recent times. I had the chance to go inside the mansion once several years ago, and I would be lying if I said that I had hoped to see or feel something in the place. I went away with no supernatural encounter, but I did not go away disappointed. It was a house alive with evil history. I heard no phantom whispers or spectral wails, but I did leave with a sense of the evil legacy that Delphine Lalaurie left behind in that house. Her twisted heart and horrific actions created a legend that has lived on for nearly two centuries. Can a spirit like her, so infused with anger and evil, ever really find peace? Can her victims?

Ghosts may no longer walk in the house on Royal Street, but history has left a dark and indelible impression there. The ghosts may be gone, but how much more "haunted" can one house be?

A BOX OF LETTERS
The Story of the "Watseka Wonder"

The strange tale of the so-called "Watseka Wonder," a baffling phenomenon that occurred in a small Illinois town in the latter part of the nineteenth century, still stands today as one of the weirdest and most authentic accounts of the supernatural in American history. It has been investigated, dissected and ridiculed but, as of this writing, no clear explanation for the events that took place has ever been offered. There are many theories that exist and yet there is not a single explanation that can encompass all of the strange happenings that are associated with this eerie case.

We have to accept the fact that we simply do not know as much about the unexplained as we think we do.

The town of Watseka, which boasted about 1,500 souls in the late 1870s, was little more than a sleepy farming community at the time when the "Watseka Wonder" left its indelible mark. Not much happened there, aside from the ordinary gossip and minor scandals that plague all small towns, until the peace of the community was shattered on July 11, 1877.

It was on this day that a thirteen-year-old girl named Lurancy Vennum first fell into a mysterious, catatonic trance during which she claimed that she was able to speak to angels and the spirits of the dead. The strange spells would often occur many times each day and some of them would last for hours. During the trances, Lurancy would speak in different voices and tell of places far away that she had no real knowledge about. When she woke up, she wouldn't remember anything that she said or did while she was under the influence of these spells. Word quickly spread around town that odd things were happening at the home of Thomas and Lurinda Vennum and soon the news began to spread out of town, to Chicago and around the state. Soon, many visitors began to arrive in Watseka, all hoping to see the young girl.

The news of these strange trances gained much attention within the Spiritualist community for many believed that Lurancy was manifesting mediumistic abilities during her trances. Soon, Spiritualists from all over Illinois, and from throughout the country, came to Watseka to see if the stories were true.

The Vennum family was not interested in mediums and Spiritualists, however. They were only concerned with the health and welfare of their daughter. They took her to one physician after another in hopes that someone would be able to help her. The doctors could find nothing physically wrong with Lurancy and they eventually diagnosed her as being mentally ill. It was recommended that she be sent to the state insane asylum. Heartbroken, the Vennums felt they had no other choice, and after the holiday season of 1877, they began to make arrangements to have their daughter committed. They knew there was little chance that Lurancy would ever come home again.

But before Lurancy could be sent away, in January 1878, a man named Asa Roff arrived at the Vennum home. He explained to them that his own daughter, Mary, had been afflicted with the same condition that Lurancy was suffering from. He begged the Vennums not to send Lurancy to the asylum. He had mistakenly sent his own daughter away years before and she had later died. Despite her death, though, he was convinced that his daughter's spirit still existed. Little did he know it would soon become apparent to many that his daughter's spirit was now inside of the body of Lurancy Vennum.

This was the beginning of a series of strange and fantastic events that rocked the little town of Watseka and created a mystery that remains unsolved to this day. To understand the events, we must first start at the beginning of the story and try to put together the pieces of the puzzle that has fascinated researchers, historians and the general public for more than a century.

Asa Roff's daughter Mary was born on October 8, 1846 in Warren County, Indiana, a little less than a year before the Roff family came to Illinois and settled in the town that would become Watseka. Starting at the age of six months, Mary began to suffer from seizures, which over the course of her life gradually increased in violence. When the attacks began, she was a tiny infant and her condition paralyzed the Roffs with fear, especially after the earlier deaths of two of their children, William and George. Strangely, though, even though Mary lay in a coma-like state for several days, she soon recovered and, within few weeks, seemed perfectly fine.

Unfortunately, her periods of good health would not last. A few weeks later, another spell seized her. Her pupils would dilate, her body would become very stiff and her muscles would twitch uncontrollably for a short time. The seizure would then be followed by a period of eerie calm that could last for minutes, hours or even days. Once it came to an end, she would behave normally, as if no illness afflicted her --- at least until she suffered from another bout with the puzzling illness. The spells came every three to five weeks and as she grew older, they became more violent and more prolonged.

As Mary grew older, and the seizures became more horrifying, she began to complain of hearing mysterious voices in her head. The voices, she said, came from nowhere and told her to do things that she knew she shouldn't. Even her periods of good health seemed to be marked by a depression and despondency that should not have been present in a beautiful young girl who was dearly loved by her parents and her sister, Minerva. Mary could often be found sitting in the parlor of their home, playing mournful music and singing sad songs. A feeling of doom seemed to linger about her, as if she knew terrible events were coming.

By the time Mary was fifteen, her health had grown worse. The Roffs had taken her to see doctors all over the region, including Dr. Jesse Bennett and Dr. Franklin Blades of Watseka, and several prominent physicians in Chicago, including Dr. N.S. Davis. Davis was a professor at the Northwestern University Medical School and a well-known homeopathic physician. He not only helped to charter a homeopathic medical college in Chicago but also pressed for reforms for the city's healthcare system. He led the campaign in 1862 for the city to hire a health officer and to start a citywide board of health. Asa Roff spared no expense in trying to get treatment for Mary, seeking out the best Illinois medical men of the time, but it was all to no avail. No one could discover what was wrong with her. It eventually was suggested that she be sent to a sanitarium run by a Dr. Nevins in Peoria for treatment.

The sanitarium was similar to many that dotted the American landscape during the 1850s and 1860s. It was known simply as a "water cure," or hydropathic institution, and it offered an alternative to the usual practice of medicine by promising a healthier life through simple, natural drug-free means. It was based on the use of pure, soft, mineral-free water in various forms of baths, wet wraps and internal cleansing. Treatment also included other "natural" treatments like exercise, fresh air, and a vegetarian diet that was rich in fruits and grains. The use of alcohol and tobacco was strictly prohibited and ladies who came to the clinic were encouraged to cast off the tight-fitting corsets that were fashionable at the time and to wear loose-fitting clothing.

By this time, Mary's doctors had come to believe that her spells and seizures were caused by some sort of "female ailment" and so a water cure seemed to be the perfect answer. Water cure sanitariums held a special appeal for women. Most members of the medical community at this time treated women's issues, like menstruation, childbirth and menopause as unnatural occurrences to be dealt with aggressively but the water cure advocates treated them as natural events that they believed could be eased by exercise, diet, calmness and baths. In addition, there were usually female doctors on staff to attend to the ladies, since hydropathic medical schools were among the only places that women who wanted to study medicine found acceptance.

Patients like Mary who came for a water cure were instructed to bring with them certain items that were needed for treatment: two large wool blankets, three comforters, two coarse cotton sheets, one coarse linen sheet, six towels and pieces of cotton for bandages. During the course of water treatments, Mary was immersed naked into a tub of water and then placed into a tub of very hot water. She would also receive a cold water douche and wet sheets were wrapped tightly around her body to restrict her circulation, followed by vigorous rubbing to restore her circulation to normal. She would later go for a strenuous walk and then return to her room for a nap, where she would be wrapped with several blankets and comforters, leaving only her face exposed.

There were few illnesses that could not be "treated" by a water cure, which purported to cure colds, weak constitutions, fevers, poor circulation, gout, alcoholism and even seizures and insanity. And while the treatment may seem harsh, or even shocking, it was preferable to most general medicine of the day, which relied heavily on purgatives, enemas, laxatives and bloodletting for treating illnesses. The water cure was not only gentler but could actually be effective.

Mary remained at Dr. Nevins' sanitarium for eighteen months, during which time she improved and relapsed several times. Her weird seizures continued, frightening the other patients, until finally, in the late spring of 1864, she was markedly improved and the doctor was able to send her home to Watseka. He truly believed that she had been cured and Mary finally seemed to be well --- at least for a time.

As summer approached, Mary began to complain of sharp, stabbing pains in her head. She called it a "lump of pain" and the only way that she seemed to be able to alleviate the discomfort was by cutting herself. She developed an obsession with blood and began stabbing herself with pins and cutting herself with a straight razor. A local doctor and druggist, F. Conrad Secrest, was called in he began applying leeches to Mary.

Bloodletting was a part of medical practice that dated back to ancient times and became particularly popular in America during the middle part of the 1800s. It was believed that by draining the blood, balance could be restored to the body. It was accomplished in two ways - either by cutting into a vein and letting blood escape, or by applying leeches, which took blood at a slow, predictable rate and then fell off when full.

Leeches were used for bloodletting in ancient Greece and Rome and they continued to be a part of European medical practice throughout the ages. The word "leech" even comes from an Old English word for physician. The practice remained popular for years and with the dawn of science, leeches became even more widely used. In the first half of the nineteenth century, scientific journals were full of articles extolling their virtues and trade in medicinal leeches became a major industry.

The use of leeches was often quite gruesome. They could be applied almost anywhere, including the gums, lips, nose, fingers, breasts, and even "the mouth of the womb." They were most commonly applied to the temples and prolonged use would leave the patient with small x-shaped scars where the leeches had fed. Dozens of leeches could be applied at a time. When they were full, they were stored in special jars until they were ready to be used again. Sometimes, a patient would be bled continuously for days at a time.

For some reason, Dr. Secrest left a supply of leeches at the Roff home and Mary would apply them to herself whenever she felt anxious or complained of a headache. She applied them to her temples and it was said that she treated them like pets. A bleeding session, which could last for thirty-five minutes or so, usually alleviated whatever pain she was feeling.

But on some days, the small amount of blood drawn by a leech or a straight pin was not enough. On Saturday morning, July 16, 1864, Mary took a knife and slipped outside to a hiding place in the backyard. She began cutting her arm and lost so much blood that she fainted. She was found several hours later and was carried into the house. It was some time before she stirred but when she did, she began to thrash violently about and scream as though she were being tortured. Her convulsions and screams continued almost non-stop for the next five days and nights. Mary oly weighed about 100 pounds, but the Roffs required the almost constant services of five strong men to hold her down on the bed. The girl bucked and kicked, punched and thrashed throughout the night and into the daylight hours. No one could explain the brutal force being manifested by this slender girl.

Finally, on the fifth day, the ravings ceased and Mary's demeanor became strangely serene. She regained consciousness and appeared to be quite normal, expect for one thing - she claimed not to recognize anyone in her family, nor her doctors, friends or neighbors. The house was filled with well-meaning acquaintances, as well as friends of Asa Roff, but Mary did not appear to know any of them. In addition to this peculiar development, Mary was able to speak of places where she had never been, often with uncanny accuracy. In addition, she was reportedly able to predict future events and she knew things about people that she should have had no way of knowing.

She also began to manifest a very strange, clairvoyant ability that allowed her to read and do anything else that she normally did in the course of her daily life, all while wearing a blindfold. Her eyes covered by a heavy blindfold, Mary would dress, stand before the mirror, open and search drawers, pick up various items and do whatever she customarily did.

The Roffs and their friends were amazed by this startling new ability and Mary was frequently put to the test by various ministers, newspaper reporters and "all of the prominent citizens of Watseka at that time."

During one of these tests, Mary was handed a thick medical encyclopedia and asked to find a listing for "blood." She turned to the index, while blindfolded, traced her fingers along the thousands of entries, pointed to the word "blood" and then opened the book to the page that was indicated and managed to read the entry. On another occasion, she took a box of letters that had been sent to her by friends and sat down, with a blindfold on, and read them aloud for the doctors, ministers and businessmen who were present. When the Reverend J.H. Rhea, newspaper editor A.G. Smith, Asa Roff and several others added some of their own letters to those that had been written to Mary, she proceeded to pull out these letters and examine them. If any were turned wrong-side up, she would reverse them, read aloud the addresses that were written on them and violently toss aside any letter that was not her own.

No one could explain how she was able to do these things. They were as mysterious as the spells that had been troubling her since she was an infant. Most of the physicians who treated Mary referred to her condition as catalepsy, a popular diagnosis of the nineteenth century.

Catalepsy is a condition that is characterized by rigid muscles and limbs, a loss of muscle control and a slowing down of bodily functions, like breathing. For this reason, many sufferers were mistakenly declared dead and this allegedly led to many premature burials in years past. In modern times, it has been learned that catalepsy does not appear of its own accord and instead, manifests as one of many symptom caused by disorders that have physical causes, ranging from

Parkinson's disease to epilepsy. In some cases, isolated cataleptic instances can also be precipitated by extreme emotional shock, but this is rare.

Most medical professionals in years past, especially those in the time of Mary Roff, believed that catalepsy was caused by a mental disorder. For this reason, they suspected that Mary was slipping into a cataleptic trance whenever she was by seized by one of her spells. However, this diagnosis did not explain how she obtained knowledge that she should not have had, was able to foresee future events, and could use clairvoyant powers to see and read through a blindfold. All of these "symptoms" remained unexplained.

For just this reason, some of the ministers who were called to the Roff home to examine Mary and witness her strange feats called her powers "a mystery of God's providence." They could find no explanation for how she was accomplishing the uncanny things she did and merely left the answers to the mysteries of divine intervention.

Perhaps the most perplexed by what was occurring were the newspaper editors and writers who came to visit the Roffs. These men could not look toward medical science for answers and their cynicism kept them from simply leaving the mystery in the hands of God. They knew that Mary's abilities, and her illness, were the result of some unaccountable phenomenon, but just what that was, they were unprepared to say.

A.G. Smith, the editor of the *Iroquois County Republican* at the time of Mary Roff's death and the editor of the *Danville Times* during Lurancy Vennum's possession, later wrote about Mary:

Now, as to Mary Roff, it was our fortune to know the sweet girl, who was herself a cataleptic, and who died twelve years ago. Disease dethroned her reason and maddened her brain until she sought her own and other's lives, and the modest young lady was transformed into a screaming maniac. She had periods of exemption from raving, and thus her aberrant mind conceived fancies of the queerest hue, creating the most impossible beings for associates, and conversing with them, she maintained her own side of the conversation in a usual tone of voice, while imagination supplied her created associates with language and intelligence. When in this condition, her father and mother asserted the discovery that Mary could read a book with its lid closed, and they desired us to test the correctness of what they claimed. We therefore took from our side pocket a letter enclosed in an envelope, and holding it before he bandaged eyes, said to her. "Mary, read the signature to that letter." Immediately, the proper name was pronounced.

Mary remained in what was referred to as her "clairvoyant state" for three or four days, still not recognizing anyone, and then finally, she seemed to regain her wits and began acting like herself again. She was once again conscious of those around her, recognized her family and friends and lost the ability to psychically "see" through a blindfold. Unfortunately, her return to what passed for normalcy meant the loss of the serene calmness that had accompanied her clairvoyant abilities and the return of her violent seizures.

The episodes came over and over again, causing Mary great pain and distress, and she would sometimes remain unconscious and rigid on the floor, or in her bed, for hours or days at a time. She never moved except when she was first seized by a spell, which often elicited horrifying screams. Her return to consciousness was often accompanied by the violent thrashing about that sometimes required several men to hold her down.

After coming out of her seizures, Mary began to speak of what she saw when she was unconscious. Angels and spirits spoke to her and traveled with her as she looked over places that she had never before visited. In time, she began to claim that these beings accompanied her back from "the other side" and were present in the Roff house. When Mary spoke with them, her friends and family saw nothing and never heard the other side of the conversations that she claimed to be having with the spirits.

Mary's condition worsened until finally, feeling they had no other choice, Asa and Dorothy Ann Roff accepted the advice that they had been given by several of Mary's doctors: they would place the girl in an insane asylum. All of the other possible avenues had been exhausted. No doctor could find a cure for her bizarre problem and, in fact, none of them could even agree on what the problem actually was. Despite the eerie abilities that Mary manifested for a time, there seemed to be no explanation for what was wrong with her other than that she was mentally ill.

Arrangements were made to send her away and all of this was carried out with the Roffs never realizing that Mary would not return home alive.

Placing Mary in an insane asylum was not a step that the Roffs took lightly. They had done everything that they could think of to find a cure for her baffling condition. They had allowed her to stay at Dr. Nevins' water cure facility, at great expense, for nearly eighteen months and had spent a small fortune on doctors, treatments and possible solutions. All of it had been to no avail and they had little choice but to consider the idea that Mary was mentally ill.

Tragically, though, sending her to the asylum offered no real chance for a cure. An insane asylum of the 1860s was not a place that was designed to treat the mentally ill. It was where those afflicted were warehoused and kept away from mainstream society in the same way that prisons were used to house criminals. Conditions were often extremely poor and treatment was not yet an option. Many asylums were barely fit for human habitation. They were filthy places of confinement where patients were often left in straitjackets, locked in restraints or even placed in cages if they were especially violent. Many of the inmates spent every day in shackles and chains.

This would have been the type of asylum that Mary Roff would have been sent to 1865. According to records, she was sent to Illinois' only state asylum at the time, located in Jacksonville. This asylum, known as the Illinois State Hospital for the Insane, was established in 1847 due to an act of the legislature and the efforts of Dorothea L. Dix, a social reformer and advocate for the insane and the incarcerated. Construction was started on the asylum in 1848 and it opened in 1851. By the time that Mary was sent there in 1865, conditions at the state asylum were similar to those that were being reported around the country at that time and it's likely that Mary found her stay to be a terrifying ordeal. Her physical health began to fail as she continued to endure her seizures while being subjected to the grim conditions of the hospital.

Asa and Dorothy Roff made as many trips to see their daughter as possible. Visiting time was restricted by hospital officials but the Roffs were able to come on successive days if they stayed somewhere locally. On July 5, 1865, they were on the third day of a visit to the hospital when Mary died. She had been able to sit down with them for breakfast but soon after had returned to her room for a nap. She drifted off to sleep but a few minutes later, she began to let out the familiar screams. They were the same bloodcurdling cries that came before Mary was gripped by one of her spells. Her parents were summoned, in hopes that they might be able to calm her down, but by the time they arrived at her room, the girl had gone quiet.

Mary's had died. At the age of 18, Mary Roff had been taken from this world, leaving a scar on her parent's hearts that was so deep that they turned to the Spiritualist movement to make sense of what had happened to her.

At the time of Mary Roff's death, Lurancy Vennum was a little more than one year old. In just over a decade, though, the two girls' lives would be forever connected in a case that still remains one of the strangest, and most authentic, cases of spirit possession ever recorded.

Mary Lurancy Vennum, or 'Rancy as she was usually called, was born on April 16, 1864, in Milford, a small community about seven miles south of Watseka. After living in Iowa for a year, the Vennums returned to Milford and a few years later, when Lurancy, was about seven, they moved to Watseka. This was long after Mary Roff's brief notoriety in town and her tragic death. The Vennum family knew nothing of the girl, her strange illness or anything about the Roff family. The only acquaintance between the two families came during one brief call that Mrs. Roff made on Mrs. Vennum after they moved to Watseka in 1871. Mr. Roff and Mr. Vennum were on formal speaking terms but that was all. The families lived on opposite sides of town.

Lurancy was the daughter of Thomas Jefferson Vennum, who was born in Washington County, Pennsylvania, in 1832. He had come to Illinois with his family when he was still a child and a number of Vennums were some of the first settlers of Iroquois County. His wife, Lurinda J. Smith, was born in Indiana in 1837 and they were married in Fayette County, Iowa in 1855. Thomas Vennum had been a farmer all of his life but his wife had asked him to move the family into town after he received a small inheritance from the sale of a farm in Iowa. Vennum was well liked in the community when his family's trouble began in July 1877.

Lurancy had never been a sickly girl, nor an especially imaginative one. For both reasons, her family was surprised when the strange events began. Save for a bout with measles in 1873, she had never been seriously ill and until 1877, she had never made up stories or told fanciful tales about much of anything at all. However, in the early days of July, she began speaking of mysterious voices that came to her in the night.

According to her story, they had roused her from her sleep. She stated: "There were persons in my room last night, and they called 'Rancy, Rancy...' and I felt their breath upon my face." She seemed to be frightened by what had occurred and was convinced that she had not dreamed it. Her parents had never known her to lie but, not believing in such things, they were not inclined to give credence to her story. They merely assumed that their daughter had experienced a very vivid nightmare, one so real that she believed that she was awake when it happened.

The following night, the same thing happened again. Lurancy was terrified and refused to stay in her room. She rose in the dead of night and nervously paced the parlor, too frightened to return to her second-floor bedroom. She told her mother that each time she tried to sleep, the presences would return, whispering her name. Finally, Lurinda took Lurancy back to her room and they lay down together on the bed. She wrapped her arms around her daughter and coaxed her back to sleep. The rest of the night passed without incident.

But on July 11, 1877, the possession truly began.

On that otherwise ordinary morning, Lurancy got out of bed feeling dizzy and nauseated. She complained to her mother about feeling sick but went about her household chores as usual. Around six o'clock that evening, after the day's heat had begun to fade, Lurinda asked Lurancy to help her start supper. Lurancy had been sewing a carpet that afternoon and she put aside her things and rose to come into the kitchen.

Suddenly, she spoke: "Ma, I feel bad. I feel so queer." She grabbed at her left breast with her hand, then collapsed to the floor. She was so quiet that she seemed to be dead and every muscle in her body had gone rigid and cold.

She stayed in a deep, catatonic sleep for the next five hours but when she woke up, she said she felt fine. The following day, Lurancy again slipped into a trance-like sleep but this time was different. This time, as she lay perfectly still, she began to speak out loud, talking of visions and spirits and carrying on conversations with people that no one else could see. She told her family that she was in heaven and that she could see and hear spirits. She described them and called some of them by name. Among them was her brother, who she affectionately called "Bertie." He had died in when Lurancy was only three years old.

In the days and weeks that followed, Lurancy's spells came more and more frequently and they sometimes lasted for more than eight hours at a time. While she was in her trance state, she continued to speak about her visions, which were sometimes terrifying. She began to see more and more spirits, including those who had terrorized her at night in her bedroom. So many of them were unfamiliar and frightening to her and she would cry out while in the midst of her spells. At times, Lurancy reportedly spoke in other languages, or at least spouted nonsense words that no one could understand. She lapsed into lengthy trances that would sometimes last for hours each day. When she awoke, she would remember nothing of what had happened during the trance and was always ignorant of her weird ramblings.

The frightening trances lasted throughout the summer months but at some point in September 1877, they stopped. Lurancy seemed to be herself again. Although her mother watched her cautiously for several weeks, the bizarre illness seemed to be gone. Gradually, life in the Vennum household began to return to normal.

But these times of normalcy were not destined to last.

On November 27, 1877, Lurancy began to complain of a violent pain in her stomach. The pain remained a dull, throbbing ache but several times each day, it became excruciating. The sharp, stabbing pain would always come on quite suddenly, making Lurancy scream and moan in torment. She would fall to the floor, her teeth grinding in agony, as the pain ripped through her body. It was later reported: "In these painful paroxysms, she would double herself back until her head and feet actually touched."

These horrendous episodes went on for about two weeks, only coming to an end on December 11, when Lurancy slipped once more into one of the dreaded trances that her parents thought had gone away. She was seized by one of these spells and slowly sank to the floor, completely unconscious. Her body rigidly remained in the same position for the next several hours. When she awakened, the abdominal pains were gone.

Unfortunately, though, the spells had returned. For the next several weeks, the trances came over her and lasted for two hours, three hours or even as long as eight hours. They occurred as many as twelve times each day, sending Lurancy into a place where she once again began to speak with the spirits that she saw there. She called them "angels" and held long eerie conversations with them, of which she would remember nothing when she finally regained consciousness.

Shortly after the trances had begun, Lurancy was placed under the care of Dr. L.N. Pittwood, who, one of the city's best-known medical practitioners. He could find nothing physically wrong with her. The family turned to a physician called Dr. Jewett for answers after the stomach pains and new spells, but he was also at a loss as to what was causing the illness. Many of the friends and family members of the Vennums believed that Lurancy had gone insane and the family's minister, the Reverend B.M. Baker from the Methodist church, went as far as to contact the state asylum in Jacksonville to see if the girl could be admitted there. It was the general opinion among those whose counsel the Vennums valued, that the girl should be institutionalized.

Stories and rumors about Lurancy and her visions began to circulate in Watseka. People were talking about the weird happenings and the local newspaper printed stories about them. No one followed the case more closely than Asa Roff. During his own daughter's illness, she had also claimed to communicate with spirits and she fell into long, sometimes violent, trances. He became convinced that Lurancy Vennum was suffering with the same affliction that Mary had. In spite of this, Roff said nothing until the Vennum family had exhausted every known cure for Lurancy and it appeared that she was going to be sent away to the asylum. At this point, he became determined to try and help.

Asa Roff called on the Vennum family in late January 1878. The family was naturally skeptical of the reason for his visit. Roff had little more than a casual acquaintance with Thomas Vennum but he explained that he had become interested in Lurancy's case after hearing the rumors that were going around town. Lurancy claimed to have had contact with the spirits of the dead, the possibility of which, being a devout Spiritualist, he did not doubt in the slightest. However, his real interest was concerning her illness. His late daughter Mary had suffered from an identical condition and she had also given incontrovertible evidence of supernatural powers in the form of clairvoyance. In her time, Mary had also been regarded as insane, although now, years later, Roff was convinced that she had been of sound mind but had been the victim of a "spirit infestation."

He believed that the same could be said of Lurancy and he begged the Vennums not to send her to an asylum.

He believed there was a way to help the girl and he convinced the Vennums to allow him to call in one more physician. If there was nothing that this man could do, then they could take whatever steps they believed were necessary to try and help Lurancy.

With some reluctance, the Vennums agreed to his plea. Although they didn't know it at the time, their lives would never be the same again.

Roff returned to the Vennum house in the company of Dr. E. Winchester Stevens on January 31. Dr. Stevens was a physician from Janesville, Wisconsin, who, like Roff, was a devout Spiritualist. He was curious about the case, having visited Watseka a few times and had heard about it during the preceding fall. He wanted to offer whatever help he could to the beleaguered family. His interest had been piqued by the medical aspects of the case and by the possibility that Lurancy might be "spirit infested," as he had come to believe that his friend's daughter, Mary Roff, had been.

Stevens and Roff were considering the idea that Lurancy was a sort of vessel through which the dead were communicating. Roff only wished that he had seen the same evidence in his own daughter years before. He believed that if Mary had actually been insane, that she had been driven to madness by the bizarre gifts and abilities that she possessed. No one had been able to help Mary but he believed that Stevens could help Lurancy Vennum. He didn't want to see what had happened to Mary befall someone else's daughter, and so he had brought Dr. Stevens to Watseka in order for him to examine Lurancy.

When they arrived at the house that afternoon, Dr. Stevens found Lurancy sitting in the kitchen next to the stove. She sat in a chair with her feet curled up under her. Her chin was in her hands and her elbows rested on her knees. She was slumped over, staring at the stove as though entranced by something in the dancing flames. Mrs. Vennum spoke to her but she did not respond. She remained with her eyes fixed straight ahead, as if she was unaware of anyone else in the room.

Dr. Stevens tried to speak to her but she ignored him. Finally, he grabbed one of the chairs that surrounded the kitchen table and pulled it over next to the girl. Lurancy's head snapped around in his direction and she savagely warned him not to come any closer. Stevens raised his hands in surrender but he did sit down, his chair a short distance from where Lurancy sat. He introduced himself and offered his hand to her in greeting but Lurancy refused to take it. When her parents reprimanded her for being rude, she snapped at them, calling her father "Old Black Dick" and her mother, "Old Granny." She had a strange look in her eyes, as if she really did not recognize her parents and when her mother reached out to touch her arm, she quickly jerked away from her. She yelled at everyone to leave her alone.

Stevens refused to move and he continued speaking to Lurancy in a calm, quiet voice. She stared at him sullenly for a time and then suddenly, she smiled and brightened up, as if hearing something that made her happy. She told Stevens that she had just discovered that he was a "spiritual doctor" and that she would answer any questions that he asked her. Stevens and Roff exchanged glances. Everyone present was confused. Dr. Stevens had told Lurancy nothing about himself and there seemed to be no way that she could have known that he was a Spiritualist. He had been introduced as a merely a doctor and yet, somehow, Lurancy had known.

Stevens began by asking her name. She said that she was not Lurancy Vennum but a woman named Katrina Hogan.

Stevens then asked: "How old are you?"
"Sixty-three."
"Where do you come from?"
"Germany."
"How long ago?"
"Three days."
"How did you come?"
"Through the air."
"How long will you stay?"
"Three weeks."

During this dialogue, Lurancy's demeanor had changed. She hunched herself over in the chair and her voice cracked, as though she really was an old woman. Then, she changed again. Guiltily, she admitted that she was not a woman but a young man whose name was Willie Canning. He had been a troubled young boy who had lost his life and now his spirit was inside of Lurancy. He stated: "I am here now because I want to be."

Lurancy answered every question that the doctor asked of her, going into great detail about the life of Willie Canning. Eventually, she seemed to tire of the questions and turned to the doctor and began asking questions of her own, such as "Where do you live? Are you married? Do you have children? What kind of doctor are you? Why did you come to Watseka?" This went on for a time and Stevens answered her as best he could, describing his home and life and travels that he had taken around the country. He believed that the questions that he was asked about his travels showed a greater knowledge of geography than Lurancy would have known at her age. Unfortunately, Dr. Stevens failed to record much of this session, except in very general details.

Lurancy's voice soon took on a devious tone and her questions changed. She began asking questions about the doctor's habits and morals, questioning him about whether he lied, stole, swore, attended church, prayed regularly and more. She then asked the same questions to be put to Mr. Roff and Mr. Vennum. She declined to ask them directly but forced Stevens to ask them on her behalf. As the other two men answered the questions, Lurancy made "some very unpleasant retorts," Dr. Stevens later wrote.

The situation continued for nearly an hour and a half and then Lurancy began to grow quiet and sullen, refusing to talk or answer any questions that Dr. Stevens asked of her. This went on for several minutes and then, perhaps believing that the girl was too tired to continue, Stevens got up to leave. As he did, Lurancy also stood up. Almost immediately, her hands fluttered in the air and her eyes rolled back into her head. Her body stiffened and she fell, crashing to the hard wooden floor. Her body was rigid and it appeared that she had gone into another of her mysterious trances.

Dr. Stevens later stated that he had seen this kind of trance before, describing how "sensitives" fall under the "power of God" during religious revival meetings. He believed that he could restore the girl to consciousness by "magnetizing" her, which was a form of mesmerism or hypnotism.

Mr. Vennum and Mr. Roff managed to get Lurancy back into her chair and Dr. Stevens sat down in front of her again. He managed to pry her hands, which were stiffly held against her chest, away from her body and took them into his own. His voice lowered to a soft, even tone and he began to speak to her, stroking her hands and easing her from out of the control of the spell. Soon, Lurancy's voice became her own and she began to speak to Dr. Stevens, maintaining that while her body was in the Vennum house, her consciousness was in heaven, where she was conversing with angels.

In this hypnotized condition, Lurancy answered the doctor's questions and spoke of her seemingly insane condition and the influences that were controlling her. She told him that she regretted allowing some of the spirits around her to take control over her body, stating that Katrina Hogan and Willie Canning were evil and forced her to do and say horrible things. Stevens explained to her that she was able to control what spirits influenced her and then asked her that, if she was going to be controlled by spirits, wouldn't it be better to be controlled by a happier, more intelligent and rational being? Lurancy agreed that this would be preferable if she could do it.

Lurancy sat for several minutes in eerie silence. By this time, the winter sun had long since set and the Vennum kitchen was dimly lighted by the fire from the stove and one kerosene lamp that had been placed on the table. The lengthening shadows danced across the room as Lurancy waited, then let out a long sigh before she spoke again. She said that she had looked about, and had inquired of those around her, to find someone who would prevent the cruel and insane spirits on the other side from returning to annoy her and her family.

She said: "There are a great many spirits here who would be glad to come."

Lurancy proceeded to give names and descriptions of people that Dr. Stevens wrote were "long since deceased" and who were unknown to the girl but often recognized by the older people who were present. Lurancy waited for several more minutes and then explained that she had found one spirit who wanted to come with her. The spirit was a young woman who believed that she could help Lurancy in a way that no other spirit could.

Dr. Stevens asked her the name of the spirit and her whispered reply echoed in the kitchen. Lurancy spoke: "Her name is Mary Roff."

While the name of Mary Roff may have sent shivers down the spines of some of the adults who were present, the name meant nothing to Lurancy herself. She had never heard of the girl and could not have known what had happened to her years before. Even if we take into consideration that rumors may have circulated about the Roff family and their crazy daughter that they once had to lock up in an asylum and who had subsequently died, it's likely that Lurancy would not have been exposed to them. The Roff and Vennum families had never had any real contact with one another and Lurancy had been a very young child when Mary had died.

Asa Roff soon recovered from the surprise of hearing his daughter's name on Lurancy's lips. He quickly assured the girl that Mary had been a good and intelligent young woman and would certainly help her in any way that she could. He added that Mary had once suffered from an affliction much like the one that was now bothering Lurancy.

Silence again filled the kitchen as Lurancy's unconscious mind appeared to deliberate about Mary's presence. Finally, she agreed that Mary would take the place of the troubled and disturbed spirits who had initially possessed her body.

Dr. Stevens and Mr. Roff left from the house a few hours later. Dr. Stevens wrote: "Leaving the family satisfied that a new fountain of light and source of help had been reached. A new beam of truth reached and touched the hearts of the sorrowing family. And to use the language of Mary Roff, 'Dr. Stevens opened the gate for her,' and for the inflowing light where before was darkness."

Lurancy remained in her trance for the rest of the evening and into the next day. During this time, she claimed to be Mary Roff. She was not a spirit inhabiting another girl's body; she insisted that she actually was Mary! She claimed that she had no idea where she was, was unable to recognize the Vennum house, which was a place where Mary Roff had never been. She wanted to go home, she said, which meant back to the Roff house.

Lurancy was so insistent about this that on the following morning, Friday, February 1, Thomas Vennum called at the office of Asa Roff and explained to him what was happening. He said that his daughter continued to claim that she was Mary and demanded that she be allowed to go home. Vennum said: "She seems like a child real homesick, wants to see her pa and ma and her brothers."

The Vennums had mixed feelings about these latest developments. They were happy to see that the rigid, corpse-like spells, excruciating pain and weird trances had passed but now they faced having had a stranger on their hands. She was very polite, mild and docile but she constantly begged the Vennums to let her go home. They tried to convince her, as did Mr. Roff, that she was already at home but the girl was having none of it. She would not be pacified. The Vennums were becoming more and more convinced that this girl was no longer their daughter.

The news of this amazing new development quickly spread and when Mrs. Roff heard what had happened, she hurried to the Vennum house in the company of her married daughter, Minerva Alter. The two women hurried up the sidewalk of the Vennum house and saw Lurancy sitting by the window. When she saw them approaching, she cried out: "Here comes Ma and Nervie!" As they came into the house, she hugged and kissed the surprised women and wept for joy. It was said that no one had called Minerva by the nickname "Nervie" since Mary's death in 1865.

From this time on, Lurancy seemed even more homesick than before, frantically wanting to leave and go home with the Roffs. It now seemed entirely possible to everyone involved that Mary Roff had taken control of Lurancy. Even though the girl still looked like Lurancy Vennum, she knew everything about the Roff family and she treated them as her loved ones. To the Vennums, she was distantly polite, as though they were strangers. The Vennums were understandably shocked and unnerved by the turn of events. Their daughter had become someone completely unknown to them.

Finally, some friends of the family insisted that the Vennums allow the girl to go home with the Roffs for a time. The Vennums were reluctant to do so. They were still befuddled by what was going on and they felt that it would be an imposition to send their daughter to be cared for by strangers, no matter whom she claimed to be.

After a few more days of the girl's weeping and begging to "go home," the Vennums decided to discuss the situation with the Roffs. It was a delicate problem but one that Mr. And Mrs. Roff agreed to take on. Braving the ridicule of people in town, and with no other motive but one of kindness, they opened their home to receive Lurancy.

On February 11, Lurancy --- or rather "Mary" --- was allowed to go to the Roff home. The Vennums agreed that this arrangement would be for the best, at least temporarily. They desperately hoped that Lurancy would regain her true identity. The Roffs, meanwhile, saw the possession as a "miracle," as though Mary had returned from the grave. They took Lurancy across town and as they were riding in the buggy, they passed by the former Roff home, where they had been living when Mary died. The home now belonged to Minerva and her husband, Henry Alter. The girl demanded to know why they were not stopping there and the Roffs had to explain that they had moved several years before to a brick home on Fifth Street. The young woman's lack of knowledge about this move, as well as her identification of the old house, was further proof to the Roffs that Lurancy had been possessed by their dead daughter.

Lurancy's arrival in the Roff home, as Mary, was met with great excitement. She immediately began calling the Roffs "ma and pa" and recognized each member of the family. Even though Lurancy knew none of them herself, she greeted them, as Mary, with affection. One of them asked her how long she would stay and she replied: "The angels will let me stay until sometime in May."

For the next several months, Lurancy lived as Mary and seemed to have forgotten about her former life. As the days passed, Lurancy continued to show that she knew more about the Roff family, their possessions and their habits than she could have possibly known if she had been merely faking. Many of the incidents that she referred to had taken place years before Lurancy had been born. Her physical condition began to improve while staying with the Roffs and she no longer suffered from the frightening attacks that had plagued her.

She appeared to be quite contented while living in the Roff home, and she recognized and called by name many of the neighbors and family friends known to Mary during her lifetime. In contrast, she claimed not to recognize any family members, friends or associates of the Vennums. Even though the Vennums allowed their daughter to live with the Roff family, they visited her often. Lurancy, while living as Mary, soon learned to love these "strangers" as friends.

Her day-to-day life in the Roff home was anything but unusual. She was easygoing, affable and hardworking, helping with the household chores, cooking and cleaning and going about the activities of any young girl of the time. She liked to read and sing, as Mary always had, and she loved sitting with her father and talking about anything that came to her mind. One day she asked him: "Pa, who was it that used to say 'confound it'?" She began laughing when she realized that the saying was one that he often used when Mary was a young girl --- nearly twenty years before.

One day, she met an old friend and neighbor of the Roffs, who had been a widow with the surname Lord when Mary was a girl. Some years after Mary had died, the woman had married a Mr. Wagoner. This seemed to be unknown to the girl. When the two were reunited, Lurancy hugged her tightly and called her by the last name of her late husband. She did not seem to be able to comprehend that this family friend had remarried.

A few weeks after Lurancy was settled into the Roff home, Mrs. Parker, who lived next door to the Roff family in 1852, moved and then lived next door to them again in 1860, came to the house with her daughter-in-law, Nellie Parker. Lurancy -- or Mary -- recognized both women immediately, calling Mrs. Parker "Auntie Parker," and the other "Nellie," just as she had known them years before. Mary sat down to speak to the two ladies and right away, she asked Mrs. Parker, "Do you remember how Nervie and I used to come to your house and sing?"

Mrs. Parker said that she did and she would later recall this incident and swear that no one had mentioned this to Lurancy before her visit. The young girl had brought it up on her own. She testified that Mary and Minerva often visited her house and loved to sing "Mary had a Little Lamb." Minerva also recalled doing this and added that they came to Mrs. Parker's house during the time when Mr. Roff was the town's postmaster, before 1852. This would have been more than a decade before Lurancy Vennum was born.

One evening in late March, Mr. Roff was reading a newspaper and drinking tea. He asked his wife if she could find a certain velvet head-dress that Mary had worn before she had died. If she knew where it was, he asked her to bring it out and say nothing of it, but to wait and see if Lurancy recognized it. Dorothy Ann quickly found the piece and placed it where she had been instructed. Lurancy was outside at the time but she soon came in and glanced over as she passed the stand where the head-dress was. She immediately exclaimed: "Oh, there is my head-dress that I wore when my hair was short!"

Lurancy took the velvet piece and lovingly caressed it. The Roffs were pleased and amazed, seeing this as further evidence that the spirit of Mary was alive within the body of Lurancy. It was yet another thing that Lurancy could not have known anything about, and such a trivial matter that even the cleverest hoaxer could not have uncovered it if she planned to try and fool the family. But Lurancy, or Mary, was not finished yet.

She turned to Mrs. Roff: "Ma, where is my box of letters? Have you got them yet?"

Mrs. Roff found a box filled with letters that had been saved after Mary had died. They were the same letters that Mary had been able to read blindfolded during the eerie tests that she had been subjected to by her father, the ministers and the newspapermen.

Lurancy began to examine them: "Oh, Ma, here is the collar I tatted! Why did you not show me my letters and things before?"

The collar had been preserved among the things that had been saved as mementoes of a lost child and it was something that Mary had made long before Lurancy had even been born. Like so many other things from her childhood, the spirit of Mary recognized it and spoke of it through the voice and body of another girl. The Roffs needed no further convincing. This was their daughter Mary, no matter what physical form she might be in.

Of course, not everyone in Watseka believed that Lurancy had been possessed by the spirit of Mary Roff. The Vennums' minister, Reverend Baker, after learning that Lurancy was staying with the Roffs, pleaded with the family once again to have the girl committed to the state asylum. He told them: "I think you will see the time when you will wish that you had sent her to the asylum." He said others in the congregation shared his opinion, and added: "I would sooner follow a girl of mine to the grave than have her go to the Roffs' and be made a Spiritualist."

Several of the doctors who had attempted to treat Lurancy started spreading scathing rumors about Dr. Stevens and dismissed the case as nothing more than catalepsy and "humbug." They believed that Lurancy was faking the whole thing and making fools of her parents and the Roff family. Of course, no one who voiced these opinions in Watseka had actually visited either family and had no in-depth knowledge of the situation. This ignorance did not stop the rumors from being spread, though, and the Roffs and Vennums were ridiculed by many in the community. For the most part, they ignored the laughter and the disdain, believing that something truly authentic and supernatural was taking place.

Dr. Stevens continued to play an important role in the case and he visited Watseka often, staying with the Roffs and investigating the phenomenon of Lurancy and Mary. When he returned to Janesville, he was kept in touch with the strange happenings through a series of letters that were sent from Asa Roff, Minerva Alter and from Lurancy, writing as Mary. Portions of these letters are relevant to the mysteries of the case and they are quoted here.

From Asa Roff, February 19, 1878:

You know how we took the poor, dear girl Lurancy Mary . Some appreciate our motives, but the many, without investigation and without knowledge of the facts, cry out against us and against that angel girl. Some say she pretends; others that she is crazy; and we hear that some say it is the devil.

Mary is perfectly happy; she recognizes everybody and everything that she knew when in her body twelve or more years ago. She knows nobody nor anything whatever that is known to Lurancy.

Mr. Vennum has been to see her, and also her brother Henry, at different times, but she don't know anything about them. Mrs. Vennum is still unable to come and see her daughter. She has been nothing but Mary since she has been here, and knows nothing but what Mary knew. She has entered the trance once every other day for some days. She is perfectly happy. You don't know how much comfort we take with the dear angel.

Lurancy often stated that she loved Dr. Stevens second only to her father meaning Mr. Roff because he had done so many kind things for her. He had opened the gate for her to return to life, had provided comfort for her family, and was helping to heal Lurancy's body. Because she was so grateful, she received the Roffs' permission to write to him. Her first letter was dated February 20, 1878:

I am yet here. Frank is better. Nervie is here for dinner; Allie Alter is going to stay the night; Mrs. Marsh was here today and read a beautiful letter to us. I wish you could spend the evening with us. I would like to have your picture to look at. Please write to pa when you get time. We all send our love to you. I like it here very much, and am going to stay all the time. I went to heaven and stayed about an hour. It seems a long time since I saw you.
Forget me not. Good night.
Mary Roff

She wrote to the doctor again on February 21. This is an excerpt from that letter:

I have just finished a letter to brother Frank. He went back to his store feeling quite well. The boys have gone out to play for a dance. In the evening, I went to heaven, and I saw some of the beautiful things, and talked with angels, and be sure I don't forget them when I got to heaven and come back. 'Fear the Lord, depart from evil.' Proverbs 3:7
Mary Roff

As noted in her letter, Lurancy or Mary was able to slip into trances and go to the other side, where she spoke to the spirits. However, on occasion, some of those spirits reportedly returned with her and Lurancy acted as a spirit medium would, allowing them to communicate through her. In March, Asa Roff sent a letter to Dr. Stevens, detailing an incident that occurred at one of these impromptu séances:

A lady came through at our house, who claimed to have lived and died in Tennessee, and she says that she was afflicted from eight years of age till twenty-five, when she died with a similar disease, and in a similar way that Mary died. She says that Mary has control of Lurancy Vennum, and will retain control till she is restored to her normal condition, when Mary will leave.

Mary is happy as a lark and gives daily, almost hourly, proofs of being Mary's intelligence. She don't recognize Lurancy's family or friends at all. She knows and recognizes everything that our Mary used to know, and nothing whatever of what the Vennum girl knows. She now enters the trance without any rigidity of the muscles whatever, very gently, and at her own will, describes heavenly scenes, etc. We think all will be well, and Lurancy restored to her orthodox friends yet.

Some of the relatives are yielding by calling Mary's attention to things of thirteen years ago, that transpired between her and them. It wakes them up. It is wonderful. It would take a volume to give the important items that have occurred.

Minerva Alter wrote a letter to Dr. Stevens on April 16, 1878:

My angel sister says that she is going away from us again soon, but says she will often be with us. She says Lurancy is a beautiful girl; says she sees her nearly every day, and we do know she is getting better every day. Oh, the lessons that are being taught us are worth treasures of rare diamonds; they are stamped upon the mind so firmly that heaven and earth shall pass away before one jot or one tittle shall be forgotten. I have learned so much that is grand and beautiful. I cannot express it; I am dumb.

A few days ago, Mary was caressing her father and mother, and they became a little tired of it, and asked why she hugged and kissed them. She sorrowfully looked at them, and said 'Oh, pa and ma! I want to kiss you while I have lips to kiss you with, and hug you while I have arms to hug you with, for I am going back to heaven before long, and then I can only be with you in spirit, and you will not always know when I come, and I cannot love you as I can now. Oh, how much I love you all!'

On May 7, 1878, Lurancy writing as Mary included a letter to Dr. Stevens in the same envelope that contained a letter from Asa Roff. She wrote:

Dear Doctor - I thought I would write you. I am at Aunt Carrie's. I am going to take dinner with her. Yesterday, I went and spent the day with Mrs. Vennum. She had a dreadful headache and I rubbed it away. Pa is quite busy in his office today. Ma is feeling a good deal better. I am feeling quite well, except my breast hurts me some today. It commenced hurting me last night. I treat ma in the morning and Nervie at night for hard colds and cold feet. We all went to the Reform Club last Saturday. Aunt Carrie's essay was splendid and very affecting. We all read that letter in the Religio-Philosophical Journal *from your daughter, and liked it very much.*
Mary Roff

In the same envelope was a letter from Mr. Roff, which read, in part:

I want to give you a little scene; time; Monday morning, May 6th; place, A.B. Roff's office, Watseka; present, A.B. Roff at the table writing; Frank Roff at the table at the right of A.B.R.; door behind A.B., and a little to the left; enters unheard the person of Lurancy Vennum; places her arm around the neck of A.B. Roff, kissing him and saying, 'Pa, I am going to visit with Mrs. Vennum today.' A.B. Roff looks around and discovers standing in the door Mrs. Vennum, Lurancy's mother, looking on the scene. The girl then bade an affectionate goodbye to Frank; A.B.R. asks, 'How long will you stay?' She replies, 'Till two or three o'clock.' Mrs. Vennum then said to Mr. Roff: 'If she does not get back at that time, don't get alarmed, we will take care of her.' Exit Mrs. V. and the girl.

You don't know how much my heart aches for that poor mother, yet she is much happier than she was last winter with Lurancy as she was.

On May 7, the day that the preceding letter was written, Lurancy as Mary called Mrs. Roff to a private room and there, in tears, informed her that Lurancy Vennum would be coming back soon. She could feel the other girl's spirit returning and she had no idea whether or not Lurancy would be staying or not. If Mary was going to be released from the body, then she hoped that she would have time to see Allie, Minerva and Henry so that she could tell them goodbye. The girl wept as she told these things to Mrs. Roff and it was almost as if, no matter how much she wanted to help Lurancy, Mary didn't want to let go of the earthly form that she had managed to obtain.

The young woman sat down in a chair and over the course of the next few minutes, a battle took place for control of her physical form. Her eyes slowly closed and her face shifted expressions several times before her eyes fluttered open again. The girl, confused, looked wildly about before exclaiming: "Where am I? I have never been here before!"

Lurancy Vennum had returned.

Mrs. Roff sat down next to the girl and held her hand, gently rubbing her arm. She tried to calm the girl: "You are at Mr. Roff's, brought here by Mary to cure your body."

Lurancy burst into tears. "I want to go home!"

Mrs. Roff soothed her and told her that someone would send for her parents. She then asked the girl if she felt any pain in her breast. Lurancy, or Mary, had been complaining of the pain for a few days, continually holding her left breast and pressing on it with her fingers .

Lurancy looked puzzled for a moment and then seemed surprised when she spoke with some confusion: "No, but Mary did."

Lurancy remained with Mrs. Roff for only a few minutes and then a subtle change seemed to sweep over her body and her features. A quiet humming sound came from the girl's lips and then softly turned into song. It was "We are Coming, Sister Mary," a childhood favorite of Mary Roff's. The dead girl had returned to the body of Lurancy Vennum.

Mary's return was marked by sadness. Everyone knew that, after the brief return of Lurancy, it was nearly time for her to leave. Over the next two weeks, a battle raged for the control of Lurancy's body. At one moment, Lurancy would announce that she had to leave and at the next she would cling to her father and cry at the idea of leaving him. She spent nearly every day going from one family member to another, hugging them and touching them at every opportunity. She became increasingly upset with each passing day, weeping at the thought of leaving her "real family."

Dr. Stevens returned to town to have as much contact with Mary as he could before she was gone. He found that over the last two weeks, she seemed to be more aware of not only her past life as Mary Roff but also about the fact that she was masquerading, as it were, in a borrowed form. One day, Stevens asked her: "Do you remember the time you cut your arm?"

Lurancy or Mary admitted that she did and she rolled up her sleeve to show him the scar. She started to speak and then paused in confusion, saying: "Oh, this is not the arm; that one is in the ground." Then, she went on to describe the spot where Mary had been buried and the circumstances of her funeral.

Dr. Stevens also noted that she began to tell of supernatural incidents that occurred after her death. He wrote:

I heard her tell Mr. Roff and the friends present, how she wrote to him a message some years ago through the hand of a medium, giving him name, time and place. Also of rapping and of spelling out a message by another medium, giving time, name, place, etc. which the parents admitted to be true.

The spirit of Mary, dwelling in Lurancy, seemed also to have held on to the clairvoyant abilities that Mary manifested before her death. One afternoon, Lurancy came to her mother and told her that Mary's brother, Frank, had to be carefully watched over during the coming night. He was going to become very sick and he could die if he was not properly cared for. At the time of this announcement, Frank was feeling just fine and, in fact, was uptown playing in a band that had been put together by the Roff brothers and their friends. That same evening, Dr. Stevens had stopped by to visit the family but then had left by 9:30 p.m.

During the early morning hours, Frank was suddenly afflicted with something like spasms and a terrible chill, which caused him to tremble and shake so badly that he almost fainted. Lurancy rushed into his room and saw the situation exactly as she had predicted it. She told her father: "Send to Mr. Marsh's for Dr. Stevens."

Roff replied: "No, Dr. Stevens is at the old town."

Mary shook her head: "No, he is at Mr. Marsh's, go quick for him, Pa!"

Mr. Roff ran from the house and went next door to the Marsh's. Here, he found Dr. Stevens but by the time the doctor could get dressed and hurry to the Roff home, Lurancy had things well in hand. She had made Mrs. Roff sit down, had provided hot water and cloths for Frank, and was doing all that could be done for him. The doctor agreed with her methods and allowed her to continue. Mary's spirit, working through Lurancy, had likely saved the young man's life.

The girl also told Dr. Stevens of seeing some of his deceased children on the other side. They were about Mary's age but had been there longer than she had. She told him that she was with them quite often and even traveled to the doctor's home with them. She correctly described his home in Wisconsin, even though she had never been there, gave the names and ages of his children, and as evidence that she was telling the truth, told the doctor of a supernatural experience that had occurred to Mrs. E.W. Wood, one of the doctor's married daughters. Stevens never revealed the details behind the story but attested to the fact that what Lurancy told him had actually taken place.

Strangely, another of the doctors' daughters, Emma Angelia, who had died in 1849, allegedly sought through Mary to take control of Lurancy's body and go home with her father to Wisconsin, to visit her family for a week. Mary wanted to do this and asked the Roffs if they would mind if she went, so that the Stevens family could spend some time with Emma. The Roffs did not think that it was advisable and the matter was dropped.

As more time passed, Lurancy's control over her own body began to slowly return. Mary's spirit would sometimes recede for a time. Mary's identity was not lost, nor did Lurancy's personality return, but it was enough to provide evidence that she was slowly returning to her own body.

On the afternoon of Sunday, May 19, Lurancy was sitting in the parlor with Mr. Roff. Henry Vennum, Lurancy's brother, was seated in a chair in the hallway. Other members of the Roff family waited with him in the corridor. He had come to the house to visit his sister and Roff, based on recent experiences, felt that Lurancy's spirit was near. It soon turned out that he was correct in his assumptions. In a matter of moments, Mary departed and Lurancy took control of her body again. Henry was called in and when he stepped into the room, Lurancy wrapped her arms around his neck, kissed his cheek and burst into tears. She was so happy to see him that Henry started to cry, which caused everyone else in the household to weep.

Mr. Roff asked Lurancy if she would be able to stay with them until someone could go to the Vennum house and bring back her mother. Lurancy answered that she could not, but if her mother were brought over, she would come again and be able to talk with her. Her eyes seemed to waver for a moment and her body shook slightly --- Lurancy was gone.

It was obvious to everyone gathered in the parlor that Mary had returned. When someone asked her where she had gone, she replied: "I have seen Dr. Stevens and he looks as good as ever again." Dr. Stevens had recently returned to Wisconsin and Mary implied that she had gone there to see him during the brief time that Lurancy had control over her body.

Lurinda Vennum was brought to the Roff house within the hour and when she came into the parlor, Lurancy once again regained full control of her body. Mother and daughter embraced one another, kissed and wept until everyone assembled was crying in sympathy. Lurancy stayed for a few minutes and then, as mysteriously as she had gone, Mary Roff returned and Mrs. Vennum was a beloved stranger once more.

But it would not stay that way for much longer.

On the morning of May 21, Asa Roff wrote to Dr. Stevens:

Mary is to leave the body of Rancy today, about eleven o'clock, so she says. She is bidding neighbors and friends good-bye. Rancy is to return home all right today. Mary came from her room upstairs where she was sleeping with Lottie, at ten o'clock last night, lay down by us, hugged and kissed us, and cried because she must bid us goodbye, telling us to give all her pictures, marbles and cards, and twenty-five cents Mrs. Vennum had given her, to Rancy, and had us promise to visit Rancy often. She tells me to write to Dr. Stevens as follows:

'Tell him I am going to heaven and Rancy is coming home well.' She says she will see your dear children in spirit-life; says she saw you on Sunday last.

She said last night, weeping, 'Oh, pa, I am going to heaven tomorrow at eleven o'clock, and Rancy is coming back cured, and going home all right.' She talked most lovingly about the separation to take place and the most beautiful was her talk about heaven and her home.

Mary sent word to her sister, Minerva, to come to the Roff house and stay with her for an hour so that she could say goodbye. After that, when Lurancy returned, Minerva was to take the girl to Mr. Roff's office and then he would take her to the Vennums. Mary said: "I will come in spirit as close to you as I can, and comfort you in sorrow, and you will feel me near you sometimes."

As 11:00 a.m. approached, Mary seemed to fight the idea of leaving and allowing Lurancy to return. Minerva was a little upset with her. She spoke, saying, "Mary, you have always done the things that you said you would, but as I don't understand these things, will you please let Lurancy come back just now, and then you can come again if you want to?"

Mary agreed that she would and kissed her mother and sister goodbye. The girl's eyes rolled back for an instant and immediately, she was Lurancy Vennum again. She found herself walking outside with Minerva, starting toward Mr. Roff's office. Lurancy asked Minerva: "Why Mrs. Alter, where are we going?" The girl then paused for a moment and smiled slightly to herself before she spoke again: "Oh yes, I know, Mary told me."

On the way, they met Mrs. Marsh and Mrs. Hoober, who were the nearest neighbors and some of Mary's closest friends. Lurancy did not recognize either of the women, but she was polite to them and greeted them warmly. When she and Minerva walked on, she remarked: "Mary thinks so much of these neighbors."

She then turned to Minerva, with whom Lurancy had been only slightly acquainted two years before, and said: "Mrs. Alter, Mary can come and talk to you nearly all the way home, if you want her to, and then I will come back."

Minerva agreed: "I have trusted you in the past, and of course, I would love to talk with my sister."

Mary's spirit enveloped Lurancy again and according to Minerva, the two of them talked about many things and family matters as they walked. As the hour for Mary's departure finally arrived, Lurancy returned. She told Minerva and Mr. Roff that she felt as though she had been asleep for a very long time, yet knew that she had not. She asked Mr. Roff if he would take her home and he immediately agreed to do so.

On May 22, Mr. Roff wrote to Dr. Stevens:

Thank God and the good angels, the dead is alive and the lost is found. I mailed you a letter yesterday at half-past ten o'clock a.m. stating that Mary told us she would go away, and Rancy would return at eleven o'clock on the 21st of May. Now I write you that at half past eleven o'clock a.m., Minerva called at my office with Rancy Vennum, and wanted me to take her home, which I did. She called me Mr. Roff, and talked with me as a young girl would, not being acquainted. I asked her how things appeared to her - if they seemed natural. She said it seemed like a dream to her. She met her parents and brothers in a very affectionate manner, hugging and kissing each one in tears of gladness. She clasped her arms around her father's neck a long time, fairly smothering him with kisses. I saw her father just now eleven o'clock . He says she has been perfectly natural, and seems entirely well. You see my faith in writing you yesterday morning instead of waiting till she came.

Lurancy returned home to the Vennum house. She displayed none of the strange symptoms of her earlier illness and her parents were convinced that she had somehow been cured, thanks to the intervention of the spirit of Mary Roff. She soon became a healthy and happy young woman, suffering no ill effects from her strange experience. She had no memories of the possession, other than of those things that Mary allowed her to know. It was as if the months that she spent as Mary Roff had never happened at all.

In June 1878, Dr. Stevens returned to Watseka to renew his friendship with the Roff and Vennum families. He was especially curious as to whether or not any of Lurancy's spells or trances had returned and whether Mary Roff had actually managed to cure the girl of her affliction.

On Sunday, June 2, Stevens met with Lurancy and her parents at the house of a friend, who lived about two miles away from the Vennums. Lurancy was introduced to him by her father. She was sure that she had never met the man before and came across as a little shy, as one might expect from a young girl meeting a stranger for the first time. They spoke very little that day and Stevens left the meeting feeling both disappointed that he could learn nothing more from the girl and excited that she truly seemed to have been the victim of a possession. She remembered nothing of meeting the doctor during the time that she was living as Mary Roff.

The next day, June 3, brought him a great surprise. Without any notice to anyone as to where he was going that day, Dr. Stevens stopped unannounced at the home of a friend, a noted attorney in Watseka. As he was entering the gate, Lurancy Vennum walked up beside him and greeted him warmly. The doctor was surprised by her presence, especially as she had seemed so reluctant to talk with him the previous day. Lurancy said: "How do you do, Doctor? Mary Roff told me to come here and meet you. Somehow she makes me feel that you have been a very kind friend to me." Lurancy then went on to deliver a long message for the doctor that she claimed that she had received from Mary.

Dr. Stevens later wrote that since the June 3 meeting, he had seen Lurancy many times and on every occasion, she was very friendly and forthcoming. Something about her demeanor had changed and he was convinced that it was because of the intervention of Mary Roff.

On June 25, Lurancy wrote to Dr. Stevens in Wisconsin:

Dear Doctor,
I am feeling quite well today. I was up to Mrs. Alter's today; she is very well at present. This afternoon I called at Mr. Roff's office, and had quite a long talk with him; but of course it was about the loving angels that you and I know so well. Let them twine around your neck their arms and press upon your brow their kiss. Kiss your loving wife for me, and tell her we shall all meet in heaven if not on earth.

I shall visit Mrs. Roff tomorrow. I shall have my picture taken and send it to you in my next letter. I get up early to take the morning air. I should like to have you write a line to me.
Your friend,
Lurancy Vennum

This was the first letter that Dr. Stevens ever received from Lurancy and he was astounded when he saw it. Having been the recipient of a number of letters from the girl when she was manifesting the personality of Mary Roff, Stevens found that this letter was very different in its makeup and penmanship that the letters that he had gotten, written with the same hand, but signed as Mary. Stevens felt this was further proof of the presence of another personality within the girl's body.

As weeks passed, everyone involved in the case watched very closely to see how Lurancy behaved. Would they see a return of the strange seizures and spells? Would they see the possession by Mary Roff return? We can only imagine the anxiety that must have filled the hearts of the Vennums, and even those of the Roffs, who had come to consider Lurancy almost a part of their own family.

Needless to say, the two families involved were not the only ones with an interest in the strange story. The people of Watseka had watched avidly as this curious drama played out in their city. But it was not until three months after the affair had ended that the public at large obtained any knowledge about it. Newspapers in Watseka, and in the surrounding area, had quickly reported the final outcome of the case.

The *Watseka Republican* newspaper wrote:

The meeting with her parents at the home was very affecting, and she now seems to be a very healthy, happy little girl, going about noting things she saw before she was stricken, and recognizes changes that have since taken place. This is a remarkable case, and the fact that we cannot understand such things, does not do away with the existence of these unaccountable manifestations.

The editor for the *Iroquois County Times*, under a banner of "Mesmeric Mysteries" wrote of Lurancy Vennum:

It was hard for even the most skeptical not to believe there was something supernatural about her. If she was not prompted by the spirit of Mary Roff, how could she know so much about the family, people with whom she was not acquainted, and whom she had never visited? No stranger would have suspected her of being the victim of disease, though her eyes were unusually bright.

There are yet numberless mysteries in this world, though science has dissipated many wonders, and philosophy has made plain many marvels. There is much that is unaccountable in the actions of Spiritualistic mediums, and they do many things which puzzle the greatest philosophers. Skeptical and unbelieving as we are, and slight as our evidence has been, we have seen enough to convince us that Spiritualism is not all humbug. The case of Lurancy Vennum, a bright young girl of fourteen years, has been the subject of much discussion in Watseka during the past year, and there is a good deal in it beyond human comprehension...

The first news of the story, outside of local newspapers, came from two articles that were contributed by Dr. Stevens to the August 3 and 10, 1878 issues of the *Religio-Philosophical Journal*, one of the leading Spiritualist newspapers of the day. In the articles, Stevens discussed the case in great detail, emphasizing the fact that, as of the time of writing, no return of the ailments, trances and spells had returned to bother Lurancy. Stevens said he was convinced that the spirit of Mary Roff had returned to earth to possess Lurancy Vennum and had been the instrument of her cure.

But not everyone was as convinced. While Spiritualists were more than willing to believe in the possibility of Lurancy being possessed and healed by Mary's spirit, many members of the general public were not so easily impressed. A number of letters were sent to the *Journal,* insinuating and openly alleging that Dr. Steven's narrative of the case was nothing more than a work of fiction.

The veracity of the Roffs was also attacked. Letters were forwarded to Asa Roff from the editors of the *Journal,* inquiring as to the truthfulness of Stevens' account of what he called "The Watseka Wonder." Some of them merely wanted to hear Roff's side of things but others accused him of collaborating with Stevens to fool the public.

Roff was indignant over the content of many of the letters he received, including those that were so rude that he never shared their content with anyone. He knew what he and his family had experienced and was convinced of the authenticity of the events. He felt he had no need to defend himself but as a believer in the wonders of Spiritualism, and in defense of his friend, Dr. Stevens, and the reputations of Lurancy and Mary, he wrote a lengthy letter to the editors of the *Religio-Philosophical Journal* that served as his reply to the many critics who attacked him, his family, Dr. Stevens and the Vennums. He noted in the letter: "Persons hereafter writing me, who do not receive an answer to their letters, will seek for the information desired in this article."

His reply to the critics read:

I furnished Dr. Stevens will all the material facts in the case, except such as were within his own knowledge. The history of the Vennum family and Lurancy's condition up to the time he and I went to see her January 31 I obtained from the members thereof, and the neighbors intimately acquainted with them. The narrative, as written by Dr. Stevens, is substantially true in every part and particular, yet the half has not been told, and never can be; it is impossible for pen to describe or language portray the wonderful events that transpired during the memorable fourteen weeks that the girl was at our house. The material facts of the case can be substantiated by disinterested witnesses, whose veracity cannot be questioned and whose evidence would settle any case in a court of law. I refer you to Robert Doyle, Chas. Sherman, S.R. Hawks, Lile Marsh, J.M. Hoober, and their wives, and to Mrs. Mary Wagoner, formerly Mary Lord, all residents of Watseka. As to "collusion," "arrangement," or "ourselves being deceived," that is simply impossible, as you will see if you carefully read the whole narrative over again. I, too, doubt whether newspapers are always "embodiments of sacred truths," but in this case I assure the writer, the Journal *does embody a very sacred truth, that of man's immortality.*

Talking with Mary, we sometimes spoke of her death. She would quickly reply: "I never died" or "I did not die." She never tired of talking of the life beyond this. She would at any time leave her play, her reading or her jovial companions, to talk with her "pa" and "ma" about heaven and the angels, as she termed spirit-life, and spirits that have left the body.

I have questioned Lurancy Vennum on different occasions, as to whether she remembered anything that occurred during the time that Mary had control of her organism, and she states that a very few things occurring the last month that she was controlled, she recollects, but that in all cases the information was imparted by Mary.

In conclusion, let me say to those who doubt or disbelieve the "strange, mysterious and wonderful story." Call to mind Lurancy's condition at her home last January, surrounded with all the kind care of parents, friends and physicians, everything done to alleviate her suffering and perform a cure that human minds and hands could possibly do, yet growing continually worse if that were possible, given up by her physicians, her friends, without a ray of hope, the insane asylum ready to receive her, a condition terrible to behold! Then view her condition from May 21 until today, over three months, a bright, beautiful, happy, healthy girl, and then tell me what produced the change. The narrative furnishes the facts; account for them if you can on any other hypothesis, than power exercised through or by the spirit of Mary Roff having control of Lurancy's body.

I am now sixty years old; have resided in Iroquois County thirty years, and would not sacrifice what reputation I may have by being party to a publication of such narrative, if it was not perfectly true. If any should desire testimonials of my standing, Col. Bundy has some to use as he deems best.

Asa Roff
Watseka, Ill. August 23, 1878

The letter appeared in the August 31 edition of the *Journal* and the editors followed it with a number of statements attesting to the reputation of Asa B. Roff. The writers of these testimonials included Matthew H. Peters, the mayor of Watseka; Charles H. Wood, a former judge of the Twentieth Circuit of Illinois; O.F. McNeill, a former county judge; O.C. Munhall, the Watseka postmaster;

attorney Robert Doyle; attorney John W. Riggs; Henry Butzow, circuit clerk; Thomas Vennum not Lurancy's father , who was the former circuit clerk; Franklin Blades, a judge on the Eleventh Judicial Circuit, and former county judge M.B. Wright.

The letters were followed by an announcement from Colonel J.C. Bundy, the editor of the *Journal.* He wrote to the effect that he had "entire confidence in the truthfulness of the narrative, and believes from his knowledge of the witnesses that the account is unimpeachable, in every particular." As for Dr. Stevens, Colonel Bundy stated that he had been personally acquainted with the physician for many years and had "implicit confidence in his veracity."

After all of this, accusations of perjury and deception were obviously futile and aside from saying that it was simply "fraud" which no one could explain , there were no adequate interpretations for the events that took place in Watseka. There was an increasing tendency to accept the view advanced by those who had participated in the affair.

But not everyone was so inclined, as the people of Watseka would find out a few years later.

In 1890, controversial psychical researcher Richard Hodgson came to Watseka. Prior to this, Hodgson had made a name for himself in the field, especially concerning research into famed psychic medium Leonora Piper. It was during these investigations that Hodgson heard about the events in Watseka and came to Illinois to study them further.

Richard Hodgson is believed to be the first full-time, salaried psychical researcher. During more than twenty years of research, Hodgson moved from skeptic and debunker to a staunch believer in psychic phenomena and the paranormal. Hodgson was born in Melbourne, Australia, on September 24, 1855 and attended college there, receiving several degrees. He moved to England, where he attended Cambridge, and after taking honors in 1881, he began teaching poetry and philosophy. While at Cambridge, he joined an organization called the Cambridge Society for Psychical Research, which was started in 1879 and was a forerunner of the Society for Psychical Research SPR . The SPR became widely known as the first established group that investigated psychic phenomena.

Hodgson took an active role in the society, exposing a number of fraudulent mediums. When the SPR formed in 1882, Hodgson became one of the first members. He was asked by the SPR to travel to India and investigate the Theosophical Society and its leaders, including Madame Helena Blavatsky. After more than four months in India, Hodgson concluded that Blavatsky was a fraud. A bitter controversy resulted from this with the Theosophists claiming that

Hodgson did not understand the psychic phenomena connected to Blavatsky's mediumship and that he was too harsh in his judgment.

Psychologist William James was keenly interested in psychic phenomena and was at the center of the SPR's sister society in America, the ASPR, which had been started in Boston in 1885. The society always seemed to be short of keen investigators and funds, so James appealed to the SPR for help. In 1887, Hodgson moved to Boston to assist and became invaluable as the executive secretary. He also took over from James the research management of the extraordinary mental medium Leonora Piper. James had been astounded with the work that he had done with Piper and believed her to be an authentic, gifted psychic. Hodgson was not convinced and he began a regular recording of her séances and even hired private detectives to have her followed.

His opinion of her soon changed. He wrote: "During the first few years, I absolutely disbelieved in her power. I had but one object, to discover fraud and trickery, of unmasking her. Today, I am prepared to say that I believe in the possibility of receiving messages from which is called the world of spirits. I entered the house profoundly materialistic, not believing in the continuance of life after death; today I say I believe. The truth has been given to me in such a way as to remove from me the possibility of doubt."

Hodgson experienced hundreds of sittings with Piper and published two reports about her work, stating that he believed that "survival after death" was the most reasonable interpretation of the results obtained by her séances. This conclusion astonished many of his friends, who had expected him to unmask Piper, as he had done so many other mediums. Hodgson, however, became one of many psychical researchers who became convinced of the validity of the paranormal after being exposed to Leonora Piper's mediumship.

In April 1890, Hodgson was in the midst of his investigations into Leonora Piper and was not yet convinced that the abilities that she seemed to manifest were genuine. He got sidetracked by the story of the "Watseka Wonder" and decided to travel to Illinois and organize a rigorous investigation into the incident. When he arrived, he found that several of the key participants in the case were unavailable. Dr. Stevens had died and Lurancy had married a farmer named George Binning and moved to Kansas with him. However, Hodgson was able to interview Asa Roff, Minerva Alter and a number of friends and neighbors who had first-hand knowledge about the possession.

Hodgson found that the witnesses were completely cooperative and all of them freely answered his questions, reiterating the facts that were given in Dr. Stevens' articles, and adding more information that had been made public. He spent several days in Watseka, going over and over the case. Although Hodgson knew that he had to be careful of unconscious exaggeration and misstatement, he nevertheless deemed the evidence presented to him to be too strong to be dismissed or explained away by ordinary means. The skeptic and debunker had been swayed by the convictions of the people in Watseka and Hodgson believed that they had been touched by something that was far beyond the ordinary. He wrote in a report:

I have no doubt that the incidents occurred substantially as described in the narrative by Dr. Stevens, and in my view the only other interpretation of the case -- besides the spiritualistic-- that seems at all plausible is that which has been put forward as the alternative to the spiritualistic theory to account for the trance-communications of Mrs. Piper and similar cases, viz., secondary personality with supernormal powers. It would be difficult to disprove this hypothesis in the case of the Watseka Wonder, owing to the comparative meagerness of the record and the probable abundance of "suggestion" in the environment, and any conclusion that we may reach would probably be determined largely by our convictions concerning other cases. My personal opinion is that the "Watseka Wonder" case belongs in the main manifestations to the spiritualistic category.

Hodgson followed up his report with an article that he wrote for the *Religio-Philosophical Journal* in December 1890 that contained an account of his inquiry and of the additional information that had been brought to light. He concluded his investigation into the case and stated that it was "unique among the record of supernormal occurrences" and freely admitted that he could not "find any satisfactory interpretation of it except the spiritualistic."

Lurancy remained in touch with the Roff family for the rest of her life. Although she had no real memories of her time as Mary, she still felt a curious closeness to them that she could never explain. On January 1, 1882, Lurancy married to George Binning, a farmer who lived about three miles west of Watseka. In 1884, they moved west to Rawlins County, Kansas, in the northwestern corner of the state.

The Roffs visited with Lurancy often, and saw her at least once each year after she moved to Kansas. Whenever she returned home to Watseka to see her parents, she always stayed with the Roffs for part of the time. During these visits, she would allow Mary to take control of her, just as she did when living with them in 1878.

Aside from this, Lurancy had little occasion to use the mediumistic skills that she had acquired. Her parents rarely spoke with her on the subject, fearing that it would cause a return of the "spells" that plagued her before she was possessed by Mary. Her husband had no interest in Spiritualism and Asa Roff wrote rather disapprovingly that he "furnished poor conditions for further development in that direction." This, combined with her household chores and care of her children, made her spirit possessions and talking with the dead things of the past.

Oddly, Lurancy told the Roffs that she was never sick a day in her life after Mary cured her in 1878.

Lurancy lived in Kansas until the death of her husband when he was in his 50s. After that, she moved to Oklahoma for a time and then eventually settled down in Long Beach, California, in 1910. She died there, at the age of 88, in 1952. She raised eleven children but it was said that none of them knew of her strange time as the "Watseka Wonder" until they were informed of it after her death by a cousin.

The Vennum family stayed on in Watseka for many years but after the death of her husband, Lurinda Vennum moved to Kansas to live with Lurancy and her grandchildren. Both of the Vennums are buried in Oak Hill Cemetery in Watseka.

Dr. Stevens lectured on the "Watseka Wonder" for eight years before dying in Chicago in 1886. He was convinced that what had occurred had been genuine and that Mary Roff had actually taken over the body of Lurancy Vennum for a time.

Minerva Alter wrote a short follow-up article to Dr. Stevens' accounts in 1908, when she was sixty-four years old. In it, she stated that neither she nor her family had any interest in deceiving or misleading people. She vowed the possession had been real, and talked about the great joy that she and her parents had felt when they were reunited with a daughter and a sister who had been dead for twelve years. At the time of the writing, she stated that Lurancy was a healthy, middle-aged woman with eleven children, respected as a neighbor and honored as a friend. She added: "Of the part she played in a great drama staged by heaven and earth, and of what she experienced, she has but a dim remembrance."

Asa and Dorothy Ann Roff received hundreds of letters, from believers and skeptics alike, after the story of the possession was printed in newspapers and appeared in magazines all over the country. In 1879, Roff was elected as justice of the peace in Watseka but resigned the position in June of that same year. Without much explanation, he moved to Garden City, Kansas, where his sons lived and where the family had invested considerable amounts of money. He invested in farmland but found that the climate was too dry for it to be profitable and moved to Emporia, Kansas, where he and his wife lived for a year. From Kansas, Roff moved to Council Bluffs, Iowa for two years and then moved to Kansas City, where he lived for several more years.

In 1885, Roff moved back to Watseka and there he and his wife lived the rest of their lives. In the spring of 1889, he was elected police magistrate for a term of four years and once more served as justice of the peace. He and Dorothy Ann were both buried in Oak Hill Cemetery.

The grave of Mary Roff rests silently in Oak Hill Cemetery, on the edge of Watseka, just steps away from the final resting places of her parents and her beloved sister, Minerva. For many years, locals made sure that Mary's grave marker was always covered with dirt, for fear that someone might vandalize it. Today, though, the stone is easy to find, although the elements have not been kind and a casual visitor has to look hard to see the name carved across the top.

It is here that she rests - this elusive and mysterious enigma of another time and place. Did Mary Roff really return from the grave? And if she did, what dark secrets did she bring with her - and take back again from this side to the next?

The story of the Watseka Wonder remains one of the strangest unsolved mysteries in the annals of American history. What really happened in this small Illinois town in 1878? Did the spirit of Mary Roff really possess the body of Lurancy Vennum? It seems almost impossible to believe but the families of both young women, as well as hundreds of friends and supporters, certainly believed that it happened. One thing is certain --- something extraordinary happened in Watseka involving Lurancy Vennum, her family and the family of a dead girl named Mary Roff. Was it a true spirit possession, a case of mental illness, or the most elaborate and carefully constructed hoax of the 1870s?

The reader will have to decide that for himself but I'll warn you, keep an open mind and be sure to explore all of the possibilities. There is much more to the story of the Watseka Wonder than first meets the eye.

The Hoax

By all accounts, Lurancy Vennum had the memories and personality of a young woman who had been dead for more than twelve years. She had knowledge about the other girl's family that no one outside of it could possibly have known. Or did she?

That seems to be the main question asked whenever anyone considers the idea that the Watseka Wonder case might have been a clever fraud. When examining the case from that possibility, we have to leave out the arguments of those who make statements like "I don't believe in that sort of thing, so it couldn't possibly have happened." Asa Roff received many letters of this sort in the months following the publication of Dr. Stevens' articles but arguments of this sort offer no proof. Like those in Watseka who scoffed at the possession in 1878, these arguments normally come from people who have little, or no, knowledge of the case and have done no research into the events to try and understand them.

Even so, an open-minded researcher into the case cannot ignore the possibility of fraud, no matter how unlikely it might seem. The case of a teenager being possessed by the spirit of a dead girl does stretch the bounds of belief. But could it have actually happened? Of course, it *could* have, for, to paraphrase Hamlet, there are things that are possible that have not even been dreamt of in our limited philosophies. But whether or not it *did* happen is open for debate.

If we examine the case as possible fraud, we first have to look at those involved and their possible agendas:

Lurancy Vennum: If this were a hoax, it would have to have been started by Lurancy, who managed to fool her family, an eminent physician, friends and scores of townspeople. Not to mention, such a stunt would have been unbelievably cruel on her part to take advantage of the Roff family the way that she did. There is nothing about her personality, save for her erratic behavior in late 1877, to suggest that she was anything more than a kind, considerate and well-liked young woman.

Those who have suggested that she hoaxed the affair claim that she did so because she had fallen in love with Frank, Asa Roff's son, and that she pretended to be Mary so that she could move into the Roff home and be close to him. However, it's hard to take this seriously since, to all intents and purposes, Frank considered Lurancy to be his sister Mary reincarnated. He would have had no romantic interest in her and such desperation would have gained very little on the part of Lurancy.

When considering this scenario, or any other scenario involving a hoax on the part of Lurancy, we have to question how she could have been coached so well that she could know the intimate details of the lives of the Roffs in the way that she did. Could this have been possible? Could she have fooled that many people by simply listening to gossip and information about the family? Prior to the beginning of 1878, the Vennums had almost no contact with the Roff family whatsoever. Mrs. Vennum and Mrs. Roff had met one time and Thomas Vennum and Asa Roff were formal acquaintances, at best. There seems to be no possible way that Lurancy could have acquired the information that she spoke of while being possessed by Mary Roff. There were hundreds of details, friends whom she recognized, small bits of daily life and much more that could not have come from casual conversation. She would have had to have employed a firm of private detectives, plus learned to be a first-rate actress, to be able to pull off an impersonation of Mary Roff.

Asa Roff: The other main suspect when it comes to a hoax is Asa Roff, Mary's father. While his motives remain a mystery, it's possible that he could have somehow convinced Lurancy, with the help of Dr. Stevens, that she really was Mary Roff. But why? Those who worked to expose the Spiritualist movement as a fraud in the late 1800s claimed that Roff wanted to bring publicity to the movement, even using his own dead daughter to do so. They claimed that he, along with Stevens, would have done anything to turn this into a big story. Of course, in order to do this, he would have to have enlisted the help of Lurancy, her parents, his own family, dozens of neighbors and even some of the most respected men in Watseka and Iroquois County at the time. Again, this seems rather hard to believe. Roff was one of the best-liked men in town in the 1870s, was one of the founders of Watseka and served in a variety of public offices that required general elections. If he had been a fraud, someone would have spoken out against him but no one did. In fact, many went out of their way to sign affidavits and write letters of support for him concerning the events in question.

There have also been suggestions made that Roff may not have purposely hoaxed the events in the case but had been somehow misled into believing they were genuine. Of course, this would have to mean that Lurancy faked the possession and managed to fool Asa Roff. Those who believe this is a possibility state that Roff was obviously gullible since he was an ardent Spiritualist. In my opinion, such statements are hardly useful since the ranks of Spiritualism in the late 1800s included scientists, scholars, authors, and some of the most esteemed individuals of the day.

So, does a hoax seem likely? Not particularly, since it would have to have involved multiple people, hundreds of confederates the population of Watseka, and an ongoing series of lies and deceptions. The story of the Watseka Wonder was not a work of fiction, but what really occurred remains to be seen.

Multiple Personality & Power of Suggestion

For those who are not inclined to believe in the possibility that Lurancy was truly possessed by the spirit of Mary Roff, there are other, more scientific possibilities available. Some of these options don't do anything to impeach the truthfulness of the testimony given by Dr. Stevens, the Roffs and the numerous other witnesses.

One of the other options given in the case is that Lurancy manifested a "secondary personality" in addition to her own. While rare, such cases do exist today, although they were largely unheard of in the 1870s. For those who have rejected the idea of spirit possession, this seems a likely alternative and, on the surface, the incident does bear a striking resemblance to such cases. In 1908, the Watseka Wonder case was re-examined and it was at that time that the idea of a "secondary" or "multiple" personality was presented. Author H. Addington

Bruce stated: "Recent research has reported these cases in such numbers, which are due to perfectly natural, although often obscure, causes. In these, as the result of an illness, a blow, a shock, or some other unusual stimulus, there is a partial or complete effacement of the original personality of the victim, and its replacement by a new personality, sometimes of radically different characteristics from the normal self."

One of the cases cited, one bearing a resemblance to the Watseka Wonder case is the account of Reverend Thomas Hanna. Following a carriage accident, Hanna, a Connecticut clergyman, completely lost his identity. He had no memory of any events prior to the accident, recognized none of his friends and in fact, couldn't walk, talk, read or write. He had mentally become a newborn child. However, as soon as the rudiments of education were acquired by him once more, he showed himself to be the possessor of an independent and self-reliant personality --- completely separate from his original one. He had absolutely no memory of his previous personality and had become a new person. Eventually, through hypnosis, Hanna was able to recall his vanished self and, fusing the secondary personality with it, to restore himself to the person that he once was.

At that time, it was believed that the secondary personality was able to retain some of the characteristics of the original self, such as the ability to read and write and other aspects of daily life. In this way, Ansel Bourne, an itinerant preacher from Rhode Island, became "metamorphosed" into a man named A.J. Brown and, without any recollection of his former career, family or friends, drifted to Pennsylvania and began an entirely new existence as a shopkeeper in a small country town.

Another case, studied by Dr. R. Osgood Mason, involved a young woman who was called Alma Z. for privacy reasons. In this situation, she manifested a secondary personality called "Twoey." Dr. Mason reported that this personality spoke in a peculiar child-like and Indian-like dialect and announced that her mission was to cure the broken-down physical body of the original self. Alma's original personality remained completely dormant as long as "Twoey" was in place. In this regard, the case is very similar to that of Lurancy Vennum with the main difference being that "Twoey" - who, by the way, was credited with having seemingly supernatural powers - did not claim to be a returned spirit from the other side.

By using examples like this, many have drawn distinct parallels between the case of the Watseka Wonder and cases like those just mentioned. In the Watseka case, as in the others, we have the loss of the original self, development of a new self, and the enactment of a role by the new personality that is completely opposite that of the original being. The main difference is the character of the personality that replaced Lurancy's original personality. Here, the claim was made that the secondary personality was that of a girl long dead and by way of proof, vivid knowledge of the life, circumstances and behavior of the dead girl was offered. So, how do we explain this? How did Lurancy conjure up a real personality from the inner depths of her mind? How did her mental illness so perfectly create the identity of a girl who had once lived?

Author H. Addington Bruce submitted what he believed was a credible explanation for this: "On this point, considerable light is shed by the discover that in many instances of secondary personality in which no supernatural pretensions are advanced there is a notable sharpening of the faculties, knowledge being obtained telepathically or clairvoyantly; and by the further discovery that it is quite possible to create experimentally secondary selves assuming the characteristics of real persons that have died."

Subscribers to this theory believe that such a creative force is nothing more than suggestion. To prove this, they cite the case of an instance of mediumship in which the medium, an amateur investigator of psychic phenomena, clearly recognized that his spirit possessions were suggested to him by the spectators at his séances. The medium, a Vancouver schoolteacher named Charles Tout, reported that after attending a few séances with friends, he felt the strong need to become a medium himself and assume a foreign personality. Yielding to the impulse, he discovered, much to his amazement, without losing control of his consciousness, he could develop a secondary personality that could be presented as a discarnate "spirit." On one occasion, he took on the part of a dead woman, the mother of a friend who was present, and it was accepted as a genuine case of "spirit control."

On another night, having given several successful impersonations, he suddenly felt sick and weak and collapsed onto the floor. At this point, one of the sitters remarked: "It is father controlling him." Tout went on to write:

And then I seemed to realize who I was and whom I was seeking. I began to be distressed in my lungs, and should have fallen if they had not held me by the hands and let me gently back to the floor. I was in a measure still conscious of my actions, though not of my surroundings, and I have a clear memory of seeing myself in character of my dying father lying in bed and in the room in which he died. It was a most curious sensation. I saw his shrunken hands and face, and lived again through his dying moments; only now I was both myself, in an indistinct sort of way, and my father, with his feelings and appearance.

Tout explained away the occurrence as nothing supernatural but rather the working out, by some half-conscious part of his personality, of suggestions made at the time by members of his circle, or by something from experience.

This case seems to be the exception rather than the rule when it comes to this sort of thing. In most instances, it seems the original personality is completely effaced and no consciousness is retained of the actions of the secondary self. However, researchers do claim that an avenue of sense remains open and makes it possible for hypnotic suggestions to be made to the original personality. In this way, these personalities can be restored and suggestions can be made as to the actions of the dominant personality.

It is here where some believe the solution to the mystery of Lurancy Vennum lies. According to their theory, Lurancy Vennum was the subject of some "psychic catastrophe" they do not explain what this might have been and her mind was opened. That is to say that she momentarily lost all knowledge and control of her personality. When that occurred, it made it possible for a secondary personality to emerge, or as with the medium Charles Tout, for suggestions to create that personality for her.

Proponents of this theory feel that Lurancy may have been predetermined to be "possessed" by a ghost. A few days before her first attack, she informed her family that there were people in her room at night, whispering her name. The next night, she was so frightened that she would only rest if her mother came to her bed with her. These notions of ghostly figures proved to be foreshadowing of the coming trouble and possibly provocative of it. They would act as a powerful autosuggestion and Lurancy would be willing to easily accept the idea that she was possessed by the spirit of a dead girl.

And what of the other spirits that came through first? Those who suggest this theory have an answer to that also. They believe that Lurancy was unconsciously looking for a satisfactory self of ghostly origins. First there was the aged Katrina Hogan, then the troublesome and dangerous Willie Canning, both of which she tried and rejected, likely because her young girl's imagination was unable to invest them with satisfactory attributes. From her family, she received no assistance in her strange quest. They, disbelieving in spirits, persisted in seeing her as insane - a suggestion that was not comforting and far from beneficial. But with the intervention of Asa Roff and Dr. Stevens, everything changed. Not questioning the truth of her assertions, they confirmed them and offered her the gift of a ready-made personality.

Mary Roff was a real person, had a real existence, and once had thoughts, feelings and desires. And Mary, they assured the disintegrated Lurancy, could help her to regain all that she had lost. Needless to say, this was an enticing idea for the disturbed young girl and the sooner that Mary could take her over and help her, the better. For knowledge of Mary, of her characteristics, her relationships, friends, and more theorists believe , it was only necessary for Lurancy to tap telepathically into the reservoir possessed by Mary's family. Here, there would be, besides general information, a wealth of chance remarks, unconscious hints, unnoticed promptings - all of the suggestions that Lurancy needed to assume this new personality. Her shattered psyche, searching for a secondary personality, eagerly took what was offered to her and Lurancy became, at least for a time, Mary Roff.

Theorists also believe that suggestion was instrumental in not only creating Mary's personality, but expelling it and restoring Lurancy to health. If the responsibility for the creation of the spirit lies with Dr. Stevens and the Roffs, then likewise credit belongs to them for the cure. Their insistence on the fact that Mary's spirit could provide a cure for the girl was itself as powerful a suggestion as anything that could be given by a modern practitioner of mental health science. It unconsciously set a limit to the time of the possession and also created the fixed idea that she was not Lurancy Vennum but Mary Roff and in the month of May, she would become Lurancy again. It was as though Stevens and the Roffs had actually hypnotized her and given her commands that were to be obeyed.

When the time came for the transformation, it occurred with some amount of struggle, a period of alternating personality, with Mary in charge at one moment and Lurancy in control at another. Proponents of the theory that Lurancy was somehow "hypnotized" into believing she was Mary Roff see this as normal and point out that Mary only returned in the future when Lurancy was in the presence of the Roffs.

Mystery solved.

But is it really? Isn't it interesting when theories to debunk a case seem to be more complex, more convoluted and harder to believe than if we simply say "it must have been a ghost?" While the secondary personality theory does have some interesting - and believable - components to it, overall it's still pretty hard to swallow. For one thing, this theory requires us to believe that Lurancy was somehow capable of reading the minds of the Roff family, their relatives, friends and neighbors. This is in spite of the fact that she had never manifested any such ability before, or after, the case. Secondly, we also have to make the leap that Lurancy suffered some sort of psychic trauma that would have caused her personality to split, or for her to assume a secondary one. There is nothing in the records to indicate how, or when, this might have occurred. Since the start of her seizures and spells seemed to take the Vennum family by surprise, it seems likely that there would have been something in the record about her having mental issues prior to this, if they had actually occurred.

In each of the cases cited but those who believe that Lurancy Vennum created Mary as a secondary personality, these alternate personalities were always fictional characters that were created by the victim. Even in the case of the medium Charles Tout, he manifested the "spirit" of his own dead father, a person he knew well. However, Lurancy did not know Mary, had never met her, did not know her family, her friends or anyone connected to her. To try and explain that her in-depth, intimate knowledge of Mary came because she could suddenly "read minds" is a rather ridiculous and lame attempt to explain away the unexplainable. Even a casual reader of this account will see that there was much more to this case than this weak theory can provide.

Could there have been a scientific explanation for what occurred? There certainly could have been, however, no one has been able to find it. Which leaves us with only one more possible explanation for what took place in Watseka...

Sir Arthur Conan Doyle, himself a devout Spiritualist, once wrote for his master detective Sherlock Holmes: "Eliminate the impossible and whatever remains, however improbable, must be the truth." In this case, if we have ruled out the idea that the Watseka Wonder incident was hoax and have rejected the idea that Lurancy created a secondary personality, then what do we have left? All that remains is that in January 1878, Lurancy Vennum became possessed by the spirit of Mary Roff, a girl who had died more than a decade before.

That's what many people believe. Is it the truth? That is, of course, up to you as the reader to decide. As for my own thoughts on this mysterious case? Well, I still don't know. I do believe that something amazing occurred in Watseka in the spring of 1878 and I believe that it permanently affected not only the Vennum and Roff families, but also the entire town of Watseka itself.

Was Lurancy actually possessed by the spirit of Mary Roff? Logic tells me that it couldn't have happened but this case certainly gives me pause. The story of the "Watseka Wonder" can make just about anyone wonder if we know as much about the unexplained as we think we do.

It certainly inspires that feeling in me.

A CAMERA
The Story of Spirit Photography

The birth of photography and the beginnings of psychical research came within a few decades of one another. Photography, which began as little more than a few tentative experiments in the early 1800s, became commonplace by the middle part of the nineteenth century. It was about this same time when so-called "spirit rappings" began at the Fox family home in Hydesville, New York, and launched the Spiritualist movement and the scientific investigations of the movement that followed. By the early 1900s, with the introduction of the Brownie camera, photography had become wildly popular and so had the Spiritualist movement, with séances routinely held in family homes and mediums not only contacting the dead but allegedly taking photographs of the departed, as well. It seemed that practically anyone could "capture" anything at any time on film.

With all of these photos have come many mysteries, especially when we begin delving into the realm of the supernatural. Could a seemingly inexplicable photo be merely a defect of the camera or the film? Could that photo purporting to be of a ghost really be nothing more than a double exposure?

And most importantly, can a ghost really be captured on film?

Since the beginning of recorded time, man has created images of the things that surrounded him. In the earliest times, cave dwellers rendered likenesses of animals on the walls of their shelters. Ancient people crafted images on pottery and stone and the Middle Ages saw the birth of thousands of pieces of classic artwork. The eighteenth century saw a demand for portraits that were far less expensive than the formal oil paintings that were commissioned by wealthy patrons. Those of the middle class were able to obtain miniature portraits that were silhouettes, created by a shadow cast from a lamp and then traced and cut out by the artist from black paper. These shadow portraits were one-of-a-kind originals until 1786, when a device called a Physionotrace made it possible to make multiple images. When the pointer of the device was traced over the lamp-created profile, a system of levers caused an engraving tool to reproduce the outline on a copper plate. Details, facial features and clothing could also be added and then the plate was inked and printed to make as many copies as were needed. Soon artists and inventors began to speculate that there might be an optical device that could produce the images directly.

An device like this, known as the *camera obscura*, was known in ancient times but there was no way to permanently record the images it obtained. Various portable models of the *camera obscura* were invented and in 1589, Giovanni Battista della Porta made note of using a lens rather than a hole to show the images. About 1665, Robert Boyle constructed a model that was the size of a small box and added a lens that could be extended or shortened like a telescope. This way, the image could be projected on a piece of paper placed across the back of the box directly across from the lens. Scientists began using the *camera obscura* for solar observations and artists adapted it as an aid in drawing since they could easily trace the projected image.

Around 1800, the first experiments were conducted to try and enhance the *camera obscura* images. They were carried out in England by Thomas Wedgwood, who tried to copy paintings that were done on glass onto sheets of paper that were treated with silver nitrate. Unfortunately, the dark images were not permanent and because of their sensitivity to the light, could only be viewed by candlelight.

The first permanent images created by light were produced by a French inventor named Joseph Nicephore Niepce, who was also an amateur artist. He wanted to create a new printmaking technique of lithography but was not very skilled at drawing. He sought ways of transferring images directly onto the printing plate and even tried Wedgwood's methods but also found that the faint, disappearing images created a problem. Over time, Niepce discovered a varnish that was sensitive to light, remaining soft where protected from light and hardening wherever exposed. A plate coated with varnish and exposed by passing light through a drawing or print made on translucent paper could then be washed with a solvent that dissolved the soft areas and left a permanent image on the plate. These first "heliographs" came about in 1822 and Niepce continued working with them for five years before using a *camera obscura* to record an image on a coated pewter plate. This view was made from the window of his home and required an eight-hour exposure. It is regarded today as the oldest surviving image produced by a camera.

In 1835, William Henry Fox Talbot discovered the fundamental principle on which modern photography is based: the photographic negative from which many copies can be made. He also identified silver chloride as the silver compound that is most suitable for photographic prints. In 1840, he gave the name "calotype" to his improved process in which a latent image could be developed onto paper. Unfortunately, his work at that time was being overshadowed by a French process that produced a very different photographic image known as the daguerreotype.

This process was discovered in 1837 by an inventor named Louis Daguerre. The biggest drawback to this new form of photography was that to expose and process a daguerreotype plate, a lot of apparatus and labor was required. First, the plate had to be placed in a hand vise and polished with a piece of leather, using powdered pumice stone and olive oil. It was finished to a high polish and then placed in a box that had two compartments for iodine crystals and bromide water. The developer then had to watch the plate carefully and estimate when the desired degree of sensitivity had been reached. The prepared plate, loaded into a plate holder, was then placed in the camera, which consisted of two wooden boxes, one of which contained the lens and the other the focusing screen and holder for the plate. After the plate was exposed, which took about thirty seconds, it was removed and taken to the darkroom, where it was placed facedown in the top of the developing box. In the bottom was a dish of mercury, heated by a lamp. As the mercury vapor developed the image, the process could be seen by candlelight through a yellow glass window in the box. When fully developed, the image was then fixed by a chemical treatment that removed the unused silver salts. The plate was then placed on a level stand so that it remained completely horizontal, then covered with a gold-bearing solution and heated. Finally, after it was washed and dried, the finished plate was covered with a decorated covering and a piece of protective glass and then sealed in a brass or foil frame. The frame had to be airtight because the silver plate would tarnish rapidly if it was exposed to air.

As the reader can see, working with daguerreotypes was highly labor-intensive, expensive and complicated. The work was so cumbersome that a photographer literally had to travel with a small laboratory that limited him to producing fragile, one-of-a-kind pictures that were "direct positives," or mirror images. In the portraits, the faces of the sitters were flattened in a way that made them look tormented. So not only were they a burden to work with, daguerreotypes were not exactly flattering to their subjects.

Even with all of their disadvantages, daguerreotypes captured the popular imagination. The daguerreotype flourished. In March 1840, dentist and machinist Alexander Wolcott and John Johnson, a former jeweler's assistant, both of whom were associates of Samuel Morse, opened the first portrait studio in the United States in New York City. The process caught on and soon attendance at the daguerreotype portrait studio became essential in the social circles of the fashion conscious.

By 1844, the daguerreotype process was virtually perfected, but even so, it was never meant to last. By the middle 1850s, a new photographic process, called the collodion or "wet plate" method, began to overshadow the daguerreotype and it lasted for several years in America.

The first "wet plate" method, the ambrotype, had a very short lifespan. This process, which used paper plates instead of silver ones, required much less work and was cheaper to produce than the daguerreotype method. Despite its advantages, there were problems. Like the daguerreotype, each ambrotype was a one-of-a-kind image. If the subject desired an additional picture, he had to sit for another exposure or have the original copied. Because the image was quite fragile, the collodion positive had to be carefully packaged. It had to be fitted with a brass covering and then covered with glass, followed by a brass rim called a "preserver." The package was then placed in a folding case that would protect it from damage.

The popularity of the ambrotype was sudden and far-reaching, lasting from the middle 1850s and into the early 1860s. Many Civil War soldiers chose this inexpensive process to immortalize themselves for their loved ones back home. But the process was not meant to last and was soon replaced by another type of collodion positive method that gained its greatest fame during the Civil War.

The tintype came about in the latter part of the 1850s but did not become popular for several years afterward. Like the ambrotype, the tintype used the same type of collodion, wet plate process but in this case, the process utilized a thin sheet of blackened iron. Thanks to this, it was nicknamed the "tintype" and the name stuck.

While tintypes lasted well into the twentieth century, when they were produced by the gelatin-silver bromide process, early tintypes were made by the collodion wet plate method. The thin iron plate that was used was coated with a black varnish and then cut to size to be inserted into the camera. It was then exposed in a camera that was often designed to contain all of the chemical operations that needed to be conducted to produce the final image. To prevent damage, the exposed plates were then given a protective coat of clear varnish.

Unlike the ambrotype, the tintype was developed as a positive image and so it did not have to be backed or even mounted in an elaborate matter that would allow the image to be clearly seen. The metal base was also less fragile, which is the reason that so many tintype images have survived into the modern era. Another advantage was that even though the tintype was also a one-of-a-kind photograph, multiple identical images could be created with a multiple lens camera. They were capable of exposing four, six or more photographs simultaneously on a single plate. After processing, the duplicate pictures were then snipped apart with metal-cutting shears.

Although the tintype photograph lacked the tonal range of the ambrotype, its relative inexpensiveness made it very popular. The low cost also appealed to soldiers during the war, especially the lower-paid Union enlisted men. Confederate tintypes became progressively less common, thanks to wartime shortages of sheet metal.

This practical and profitable method of photography continued to be in use for decades, despite the clamor for paper prints. The process even remained in use, generally at beaches and fairgrounds, until after World War II.

As successful as the wet plate process was, there was still a need for a process during which a prepared plate could be kept for some time before being exposed to the camera. There were many early attempts to keep the plates wet for extended periods but all of them failed until 1855, when J.N. Taupenot devised the first successful "dry plate" method. He did it using sensitized layers of collodion and albumen, which allowed the plates to be stored for weeks before exposure.

Another major development was achieved by Dr. Richard Leach Maddox in 1871 when he returned to a substance that was earlier used in photography: gelatin. He found that a mixture of silver nitrate and cadmium bromide in a solution of warm gelatin yielded a silver bromide emulsion that produced effective dry plates.

Two years later, John Burgess began to sell an already-mixed gelatin emulsion for coating glass plates and the following year, another inventor, Richard Kennett, marketed the emulsion in a dried form that could be mixed with water before use. Called Kennett's Patented Sensitized Pellicle, it inadvertently gained sensitivity from the heat-drying process by which the gelatin "pellicle" was prepared. This created the most sensitive plate so far but it remained for Charles Bennett to investigate the increased sensitivity and to use prolonged heating to develop highly sensitive plates and ones that could be easily manufactured. The new process was successful and by 1880, photographers could travel without the dark tent and wagon full of chemicals that were previously required. Now, photographers could make an excursion with just a camera and tripod and a few plate holders loaded with prepared dry plates. They could later be processed on the photographer's return to his studio. Remaining popular until the 1920s, the gelatin dry plate glass negatives brought several important changes to photography, especially the means to measure sensitivity of the plate. This was notable since unlike the wet plates which were developed in the field and permitted the photographer to make successively corrected exposures the results of dry plate photography were not immediately apparent.

Along with plates for which the sensitivity could be measured came methods of calculating the necessary lens aperture and exposure time. By 1886, this was accomplished by pocket watch-size devices that were used until the 1920s. With the reduction of exposure times, which were accomplished by increasing the aperture of the lens, came radical advancements in photography. For the first time, photographs could be achieved that required exposures of fractions of seconds and photographing moving subjects became practicable at last.

Because of the lengthy exposure times needed by the earlier photographic plates, any movement produced a blur. For this reason, not only were photos of moving people or objects out of the question, but even those who sat quietly for portraits had to have their heads held by clamps fixed to the backs of chairs. This is the reason why you never see any photos from the Civil War era that are anything other than posed portraits or still landscapes. And also why people are rarely smiling in photographs from the 1800s; it was just too hard to maintain anything resembling a natural smile for that long a time.

Shuttered cameras first came into use with stereographs and were made possible by the small images that were produced. When stereo views were made of scenes involving movement, both pictures had to be exposed at precisely the same instant. In that way, simple shutters, consisting of flaps or sliding plates, could create exposures as brief as one-fourth of a second.

The instantaneous photo was characterized as a "snapshot" a term applied to a hurriedly aimed shot by Sir John Herschel in 1860. Such brief exposures permitted cameras to be freed from the tripod, which had been used by the photographer to prevent movement and then blurring of the picture. Now, with the addition of a viewfinder to aid in the framing of the photo, cameras could be handheld. In 1881, Thomas Bola called his small, box-type camera a "Detective" camera, and soon diminutive models were hidden in bags, hats and even in the handles of walking sticks. The glass plates remained a problem though, thanks to rather awkward mechanisms that held several dry plates at once. Such cameras came to be known as "magazine" cameras and became the forerunner to a revolutionary development in America that allowed successive snapshots to be made quickly.

The dry photo process that had been devised by Charles Bennett gained the attention of a man named George Eastman. The Rochester, New York, bank clerk turned amateur photographer was so impressed with the plates that he began manufacturing gelatin dry plates and selling them through a photographic supply house as early as 1880. He became the first person to do so in the United States.

Eastman soon sought additional ways to simplify photography, realizing that its complexity, along with the messy processes, was keeping it from being enjoyed by everyday people. Working with camera manufacturer William H. Walker, Eastman developed a holder for a lengthy roll of paper negative film. Although there had been earlier experiments with such things, the Eastman-Walker invention combined a roll-holding feature with very sensitive, lightweight material. It became an immediate success.

Soon after, Eastman designed a small, hand-held camera that utilized the roll holder. Patented in 1886 with an Eastman employee named F.M. Cossitt, the small model was produced with a run of only fifty cameras. Too complicated and too expensive to be popular, the entire lot was sold off to a dealer the following year. Two years later, in 1888, Eastman developed a new model that was made up of a small box that contained a roll of paper-based film that was sufficient for about one hundred exposures. It was simple to operate but the photographer had to keep track of the number of pictures taken for there was no exposure counter. Eastman gave his camera the invented name of "Kodak," which he felt sounded firm and uncompromising.

Although there had been earlier roll-film cameras, the Kodak was the first to be backed up by a service that processed the exposed pictures. Realizing that most people did not have the time, skill or inclination to develop their own film, Eastman adopted the slogan "You Press the Button, We Do the Rest." After completing the roll, the customer sent the camera to Eastman's factory in New York, where the film was unloaded, developed and printed. After that, a reloaded camera was shipped back to the owner, along with the processed prints. After much success, Eastman introduced a new camera in 1889 with an improved shutter. He called it the No. 2 Kodak.

At the end of that year, Eastman introduced a new product that replaced the old paper-based film, which was complicated to handle since it required the processed negative image to be stripped from the paper base before printing. The new product was a roll film on a celluloid base and with this clear, flexible material, the roll-film camera finally became practical.

The Kodak camera and the development of celluloid roll film launched the heyday of popular snapshot photography, although it took years to solve all of the problems that remained. The need to expose a hundred images, for example, was solved by shorter films and simpler methods of loading that did not involve sending the camera back to the factory. By 1891, cameras had been devised that even allowed the film to be loaded in daylight. Numbered markings were placed on the black backing paper that helped protect the celluloid film from light when it was wound on a spool. These numbers could be read through a window on the camera's back, permitting the film to be wound a precise distance each time until a new number was centered in the window. Eastman incorporated the idea in his pocket Kodak of 1895 and the first of his folding Kodak cameras in 1897.

Despite all of this, Eastman still felt that photography was too expensive for the masses and he assigned his camera designer, Frank Brownell, to develop a simple model that could be cheaply reproduced. The result was the Brownie Kodak, introduced in February 1900. Even though most assumed that the name for the camera came from its creator, Frank Brownell, the designation was actually supposed to have been sparked by the popularity of the Brownies, the little fairies in Palmer Cox's children's stories. This was tied to Eastman's advertising strategy that asserted that the Brownie camera had a "simple Kodak method that enables even a child to make successful and charming photographs."

The Brownie captured the public's imagination, but not everyone was pleased with the popular revolution in photography. According to one newspaper report, "Several decent young men are forming a Vigilance Committee for the purpose of thrashing the cads with cameras who go about seaside places taking snapshots of ladies emerging from the deep."

Regardless, photographic enthusiasm continued to spread and further advancements were made. In 1893, the first practical motion pictures were made using Eastman's film and were shown on Thomas Edison's Kinetoscope viewing machine. The motion pictures were based on earlier experiments conducted by Edward Muybridge in 1878. He had arranged a series of cameras with shutters that were triggered by trip wires across the path of a galloping horse. This produced a picture sequence that showed the horse in motion. The 1893 images, shown at the Columbian Exposition in Chicago, were the first to show motion using a steady roll of film.

More significant steps in photography followed. One of the most important was the development of the camera flash. Although flash powder had been used for the illumination of subjects almost from the beginning of snapshot photography, it was, not surprisingly, very dangerous. The flashbulb was invented in the 1920s and automatically triggered flashes came with professional cameras in the middle 1930s. The first simple flash camera, the Falcon Press Flash, came along in 1939.

Another development came in 1938, when the first fully automatic camera was developed. It used a photoelectric cell to move a meter needle, which was locked in place by the initial pressure on the shutter release. Then, a spring-loaded sensor linked to the aperture setting moved until it was stopped by a locked needle, automatically setting the exposure.

Among the most important developments in the field was the introduction of color photography. Although its possibilities were considered early in the history of photography, the earliest color pictures were nothing more than black and white Daguerreotypes that were hand-colored. The first color photograph was produced as early as 1861 by James Clerk Maxwell, but the first color plates were not produced until 1896. The first genuinely successful plates were marketed by the Lumiere Brothers in 1907 and were called Autochrome plates. They ceased making them in 1932 but three-color "carbro" plates began to be used by fashion photographers in the 1930s. In 1935, the great breakthrough in color photography came with the introduction of Kodachrome film.

Kodachrome was produced at the suggestion of two musicians, Leopold Godowsky, Jr. and Leopold Mannes. They proposed coating film with three different black and white emulsions, each sensitive to one of the primary colors of light. A single exposure, when processed, produced three superimposed images, each of which could be selectively dyed to yield a full color picture. Kodachrome was initially introduced as a motion picture film but a version for still cameras was soon created.

About that same time, Agfa, in Germany, produced a film that used the same three layers sensitive to red, blue and green light but the color-forming compounds were placed directly into the film's emulsion. The Agfa and Kodachrome systems are the basis for almost all color photography in use today.

More improvements in photography involved cameras that had "instant" features. The Polaroid Land Camera was marketed starting in 1948. Within a minute of being removed from the camera, the print yielded a sepia-toned image. It was a huge success and many improved cameras and film followed, including Polaroid color film in 1963. The Kodak Pocket Instamatic later simplified a common problem for the average person who wanted to dabble in photography: loading the film. The Instamatic came about in 1963 and was similar to the Brownie but introduced simple load-in cartridges that could be inserted only one way. In 1982, Kodak also introduced the so-called Disc Camera that had cartridges in the form of a circular disc that contained the negatives. But the small size of the negatives resulted in grainy images and the camera failed to interest the public in the way the Instamatic had. One of the most popular types of cameras a few years ago were the APS cameras that featured simple drop-in cartridges and also allowed the photographer to photograph at various sizes, including classic size and wide panoramic prints.

Today, most film cameras have been replaced by digital cameras, which save money on film and developing and offer instant results when a shot is taken.

The origins of digital cameras can be linked back to the computer imaging that was being done by NASA back in the 1960s. During this time, NASA was preparing for the Apollo Lunar Exploration missions and in advance of men landing on the moon, they sent out a series of probes to map the surface. The probes relied on video cameras that were outfitted with transmitters that could broadcast analog signals back to mission control. The weak transmissions were often plagued by natural interference and television at that time could not transform them into coherent images.

NASA researchers soon began searching for ways to enhance the signals by processing them through computers. The signals were analyzed by the computer and then converted into digital information. The interference was removed and the critical data could be enhanced to produce clear images of the moon. This was the first real digital imaging to be done and it would soon revolutionize photography as we know it.

Digital technology was not only used by NASA to explore the solar system but it also created a number of medical imaging devices, changed the world of entertainment and made photography and video accessible to people who had never used it before.

The digital cameras of today capture images electronically and convert them into digital data that can be stored on a chip inside the camera. The images can then be transferred and manipulated using a computer. Like conventional cameras, digital devices have a lens, a shutter and an aperture but they do not use film. When light passes through the lens, it is directed to a light-sensitive chip called a "charged coupling device" CCD . The CCD converts the light into electrical impulses, feeds it into the processing chip and then transforms that into digital information. Digital images offer many advantages over a standard camera, freeing the photographer from film and optics and allowing the images captured to be transformed in ways that have never been available before.

All images that are seen by the human eye are formed from energy given off by light. In order for the digital camera to store an optical image, it must be converted into digital information. A simple photograph is composed of a wide range of color and light variations and like the spectrum of natural light that it represents, the tones of the photo are continuous and unbroken. However, a digital image consists of scores of points of light that have been sampled from the light spectrum. The range of tone is determined by the camera's capacity to store and sample different light values. The more expensive the camera, or at least the greater number of megapixels of light that it offers, the better image the photographer will obtain. When a photo is taken, the pixels in the image are assigned a place on the color scale that corresponds to its place and value in the optical image. The more pixels, the greater the range of tone for the image. Once the camera has determined the proper colors and tone, the CCD calculates a sampling rate for the entire image.

Most digital images form within a fraction of a second and in that instant, an image made of light is transformed into a stream of numerical data that can be changed and altered to look like anything that the creative photographer wants. There is no question that digital cameras have permanently changed the world of photography--- whether it is the photography of the mundane or that of the spirit world.

The history of photography is long and often convoluted, as noted in the preceding pages. How does all of this fit in the world of the supernatural? Over the years, there have been scores of photographs that allege to be ghosts captured on film. Are they? It's possible - but it should also be noted that a camera does not operate like the human eye. Many have written about "seeing the world through the camera lens," perhaps never realizing how radically different it is to actually see something rather than to capture it with a camera.

The human eye works in some ways like the shutter of the camera. It opens and closes in a blink or can be closed at the speed of a long exposure. The lens of the human eye works to focus on what it is looking at in the same way as focus ring on a camera. The human eye does this by reflex but the camera has to be manually focused, either by hand or by the camera's inner workings. The iris of the eye dilates to let in more or less light in the same way that the f-stop on a camera does. The retina of the eye receives an image and imprints it on the consciousness in the same way that images are captured on the camera's film. At that point, though, the comparison comes to an end. The images that we see with our eyes are collected and analyzed by our brain and anything that we see is subject to adaptation and censorship by our personality. Images that are collected by the camera are captured just as they are and are not distorted by emotion or disbelief, freezing a moment of time and space in a way that our eyes cannot. Could this be why, as some believe, ghosts can be captured with a camera but sometimes are invisible to the human eye?

As the reader has already learned in the previous pages, the camera basically consists of two things: a box that is tight enough to keep out light and a lens. The lens collects the light from the object that is being photographed and focuses on the image. The box is sealed so that it does not take in any other light than what is coming in through the lens. Beyond that, cameras are also equipped with a shutter, a simple timing device that restricts the length of time that light is allowed to reach the film, and an aperture, which is a hole that is located just behind the lens. The aperture is opened wider or smaller to brighten the image. This is known as the f-stop and the larger the number, the smaller the aperture. A higher number allows more light to be admitted than a smaller number f-stop. All of these items can be adjusted with manual cameras, although today, most cameras are automatic and these settings are handled by the mechanism of the camera itself.

These Single Lens Reflex or SLR cameras are the most commonly used by photographers and ghost hunters alike. A single lens handles the viewing and the taking of the picture but this type of device also allows manual focusing and changes in f-stop settings, exposure settings and more. They can be a little complicated for the amateur but are well worth the trouble of learning to use them. Many others prefer the simple "point and shoot" type cameras, which handle all of the settings automatically.

But how do we "capture the light," so to speak, and make the camera work?

The light around us can be thought of as rays of energy that emanate from or reflect off of every point of an object and travel from it in straight lines. These lines travel randomly, so the lens of the camera serves to control their progress. The curved lens collects and redirects the light, bending it as it does so. The thicker and more curved the lens is, the greater its ability is to bend the light and the more the light is bent, the shorter the focal length will be. When the lens is focused at infinity, it is one focal length away from the "focal plane," where an image is actually formed. The operation of focusing the lens, whether done either manually or automatically, brings the lens away from the focal plane and brings nearer objects into focus. When the lens is focused on a point a certain distance away, there will be an area in front of and behind this point that appears very sharp on film. This is referred to as "depth of field." Using the depth of field can be helpful to the photographer and not just to create better-looking pictures. One way that it's useful is allowing the photographer to focus the camera in advance of taking photos when there may not be time to manually focus an SLR camera.

The light captured by the camera is also connected to the camera's shutter, which has been mentioned previously. The shutter allows light to reach the camera by opening and closing at various speeds, from very fast to very slow. Using a fast shutter and a high-speed film, the photographer can literally freeze even fast-moving objects and also take pictures under very low light conditions.

With our primer on the history of photography, and the basic operations of cameras and film, completed, we can begin to take a look at the other side of photography -- a side that is totally ignored by most scholars and experts in the field: capturing of the spirit world on film.

Spirit photography is nearly as old as photography itself but when the first photographers found inexplicable images in their work, they assumed they were caused by unknown variables in the strange chemicals and new apparatus they were using. At the dawn of photography, it was nearly impossible to take pictures of people. With the exposure times of a half hour or more needed to impress an image on the paper films and coated plates of the day, it was impractical to expect anyone to sit still for so long. It was not until improvements came along in cameras, lenses, photographic chemicals and processes that exposure times were reduced to a matter of seconds. By this time, people were flocking to the portrait studios to have their images immortalized.

Interest in the Spiritualist movement had been on the rise since the announcement of spirit rappings at the home of the Fox family of New York in 1848. Of course, no photographs were taken of the weird events at the Fox home because indoor photography was impossible at that time and for a number of years afterward. But the days of spirit photography were coming.

In those days, the photographer had to first prepare a plate by coating it with collodion, bathing it in silver nitrate, and then take the photo while the plate was still wet. Each new exposure was an exciting event but imagine how excited W. Campbell of Jersey City must have been when he achieved what is considered to be the first spirit photograph. At the American Photographic Society meeting of 1860, he displayed a test photograph that he had taken of an empty chair. There had been no one else in the studio at the time but when the plate was developed, it showed the image of a small boy seated in the chair. It is not known why Campbell wanted to take a picture of an empty chair in the first place, but whatever his reasons, he was never able to produce any other photographs of this sort. It would not be until the following year that the real history of spirit photography began.

On October 5, 1861, in a photographic studio at 258 Washington Street, a Boston jewelry engraver and amateur photographer named William H. Mumler developed some experimental self-portraits that he had taken and was startled to find that the image of a ghostly young woman appeared in one of the photos with him. He was said to have recognized her as a cousin who had died twelve years before. He later recalled that while posing for the portrait, he had experienced a trembling sensation in his right arm that left him particularly exhausted. The photograph attracted great attention and it was examined by not only Spiritualists but by some of the leading photographers of the day. Perhaps his most well-known spirit photograph shows a seated Mary Todd Lincoln seemingly being consoled by the ghost of her husband, Abraham Lincoln, who is standing behind her with his hand on her shoulder. Mumler was soon overwhelmed by demands for his photographs and he gave up his regular job as an engraver to devote himself entirely to spirit photography.

William Black, a leading Boston photographer who was known as the inventor of the acid nitrate bath for photographic plates, was one of the professionals who investigated Mumler and his methods. After sitting for Mumler in his studio, Black examined his camera, plate and bath and kept his eye on the plate from the moment its preparations began until it was locked into the camera. After his portrait was taken, Black removed it from the camera and personally took it into the darkroom, where, as it developed, he was stunned to see the image of a man leaning over his shoulder. Black was convinced that Mumler was the genuine article and could somehow entice the spirits to appear on film.

Others were not so sure. Mumler had never before been interested in the spirits or Spiritualism and his charge of $5 per photograph began to arouse suspicion that he was just in it for the money. He became the object of great controversy and he eventually moved to New York, where he doubled the price for his photographs. The critics and the disbelievers howled once more. In spite of this, he still had many supporters. One of them was U.S. Court of Appeals Judge John Edmonds, who had originally come to Mumler's studio convinced the man was a con artist, but left believing that he could actually conjure up genuine psychic photos.

In 1863, Dr. Henry T. Child of Philadelphia reported that Mumler was willing to allow him to thoroughly investigate the matter of his spirit photos to try and find a rational explanation for the mystery. Mumler permitted Child to watch all of his operations inside and outside the darkroom, and also allowed him to examine his apparatus. Dr. Child displayed the pictures made at the time, while he and several friends watched the entire process, from the plate cleaning to the fixing. He took the precaution to mark each plate with a diamond before it was used and yet on each one of them was a spirit image. Child had failed to discover any human agent that was responsible for the formation of the spirit pictures. Each photograph differed considerably from the others and Child could not come up with either an explanation or a way to duplicate them.

However, the "extras," as they came to be called, in Mumler's photographs did not amaze everyone. After much controversy, pressure from city officials led to him being arrested and charged with fraud. But the testimony of a number of leading New Yorkers, including famed Broadway producer Jeremiah Gurney, who affirmed that as a professional photographer he had never seen anything like the images that Mumler produced, led to the beleaguered spirit photographer being exonerated and his case dismissed.

As it would turn out later, the courts may have been a little too hasty about dropping all of the charges against Mumler.

According to an article in *Scientific American* magazine in 1902, William

Mumler may have been cleverer than anyone ever gave him credit for --- and a much bigger fraud. Experiments in duplicating spirit photos that came about after his heyday achieved a simple way of creating spectral images that would have passed inspection by those who examined Mumler's plates and apparatus at the time. This method involved making a very thin positive image on glass, the same size as the plate that was to be used in producing the spirit photo. The glass was then placed in the holder where the plate would later be positioned. With the glass in place, the plate could be inserted under the watchful eye of the examiner and the photograph produced. With the weak positive superimposed, the ghostly image would appear, along with the sitter, on the negative plate. In this way, the plates would never be tampered with and in examinations like those conducted by Dr. Child, his mark would appear on the plate that was used and he would never conclude that anything fraudulent was taking place.

Could this have been Mumler's secret? If we assume that fraud must have been involved with the creation of his photos, then yes, it could have been. But what about those photos that contained the images of loved ones that Mumler knew nothing about? Could his research have been so thorough that he was somehow able to delve into the private lives --- and photographs --- of the hundreds of people who made appointments with him so that he was able to obtain photos of dead relatives that could appear in his spirit photographs? And what of those who came to him without an appointment and yet their loved ones still managed to appear on film? Was it wishful thinking that the extras appeared to be departed loved ones? Perhaps --- or perhaps not.

Other spirit photographers, both amateur and professional, soon began to appear, eager to capitalize on the success of William Mumler. In America and Great Britain, a flurry of new studios began to open and the photographers began to call themselves "mediums," claiming the ability to make the dead appear in photographs. Spirit photography soon became a popular pastime and literally thousands of dollars were made from those who came to have their portraits taken. One photographer, William Hope, claimed to take more than 2,500 spirit photographs during a period of about two decades.

Hope was one of the premiere spirit photographers of the era and was considered by his supporters to be a true master of the art of producing spirits on ordinary photographic plates. To others, he was a clever trickster and while he had more than his share of detractors and was often accused of fraud, he was never caught at it, largely thanks to the controversy that surrounded the main attempt to expose him.

Hope was born in Crewe, England, in 1863 and as a young man, went to work as a carpenter. His talent for capturing spirits in photographs allegedly came about around 1905 when he and a friend were taking turns photographing one another. In a photo that was taken by Hope, there appeared an "extra" of his subject's deceased mother.

Not long after this incident, a group of six people organized a Spiritualist hall in Crewe for the purpose of creating spirit photographs. The group became renowned as the "Crewe Circle" with William Hope as its leader. During their early efforts, the circle destroyed all of the negatives of the photos they took for fear of being suspected of witchcraft. However, when Archbishop Thomas Colley, a lifelong enthusiast of both the supernatural and Spiritualism, joined the circle, they began to make their work public.

Ironically, Hope's first brush with exposure as a fraud came when Archbishop Colley arranged his first sitting. According to the story, Hope doctored the photograph with the wrong spirit extra, substituting another elderly woman for Colley's mother. When Hope tried to confess his fraud to Colley, the other man dismissed his confession as "nonsense." He said he could recognize his mother when he saw her and the extra in the photo was certainly his mother. To prove his case, he even put a notice in the local newspaper asking all of those who remembered his mother to call at the rectory. No fewer than eighteen people selected Hope's mistake from among several others and said that it definitely showed the ghost of the late Mrs. Colley.

In February 1922, Hope was almost exposed again but this time, the attempt almost backfired on the accuser and there remain some questions about the incident to this day. By that time, Hope had moved to London and had established himself as a professional medium. The Society for Psychical Research SPR decided to investigate Hope's claims and sent a new member, the indefatigable Harry Price, to look into it. The young Price had a good working knowledge of sleight of hand. During the investigation, Price claimed to detect evidence of trickery by Hope but questions immediately arose as to whether it was Price, and not Hope, who had tampered with the photographic plates.

Price told a different story of the incident and blamed his problems with the Spiritualist community on the controversy. Even though he had recently joined the SPR, Price had already exposed a number of fraudulent mediums, earning him the dislike of much of the community. During the sitting, which was organized with hymn singing and prayers like a standard séance, Hope and Price went into the adjoining dark room. While examining the photographic slide that Hope planned to use, Price secretly impressed twelve small punctures into it with a needle. He then was asked to open a packet of plates that he had brought with him. These plates had come from the Imperial Dry Plate Co. and had been imprinted at Price's suggestion with their trademark in the corner. The trademark would then appear on the negative of whatever picture was developed.

Price loaded two plates into the slide and then Hope asked for the slide.

As he took it from Price's hand, the investigator watched Hope's movements very carefully, which was hard to do in the dull, red darkness of the room. Very quickly, in one smooth movement, Hope placed the dark slide into the left breast pocket of his coat and then, apparently, pulled it back out again. Price knew that the slide had been changed but sat down and posed for the photograph to be taken anyway. When it was over, he refused to sign the plates, as Hope wanted him to, and as he examined the slide, he discovered that his twelve needle marks had "mysteriously" vanished. It was clearly not the same slide that he had given Hope. He did not accuse Hope of a swindle on the spot, fearing that his evidence of deception would be destroyed, but took away two photographs that had been taken of him, one of which contained a beautiful female "extra," but on neither plate was the Imperial Dry Plate trademark! Hope had managed to switch the plates as well. Price was able to show that they were not the same type of plates that he had given to Hope to use, as they were a different thickness, weight and color and were "fast" plates, while the ones that Hope gave back to him were "slow" ones.

In the May issue of the *Journal of the London SPR*, Price published a report about the incident under the title "Cold Light on Spiritualistic Phenomena," which was later reprinted as a separate booklet. Immediately, he was attacked by the Spiritualist camp. They accused Price of trickery and of switching the plates himself in order to discredit the medium. Sir Oliver Lodge however, who was a proponent of Spiritualism, believed that Hope was a fraud and wrote to Price saying: "I don't see how your proofs of Hope's duplicity could be more complete."

More than eleven years after this incident, the widow of a man who worked for Hope admitted in an article that, after Price's séance, her husband went through Hope's luggage and "found in a suitcase a flash lamp with a bulb attachment, some cut-out photographic heads and some hairs." Unfortunately, these devastating facts were suppressed in 1922 and Price would later comment that if not for this suppression, his accusations in the affair would have convinced even the Spiritualists that Hope was a fraud.

However, to make matters more perplexing, not all of the sittings that Hope conducted ended with questionable results. Throughout his career, Hope gained support from many quarters and figured prominently in a book about survival after death by the Reverend Charles Tweedale, who resided in a purportedly haunted Yorkshire vicarage. In his writings, Tweedale gives many accounts of Hope's prowess as a spirit photographer, stating that there was no fraud evident in the majority of Hope's cases in which people called upon him unannounced, even with secret identities, and obtained clearly recognizable spirit images. One such case was that of Mrs. Hortense Leverson, who came to Hope and was given a psychic photograph of her recently deceased husband, Major Leverson, who had been on the staff of the War Office. She was absolutely convinced that the photograph was legitimate. She, along with dozens perhaps hundreds of others, believed that Hope was absolutely genuine.

William Hope died on March 7, 1933, leaving a number of mysteries behind. Was he real - or was he a fraud? No one can say for sure, and like so many of the other enigmas connected to the practice of spirit photography, this one also remained unsolved.

In many cases, though, the answers are not as mysterious. Typically in spirit photographs, ghostly faces materialized, floating above and behind the living subjects. In others, fully formed figures would appear, usually draped in white sheets. Unfortunately, the methods of producing such images were simple. The fraudulent photographers became adept at doctoring their work, superimposing images on plates with living sitters and adding ghostly apparitions and double exposures. The appearance of the fully formed apparition was even easier. Many cameras demanded that the subject of the photo remain absolutely still, sometimes for periods of up to one minute, all the while, the shutter of the camera remains open. During this time, it was very simple for the photographer's assistant to quietly slip behind the sitter, dressed in appropriate "spirit attire." The assistant would remained in place for a few moments and then duck back out of the photo. On the finished plate, it would seem that a transparent figure had made an appearance. This could be done with cameras that required even a brief exposure time of a few seconds with an assistant popping out for only a second or two from behind a curtain.

This type of trick photo was first mentioned in photography journals in 1856. Ten years later, Sir David Brewster recalled the technique when he saw some of the early spirit photos that were produced. He remembered another photo that he had seen of a young boy who had been sitting on a step near a doorway and who had apparently gotten up and left about halfway through the exposure. As a result, the seated image was transparent in the finished photo. Brewster wrote: "The value and application of this fact did not at first present itself to me, but after I had contrived the lenticular stereoscope I saw that such transparent pictures might be used for the various purposes of entertainment." Photographs and stereographs of this type were sold commercially through the 1860s and 1870s but were nothing more than a novelty and were not meant to be taken as genuine spirit photographs.

Other methods of obtaining fraudulent photographs were used, as well. Prepared plates and cut films were often switched and substituted by sleight of hand, replacing those provided by the investigator. While this might have fooled a credulous member of the general public, legerdemain and instances of assistants prancing through photographic studios draped in sheets did not convince hardened and skeptical investigators that the work of the spirit photographers was credible or genuine. However, in case after case, investigators walked away stumped as to how the bizarre images managed to appear on film. For every fraud who was exposed, there was at least one other photographer who was never caught cheating. This is what has kept the public curious about the early spirit photographers after more than a century has gone by.

But, unfortunately, there were many who were not so honest. In 1874, a French photographer named E. Buguet opened up a studio and also began a profitable sideline career of capturing spirits on film. Most of his photographs were of famous people, most of whom claimed to recognize the extras as deceased loved ones and family members. This did not stop him from being arrested for fraud and tried by the French government. He admitted deception but even then, there were many who refused to accept his confession as genuine, claiming that he had been paid off by the Catholic Church to plead guilty. In his confession, he stated that his photographs were created by double exposure. He would dress his assistants to play the part of a ghost, or would dress up a doll in a sheet. The doll, along with a stock of mannequin heads, was seized by the police when they raided his studio. Buguet was fined and sentenced to a year in prison. Even after this, his supporters continued to insist his photographs were real. Reverend Stainton Moses, the famous medium, was convinced that at least some of Buguet's spirit photographs were authentic. He said that the prosecution of the case was tainted by interference by religious officials, that the judge was biased or that Buguet must have been bribed or terrorized to confess.

The 1870s saw the first general acceptance that there might be something credible to at least some aspects of spirit photography. A number of references to it appeared in issues of the *British Journal of Photography* and in other periodicals of the time. In the 1890's, J. Traille Taylor, the editor of the *Journal*, reviewed the history of spirit photography and detailed the methods by which fraudulent photos were sometimes produced. He approached the phenomenon as a true skeptic, not immediately disbelieving it, but studying it in a scientific manner. He used a stereoscopic camera and noted that the psychically produced images did not appear to be in three dimensions. He used his own camera and he and his assistants did all of the developing and photographing. Strangely, they were still able to produce mysterious results.

In 1891, the practice of spirit photography gained more credibility when Alfred Russell Wallace, the co-developer of the theory of evolution, spoke out with the belief that spirit photography should be studied scientifically. He later wrote about his own investigations into it and included a statement that he believed it could possibly be real. He felt that just because some of the photos that had been documented were obviously fraudulent, not all of them could be dismissed as hoaxes.

Despite such notable interest in the field, little was heard of spirit photography outside of Spiritualist circles for a number of years. In 1911, spirit photography entered the mainstream with the publication of the book *Photographing the Invisible* by James Coates. It covered dozens of cases of spirit photographs in detail and was later revised and expanded in 1921. It remains one of the most comprehensive books on the subject during this period and it managed to bring spirit photography into the mainstream for the first time.

Following the publication of the book, several noteworthy articles appeared on spirit photography, including one by James Hyslop, a Columbia University professor. He wrote an introduction to a series of experiments carried out by Charles Cook of two American spirit photographers, Edward Wyllie of Los Angeles and Alex Martin of Denver. Cook did extensive work with the two men in 1916, providing them with his own plates and having them developed by a commercial studio. In this way, he eliminated any opportunity that the pair might have had to doctor the images. Cook concluded that the photographs submitted were genuine but in these cases thought the name "psychic photography" better matched the phenomenon. He believed that Wylie and Martin actually produced the images through some psychical means, rather than actually photographing ghosts.

In addition to the photos created by Wyllie and Martin, there were a number of spirit photographs that appeared in those days for which critics could find no plausible explanation. Despite the failure to debunk many of these photographs, the reality of them was not accepted by the scientists of the day. As it is today, the majority of them simply refused to examine the data and assumed that the possibility of fraud was more than adequate to explain the findings. One of the few exceptions was Sir William Crookes, the distinguished chemist and physicist. For thirty years, he was a member of the Royal Society and was known for his discovery of thallium, his studies of photography and other scientific work. At the invitation of several skeptical members of the Royal Society, he agreed to take on a six-month study of psychic phenomenon. Instead of just six months, his work continued for years and he came to the conclusion that much of what he studied including psychic photographs was genuine. He presented his findings in both book and article form but soon became discouraged about convincing most of his scientific colleagues of the reality of what he was doing. He endured ridicule and disdain, but never wavered from his beliefs. More than twenty-five years later, he would maintain that spirit photography could, and did, exist.

As time passed and photographic techniques and equipment became more advanced, researchers began to discover that some of the photographs being taken in allegedly haunted locations could not be explained away as film flaws and tricks of light. Gone were the days of fake photos that were taken by so-called spirit mediums in studios. They had been replaced by often-accidental photos that defied all logic.

There have been those who have been attempting to take photographs of ghosts since the days when cameras were little more than newly invented curiosities. What could be better proof of their existence than the ability to capture a spirit's image on film? Unfortunately, many "spirited" efforts have led to failure and, even worse, outright fraud.

Trickery was introduced in the early days of the photographic process, which coincided with the heyday of the Spiritualist movement. In those days, scores of photographers began capturing photos that included faint images that were alleged to be their customer's deceased loved ones. Business boomed until someone noticed that the "spirit faces" resembled a number of people who were still alive. The "spirits" in the photographs were soon recognized as double exposures and over-printed images and many of these new mediums were arrested on charges of fraud.

But that's certainly not to say that no authentic photos of ghosts exist!

In fact, there have been a number of such photos that have been taken over the years for which no clear explanations exist. Photos have sometimes appeared for which no evidence of fraud, trickery or mistakes can be discovered. There have been many taken that have been deemed legitimate by a variety of sources over the years. In each case, the photographer claimed to be surprised by the end results of the photograph and experts have looked over the photos and yet have found no explanations for the strange images that were captured on film. However, the authenticity of each remains for the viewer to decide.

Whatever questions remain, though, there is no doubt that the camera has become one of the most important tools used by researchers of the supernatural to collect evidence of ghosts and paranormal phenomena. Since the days when investigators were debunking mediums and ghost hunters were hanging trip wires to prevent fraud, the camera has been an essential part of paranormal investigations and an important method of chronicling the supernatural.

OUIJA BOARD
Talking with the Dead

During the heyday of the Spiritualist movement in the middle nineteenth century, spirit mediums were regularly conducting séances for those who wanted to make contact with the other side. Ordinary people who possessed no psychic abilities also wanted to try and get in touch with the spirits. They formed what were called "home circles." These were groups of friends and neighbors who experimented with table tipping, knocking and rapping in reply to questions that were posed to the spirit world. Soon, they began looking for more efficient ways to contact the dead.

In 1853, a French educator who went by the pen name of Allen Kardec attended a séance where the participants used a little basket with a pencil attached to receive written messages from the spirit world. Kardec was so impressed by this new method of contacting spirits, which was far less time-consuming than calling out letters of the alphabet and waiting for rapped responses, that he made a note of it in his journal. Soon afterwards, the little baskets were replaced with a device called a planchette, a French word meaning "little plank." The first planchettes were small, heart-shaped pieces of wood with three little wheels on the bottom. The point of the heart held a downward-facing pencil. The idea was for a medium to place his or her hand on the planchette and then the pencil would write out messages from the spirit controlling the medium. This method of receiving spirit communications soon became a sensation in Europe. American tourists who were interested in Spiritualism brought back planchettes from their trips abroad. Word spread of their remarkable results and by 1868, when the planchette became widely available in America, thousands were sold. The invention was often used by mediums as a more elaborate form of automatic writing, but it really did not hold a wide appeal for use by general public.

A short time later, though, another invention came along that could be used by anyone. No experience was required and no real psychic skills were needed. This new device would revolutionize the Spiritualist movement and have an impact that still resounds today. The "talking board" - better known by its trademark name as the "Ouija board" - was born.

Legend has it that shortly after the planchette came to America, a cabinet and coffin maker from Maryland named E.C. Reichie created a new method of communicating with the dead. He devised a wooden lap tray with the letters of the alphabet arranged in two lines across the center of the board. Below these letters, he placed the numbers 1-10 and the words YES and NO in each lower corner. He used the planchette with his board but removed the pencil tip and the wheels and placed wooden pegs on the bottom. In this way, the planchette was free to move about the board.

It was said that Reichie named his board the "Ouija" because the name represented the French and German words for "yes" *oui* and *ja* , however, legend has it that he believed that the word "Ouija" which came to him through his talking board was actually the Egyptian word for "luck." Suffice it to say, it's not, but wherever it came from, the name stuck.

The history of how the Ouija board became a part of our culture is not as mysterious as the strange messages from the other side that it was said to impart, but it does have a number of unusual elements to it. It actually took seven men, from very different backgrounds, to create the first mass-produced American talking boards. Those men were Charles Kennard, Harry Welles Rusk, Colonel Washington Bowie, Elijah J. Bond, William H. A. Maupin, William Fuld and the elusive E.C. Reichie a man about whom almost nothing is known and who may not have existed at all . These men pooled their cash and resources to create the Kennard Novelty Co. of Baltimore, Maryland. All of the men had two things in common: Each was a wealthy entrepreneur who was not opposed to taking risks and all of them were Freemasons. It is believed that they met through their association with this secret society and they soon made a pact to start the company.

Colonel Bowie initially handled most of the matters involving the company. Rusk was named as president, as he had the most experience with patent law and was able to file all of the necessary papers himself. Kennard owned some land and buildings from a defunct fertilizer company and he offered this property, located at 220 South Charles Street in Baltimore, for use by the new firm. Because of this, his name was used on the masthead. Elijah Bond contributed little to the firm, save for some ideas, and shortly after the patents were filed, he disappeared.

William Maupin remains a mystery to this day. He was gone before the company even got started and the only proof that he even existed at all was his name on the patent filings. The most active investor in the company was a young varnisher named William Fuld. He played a major role in the daily operations of the company, including production, and had many ideas of his own. Due to his age and lack of finances, he had to work much harder than the other officers of the company to achieve success. It took him nearly a year to begin his climb to the top.

Historically, William Fuld has been acknowledged as the inventor of the Ouija Board, a fact that is confirmed by his descendants and those of Colonel Bowie. At the time the company was created, Fuld had little money to invest, but it is believed the idea for the board became his contribution, thus earning him a partnership and his name on the patent papers. He remains the name most connected to the boards today, despite the apocryphal legend of E.C. Reichie.

By 1891, the Ouija board was selling well, and on November 10 of that year, Charles Kennard filed a patent that would improve the performance of the board's planchette. This turned out to be his last act as a member of the Kennard Novelty Co. One day later, he was removed from the board of directors. Although the company bore his name and used his land, Kennard was said to have been a poor businessman and so he was voted out. Years later, his descendants would claim that William Fuld drove Kennard out of the business, but most likely it was Colonel Bowie. By 1892, Kennard's name was no longer listed in connection with the company but Bowie was named as manager and Fuld as supervisor. The company was moved to 909 East Pratt Street and the name was changed to the Ouija Novelty Company.

Soon after, Kennard tried to sell another version of the talking board that he called the "Volo." Bowie and Fuld responded by purchasing the Espirito trademark from the well-known W.S. Reed Toy Company. They placed an exact copy of the Kennard's Volo design on the back of their Ouija boards. Consumers loved getting two boards for the price of one and soon, Kennard's business was destroyed. He had no trademark for the Volo, so he tried to advertise the "Igili - the marvelous talking board" instead. It also failed and Kennard would vanish from the scene until 1919.

In 1894, the Ouija Novelty Co. moved to larger quarters at 20 North High Street, thanks to the fact that they were turning out huge numbers of talking boards. Bowie remained in charge of the company with Fuld and Rusk as his side. A few years later, Bowie's other business interests caused him to sell out his share of the patents and he and Rusk both stepped into the background of the company. Production was turned over to Fuld, although Bowie would remain a financial partner in the company for another twenty years.

Fuld now needed a partner. He had a day job as a customs inspector and was unable to devote himself full-time to the Ouija business. In 1898, he and his brother, Isaac, went into business together and they leased the rights to make the Ouija Board from Colonel Bowie. They split the proceeds from the talking board production and from other games. By April 1901, though, the partnership was over. William and Isaac had a falling out and Isaac was fired. They never spoke to one another again, except in court. Colonel Bowie employed his son, Washington Bowie, Jr., to represent William Fuld against his brother. The brothers returned to court again and again over the years, bickering about money, rights and even who had the authority to open mail that was addressed to the company. This would be just one of the relationships that was utterly destroyed over what most people claim is just a game.

Fuld soon changed the name of the company to the William Fuld Manufacturing Co. and moved the Ouija business to 1208 Federal Street. Business started to slow down and from 1905 to 1907, Fuld moved the company into his home at 1306 North Central Avenue. By 1908, business had improved once more and he relocated to 331 North Gay Street and then on to 1226-1228 North Central Avenue. This building would remain the home of the Ouija board until an enormous sales boom in 1919.

Meanwhile, Isaac Fuld was breaking an injunction that had been filed against him in 1901 by sending out samples of a talking board that he had created called the Oriole board. They were exact duplicates of the Ouija board, with the "Ouija" logo replaced with "Oriole." He named his business the Southern Toy Co. and operated it from his home.

At this same time, William decided to expand his company and issued press releases that stated that he was preparing for "big business." He took a risk and moved his factory to an enormous, three-story building. The gamble paid off and Ouija board sales began to climb. This made 1919 perhaps the greatest year in the history of the company. Not only did William enjoy an income from national sales of the boards, he also began to see national acclaim. The remaining rights to the boards were assigned to him by Colonel Bowie, which only served to stir up the ongoing feud with his brother. The battle was soon to come to an end, however.

In April of that year, William began mailing letters to stores who placed orders for Isaac's Oriole board. He warned them that the boards violated his patents and anyone who bought them was breaking the law. When Isaac found out about the letters, he filed suit against William. But William countered with the allegation that Isaac had violated the injunctions filed against him in 1901. Isaac's case was dismissed and the judge ruled that he had copied and distributed the Oriole boards in violation of the injunction. A review of the trademark that he had filed revealed that it had nothing to do with a talking board - it was for a pool table. Isaac was ordered to pay all of the court costs associated with the case and to never make another talking board.

Once the court battles with his brother were behind him, William continued to expand. He retired from his customs job to dedicate more of his time to the Ouija business. He later served in the Maryland General Assembly in 1924. Washington Bowie, Jr. continued as his legal counsel and years later, he would recall his father sitting down with all of the children to look through toy catalogs. They were instructed to circle any talking boards that might infringe on the Ouija trademarks, and he recalled finding many of them. The younger Bowie aggressively pursued each of the manufacturers and never accepted any payment for this service.

In 1920, another talking board company appeared in the news. The Baltimore Talking Board Co. was started by two men named Charles Cahn and Gilbert Michael. They had absolutely no connection with Fuld or his business. They did, however, pay a fee to call their boards Ouija. The Internal Revenue Service collected tax on their Ouija boards in 1920, but the Baltimore Talking Board Co. resisted the tax payments, claiming that the boards were not a game but a spiritual tool, and therefore should not be taxed. They took the IRS to court and mysteriously, they were represented by Washington Bowie, Jr. in the proceedings. They lost and Ouija boards were considered taxable. They appealed the decision all of the way to the U.S. Supreme Court, but the case was never heard. Talking boards are legally not considered to be a tool to communicate with spirits – to this day.

From 1919 to 1927, William Fuld continued to expand his business, offering cheaper forms of his board in an effort to combat knock-offs. He also sold a line of Ouija jewelry and even Ouija oil for rheumatism. He trademarked the Ouija board as the Egyptian Luck Board, the Mystifying Oracle and the Hindu Luck Board. Everything seemed to be going his way, but then on February 24, 1927, disaster struck the Fuld family. William always supervised any work that was done on the factory and when a flagpole needed to be affixed to the top of the three-story building, he joined the workmen on the rooftop. When an iron support that he was leaning on collapsed, he fell backwards off the structure. He caught himself for a moment on one of the window ledges, but the force of his fall slammed the window shut and he plunged to his doom. Amazingly, the fall only left Fuld with a concussion and some minor broken bones. He would have recovered if one of his broken ribs hadn't pierced his heart on the way to the hospital.

William Fuld's children took over the company. Catherine and William A. Fuld ran the business until their youngest brother, Hubert, became president in 1942. Sales sagged for years but the talking board industry saw a renewed interest in the 1940s, around the same time that the Spiritualist movement enjoyed a brief revival, likely due to grief-stricken relatives of servicemen killed in World War II hoping to contact their lost loved ones. World War I and the Influenza pandemic of 1918-1919 accounted for a similar surge in sales. Many companies introduced their own talking board designs, often with extravagant designs and colors, but eventually, disinterest and a declining market saw each of these companies collapse to the Fulds.

The Fuld heirs maintained the company until 1966, when they sold out to Parker Brothers. Hasbro Inc. purchased Parker Brothers in 1991 and it now owns all of the rights and trademarks to the "talking board," which they still produce in large numbers, including a pink Ouija board designed to appeal to little girls. For some reason, Ouija boards have been a huge hit for decades among the preteen set at sleepover parties. In spite of the fact that it is now sold in toy stores, it remains an exact duplicate albeit a more cheaply made one of the talking board that was sold in the early twentieth century.

In 1913, one of the greatest mysteries of Spiritualism - and the Ouija board -- manifested around a woman named Pearl Curran, who lived in St. Louis, Missouri. The story emerged at a time when St. Louis had reached the end of its "Gilded Age" and had entered a time when World War I was looming on the horizon. St. Louis was a different place than it had been just a few years before and the glitter of the 1904 World's Fair was beginning to tarnish. Labor troubles were beginning to plague America. During these darkening times, many people started looking for a glimmer of hope and began embracing a movement that was becoming popular in America all over again.

Interest in Spiritualism had returned, especially in the form of "home circles," where gatherings of friends and family members got involved in table-tipping, where the ghosts would knock or cause a table to tilt in reply to a question. Ouija boards were very popular. According to those who used them, the boards allowed ordinary people to communicate with the spirits. Questions were asked aloud and then the spirits would make a wooden pointer planchette on the board move about under the light touch of the sitters. The ghosts would then spell out messages to the people present.

Controversy has raged since the inception of talking boards as to whether or not these messages are real spirit communications, clever hoaxes, or simply hidden thoughts that are dredged up from the unconscious minds of the sitters. Such boards are still in use today and are as much of an enigma now as they were at the turn of the last century.

Which is, perhaps, why what happened to an ordinary St. Louis housewife in 1913 still remains such a mystery after all of these years.

Pearl Curran had no interest in the occult prior to 1913. She was born Pearl Leonore Pollard in Mound City, Illinois, in February 1883. Her father was a railroad worker and sometimes newspaperman. She grew up in Texas, playing outdoors and exploring the countryside. Her parents, George and Mary, were easy-going and never really demanded much from Pearl, which probably made her an indifferent student. She left school after the eighth grade and began to study music in Chicago, where her uncle lived. She also played the piano at her uncle's storefront Spiritualist church, where he was a medium. But Pearl and her parents were not Spiritualists and in fact, had no interest in the movement at all. Pearl had attended Sunday school as a child but few of the teachings ever stuck with her. She did not attend church as a child and never read the Bible.

In fact, she rarely read much of anything at all. She had enjoyed popular children's books of the day, like *Black Beauty* and *Little Women,* and was always entertained by fairy tales but, probably thanks to her lack of education, she had little interest in reading or writing. Her only creative outlets were playing piano and dreaming of perhaps someday acting on stage, but she gave up that idea at age twenty-four when she married John Curran, a widower with a teenage daughter.

Her marriage was as uneventful as her childhood had been. The Currans were not rich, but they made a comfortable living. Pearl had a maid to take care of the household chores and she and her husband enjoyed dining at restaurants and going to the theater. They were a social couple and enjoyed getting together with friends and playing cards with neighbors in the evening. The Currans seldom read anything, outside of the daily newspaper and some of the periodicals of the day, and never really had an opportunity to associate with well-educated writers or poets. They were happy, though, and content in their ordinary middle-class apartment on Kingsbury Avenue with their close friends and acquaintances.

They could have never imagined the changes that were coming to their lives.

In the afternoons, Pearl would often visit with a friend named Emily Grant Hutchings. Mrs. Hutchings was a Spiritualist and a well-known writer. Her poetry and fiction appeared in many magazines including *Atlantic Monthly* and *Cosmopolitan.* She was also a regular feature writer for the *Sunday-Globe Democrat.* During the St. Louis World's Fair, she was on the staff of the general press bureau, writing an article a day for every day for twenty-four weeks, which were printed all over the world.

Mrs. Hutchings and her newspaperman husband, Charles Edwin Hutchings, were on cordial terms with the author Mark Twain. She later wrote a novel and several short stories that she claimed to have been dictated by him after his death through a Ouija board with the help of a St. Louis medium with the wonderful name of Lola Viola Hays. That was in 1917, after Emily and Pearl had fallen out. They were still good friends on the hot evening of July 8, 1913, when Mrs. Hutchings brought a Ouija board to Pearl's apartment. It's very likely that Pearl had seen a talking board before, and perhaps even experimented with one, while at her Spiritualist uncle's house. She later claimed that she had, but that she didn't find it particularly interesting. In fact, she believed that using a Ouija board was a boring and silly pastime. Before July 8, she had never seen the pointer spell out anything but gibberish.

But this afternoon was different. Pearl and Emily placed their hands on the planchette and Pearl's mother sat nearby with a pad and pencil, ready to transcribe any messages that "came through." To the ladies' surprise, the message that was spelled out made perfect sense. "Many moons ago I lived. Again I come. Patience Worth is my name," it spelled out.

The three women were startled. They certainly knew no one by that name. Who was Patience Worth? Was she a real person? Pearl was the most skeptical of the three; she doubted that the dead could make contact with the living by way of a wooden board. However, at her friend's urging, she asked the sender of the message to tell them something about herself. Replies to her queries began to come through the message board and were recorded by Pearl's mother.

According to the spirit who called herself Patience Worth, she had lived in Dorsetshire, England, in either 1649 or 1694 the pointer gave them both dates but even that information was difficult to obtain. Patience spoke in an archaic fashion, using words like "thee" and "thou" and sometimes refused to answer their questions directly. When Mrs. Hutchings pushed for more information, the spirit first replied by saying "About me ye would know much. Yesterday is dead. Let thy mind rest as to the past." Eventually, though, the ladies would learn that Patience claimed to have been an unmarried woman who had emigrated to America, where she was murdered by Indians on Nantucket island.

The initial contact with Patience Worth came through the Ouija board when Pearl and Mrs. Hutchings controlled it. But it was soon evident that Pearl was mainly responsible for the contact, for no matter who sat with her, the messages from Patience would come. The messages continued to be very strange. The "spirit" seemed to have an extensive knowledge of not only seventeenth-century vernacular but of clothing, mechanical items, musical instruments and household articles of the period. Patience didn't seem to think much of Pearl's housekeeping, informing her through the board: "A good wife keepeth the floor well sanded and rushes in plenty to burn. The pewter should reflect the fire's bright glow. But in thy day housewifery is a sorry trade."

Pearl was fascinated with the messages that they were receiving and began devoting more and more time to the Ouija board. Eventually, though, the messages began coming so fast that no one could transcribe them. Pearl suddenly realized that she didn't need the board anymore. The sentences were forming in her mind at the same time they were being spelled out on the board. She began to "dictate" the messages from Patience to anyone who would write them down. She first employed a secretary, but later, Pearl recorded the words herself, using first a pencil and then a typewriter.

For the next twenty-five years, Patience Worth dictated hundreds of thousands of words through Pearl Curran. Her works were vast and consisted of not only her personal messages, but creative writings that included nearly five thousand poems, a play, many short works and several novels that were published to critical acclaim.

Shortly after Patience made her presence known, the Curran home began to overflow with friends, neighbors and curiosity-seekers. When word reached the press, Casper Yost, the Sunday editor of the *St. Louis Post-Dispatch*, began publishing articles about Pearl Curran and the mysterious spirit who seemed to be dictating to her. In 1915, he even published a book called *Patience Worth, A Psychic Mystery* and the housewife from St. Louis became a national celebrity.

People came from all over and the Currans, always gracious and unpretentious, welcomed visitors who wanted to witness the automatic writing sessions when Pearl received information from Patience Worth. Authorities in the field of psychic investigation came, as well as people from all over the country who had begun to read and admire the writings attributed to Patience. The Currans never charged any admission and all of the writing sessions were conducted with openness and candor. There were no spooky séances, darkened rooms or candles. John Curran and his friends would be in the next room, smoking cigars and playing pinochle. Patience Worth Curran, the baby girl the Currans adopted in 1916, would be playing with her toys and food would be laid out on a table, buffet-style, for guests to help themselves. Pearl would usually just sit in a brightly lit room with her notebook or typewriter and when the messages came to her, she began to write.

In addition to the stories and novels, Patience produced thousands of poems through Pearl Curran. One of her unusual abilities was to write poems that would suit any topic suggested by the company present. On January 12, 1926, at Straus's Studio in St. Louis, during a meeting of the Current Topics Club, suggestions were made by some of the members and Patience composed two poems called "Lavender and Lace" and "Gibraltar." Each poem was presented with no noticeable delay. Neither had ever been produced before. The famous poet, Edgar Lee Masters, was asked if anyone could actually write poetry that way, instantly and in response to random topics suggested by a group. He replied, "There is only one answer to that... it simply can't be done!"

Not surprisingly, many questioned the reality of the spectral Patience Worth. Critics simply refused to believe that the whole thing was not an elaborate hoax. And Patience did not offer much help in trying to get people to believe in her. Witnesses worked hard to get her to offer some details about her past but she seemed to think her origins were unimportant; however, she did mention landmarks and scenery around her former home in England. The newspaperman Casper Yost, who was one of the spirit's greatest defenders, took a trip abroad during the height of the phenomenon and when he reached Patience's alleged home in Dorset he did find the cliffs, old buildings, a monastery and scenery just as Patience had described. This was interesting, but it was hardly proof.

Perhaps the most convincing evidence that Patience Worth was not the conscious or unconscious creation of Pearl Curran is the material that she dictated for her books and stories. Patience seemed to be able to pass between old English dialects at will or could write in a semblance of modern English, as she did with most of her poetry.

The Story of Telka was one of her novels and it is a poetic drama of medieval life in rural England, written mostly in Anglo-Saxon words. It was composed during a series of sittings and as with other Patience Worth dictations, there were no revisions and no breaks where sentences left off and began again. The only comparable work to this novel is the Wickcliffe's Bible of the fourteenth Century, which is also composed of almost pure Anglo-Saxon. However, the language in *The Story of Telka* is different in that there are few words in the novel that modern readers cannot understand. It was as if the writer wanted to create something that seemed old but could still be comprehended by twentieth-century readers. Many argued that it would be impossible for a person living in turn-of-the-century St. Louis to create such a dramatic work and then limit the vocabulary to easily understood words in an ancient form of their own language. It simply could not be done, they believed.

And this was far from Patience's only book. *The Sorry Tale* was a lengthy novel about one of the thieves who was crucified with Jesus. It brought to life the Jews, Romans, Greeks and Arabs of the period. The book was also filled with an accurate knowledge of the political, social and religious conditions of the time. Critics hailed it as a masterpiece. It had been started on July 14, 1915 and two or three evenings a week were given over to the story until it was completed. The tale proceeded as fast as John Curran could take it down in abbreviated longhand and continued each night for as long as Pearl was physically able to receive it.

Professor W.T. Allison of the English Department of the University of Manitoba stated that, "No book outside of the Bible gives such an intimate picture of the earthly life of Jesus and no book has ever thrown such a clear light upon the manner of life of Jews and Romans in the Palestine of the day of our Lord."

At the same time that *The Sorry Tale* was being produced, *The Merry Tale* was started as a relief from the sadness of the previous book. For a time, work was done on both novels during a single evening.

When the first words of the next book, *Hope Trueblood*, appeared, the sitters gathered at the Curran home were astonished. For the first time since Patience Worth's arrival, four years before, the material was in plain English. Her previous stories had dealt with ancient Rome, Palestine and Medieval England. This book told the story of a young girl's effort to find her family in Victorian England. When the book appeared in England, no clues were given as to its mysterious origins and reviewers accepted it as the work of a new and promising British author. One critic stated that "the story is marked by strong individuality, and we should look with interest for further products of this author's pen."

While critics were impressed with the works she produced, those who witnessed Pearl taking dictation from the spirit were even more astounded. For instance, *The Story of Telka*, which came in at over seventy thousand words, was written over several sessions, but was completed in just thirty-five hours. This type of speed was fairly typical. Once, in a single evening, thirty-two poems were delivered, along with several short stories. On some evenings, Pearl dictated portions of four novels, always resuming the work on each one at the same place she left off. Pearl took down all of the words, usually in the presence of a number of witnesses, and never made any revisions.

Those who came to investigate the strange events often made requests of Patience in order to test her. She never hesitated to respond to questions or tasks they put to her. When asked to compose a poem on a certain subject, she would deliver the stanzas so quickly that they had to be taken down in shorthand. Weeks later, when asked to reproduce the poem, she could do so without any changes or errors. One night, author and psychic investigator Walter Franklin Prince, who was a regular visitor to the Curran house, posed an unusual task for Patience. Could she deliver a poem about the "folly of being an atheist" while simultaneously producing a dialogue that might take place between a wench and a jester at a medieval fair? He asked that she alternate the dialogue every two or three lines. Not only could Patience accomplish this, she did it so quickly that dictation was given to Pearl within eight seconds after the request was made.

When she finished, Pearl stated that she felt as if her head had been placed in a steel vise.

It should come as no surprise to learn that Pearl Curran's life was permanently changed by the arrival of Patience Worth. While the alliance was undoubtedly a wondrous affair, as Pearl often stated, it also demanded a lot from her, both physically and mentally. She never allowed herself to become obsessed with Patience, though, and the Currans never attempted to exploit the "partnership" for material gain. Pearl continued, with the help of her maid, to do all her own shopping, cooking and housework and she continued to visit with friends as she had always done. Two or three nights each week were set aside for writing sessions and Patience always dictated to Pearl no matter how many people were in the house. She only stopped when frightened by loud or sudden noises or when Pearl halted to converse with the guests.

Pearl explained that as the words flowed into her head, she would feel a pressure and then scenes and images would appear to her. She would see the details of each scene. If two characters were walking along a road, she would see the roadway, the grass on either side of it, and perhaps the landscape in the distance. If they spoke a foreign language, she would hear them speaking but above them, she would hear the voice of Patience as she interpreted the speech and indicated what part of the dialogue she wanted in the story. She would sometimes even see herself in the scenes, standing as an onlooker or moving between the characters. The experience was so sharp and so vivid that she became familiar with things that she could have never known about from living in St. Louis. These items included lamps, jugs and cooking utensils used long ago in distant countries, types of clothing and jewelry worn by people in other times and the sounds and smells of places that she had never even heard of before.

On one occasion, Pearl was shown a small yellow bird sitting on a hedge. Patience wished to include it in a poem, but Pearl had no idea what kind of bird it was. Finally, Patience became frustrated and said, "He who knoweth the hedgerows knoweth the yellow-hammer." Pearl and her husband later consulted an old encyclopedia and saw that the yellow bird in her vision was not the type of northern flicker called a yellowhammer that is known in America, but a kind seen only in England.

In spite of the visions and odd experiences, Pearl never went into a trance during the writing sessions, as a Spiritualist medium would have done. She understood the writing as it came and yet while calling out the words to the stenographer, she would smoke cigarettes, drink coffee and eat. She seemed always to be aware of her surroundings, no matter what else might be going on with her.

As time passed, Pearl was not completely satisfied with the literary reputation that was being achieved by Patience Worth. She became determined to take up writing herself, even though she had never written anything before and never had the urge to do so. Unfortunately, though, her writings reflected her lack of education and talent. She wound up selling two of her stories to the *Saturday Evening Post*, but likely more for her fame as a conduit for Patience than for her own literary ability.

Patience was tolerant but condescending of her host's abilities, which was likely what created a sort of love-hate relationship between them. Patience was often irritated with Pearl, but never failed to show her kindness. She simply seemed to think that her human counterpart was slightly stupid and that only by perseverance was she able to make herself understood, especially when Pearl failed to grasp the spellings and meanings of certain words. But they plodded on together, continuing to amass a great body of work until about 1922.

It was in that year that the connection between the two of them began to deteriorate, possibly due to changes in Pearl's life and the fact that she had become pregnant for the first time at age thirty-nine, giving birth to a daughter six months after her husband died. After her husband and her mother died, the contact between Patience and Pearl came less and less often and eventually it died away.

By that time, public interest in the mystery had also faded, especially since no solution had ever been offered as to how Pearl had accomplished such remarkable feats. The Jazz Age had taken over America and suddenly Pearl Curran and her Puritan ghost seemed stodgy and old-fashioned. After the publication of several books and hundreds of poems, interest in Patience Worth vanished and cynicism replaced it. Debunkers accused Pearl of hiding her literary talent in order to exploit it in such a bizarre way and become famous. However, exhaustive studies have shown this to be highly unlikely, if not impossible. Scholars have analyzed Patience's works and have found them accurate in historical detail and written in such a way that only someone with an intimate knowledge of the time could have created them.

Pearl Curran died of pneumonia in California on December 4, 1937. The *St. Louis Globe-Democrat* headlined her obituary with the words: "Patience Worth is Dead." And whatever the secret of the mysterious "ghost writer," it went to the grave with her.

So, what really happened in this case and why does it remain today as one of our great unsolved mysteries of all time? Did an entity speak to Pearl from beyond the grave? Or could the writings have simply come from her unconscious mind?

While there were several women with the name Patience Worth listed on passenger logs of ships sailing from England to America in the seventeenth century, there is no evidence that any of them were the Patience Worth who made contact with Pearl Curran. Yet experts who studied Pearl Curran doubted that she could have produced the works attributed to the ghost on her own. She was a woman of limited education with no knowledge of the language used or the history and subject matter that was written about by the alleged Patience Worth. Pearl simply could not have created such works of literary quality on her own.

But could the writings have come from her unconscious mind? Was Patience Worth a secondary personality of Pearl Curran? This too seems unlikely because on the rare occasions when secondary or split personalities have been documented, they have always been shown to supplant the main personality for a time. This was not true in Pearl's case. Her own personality co-existed with that of Patience Worth and Pearl was well aware of this fact.

So, what did happen at the Curran home in 1913? Was it a true case of afterlife communication or the greatest hoax ever perpetrated on both the literary and Spiritualist communities? It's unlikely that we will ever know for sure, but in the absence of any other explanation, this one will have to be filed under "unexplained."

SPIRIT CABINET
Channeling the Power of the Dead

During the heyday of Spiritualism, many of the mediums that practiced at the time made use of what were called "spirit cabinets," enclosures where the medium could be segregated from the guests while they were in a trance state. Many of the cabinets were actual wood enclosures, although it was more common for a corner of the room to be hung with a curtain and closed off from view. The cabinets became the medium's workspace and their purpose was to "attract and conserve spiritual forces." Paranormal researcher Hereward Carrington referred to a spirit cabinet as a "spiritual storage battery."

Although the spirit cabinet later became standard equipment for mediums, it was first introduced into the American Spiritualist movement by the Davenport brothers in the middle 1850s. None of the earlier mediums in the movement, including Spiritualism's founders, the Fox sisters, ever used such a device. The idea behind the cabinet was so be able to section off the medium from the sitters so that they would be out of direct view when producing strange phenomena. This would prove to be both popular and astounding to audiences, as the mediums were generally bound hand and foot in the cabinet while seemingly impossible phenomena manifested around them.

For fraudulent mediums, the spirit cabinet was a great gift. With only a limited amount of skill as an "escape artist," the mediums could amaze their sitters while hidden away from view behind curtains and wooden doors. Ropes could be easily shed and then an assortment of "spirit phenomena" could be produced. In most cases, the sitters would be invited to inspect the cabinet ahead of time so that they would be satisfied that no secret entrances or trap doors were present.

The medium would then enter the cabinet and be seated in a chair, where they would often be tied up to "prevent fraud." After slipping their bonds, the phenomena would begin. There were several ways for the mediums to collect their materials for the hoax. Often, "spirit forms" would appear. They would usually be made up of soft cloth or chiffon, which is very compressible. It could easily be secreted in the medium's clothing and when unwrapped or draped over the medium for a full materialization would appear ghostly in the dim light. The cloth could also double for ectoplasm as well, a spirit substance that allegedly exuded from the medium's body. If the medium allowed himself or herself to be searched prior to the séance, the materials could also be smuggled in by the "cabinet attendant," who acts as the medium's bodyguard. Spiritualists say that this person is present to protect malicious intruders from touching the medium's ectoplasm which could cause injury or death but in reality, they were merely accomplices in the fraud.

The medium would be dressed completely in black and when they emerged from the cabinet with the "ghostly" cloth, it would appear to be moving on its own. The ball of material would be slowly unwound and in the near total darkness, the effect would be eerily convincing. The medium could also drape his body in the material and then, while standing in front of the cabinet and moving the black curtains back and forth, he could create the illusion that the spirit form was moving sideways and up and down. Combined with spooky music and chilling dramatics, it is no wonder that so many were convinced of the reality of the spirit cabinet séances.

Not surprisingly, the claims being made by the Spiritualists about their contact with the dead inspired a need for the investigation of those claims. This research was not done so that the Spiritualists could be exposed as frauds although this sometimes happened but because the evidence that was being presented had to be questioned.

This new method of psychic investigation began shortly after the birth of Spiritualism. By the 1850s, science had managed to challenge the hold that religion maintained on society, offering a new version of the truth for people to examine. Mixed into this time period was Spiritualism, with its alleged proof of life after death, and the public became fascinated by it. Not long after, however, many of the practitioners of this new faith were exposed as frauds and a division formed between those who believed in Spiritualism and those who did not.

The scientific establishment, resentful over the fact that they had managed to break the hold that religion had on society only to lose their footing to Spiritualism, encouraged the debunking of mediums and had a blatant disregard for anything that even hinted at the supernatural. In spite of this, there were a small number of scientists who had taken the time to attend séances and who believed that there could be something to the strange phenomena that were being reported. They decided to try and apply the laws of science in investigating these reports.

By the late 1800s, there were a number of scientists who investigated the claims of mediums. Many of them operated independently, while others formed groups like the Society for Psychical Research SPR , which became one of the most esteemed investigative organizations in the world.

One of the most eminent men to become involved in psychical investigation was Sir William Crookes, one of the great scientists of the modern age. Crookes decision to delve into Spiritualism was greeted with wide approval. The popular press felt sure that Crookes would soon show that Spiritualists' claims were nothing more than ridiculous humbug. Crookes appeared to share that view. When he announced that he was going to begin his investigations, he stated that he had no preconceived notions on the subject and then added, "The increased employment of scientific methods will produce a race of observers who will drive the worthless residuum of Spiritualism hence into the unknown limbo of magic and necromancy." This grandiose statement was taken as a disclaimer of belief in Spiritualism but if Crookes' private beliefs had been better known, it could have been interpreted that he intended only to disprove the "worthless residuum" of psychic frauds without prejudice to Spiritualism's basic beliefs. Crookes had first come into contact with Spiritualism in 1867 and his diary entries for December 1870 -- within months of declaring his intention of studying Spiritualism -- showed that he was already a firm believer in the possibility of the "unknown power."

Crookes was born in London in 1832 and was largely self-taught, with no regular schooling, until he enrolled in the Royal College of Chemistry at age sixteen. He graduated in 1854 and took a position as the superintendent of the meteorological department at Radcliffe Observatory, Oxford. A year later, he took a teaching position as a professor of chemistry at Chester Training College, but resigned after one year because he was not given a laboratory in which he could do research. Although he tried to find another teaching position, he was never successful and most of his later work was done in a laboratory at his home. In 1856, Crookes married Ellen Humphrey, with whom he had eight children who survived infancy. From his home, he began writing and editing for scientific journals like the *Chemical News*. He also helped to found the *Quarterly Journal of Science* in 1864. In 1861, Crookes achieved the first of his scientific discoveries: the element thallium and the correct measurement of its atomic weight. This got him elected a Fellow of the Royal Society at age thirty-one.

Then, in 1867, a turning point came in Crookes' life with the death of his youngest brother, Phillip. The two men had been very close and Crookes was disturbed by his brother's death. Like others of the time who suffered a bereavement, he turned to Spiritualism for answers. At the urging of his friend and fellow scientist, Cromwell Varney, Crookes and his wife attended some séances to try and make contact with Phillip. Although the details of these sessions are unknown, Crookes believed they were successful. One of his first séances was with the famous medium D.D. Home, where Crookes was amazed to see phenomena that he never dreamed possible before. The scientist was not content to simply observe Home's manifestations, he also attempted to re-create them in the laboratory, and this was also successful.

Crookes applied strict scientific controls during his research with Home and the meticulous testing failed to find any evidence of fraud. He believed that Home possessed a "psychic force" which emanated from his body and he wrote a paper on the subject, believing it to be of scientific importance. Not surprisingly, the paper was first rejected and then met with scorn and derision when it was finally published. His critics, mainly other scientists, scoffed and stated that the phenomena Crookes reported could not have occurred, that it was simply impossible. "I never said that it was possible," Crookes famously replied, "I only said that it was true."

Although the scientific community frequently criticized him, Crookes doggedly continued his investigations into the spirit world, testing mediums and publishing material on the science of the afterlife. Crookes' last series of sittings were experiments conducted with a medium of rather dubious reputation named Anna Eva Fay. After this, he turned away from psychic research for a time and returned to his scientific pursuits. Although he supported the foundation of the Society for Psychical Research in 1882, and even served as its president in 1886, he did not take an active part in the group's investigations.

In 1875, Crookes earned the Royal Medal, awarded each year for "the most important contributions for the advancement of natural knowledge." One year later, he invented the radiometer, a device which demonstrated the effects of radiation on objects in a vacuum, and a device called the "Crookes Tube" that went along with it. This invention would lead to the discovery of cathode rays, X-rays and the electron.

Crookes went on to serve on scientific committees, earning prestigious awards for his discoveries and inventing an instrument that would be used to study subatomic particles, and yet he never wavered in his belief in Spiritualism. In 1916, after the death of his wife, Crookes attempted to communicate with her and was unsuccessful, but after a visit to a spirit photographer, he was able to obtain what he believed to be photographic proof that her presence was still with him. Sadly, this plate, under modern study, appears to have been double-exposed - an obvious fake.

Crookes died in April 1919, never questioning that fact that the spirit world was genuine and that there were things his beloved science would never truly be able to explain.

In addition to his work with D.D. Home, there was one medium with whom Crookes was most closely linked: the controversial Florence Cook. It would be his work with this young woman, barely out of her teens, that would not only overshadow much of the important work that Crookes did in the world of psychical research, but would lead to an alleged sex scandal that would forever taint his reputation.

During the heyday of Spiritualism, Florence Cook became one of the movement's most famous mediums. She was noted for her ability to produce full-form spirit materializations and became known as the first medium to do so in a fully lit room. Cook's manifestation was that of her spirit guide, Katie King. Katie already had a long history before being forever attached to the persona of Florence Cook. She first appeared during the initial Spiritualism craze of the 1850s and graced the séances of many famous mediums. Like her spectral father, John King, "Katie" was not her real name. In life, she was said to have been Annie Owen Morgan, daughter of the pirate Henry Morgan, who was known for his raids on the Spanish Caribbean colonies in the late seventeenth century. England was so pleased by Morgan's exploits against its old enemy that he was knighted by Charles II and appointed deputy governor of Jamaica. For reasons unexplained, he preferred to be known as "John King" in the afterlife, and his daughter adopted his name. In life, Annie Morgan had been a self-professed liar and cheat, as well as a thief and an adulteress -- all this before she died in her twenties. Her new mission, in death, was to prove to the world the truth of Spiritualism and of course, to prove the talents of a few mediums in particular. One of these was Florence Cook.

Florence or Florrie, as her mother called her was born in 1856 in London's crowded, impoverished East End. As a child, she claimed she could hear the voices of angels. Her mother would later state that the girl had always been aware of the presence of spirits but her psychic gifts only began to manifest at age fifteen, when she levitated a piece of furniture during a table-tilting session with friends. When she was still an adolescent, she began conducting séances in her home, where she became known for being able to manifest "spirit faces." To create a cabinet of the kind mediums used, Florence would sit inside a large cupboard in her family's dining room. A hole had been cut high up on the door and it was here where the faces would appear.

Florence would climb into the cabinet and would allow herself to be bound to a chair with ropes about her neck, waist and wrists. The door would be closed and the sitters would sing a hymn to create the proper mood. The cabinet door would be opened again to show that Cook was still tied to the chair, and then it would be closed. A few moments later, the faces would appear in the opening. When they finally vanished, the cabinet door would again be opened and Florence would be revealed, still tied to her chair and apparently exhausted from allowing the spirits to use her energy in order to materialize. A few people noticed that the faces, which were draped with a thin white cloth, looked an awful lot like Florence. They suggested that the girl simply slipped her ropes, stood on the chair to stick her face through the hole, then tied herself back up again. Nevertheless, the audience loved her performances and she soon gained a following. Many were impressed by the fact that she never charged a fee for her séances and others came merely because she was an exceptionally attractive young lady.

With that in mind, it's no surprise that the pretty young girl quickly became famous. In addition to her looks, her séances had other appeals as well, including the fact that the spirits had a habit of playfully tossing her into the air and -- on at least one occasion -- ripping her clothing off. While Florence basked in the newfound attention, some of her friends, and her employer, were becoming unsettled by her new gifts. Eliza Cliff, in whose school Florence worked as an assistant teacher, was reluctantly forced to discontinue her employment. The girls in the school were unsettled by the strange happenings that seemed to occur around Miss Cook and their parents were afraid that the young ladies might become affected themselves. Miss Cliff said she was quite fond of Florrie but was "compelled to part with her."

By 1872, full-form materializations had become very popular at séances and one night, in that same year, a white face appeared in the darkness outside the curtains of Florrie's cabinet. The floating mask was announced to be the face of Katie King, who was already a spirit to be reckoned with in America. But Katie was not the mysterious and ethereal figure of Spiritualist writings --- she was a proof of the resurrection of the dead, a spirit made flesh and a young woman who could walk among and talk with the sitters. Her new body was almost indistinguishable from that of a living girl. She was a beautiful young lady, one who very closely resembled Florence Cook.

As with most Spiritualist mediums of the day, Florence preferred to enter her trances within the confines of the spirit cabinet, out of sight of the sitters. As long as thirty minutes might pass before the curtain would part and a figure, dressed all in white and looking quite pale, would emerge as Florrie continued to lie unconscious in the cabinet. Occasionally, while Katie was present, Florrie could be heard sobbing and moaning inside the cabinet, as if the manifestation were draining her energy. During Katie's first appearances, the spirit would simply smile and nod at the audience, but later, she began to walk amongst them, offering her strangely solid hand and talking to them. She was fond of touching the sitters and allowing them to carefully touch her, as well. After Katie returned to the cabinet, Florence would be found, still tied up and seemingly exhausted.

It was believed that spirit forms, like Katie, were made up of that mysterious substance known as ectoplasm. It was generally regarded during the heyday of the movement that interfering with ectoplasm, or with the body of the entranced medium, could be dangerous to the medium's health. If this is true, then on one occasion, Florence Cook had a very close call.

While it was highly improper for sitters to grab at the spirits, or to touch the medium, during a séance, it did sometimes happen. On the night of December 9, 1873, one of the sitters at a Cook séance was a man named William Volckman. He apparently became quite agitated by the "obvious similarities" between the medium and the ghost. In a fit of anger, he jumped up and grabbed Katie by the wrist, announcing loudly that she was Florence in disguise. For a spirit, Katie put up quite a fight and managed to succeed in leaving several bloody scratches on the man's nose. Katie was finally rescued by Edward Elgie Corner, Florence's fiancée; by the Earl and Countess of Caithness and by barrister Henry Dunphy, who were friends of the Cook family and aware of the inherent danger in interfering with an apparition. They seized Volckman and a scuffle ensued, allowing Katie to make her escape. According to Dunphy, she disappeared, dissolving from the feet upward. Volckman was determined to follow up on his assault, though, and he rushed to the cabinet. There, he found no sign of Katie but he did find Florrie, with her clothing in disarray, but still tied up.

Was this a case of a skeptical investigator gone berserk, or something else? It is significant that shortly after this incident, Volckman married another famous London medium named Agnes Nichol Guppy, a portly widow who was very jealous of the lovely Florence and her fame. The incident with Volckman did not immediately harm Florrie's career as a medium, but it did shake the faith of some. She suffered a slight reversal of fortune for a time and began looking for a new angle to pursue to garner some much-needed favorable publicity.

At about this same time, medium D.D. Home was undergoing testing by Sir William Crookes. Florrie quickly got in touch with Crookes and offered to add her own contribution to psychical research. Crookes was delighted to investigate the now-famous partnership of Florrie and Katie King and happily agreed to a series of private séances. Shortly after, what many consider to be the most problematical investigations of the Spiritualist era began.

Once the investigations started, Crookes invited Florence, and occasionally her mother and sister, to stay with him at his home on Mornington Road in northwest London. Crookes knew that most Spiritualists had a distrust of scientists and he hoped to rectify this by inviting the young woman into his home and befriending her. Mrs. Crookes was in the house, but was not much in evidence, as she was expecting their tenth child at the time and was usually confined to her room.

The first time that Crookes had experienced Katie had been when Florrie had initially approached him about the investigations. He had visited the Cook home and took part in a séance. He was well aware of the fact that many skeptics believed that Florence and her spirit guide, Katie, were one in the same person but Crookes took note that while watching the materialized Katie, he distinctly heard "a sobbing, moaning sound from behind the curtain where the young woman was supposed to be sitting." In spite of this, critics were not impressed.

In March 1874, though, Crookes obtained what he felt was "absolute proof" that Florrie and Katie were two separate entities. During a séance, Katie had walked among the sitters for a time and then retreated behind the curtain where Florence had been bound to a chair. In a minute, she reappeared and asked Crookes to accompany her behind the curtain. According to his account, he found the unconscious form of Florence Cook, still bound with sealed tape. Katie had vanished, leaving Florence behind. He wrote, "I found Miss Cook had partially slipped off the sofa, and her head hanging in a very awkward position. I lifted her onto the sofa and in so doing, had satisfactory evidence, in spite of the darkness, that Miss Cook was not attired in 'Katie's costume but had on her ordinary black velvet dress, and was in deep trance." According to Crookes' account, he checked three different times to be sure that the woman on the floor, illuminated by a dim gas light, was actually Florence and he was convinced that she and Katie were separate individuals.

However, Crookes had still not seen them together. This opportunity came on March 29, he said, when Katie invited him into the cabinet after he had turned out the gaslight in the room. He carried with him a phosphorus light, which cast only a very dim glow. However, Crookes claimed to be able to see adequately. He wrote:

I went cautiously into the room, it being dark, and felt about for Miss Cook. I found her crouching on the floor. Kneeling down, I let air enter the phosphorus lamp, and by its light I saw the young lady dressed in black velvet, as she had been in the early part of the evening. And to all appearances perfectly senseless; she did not move when I took her hand and held the light quite close to her face, but continued quietly breathing. Raising the lamp, I looked around and saw Katie standing close behind Miss Cook. She was robed in flowing white drapery as we had seen her previously in the séance. Holding one of Miss Cook's hands in mine, and still kneeling, I passed the lamp up and down so as to illuminate Katie's whole figure, and satisfy myself thoroughly that I was really looking at the veritable Katie... and not the phantasm of a disordered brain. Three separate times did I turn the lamp to Katie and examine her with steadfast scrutiny until I had no doubt whatever of her objective reality. At last Miss Cook moved slightly, and Katie instantly motioned me to go away. I went to another part of the cabinet and then ceased to see Katie, but did not leave the room till Miss Cook woke up, and two of the visitors came in with a light.

Was this proof that Katie really was a ghost?

Perhaps --- but not all of the sitters at her séances were convinced. Many of them insisted on extreme measures to prevent Florence from practicing trickery. Customarily, before the séance would begin, Florrie would be bound with a cord or sealed with tape. Each time, the bindings were found to still be intact at the end of the evening. And although the indignities that were later inflicted on mediums, such as filling their mouths with fruit juice to prevent ventriloquism and checking all of their orifices for secreted ectoplasm, were never pressed on Florrie, her hair was nailed to the floor on at least one occasion. Believe it or not, Katie still appeared.

In 1874, Crookes began testing Florence and he produced a number of photographs of Katie King and was allowed to test her appearances with Florence in plain sight. During the test, Florence reclined on a sofa behind a curtain and wrapped a shawl about her face. Soon, Katie appeared in front of the curtain. Crookes checked to be sure that Cook was still lying on the sofa and he saw that she was --- although incredibly, he never moved the shawl to be sure that it was really her.

Crookes created fifty-five photographs of Florence and Katie but only a handful of them remain today. The rest were destroyed, along with the negatives, shortly before his death in 1919. Crookes used five cameras, two of them stereoscopic, operating simultaneously during the sessions. Many of the photos were both poorly-shot and questionable in authenticity and while many of them purported to show both Katie and Florence at the same time, they mainly played right into the hands of the debunkers.

Crookes was called into question about his testing methods but he rushed to the defense of his subject. He stated that Florence agreed to every test without question and that he had never seen the slightest inclination on her part to try and deceive him. Crookes wrote, "Indeed, I do not believe that she could carry on a deception if she were to try and if she did she would be certainly found out very quickly, for such a line of action is altogether foreign to her nature."

Crookes may have been convinced of the genuineness of the Cook-King collaboration but his critics were not. Katie looked so much like Florrie simply because that's who she was, the skeptics said. It was not good enough to cite Crookes' integrity and his stature as a scientist to convince people of the authenticity of the séances. They also said that it was possible that Crookes might have had a sexual relationship with Florrie, which would explain his willingness to help her perpetrate fraud. And while no evidence of this exists, it would be naive of us not to consider the possibility.

There are five possible explanations for the seemingly unexplainable events that occurred between Crookes, Florence and Katie:

1. That the scientist became embroiled in an affair with Florence under his wife's nose and that he colluded with her to manufacture fraudulent results for the Katie King investigation. The rumor of a possible sexual affair followed Crookes to the grave. Not only was the suggestion made during his lifetime but many years later it re-surfaced as a possible explanation for his seemingly naïve acceptance of Florence's fraud.

2. That Crookes was enamored with the girl, or her alter ego of Katie, and that he kept up the pretense that he believed her act to save face and to keep her close to him. It has also been suggested that perhaps Crooke fell in love with the girl, but the affair was one-sided. The brilliant scientist is believed by some to have immediately seen through Florence's fraud but, because he was infatuated with her, he chose to ignore it.

3. That Florence employed a double to pretend to be Katie King. This is not as outrageous as it might sound. During the investigations, a young medium named Mary Showers stayed in the Crookes' residence while Florence was there. She performed a double act with Florrie as the two of them would go into trances together and would create two materializations, one of Katie and one of

"Florence Maple," who bore more than a passing resemblance to Mary. Would it not have been possible for Mary, or even for Florence's sister, to have simply stepped in and pretended to be an unconscious Florrie, slumped over and usually covered, while Florrie walked about as Katie King?

4. That Florence truly believed that she was manifesting a "spirit," while she had actually created a split personality, which she called Katie King. To most modern readers, the accounts of Katie's manifestations contain many clues about the nature of Florence and her possible alter ego. Katie flirted and teased, wandering about the darkened room and sitting on laps, touching and being touched and, on one occasion, even stepping out of her robes to reveal her naked form. "Now you can see that I am a woman," she said. Could Katie have been a way for a repressed young lady of the Victorian era to act out her innermost desires? And if so, was she doing it consciously --- or had she actually convinced herself that the manifestation of Katie was real?

5. Our final explanation: that Florence was a genuine medium, Katie was real and Crookes' investigations were completely genuine. Although Crookes behaved strangely for a man with a scientist's regard for detail --- such as omitting names and addresses of witnesses from his record --- this may have been in response to Florrie's strict rules of secrecy.

In addition, we can look to the eyewitness accounts of the séances that survive. According to Mrs. Ross-Church, who was better known as the novelist Florence Marryat, daughter of the same Captain Marryat who famously fired a gun at the Brown Lady of Raynham Hall, Katie resembled Florrie in some ways but was remarkably different in others. She stated that Katie was taller and heavier than Florence and that Katie had red hair, while Florrie's hair was almost black. Crookes had also noted a number of differences between the two young women. Katie was taller, heavier and broader in the face, had a fairer complexion and longer fingers. Florrie had pierced ears, Katie did not. On one occasion, Florence had a large blister on her neck but when Katie appeared, her neck was as smooth as usual. Another time, Katie's lungs seemed to be clear while Florence was under treatment for a severe cough.

Unbelievably, though, as when he failed to check under the shawl, Crookes took no comparison photographs to show the pierced and unpierced ears or the length of the girls' fingers. Or if he did, he left no record of them. This seems amazing in that Crookes was investigating a phenomenon that could theoretically change the way the world believed about the afterlife.

But not everyone was so careless. Cromwell Varley, the famous electrician who worked on the Atlantic cable, believed that he had proof that Katie and Florence were not the same person. Varley, an ardent Spiritualist, designed a test to prove that Florence was still in the cabinet while Katie walked about the séance room. Florence was placed in an electrical circuit with wires connected to coins that were placed on her arms so that a small current was running through her body. A large galvanometer --- an instrument that detects and measures small electrical currents --- was positioned ten feet away from the cabinet. It was placed on a mantelpiece in full view of the sitters so that the flow of electricity could be monitored. If Florence broke the circuit in order to leave the cabinet dressed as Katie, the galvanometer would register wild fluctuations. Katie appeared as usual and there was no change in the current. Crookes asked Katie to plunge her hands into a chemical solution that would cause a change in the current flow if Florence had managed to dress as Katie and still get out of the cabinet. Again, the galvanometer showed no fluctuation in the current.

Did this prove that Katie and Florence were not the same person? Perhaps, but it still didn't prove that Katie King was a spirit. It's still very possible that she could have been Florrie's sister or her friend, Mary Showers.

In 1875, Katie sadly announced that she would soon be leaving Florence and that her time visiting earth would soon be at an end. Crookes later wrote of a scene that he witnessed when Florence and Katie said their final goodbyes. According to his account, Katie made one last appearance in the séance room and then walked over to where Florrie was lying on the floor. She touched the medium on the shoulder and implored her to wake up, explaining that she had to leave. They talked for a few moments until "Miss Cook's tears prevented her from speaking." Crookes was asked to come over and hold Florence in his arms, as she was falling to the floor and sobbing hysterically. When he looked around, the white-robed figure of Katie was gone.

With Katie now gone, there was no point in Florrie staying on at the Crookes home for further investigations. In fact, she told Crookes for the first time, she had been married about two months before to Edward Corner. Florence went into a sort of retirement for six years but then returned to the Spiritualist scene manifesting a new spirit, this one named Marie. This new spirit partner managed to provide even more entertainment that Katie had, singing and dancing for the sitters at her séances and providing contact with the spirit world.

But there was something about "Marie" that was beginning to bother people. At a séance in 1880, Sir George Sitwell noticed that Marie's spirit robes covered corset stays, so he reached out and grabbed hold of her. He held on tightly to her and when he pulled aside Florrie's curtain, he found that the medium's chair was empty. He was not surprised to discover that he was holding onto Florence, clad only in her underwear.

After that, Florence would only perform if someone were tied up in the cabinet with her. On at least one occasion, Florence Marryat participated and she later testified that during Marie's appearance, she was firmly tied to Florence in the cabinet. This wasn't enough to keep her audience, though, and Florence vanished into relative obscurity as a housewife in Monmouthshire. She gave her last séance in 1899 and passed away at age forty-eight in 1904.

PRINCESS MARY'S GIFT BOOK

How Cut-Outs from a Children's Picture Book Changed Spirit Photography Forever

In the summer of 1917, two young girls who lived in Yorkshire took a series of photographs that started off as a prank and eventually led to one man's belief that fairies were real.

That man was Arthur Conan Doyle, a former doctor turned writer who, thanks to the creation of his legendary detective, Sherlock Holmes, became world famous. Doyle achieved a remarkable career as an author and as a vivid public figure. He became personally involved in a number of causes, including using his own deductive skills to free two innocent men from prison. He also championed military and social reforms that were well ahead of their time and was knighted for his service during the Boer War. In addition, he also introduced skiing to Switzerland and chronicled the history of the British Army during World War I. In other words, he was a brilliant and multi-faceted man.

But all of these achievements, at least in Conan Doyle's mind, paled in comparison to what he believed was his greatest crusade: the promotion of Spiritualism. Around the time of World War I, Doyle converted publicly to

Spiritualism and he set aside his writing career to lecture and travel the world for the Spiritualist cause.

To the disappointment of Sherlock Holmes fans, his writings became almost solely centered on the movement and its amazing wonders. Conan Doyle pursued Spiritualism with all of the vigor that he plunged into everything else -- full steam ahead. Despite a number of setbacks, the collapse of friendships, ridiculous frauds and even the exposure of mediums he believed in, Conan Doyle would not be shaken in his beliefs. He was insulted, disparaged and forced to give up most of his paid work but he never faltered.

What could have so convinced this proper and courageous English gentleman to so heartily embrace a movement that was despised by so many? What did Conan Doyle know that so much of the rest of the world did not? And how did he become convinced that illustrated cut-outs from a children's fairy story were the real thing?

Arthur Conan Doyle was born in Edinburgh, Scotland, on May 22, 1859. He was the second child and oldest son of Charles Doyle, an assistant surveyor in the Scottish Office of Works. Charles Doyle was an artistic man but never fared well in his work. Biographies of his son painted a picture of his father as a "dreamy aesthetic figure" but it was later revealed that he was both an alcoholic and an epileptic. He left his job while in his 40s and spent most of the rest of his life in nursing homes for alcoholics and mental asylums. Conan Doyle's mother, Mary, on the other hand was the backbone of the family. She was a well-read woman and a great storyteller. Years later, Arthur would credit her for his love of literature. She bore her husband ten children in all. Five girls and two boys survived into adulthood.

Growing up, Conan Doyle spent two years at a preparatory school and then studied among the Jesuits at Stonyhurst. He had been allowed to attend this Catholic institution at no charge for it was hoped that he might dedicate his life to the church. He would eventually become disenchanted with Catholicism, though, and decided on pursuing a medical career instead. Over the next few years, he endured the spartan conditions of boarding school, the corporal punishment and the poor food. He excelled at sports, especially cricket, and at age sixteen, he passed his graduate exam with honors. Conan Doyle began working hard to obtain a scholarship for his medical studies and while awarded one, a series of official mistakes prevented him from receiving it. His family could not afford to send him to school, so he worked a series of jobs while attending medical college. It took him five years to earn his degrees as a Bachelor of Medicine and Mastery of Surgery in Edinburgh in 1881.

Conan Doyle was eager to start a medical practice and had also developed a love for writing. He hoped to supplement his practice by selling short stories to the popular magazines of the day, but while in school, he recognized the importance of working first and writing later. He wrote and sold a short story or two and then, as a third-year student, he signed on as a ship's surgeon for a whaler that was making a seven-month voyage to the Arctic. Conan Doyle got along well with the ship's crew. He was by now a massively strong young man and an all-around sportsman. His boxing skills served him well when he won a bout with the ship's steward on the first night out of port.

The trip to the Arctic so fulfilled his taste for action and adventure that he signed on to another ship the following year. This time, signed on as a medical officer with the African Steam Navigation Company for a voyage aboard the 1,500-ton *Mayumba,* taking cargo down the west coast of Africa. This adventure was far less enjoyable and he became extremely ill, likely with malaria. He came home with a small amount of money in his pocket, though, and decided to start his medical practice. Oddly for such a usually savvy man, Conan Doyle first ended up working as an assistant to an eccentric character named George Budd whom he knew from medical school, where they played rugby together. By all accounts, Budd was a charming con artist. He lived a plush life that was well above the means of a recent medical school graduate by borrowing money from people. When his creditors demanded payment, Budd spoke so movingly about the difficulties faced by a humble but ambitious young man in a harsh world that his listeners often broke down and wept in sympathy. More importantly, they usually either forgave the debt or allowed Budd extra time to pay up. True to form, Budd cheated Conan Doyle out of not only his portion of the practice but left him nearly penniless as well. Finally, Conan Doyle landed in a small village outside of Plymouth called Southsea, where he practiced for eight years.

He made little money during this period of his life but he managed to supplement his meager income with sales of short stories. As he settled into his practice, he wrote as often as time allowed and since he had few patients, he would often spend hours scratching out adventure stories at his desk. In 1886, he penned his first Sherlock Holmes story but had difficulty finding anyone to publish it. He eventually sold it outright for a small sum. The publishers told him that at the time, they didn't plan to publish it for at least a year "as the market is flooded at present by cheap fiction."

The story called "A Study in Scarlet" appeared in the *Beeton's Christmas Annual* for 1887. It met with success but Doyle had no interest in being merely a writer of short detective stories. Instead, he began doing research and wrote a lengthy historical novel called *Micah Clarke*. The book appeared in 1889 and was another immediate success. Six more stories about Sherlock Homes followed in the recently founded *Strand Magazine* and an American publisher requested a Holmes novel, spurring Conan Doyle to write *The Sign of the Four*. Doyle meant to write only those stories about Sherlock Holmes and no more. He thought of himself as a serious novelist and the Holmes stories were merely a distraction to him. However, when the publishers offered more and more money for additional tales, Conan Doyle surrendered --- and the Sherlock Holmes canon began.

Before Sherlock Homes was a sensation in England, though, Conan Doyle was already busy writing another historical novel, *The White Company* which he considered his best work and attending to his practice. His younger brother, Innes, had come to live with him in Southsea and he assisted Conan Doyle in his work. He still saw his writing as simply an added income to supplement his earnings as a doctor.

In 1885, Conan Doyle married Louise Hawkins, the older sister of one of his patients who had died. She was a sweet and docile woman who remained in the background, perhaps overshadowed by her larger-than-life spouse. In 1889, their daughter Mary was born. In 1890, a strange event occurred that may have only been a coincidence but in later years, many would wonder. Not long after Mary's birth, Conan Doyle received word of a demonstration that was taking place in Berlin by a doctor who claimed to be able to cure consumption tuberculosis. Conan Doyle became obsessed with going to the conference, even though he did not specialize in the treatment of consumption. He could not explain his interest and so went to Berlin to see what was occurring. Unfortunately, the trip turned out to be fruitless for he arrived too late to get into the presentation. Conan Doyle's interest in the lecture was never fully explained but tragically, three years later, his beloved Louise would be diagnosed with consumption and would be given only a few months to live. Was it merely a coincidence or was Conan Doyle's keen interest in the subject matter, as some have suggested, a foreshadowing of things to come?

A chance meeting with a physician in London convinced Conan Doyle to move his practice to the city. He decided to specialize in eye care but to do so, he needed to attend a six-month training session in Vienna. The Southsea practice was abandoned it was too small to be sold , Mary was sent to her grandmother and Conan Doyle and Louise set off for Austria. The entire trip turned out to be a disaster. The lectures were given in German and while Conan Doyle had a conversational knowledge of the language, he was unable to follow the technical terms. He wrote a short book, *The Doings at Raffles Haw,* about a millionaire with the ability to turn lead into gold. Conan Doyle and Louise left Vienna after two months instead of six. When the couple returned to England, he set up practice in London in Devonshire Place, at the top of Wimpole Street. It was a quiet and ideal location -- for writing anyway -- for not a single patient darkened

Conan Doyle's doorstep. He spent all of his time writing and it was here that he created the next set of Sherlock Holmes tales. The immediate success of the stories, the lack of patients and a severe bout with influenza that nearly killed him made his next decision an easy one. He would give up his medical work and turn his attention to writing.

Conan Doyle was in his early 30s when he decided to break with medicine and over the next ten years, he became increasingly more successful and increasingly more of a public figure. He emerged into the last decade of the nineteenth century as one of the most influential characters of his generation. To one segment of the public, he was the creator of Sherlock Homes, to another he was the author of historical novels and adventure stories. To another, even those who were not interested in his gripping tales, he was a man of total faith in Britain's imperial destiny and a personage who was ready and eager to play a role in public affairs.

Conan Doyle was a figure that many men aspired to imitate. He looked more like a sportsman than a man of letters. He was a robust outdoorsman and an avid boxer, adept at soccer and cricket. He was also, like many men and women of his generation, concerned about religion. He lost his Catholic faith while still a young man and for a time was mildly agnostic. While living in Southsea, he became interested in psychical research and began reading heavily on the subject. He also had the opportunity to visit séances and experiments in telepathy and thought transference. His search for answers led to a meeting with Sir Oliver Lodge, one of the leading paranormal investigators of the time, and in 1893, he joined the Society for Psychical Research. He watched with interest the public's fascination with Spiritualism but did not understand how ghostly phenomena warranted a faith and religion based around it --- at least not yet. He did become more and more interested in the Spiritualist movement, though, although at first his interested was tinged heavily with skepticism.

Sadly, Conan Doyle's personal life was not as successful as his professional one. He refused to accept the diagnosis that doctors had given to Louise and became determined to find a cure for her tuberculosis. According to the doctors, she only had a few months left but Conan Doyle was sure that he could prolong her life. He set aside his a career and began taking Louise to various places that had been recommended as being helpful to patients suffering from consumption. He traveled first to Switzerland and then was told by a friend and fellow writer, Grant Allen, who also suffered from tuberculosis, that he had found the climate in the English county of Surrey to be of great benefit. So, Conan Doyle purchased a large home there called Undershaw, which incidentally, was one of the first in the region to have electric lighting. This was Louise's home until her death in 1906.

The strain of caring for Louise took its toll on not only Conan Doyle's own peace of mind but on his relationship with his children as well. A son, Kingsley, had been born in 1892 and to Kingsley and Mary, their father was a lovable but slightly fearsome character. He could be reckless and boyish one moment and then, when tired or worried, curt and sharp with them the next. Much of his strain undoubtedly came after 1897, when he met a young woman named Jean Leckie. If one needed any evidence to prove that Conan Doyle was an honorable and respectable man, they need only examine the fact that his relations with Jean, who was fourteen years younger, remained platonic until after Louise died. A year later, they married and she bore him three more children. Some of his friends were critical of his attachment to Jean but as far as Conan Doyle was concerned, the relationship remained innocent for a number of years.

Conan Doyle's grief over the sad state of affairs at home, as well as his mixed emotions about Jean, led him to escape into his writing and into the bright lights of public life. He attended dinners, joined literary societies, went on trips and even wrote a stage play called "Waterloo," which was performed by the eminent actor Henry Irving. He took his brother Innes, who was about to enter the military, to the United States, where he went on a book tour, giving talks and readings. He became very popular with Americans. They loved his bluff manner, his cheerfulness, his Scottish accent and his simple and unpretentious ways. Conan Doyle found the wide-open spaces and outdoor life of America to be invigorating and felt very much at home. Since Americans loved the Sherlock Holmes stories as much as the British did, Conan Doyle was probably the best-known Englishman in America for many years.

During the Boer War, Conan Doyle came into his own as an adventurous public figure. The war began in October 1899 and just before Christmas of that year, in what was known as Black Week, the British military suffered three staggering defeats at the hands of an army of farmers in South Africa. There was much alarm in Britain, together with a patriotic upsurge, and on Christmas Eve, Conan Doyle decided to volunteer for South Africa. His mother was angry and distressed, believing that his life was of more value to his country at home. There were thousands who could fight, she told him, but only one who could have created Sherlock Holmes Conan Doyle's mother never understood her son's disinterest in the great detective and was very angry when he killed him off by having him plunge over Reichenbach Falls with his archenemy, Professor Moriarty . She also believed that his sympathies should belong with the Dutch settlers of the two independent Boer republics rather than with the wealthy companies who were using the military to protect their interests in South African.

Many in England shared her feelings about the Boers. The discovery of gold in the Witwaterstrand region of South Africa in the 1880s had led many who wanted to get rich quick to descend on Johannesburg. Cecil Rhodes was the operator of many commercial endeavors who used British imperialism as an excuse to run roughshod over the people of the area. Conan Doyle himself admired and respected the Boers, but his adherence to Britain and the Empire was unquestioning. He decided to enlist but the Army had little use for a forty-year-old recruit and placed him on a waiting list. When the chance came for him to join a hospital unit at his own expense that had been put together by his friend John Langman, he jumped at the chance. He became a doctor and an unofficial supervisor and shipped out to South Africa.

Conan Doyle remained in South Africa for a little more than three months. After the capture of the Boer capital of Pretoria, the war he thought had come to an end. He found the time he spent in the country to be deeply satisfying and after obtaining a number of first-hand accounts of the fighting, he wrote a book called *The Great Boer War* on his return to England. The book became very popular, although it was outdated by another history that came out later, since what seemed to be the end of the war was not. It actually continued on as a guerilla war for nearly two years. Regardless, the book was successful and in the last chapter, Conan Doyle suggested what he believed were some necessary military reforms. They caused a great stir and included the concealment of large guns two batteries had almost been lost at one battle because a commander foolishly pushed them ahead of the infantry and provided no cover for them ; the abandonment of cavalry swords and lances as outmoded; and the development of a highly trained infantry that could be supplemented by national volunteer militia units. These ideas seem quite sensible today but they shocked the Army establishment of the time.

Conan Doyle also found himself immersed in the controversy that surrounded the final months of the war. The guerilla war that continued brought a severe response from the British military. The Boers fed off the land and moved around constantly, striking at British forces and then vanishing. The military established a series of block houses to try and contain the guerillas, burned their farms and built concentration camps for the women and children who were burned out. The camps were dirty and badly run and various epidemics continually swept through them. A number of articles and pamphlets appeared that described the conditions of the camps but which also made false claims about atrocities committed by British soldiers. They articles inflamed many European countries and Britain became widely criticized. In response, Conan Doyle penned a small booklet called "The War in South Africa: Its Causes and Conduct" and it was put together from eyewitness accounts in less than a week. He made a good case against the claims that British soldiers were raping Boer women and using dum-dum bullets that expanded on impact. He also admitted that while the camps had their shortcomings, they were a necessary alternative to allowing the women and children to starve to death. The booklet had its effect, especially in Europe, and managed to counter the anti-British feelings. We would consider it to be propaganda today but it was done in support of a cause that the author truly believed in.

Before Conan Doyle wrote the booklet, he had stood for Parliament in the 1900 general election. He was a Conservative candidate and while not in opposition to the Liberal policy of social reform at home, he joined the conservative Unionist party because they were pro-military and Empire. He ran for office in Edinburgh but had little chance of winning in the mostly Liberal area. His campaign was very effective however and he spoke to workmen, gave informal speeches in the street and rented out an opera house for formal speeches in the evening. He ended up making fourteen appearances in less than three days, genially acknowledging the hecklers who called him "Sherlock Holmes" and focusing on the importance of military reforms, national defense and the Empire. Things looked well for him until, on election day, a fanatical Protestant hung posters all over the district that proclaimed Conan Doyle to be a Jesuit-educated, Catholic agent --- a lie that must have galled a man who had long ago abandoned the Catholic faith. The posters likely swayed many voters but Conan Doyle did improve the Unionist vote by 1,500. Regardless, he lost the election. Years later, he admitted that he was glad that he had never ended up in politics. He would have never have been a good party man and he disliked electioneering. He was never that interested in politics anyway, but he was a fighter by nature and fighters never like to lose.

By this time, Conan Doyle was offered a knighthood, which he immediately refused, stating that a knighthood was a discredited title. His mother was furious and persisted with her demand that he reconsider until she eventually got her way. In 1902, he became Sir Arthur. Interestingly, though, years later, in one of the last Sherlock Holmes stories, "The Three Garridebs," Dr. Watson mentions in passing that Holmes had refused a knighthood and named the year in which this occurred. Not surprisingly, it was 1902.

In 1911, Conan Doyle took part in an automobile race called Prince Henry's Tour. He had long been fascinated with the automobile, having purchased his first in 1903, and looked forward to a great sporting event. Prince Henry was Prussian and the race began in Germany and ended in London, after a circular tour of England and Scotland. It also pitted fifty British drivers against fifty German drivers and Conan Doyle drove his favorite motorcar and took Jean along as a passenger. The British team won the race and Prince Henry presented them with an ivory statuette of a lady called "Peace" but from what Conan Doyle saw and heard during the race, he feared that war with Germany was not far off. He had been accompanied by various Prussian officers as observers and several of them made the assumption that war between the two nations was inevitable.

Conan Doyle began preparing for war in the best way that he knew how --- with his pen. He told his brother Innes that he did not like the look of things and feared that England was not ready to fight. He exaggerated the effectiveness of the airship in those days but he was almost uncannily accurate about the threat posed by the submarine. He wrote a lengthy story called "Danger! Being the Log of Captain John Sirius," in which Britain's fictional enemy Norland had a fleet of submarines that ignored the British Navy but made merciless attacks on merchant shipping, causing famine and forcing England to surrender. His warning of the submarine threat was laughed about at the time it was written but three years later, the German Naval Secretary would write that Conan Doyle had been "the only prophet of the present form of economic warfare" as the Germans began preying on merchant vessels.

Conan Doyle was again galvanized into action when war was declared in August 1914. He said after the fighting had ended that the Great War was the physical climax of his life, a remarkable statement considering that he was fifty-five years old at the time it started. Within a day or two, he had organized a civilian group in Crowborough, the Sussex town where he now lived, called the Volunteers. He received requests for their rules and methods from over 1,200 other towns and villages, even though the volunteer force was disbanded by an order from the War Office a few weeks after it was founded. It was replaced by an official body that boasted more than 200,000 men. Conan Doyle served in it as a private during the entire war. Most of the men were Sir Arthur's age or older but they thought nothing of marching as much as fourteen miles each day, singing along the entire route.

He was invigorated by the war effort but it was not enough for him. He wanted to see action and volunteered for the Army, writing to the War Office, "I am fifty-five but I am very strong and hardy, and can make my voice audible at great distances, which is useful at drill." Needless to say, despite the loudness of his voice, he was not accepted but he did send the War Office a flurry of ideas, many of them ingenious and practical. Since many of the military ships had few lifeboats, the sailors on board had little chance of surviving if they lost their ship or fell into the sea. Conan Doyle suggested the idea of inflatable rubber rafts that could be used and while this idea was turned down, he did suggest the development of inflatable rubber collars for seamen to carry with them in their pockets. He also came up with an idea for soldiers to be fitted with body armor but it too was rejected. Many of those who worked in the office agreed with his innovative notions but there was little they could do about it without approval from the high command. At the Ministry of Munitions, when he went there to argue for his body armor idea, he was told: "Sir Arthur, there is no use arguing here, for there is no one in this building who does not know that you are right!"

Ideas aside, his principal endeavor during the war was to rally Britain's spirits. Within a month of the war's beginning, he published a booklet called "To Arms" and quickly set to work on a history of the British campaign in France. He maintained contact with many of the British commanders and chronicled their efforts extensively, sometimes posting and receiving as many as five letters each day to and from the front. But he was not content to work from home. In 1916, he accepted an assignment to write about the Italian Army and to visit the British front on the way. As a deputy-lieutenant of Surrey, he had the right to wear a uniform and his tailor "rigged me up in wondrous khaki garb which was something between that of a Colonel and a Brigadier, with silver roses instead of stars or crosses upon the shoulder straps." He looked impressive, especially wearing his medals from South Africa, and was treated with respect everywhere that he went. He went to France on a destroyer in the company of several generals and was allowed to meet up with his brother Innes, who was now a colonel.

His trip to the Italian front turned out to be a hazardous one. His hosts tried, without success, to keep him out of harm's way but the party was shelled and had to turn back. Conan Doyle put together volumes of notes about the Italian troops, wrote them up on his return and was told that his trip was a great success. The expedition led to his having breakfast with Lloyd George, the new Prime Minister, and also to an invitation from the Australian government to see their section of the line. While on this trip, he saw part of the battle of St. Quentin. The end of the Great War must have brought mixed feelings to Conan Doyle. He was undoubtedly overjoyed with the Allied victory but in another sense, his greatest adventure had come to an end. The marching and the drilling, the war correspondence, the dangerous journeys that took him into the heart of historical events all combined to indulge his boyish love of adventure.

But the war and its aftermath also brought him the deepest grief that he had ever known. First, his wife's brother and Conan Doyle's friend, Malcolm Leckie, had been killed, along with two nephews and several other friends and relatives. And then Kingsley, the only son of his first marriage, and his beloved brother Innes, both died within a few weeks of one another. Kingsley had been badly wounded on the Somme and had died of pneumonia in October 1918. Not long after, Innes, now a brigadier general, also came down with pneumonia and died.

Conan Doyle wrote very little about these deaths but they must have hit him quite hard, perhaps even harder than the death of his mother two years later.

Although these losses were not responsible for his belief in Spiritualism, they surely must have had a great effect on the strength of his convictions. He had long been interested in the occult, but at the beginning of the war he had merely been sympathetic to the movement. The wartime deaths and the suffering that he witnessed must have convinced him of the need for our spirits to live on. It was a time when the public at large felt a great urgency to turn toward spiritual things and just as Spiritualism had seen a great revival following the Civil War, it would see another following World War I. The movement had just entered its modern heyday and standing at the forefront was Sir Arthur Conan Doyle.

Conan Doyle's interest in Spiritualism began when he was still an almost penniless young doctor living in Southsea. It was during a time when science was just starting to question the idea that another world might exist beyond our own and Conan Doyle became caught up on the study, as well as in the burgeoning Spiritualist movement. He avidly followed the research that was being done and even attended a number of séances and kept detailed notes of what occurred there. Early in his research, he began to consider the idea that a great amount of the phenomena that he witnessed was genuine and that the knocks, raps, horn-blowing and messages from the dead were worthy of at least a cautious belief.

Somewhere along the line, his cautious skepticism gave way to outright acceptance and there has been much debate as to what finally immersed him completely into the Spiritualist movement. Most believe that it was the series of deaths that occurred during the Great War that led Conan Doyle to embrace the movement as he did. Soon after Kingsleys' death, he was convinced that he heard the voice of his son during a séance with a Welsh medium. On the other hand, two years later, he would also be convinced that he embraced the materialized spirit of his mother with the help of two American mediums, William and Eva Thompson. Within days, these mediums were exposed as frauds and were arrested at another séance by police officers who found wigs, costumes and fluorescent makeup among their belongings. In spite of this, Conan Doyle was not swayed from his newfound beliefs.

Even before this, a short time after the death of Malcolm Leckie, a sick friend of Lady Jean Doyle came to stay at the Conan Doyle home. Her name was Lily Lauder-Symonds and she had a reputation for being a gifted medium. While she was there, she offered to conduct a séance for the family and she delivered a message from Lady Jean's brother, Malcolm. He had been killed during the Great War and he and Conan Doyle had been close friends. Years before, the two men had shared a private joke about a guinea that Leckie had had given to Sir Arthur as his first "fee" when he became an Army doctor. Conan Doyle had cherished the coin and wore it on his watch chain. The message that Conan Doyle was given by Lauder-Symonds concerned the guinea, an item that most people, including the medium, knew nothing about. This was likely the incident that finally convinced Sir Arthur of the legitimacy of Spiritualism. Shortly after, he began his full-fledged conversion to the movement, although he did not go public with his beliefs right away due to his involvement with the war effort.

Soon after the war's end, though, he announced his conversion to the public in the Spiritualist magazine, *The Light*. While Spiritualists around the world applauded his valiant efforts, his critics were instantly unkind. None of them could understand how the creator of the logical detective, Sherlock Holmes, could so gullible about the so-called "wonders" of Spiritualism. But Conan Doyle's convictions came from his supreme self-confidence, and whether the public shared his beliefs of not, he never doubted that he had found the true path. Conan Doyle plunged into Spiritualism with all of the considerable vigor that he gave to everything else. Despite some setbacks and the exposure of frauds like the Thompsons, Conan Doyle could not be shaken from his beliefs. He was firmly convinced of life after death and the possibility of making contact with the spirit world.

Conan Doyle began lecturing for the Spiritualist cause in October 1917, appearing in Bradford and London. In the years that followed, he visited almost every town in Britain, finding what he described as critical but attentive audiences. It's possible and perhaps even likely that most people came to hear the creator of Sherlock Holmes rather than because of their interest in the spirit world, but if this was the case, he didn't care. After storming through London, Conan Doyle and his family visited Australia and the United States, all on behalf of Spiritualism. He also lectured all over Europe and in South Africa, Kenya and Rhodesia. In 1926, he published a spiritual adventure story called "The Land of the Mist," which featured the popular Professor Challenger character from his earlier book, *The Lost World*. He also wrote a massive, two-volume book called *The History of Spiritualism* and throughout the 1920s, spent a quarter of a million pounds advancing the Spiritualist cause.

During this same time period, Lady Jean began to develop mediumistic skills, which was in sharp contrast to her earlier feelings about the movement. She had disapproved of her husband's interest in the occult and disliked his concerns with Spiritualism, which she called "uncanny and dangerous." However, her brother Malcolm's death during the war changed her feelings and in 1921, she was suddenly given what her husband called the "gift of inspired writing." She soon began to receive messages from the other side and the loved ones they had lost soon began to make regular appearances at the Conan Doyle home circle.

In his books, writings and personal appearances, Conan Doyle recounted dozens of bizarre and seemingly unexplained occurrences, but whether they were the product of the supernatural or his own willingness to believe, is unknown. He often claimed to touch phantom hands, to see objects move about, to witness the wondrous works of talented mediums and to possess notebooks filled with information that had been given to his wife from spirits --- information that Conan Doyle insisted was "utterly beyond her ken." He also came face to face with at least one ghost and investigated a haunted house in Dorset. He chronicled this adventure in his book *On the Edge of the Unknown*, which makes compelling reading whether you believe in the mysteries of Spiritualism or not. Strangely, the house burned down after his investigation and a child's body was found buried in the garden. After the body was discovered, the haunting ceased and Conan Doyle came to believe that the child's spirit may have been responsible, since nothing out of the ordinary ever occurred at the site after the blaze.

Conan Doyle also collected a huge number of spirit photographs, most of which he believed to be genuine, including one of a ghostly woman that was taken at a haunted inn in Norwich. In 1922, he penned a book on the subject called *The Case for Spirit Photography*. Unfortunately, the vast majority of the photos that Conan Doyle championed appear blatantly fake today, the obvious results of fraud and double exposure. He became particularly involved with a group of spirit photographers led by William Hope of Crewe. The so-called "Crewe Circle" produced several hundred alleged spirit photographs during its heyday and Doyle posed for a number of them. Not surprisingly, all of the developed plates portrayed a spirit "extra" or two lurking over his shoulder. The credulous author believed all of them to be authentic.

In 1922, Conan Doyle began to develop a relationship with a man with whom he would maintain a rather strange friendship over the course of the next several years. He was the famous magician and escape artist Harry Houdini and the two of them met in England and began a good natured but antagonistic relationship that lasted for about two years. Conan Doyle believed that Spiritualism was of great importance to the world, while Houdini actively campaigned against it and its "mediumistic parlor tricks." The two men, both of whom possessed a vast knowledge of the movement, argued long and inconclusively but remained close until a series of incidents caused the friendship to abruptly end. A rift developed between them and was never repaired, resulting in both public and private battles between them until Houdini's death in 1926.

Conan Doyle and Houdini first met in 1922, during the magician's tour of England. The two of them became good friends, despite their opposing views on the supernatural. Houdini was delighted to learn that there was at least one intelligent person who believed in Spiritualism and found that man in his friend, Conan Doyle.

Before the two had met, Houdini had gained a reputation for exposing fraudulent mediums. His search for a genuine medium began after the death of his mother and in his attempts to contact her, he met scores of phony Spiritualists. Conan Doyle agreed with some of Houdini's methods in exposing fraudulent mediums because he believed that their existence damaged the legitimacy of the movement. Lacking his new friend's magical training, though, he was less able to see how fraud was accomplished. Houdini worked to try and show the secrets practiced by the fraudulent mediums to Conan Doyle but the author merely insisted that the mediums he knew were honest people who would never try and trick or cheat their followers. Besides, just because Houdini could prove that fraud was possible was not enough to convince Conan Doyle that it actually occurred.

Neither convinced the other to his respective point of view but both of them found their own interest stirred by their meeting and the lengthy correspondences that followed.

It would be a series of strange events over the next two years that would bring this unusual friendship to an end. The rift between them started when Conan Doyle began to publicly take the side of Spiritualists who believed that Houdini accomplished some of his greatest magic using supernatural powers. Houdini had long been working to expose fraudulent mediums in private, in print and during his stage shows, which made him a much-hated figure in Spiritualist circles. Some believed they had an explanation for this --- they stated that Houdini's exposure of mediums was simply to cover the fact that he was a medium himself! They claimed that many of his extraordinary escapes were actually done by Houdini "dematerializing" from the traps that he had placed himself in. "This ability," Conan Doyle stated publicly, "to unbolt locked doors is undoubtedly due to Houdini's mediumistic powers and not to any normal operation of the lock. The effort necessary to shoot a bolt from within a lock is drawn from Houdini the medium, but it must not be thought that this is the only means by which he can escape from his prison. For at times, his body can be... dematerialized and withdrawn."

Now, Houdini was placed in the classic magician's "catch" position, meaning that he could only go so far in denying the Spiritualist claims without revealing how his escapes were accomplished, which he would never do. His reply was simply that all of his escapes were managed by purely physical means. He stated that his crusade against Spiritualism was simply a way to protect the public from charlatans. He said he was able to keep an open mind on the subject and did not assume that all mediums were frauds.

Spiritualist leaders declared that Houdini's actions did not agree with his words and so the magician made a pact with a number of friends. The pact promised that whichever of them died first, he should make every attempt to contact the others by way of a secret code. But Houdini still could not escape the claims being made by Conan Doyle, so he devised a plan to make the author realize that all of his tricks were just that --- tricks. He assured Conan Doyle that he would give him proof that magic was accomplished through simple trickery.

Three persons were present at the test, Houdini, Conan Doyle and Bernard Ernst, the president of the American Society of Magicians. A slate was hung in the center of the room by Conan Doyle and he was given five plain cork balls to examine. He chose one of the balls at random and placed it in a container of white paint. Conan Doyle was then given a piece of paper and was told to walk anywhere that he wanted to and then write a message on the paper. He left the house, walked three blocks away and then turned a corner. He shielded the paper with his hand and wrote down a short message. Meanwhile, Ernst stayed in the room with Houdini to ensure that he remained in the room. When he finished writing, Conan Doyle folded the paper carefully and placed it in his pocket. He then returned to the house.

Houdini then told Conan Doyle to pick up the paint-soaked ball and stick it on the suspended slate. The ball then began to roll over the surface of the slate, spelling out the biblical phrase, *Mene Mene Tekel Upharsin*... the exact words that Conan Doyle had written on the paper!

Houdini claimed that it was all done by simple trickery but Conan Doyle was more convinced than ever of his friend's supernatural powers. Ernst begged Houdini to explain how the trick worked, either to himself or to Conan Doyle, in the strictest confidence, but Houdini refused. Strangely, he would never use the trick again in any of his shows and no one has ever been able to reproduce it.

The relationship between the two men had become tense and it was damaged even more by an event that occurred during Conan Doyle's American lecture tour in May 1922. The tour got off to a rocky start when the author landed in New York and gave a press conference that was derided and harshly criticized in the *New York Times* the following day. He gave seven lectures while in New York and while each was well attended, the schedule left Conan Doyle exhausted. Needing a break, he and his family went to Atlantic City to relax.

After arriving, Conan Doyle sent a message to Houdini and suggested that he come down for a short vacation. Houdini enthusiastically accepted and soon,

Conan Doyle was floating in the hotel swimming pool and admiring the length of time that the magician could remain under water while holding his breath. While Lady Jean and the children played with a beach ball, Conan Doyle and Houdini sat in deck chairs, looking out over the ocean and discussing aspects of Spiritualism. As Conan Doyle described the work done by a Mrs. Deane in London, Houdini maintained a stoic silence, knowing that Mrs. Deane had been caught substituting a photographic plate from her purse for one exposed at a séance. Houdini offered comments and careful observations but he had no intention of upsetting his friend and ruining their holiday.

On Sunday, Bess Houdini joined the happy group. Conan Doyle was excited to see her, as was her husband, who had been enjoying the time spent playing with the children. He had been entertaining them with small magic tricks and delighted in their laughter. He eagerly spent a few moments alone with Bess, though, and the couple of was sitting on the beach one afternoon when a lifeguard's son came running along to tell them that Lady Jean wanted to give Houdini a private séance in her suite. Houdini, who was impressed with Lady Jean's obvious sincerity and decency, was thrilled. Perhaps he could at last obtain proof of survival after death and when Conan Doyle later told him that Lady Jean would try and get a message to the magician from his adored mother, he was beside himself with excitement.

Houdini went up to the suite and Lady Jean greeted him with great affection. She sat down at a large table, where a pile of paper and a pencil lay ready. Conan Doyle sat next to his wife and Houdini sat on the opposite side of the table. Conan Doyle then offered a solemn prayer and asked his wife if she was ready. Her hand struck the table three times a Spiritualistic code for "yes" and then she sank into a deep trance.

Houdini wrote later: "I had made up my mind that I would be as religious as it was in my power to be and not at any time did I scoff during the ceremony. I excluded all earthly thoughts and gave my whole soul to the séance. I was willing to believe, even wanted to believe. It was weird to me and with a beating heart I waited, hoping that I might feel once more the presence of my beloved mother..."

Jean began to breathe deeply and her eyes fluttered. Her hand, as though moving on its own, dashed with amazing speed across sheets of paper. Conan Doyle handed them one by one over to the magician. Houdini turned pale and began to tremble. The message began: "Oh my darling, thank God, thank God, at last I'm through. I've tried, oh so often -- now I am happy. Why, of course, I want to talk to my boy -- my own beloved boy -- friends, thank you, with all my heart for this." The message continued with an expression of joy about Mrs. Weiss' new existence on the other side and the beauty of the next world. She concluded with "I wanted, oh so much -- now I can rest in peace." Doyle then asked Houdini if he wanted to ask his mother a question for "her reply will prove that she is at your side."

Houdini looked extremely upset and could not speak. Conan Doyle suggested a question. "Can my mother read my mind?" Houdini silently nodded his agreement and Lady Jean's hand began to move again. "I always wanted to read my beloved son's mind," the message continued. "There is so much that I want to say to him." The message then went on for several hundred words, mostly expressing joy at communicating with her son and her appreciation of the Conan Doyles.

At the end of the séance, Houdini sank back in his chair, utterly drained and exhausted. Then, unseen by Conan Doyle and Lady Jean, Houdini scribbled with a fragment of pencil a small note on the first sheet of paper. "Message written by Lady Doyle claiming the spirit of my dear Mother had control of her hand --- my sainted mother could not write English and spoke broken English." A moment later, he picked up a sheet of paper and boldly wrote on it a single word "Powell." He looked at Conan Doyle and his eyes issued a challenge to the other man. He had been thinking of his friend Powell, a fellow magician --- if his mother had been reading his mind, wouldn't she have known this?

But Doyle misunderstood the message completely and he stood up from his chair in shock. A good friend of Conan Doyle's, Ellis Powell, editor of the *London Financial News*, had died just three days earlier. He was convinced that Houdini, with the gift of a medium, was trying to say that Powell was in the room. Houdini didn't have the heart to disillusion them on the spot but a few days later, he sent Conan Doyle a letter to let him know that he was thinking of his magician friend and that he was not trying to tell him that a spectral presence was in the room.

Houdini left the hotel and returned to New York to wrestle with his conscience. Should he disclose the truth --- that his mother had not come through, that this had been her birthday and there was no reference made to it, that he felt no presence in the room, no smell of her favorite perfume --- and that when the message ended, he felt as alone and lost as he had when she died? If he were to reveal this, Sir Arthur and Lady Jean would be hurt and perhaps even ruined. On the other hand, if he kept quiet, he would be allowing the Spiritualists a false victory. Out of decency, he decided to withhold any statements about the séance until after the Conan Doyles left America.

Sir Arthur and Lady Jean never expected the blow that awaited them. They remained friendly with Houdini, dining and attending the theater with him and he came to the docks to see them off when they departed on a trip on June 24. For some reason, Houdini held back on speaking out about the couple until December 19, 1922. At that time, he issued a press release that stated there was not the slightest evidence that his mother had "come through" Lady Jean. His mother could not read or write and could barely speak English. In addition to that, Lady Jean had started her automatic writing by scrawling a cross on the top of the paper. His mother had been Jewish and would have never have done this.

Conan Doyle protested Houdini's claims, stating that language and earthly dates meant nothing to the spirits. Lady Jean suggested that Mrs. Weiss had learned fluent English in the afterlife. Houdini was not convinced. He did not think that his friends had deliberately tried to deceive him but had deceived themselves by their own gullibility. As for Sir Arthur and Lady Jean, they weathered Houdini's criticisms, although his statement damaged their formerly friendly relationship. Conan Doyle tried to remain loyal to the magician and convinced himself that Houdini was too nervous about the encounter with his mother's spirit to admit that it was genuine. They also claimed in some reports that another message had also come through that day --- claiming that Houdini would die soon --- and this was the reason he denied the authenticity of the communication.

For a short time after this, the two men tried to pretend that their friendship had not been ruined but it was too late to salvage it for the hurt was too deep on both sides. To Sir Arthur and lady Jean, Houdini was willfully blind and appallingly ungrateful but to Houdini, the Conan Doyles had made a terrible mockery of the deep feelings that he had for his mother. What little remained of their friendship was destroyed in 1923 with Houdini's attacks on Boston medium Mina Crandon, who appeared under the stage name of Margery. Houdini had become a member of a panel that was sponsored by *Scientific American* magazine to investigate self-proclaimed mediums and Houdini was instrumental in making sure that Margery was discredited.

The entire matter with Houdini, Margery and the *Scientific American* investigations was never settled to anyone's satisfaction. Margery was never deemed genuine by the panel but she remained triumphant in the eyes of many, including Conan Doyle. The friendship between Houdini and himself had finally reached its bitter end. "You force me to speak," he wrote to the magician, "and I have no wish to offend you but you cannot have it both ways. You cannot bitterly and offensively, often also unruly, attack a subject and yet expect courtesies from those who honor that subject. It is not reasonable."

Within a few years, in 1926, Bess Houdini would be shattered by her husband's premature death. While sorting through his papers and vast library, she uncovered a number of books on Spiritualism and the supernatural and thought they would make a nice gift to Conan Doyle, whom she still considered one of her husband's best friends. She wrote to Sir Arthur and Lady Jean and offered the books but Conan Doyle was reluctant to take them, believing that

Houdini had harbored bad feelings about him at the time of his death. Bess quickly replied that this was not the case and blamed most of the problems between the two men on the press. Houdini had never given up on the possibility of contacting his mother and told Bess so while on his deathbed. And "if, as you believe, he had psychic powers," she wrote, "I give you my word that he never knew it.... He was deeply hurt whenever any journalistic arguments arose between you and would have been the happiest man in the world had he been able to agree with your views on Spiritualism. He admired and respected you... two remarkable men with different views --- it is usually the third party that distorts the word or the meaning."

In the midst of Conan Doyle's friendship with Houdini, an incident occurred that should have been the greatest embarrassment of the author's career. It stemmed from his fascination with unusual photographs and his belief in the unseen world but instead of being embarrassed by the photographs and their outcome, he simply could not conceive of the idea that the whole thing could have been a hoax.

In 1920, Conan Doyle received a letter from a Spiritualist friend, Felicia Scatcherd, who informed him of some photographs taken in Yorkshire that appeared to prove the existence of fairies. Conan Doyle asked his friend Edward Gardner to go down and investigate and Gardner soon found himself in the possession of several photos that showed very small, winged female figures. The photographers had been two young girls, Elsie Wright, sixteen, and her nine-year-old cousin, Frances Griffiths. They claimed they had seen the fairies on an earlier occasion and had gone back with a camera and photographed them. They had been taken in July and September 1917, near the Yorkshire village of Cottingley. Doyle's acceptance of the photographs, and his writings about them, would galvanize the Spiritualist community --- and would provide ammunition for mockery by his critics.

The two girls claimed to have seen the fairies around the "beck" a local term for "stream" on an almost daily basis. At the time, they claimed to have no intention of seeking fame or notoriety. Elsie had borrowed her father's camera on a hot Saturday in July 1917 to take pictures of Frances and the beck fairies. According to their account, Arthur Wright developed the photos later that day, revealing anomalous white shapes that gradually moved toward the foreground of the photographs. They looked like sandwich papers or some sort of birds to Wright, but Elsie insisted they were fairies. Wright took no notice of it but then a month later, Frances photographed Elsie with what the girls claimed was a gnome. Arthur Wright questioned the girls about it but they stuck to their incredible story that they simply took photos of what they saw down by the beck. They were banned from borrowing the camera from that point on.

The photos amused Wright and to appease his wife who was a believer, he combed the area around the beck and searched for signs of either of fairies or fraud. He found neither and since the photos had a novelty value, he made a few prints of them to show the neighbors. Wright's wife, Polly, though was a member of the Theosophical Society, which flourished in an atmosphere of belief and excitement about the impossible. It was at a local meeting of the society --- which incidentally was a lecture on fairies --- that Polly Wright confided to her friends about the photographs of fairies taken by her daughter and her neice.

Conan Doyle's friend, Edward L. Gardner, was a Theosophist himself and had no trouble believing that the photographs were authentic. Even though the photographs were extremely questionable and the fairies later turned out to be cut-outs from *Princess Mary's Gift Book*, publishing in 1915, Gardner pronounced them genuine and obtained copies for Conan Doyle. The author was wary of them at first. He began seeking other opinions, including from Sir Oliver Lodge, who immediately pronounced them as fakes. Conan Doyle had his doubts. He was not sure that the little creatures in the photos were actually fairies but they were certainly mysterious figures. Obviously, the girls were central to the issue --- could they be gifted mediums? He sent Gardner back up north to meet with them and to investigate the "magical" beck. Conan Doyle meanwhile set off for Australia on a lecture tour and left Gardner to cope with the media storm that surrounded the revealing of the photographs. The newspapers, not surprisingly, were not open to the possibilities of fairies and the *City News* even stated that "It seems at this point that we must believe either in the almost incredible mystery of the fairy -- or in the almost incredible wonders of faked photographs."

Unknown to the newspapers and to Gardner and Conan Doyle at the time, the girls had taken three more fairy photographs during the summer of 1920. One of them showed an obviously two-dimensional fairy with fashionably bobbed hair offering a flower to Elsie and another depicted a "fairy bower" in a tree. The latter appeared to be an ectoplasm-like cocoon that was very exciting to Conan Doyle. The third was of a leaping fairy that the girls claimed was captured on film during its fifth leap.

Conan Doyle was intrigued but still bothered by the photographs and so he asked for an opinion about them from the Eastman Co., although he never waited for a response before declaring them to be genuine. He published an article about the fairies in the Christmas 1920 issue of the *Strand Magazine* and soon was deluged with photographs from other people who claimed to have seen fairies. Conan Doyle examined them all, but saw none that appeared to be as genuine as the Cottingley photographs. He later penned a book in 1922 called *The Coming of the Fairies*, which detailed the entire affair.

To look at these photographs today, the modern eye can easily see them to be fakes. In defense of Conan Doyle however, we have to realize that first and foremost, he was a gentleman and he believed that because he treated others with kindness and honesty, they would treat him in the same manner. Needless to say, he was taken advantage of on many occasions. On this occasion however, it would have never crossed his mind that the two young girls might be lying about the photographs. Even if he had doubted them, he would have never accused them of dishonesty, for it was just not his way.

In the early 1980s, the two women finally admitted the photographs were a hoax. They stated that they had faked them to get back at adults who teased them for saying they played with fairies. The joke had gotten out of hand when Gardner and Conan Doyle got involved and by that time, it was too late to back out. They promised though, that they would reveal the truth once all of the principles in the case had passed away, especially Conan Doyle, whom they did not want to embarrass when it came out the photos were not real.

Strangely, though, even though they eventually admitted the photos were fakes, they maintained that they had really seen fairies in the beck. The photographs were staged to show their parents just what they had seen. In fact, despite their confessions, Frances went to her grave maintaining that one of the famous photographs was authentic. Which one? We will never know for sure...

Until his final days, Conan Doyle clung tenaciously to his belief in the afterlife and to the reality of the Spiritualist movement. In fact, he believed that his final hours in 1930 were the beginning of perhaps his greatest adventure. Throughout the 1920s, he had suffered several small heart attacks and his doctors warned him about his excessive travel and speaking engagements. The robust author ignored them, maintaining that he simply had too much to do. Eventually, though, all the activity caught up with him and he was diagnosed with serious heart disease in the spring of 1930. He began a decline that ended in July and worsened after he caught a serious cold while lecturing about Spiritualism in Scandinavia.

On the morning of July 7, his family gathered around him and held on to his hands. Around half past eight, Conan Doyle revived a little but did not speak. He looked at each of his loved ones and then settled back and closed his eyes forever. His son Adrian gave the anxious public a short account of his father's last moments: "His last words to us were to my mother and they show just how much he thought of her. He simply smiled up at her and said that she was wonderful. He was in too much pain to say a lot, his breathing was very bad and what he said was during a brief flash of consciousness. I have never seen anyone take anything more gamely in all my life. Even when we all knew that he was suffering great pain, he always managed to keep a smile for us."

Conan Doyle's death caused an immediate sensation among the world's Spiritualist community. Mediums everywhere waited anxiously for his first message from the other side and while it took some time, they never gave up hope. Soon, Sir Arthur became a frequently reported presence at séances the world over and also began appearing in a number of questionable spirit photographs as well.

His family never had any doubts that he would return. When asked if he would, Adrian Doyle replied: "Why, of course! My father fully believed that when he passed over he would continue to keep in touch with us. All of the family believes so too. There is no question that my father will speak to us just as he did before he passed over."

There is no question that Conan Doyle lived a life of action, romance and literary greatness but what drove this brilliant author and adventurer to cling to the tenets of Spiritualism as strongly as he did, sacrificing almost everything, from his writing career to his friendships and often even his credibility, for the movement? He is often criticized today as he was then for his gullibility and foolishness but could the creator of such a coldly analytical character as Sherlock Holmes have seen something in Spiritualism that the rest of us do not? It is not up to us to judge the correctness or credulity of Conan Doyle's personal beliefs but we do know that he believed in the reality of the movement whole-heartedly, and right or wrong, we cannot find fault with him for his convictions.

It has been said that the final moments of a man's life will define his entire existence in the next world and if this is true, then Conan Doyle lived his final moments as a man who was at peace with himself and his beliefs. What more could possibly be asked for?

A FOLDING CARPENTER'S RULER
Houdini's Battle with "Margery"

After making a name for himself as an escape artist and becoming one of the most famous men in the world, Harry Houdini turned his attentions to the exposure of fraudulent Spiritualist mediums. Houdini had long been interested in Spiritualism and even posed as a medium or a short time while working with a traveling carnival in the early days of his career. After his beloved mother died, he began seeking out honest mediums to try and make contact with her spirit. Unfortunately, though, genuine mediums turned out to be in short supply and his quest turned into the exposure of dozens of frauds.

Thanks to his background in magic and illusion, Houdini could usually re-create the tricks that the phony mediums used to dupe their customers, and he eventually turned his knowledge into a book and a stage show.

Then, in 1923, Houdini learned of a Boston medium named Margery, who even the editors of *Scientific American* magazine claimed was the real thing. Houdini's confrontation with Margery would become the highest - and the lowest -- point of his Spiritualist-exposing career.

In 1923, Houdini joined a committee that was put together by *Scientific American*, which offered a reward for any medium able to prove that their psychical gifts were genuine. The initial prize for an authentic exhibition was $2,500. There was also a secondary prize for anyone who could produce a genuine spirit photograph. The committee consisted of Dr. William McDougall, professor of psychology at Harvard; Dr. Daniel Fisk Comstock, from the Massachusetts Institute of Technology; Dr. Walter Franklin Prince, research officer for the American Society for Psychical Research; Hereward Carrington, a prolific writer on the occult; and Houdini.

The committee had been Houdini's idea. He had been approached by the magazine to write a series of articles on Spiritualism but, because of his vaudeville commitments, could not accept the offer. He suggested instead the formation of an investigative committee on which he would serve for no fee -- if he were granted the right to select or reject its other members. Houdini did not exercise his power of approval to limit committee membership to people he knew would agree with him. The committee would eventually have several members with whom he could not get along. Even the original membership was problematic. Houdini's personal opinion of Carrington, for example, was that the writer was an opportunist who professed to believe in Spiritualism because it helped to sell his books about the occult.

Before Houdini left on a cross-country vaudeville tour, he promised to cancel his bookings whenever he was called for an investigation. The Water Torture Cell was the main feature of his act at the time and the open-air straitjacket escape continued to draw capacity crowds for his performances.

While Houdini was traveling, there was no rush of applicants for the *Scientific American* prizes. It was easy for a photographer to produce mysterious photos on his own plates, in his own studio, or for a medium to conjure up phenomena when surrounded by hymn-singing believers. Why would they risk their reputations being tested by observers who were well versed in psychology, physics and trickery?

A few mediums did come forward. The first to announce that she was ready to try for the prize was Elizabeth Allen Thomson, but she was never formally tested, having been caught with twenty yards of gauze taped to her groin, flowers tucked under her breasts and a live snake concealed in her armpit. A contestant who looked more promising was George Valiantine. He had given two séances for *Scientific American* while Houdini was on the road. The first had been unimpressive. During the second, a trumpet had floated in the dark, lifted by a spirit Indian, according to the medium, at least. The trumpet tapped various sitters, whacked a spectator's head, and then crashed to the floor just as Fred Keating, a young magician friend of Hereward Carrington, tried to grab it.

Houdini attended the third séance and this time, science was brought into the séance room. Unknown to the medium, men in an adjoining chamber were following his movements with light signals, a Dictaphone and a stopwatch. Valiantine's chair had been wired. Whenever he left his seat, a light flashed in the control room and a note was made of the time. By comparing the times that Valiantine got out of his chair and the times when phenomena were recorded in the séance room, it was obvious that it was the medium, not the spirits, who had been raising a ruckus in the dark. The *New York Times* quoted Houdini when the medium was exposed.

J. Malcolm Bird, an associate editor of the magazine and the secretary for the investigative committee, was annoyed by the newspaper story. The *Times* reporter should not have written the story until he, Bird, had printed an article in *Scientific American*. He resented being scooped. When the *Times* followed up with an interview with Houdini, Bird was enraged. The medium-trapping system had been devised before Houdini, who was busy with his vaudeville tour, came on the scene. Yet to the public, it appeared that the magician had exposed Valiantine. Bird disliked Houdini immensely. This would be the first time the two men clashed, but it would not be the last.

Houdini spent more time attacking fraudulent mediums than arranging spectacular escapes during his fall vaudeville tour. In late September, he spoke to a psychology class at the University of Illinois on "The Psychology of Audiences" and "The Negative Side of Spiritualism." The latter topic took up most of the class time. In October, he gave an illustrated lecture on mediums and their methods at Marquette University.

Meanwhile, medium Nino Pecoraro applied for the *Scientific American* prize money while Houdini was still on the road with his lecture tour. Sir Arthur Conan Doyle, during his first American lecture tour, had attended a séance held by Pecoraro and had been tremendously impressed by him. He noted that the medium, while bound with wire, caused a bell to ring, a tambourine to spin in the air, and a toy piano to play. Hereward Carrington had arranged the séance for Conan Doyle. There was reason to think that the committee might give Pecoraro a comparatively sympathetic hearing.

Doubtlessly believing that Pecoraro would have too easy a time of it, *Scientific American* publisher Orson Munn urgently requested Houdini, then performing in Little Rock, Arkansas, to return to New York and attend a test séance. Fellow committeemen planned to tie the Italian medium with a sixty-foot-long rope and Houdini laughed. Even amateur escapologists could free their hands when trussed up in such a manner, he told them. Houdini slashed the rope into short lengths and secured the medium himself. After that, Pecoraro produced no manifestations.

Houdini returned to his theater tour in the Midwest. He spoke at several more colleges, which became rehearsals for a lecture tour that was booked for him around the country. His anti-Spiritualism campaign had been only for his spare time during his Orpheum tour. Now he was free -- at least for twenty one-night shows -- to devote his full energy to counteracting the propaganda that was being spread by the Spiritualist community.

Houdini's lectures were a huge success. The people who attended the shows came more to see him perform than to hear about his exposures of the Spiritualists. He found that he had to mix entertainment with his message to appeal to the crowds. To say that a medium employed a trick spirit slate was not enough. He had to show how the slate was used. The demonstration drove his point home and delighted the audiences at the same time. To make sure that he had full auditoriums to educate, he broke out of packing boxes at every stop along his route to generate publicity.

The publication of Houdini's book *A Magician Among the Spirits* in 1924 brought violent attacks from believers, cheers from skeptics and the inevitable end of his friendship with Sir Arthur. Houdini wrote that he treasured Conan Doyle as a friend. Sir Arthur was a "brilliant man," he had a "great mind" -- except where Spiritualism was concerned. Houdini respected Conan Doyle's beliefs and was convinced that he was sincere, but the eminent author refused to accept the fact that many of the mediums he endorsed were frauds. Houdini listed instance after instance of mediums that Sir Arthur trusted even though others had found them to be frauds. He quoted the written message that Lady Jean claimed had come from his mother in Atlantic City --- then revealed why it could not have been from her spirit.

Conan Doyle was angered and saddened by the book. He had been fascinated with Houdini the man, but when his friend attempted to destroy his beliefs and held him up to ridicule, any further friendship between them was impossible.

Houdini and Conan Doyle never wrote or spoke to one another again.

Houdini returned to his lecture circuit after the Pecoraro fiasco, only to hear three months later that the investigative panel had deadlocked over a medium named Mina Crandon, who used the stage name of "Margery." They stated that they believed her to be genuine and were prepared to give her the $2,500 reward. J. Malcolm Bird was one of Crandon's supporters and was eager to give her the magazine's endorsement. He allowed word of the panel's favorable findings to reach the press. "Boston Medium Baffles Experts," one headline announced. "Houdini the Magician Stumped," trumpeted another.

Houdini, who had not even been present during Crandon's séances, much less stumped by them, was stunned to think the magazine would even consider approving a medium that he had never seen. Orson Munn called him in for a consultation and he publicly told *Scientific American* that he would forfeit $1,000 of his own money if he failed to expose Margery as a fraud.

When it was discovered that Houdini was now going to be involved in the investigations of Margery, Sir Arthur Conan Doyle, an avid supporter of the medium, was outraged. He called it a "capital error" placing such an enemy of Spiritualism into the investigation. He wrote: "The Commission is, in my opinion, a farce." Mina Crandon, however, seemed to welcome the opportunity to test her mettle against Houdini. The prize money meant nothing to this wealthy woman but the opportunity to win the approval of such a prestigious committee --- at the expense of the mighty Houdini --- proved too great a temptation for her to resist.

Houdini traveled with Orson Munn by train to Boston and on the way, he reviewed the findings of his colleagues on the investigative panel. To his way of thinking, the investigation had been badly handled from the start. Margery did not perform under the same test conditions that other mediums were forced to. She was allowed to hold her test séances at her home, which opened the possibility of fraud. Most of the committee members had availed themselves of the Crandons' generous hospitality during the proceedings, staying in their home, eating their food and enjoying their company. Houdini believed that this had badly compromised their objectivity and later, it was learned that accepting food and a bed from the Crandons were the least of the problems. One investigator had actually borrowed money from Margery's husband, while another hoped to win his backing for a research foundation. Worse yet, the "distinguished" panel was not unaware of Margery's physical attractions. Years later, at least one committee member would tell of his amorous encounters with the shapely medium.

Mina Crandon certainly created a firestorm of controversy in the early 1920s. In truth, she was a rather unlikely medium.

Mina Stinson had been born in Ontario in 1888, the daughter of a farmer. She moved to Boston when she was sixteen so that she could play the piano, coronet and cello in local bands and orchestras. After working as a secretary, an actress and an ambulance driver, she married a grocer named Earl P. Rand, with whom she had a son. They remained happily married until a medical operation introduced her to Le Roi Goddard Crandon, a prominent surgeon and a former instructor at Harvard Medical School. She divorced Rand in 1918 and married Crandon a short time later.

Mina had no psychic experiences early in her life and in fact, had no interest in the spirit world at all until her husband became enthralled with the paranormal in the early 1920s. One evening in May 1923, Dr. Crandon invited a number of friends to his home for a "home circle" meeting. The group gathered around a small table and soon had it tilting in response to the sitters' questions. Crandon suggested that they each remove their hands from the table, one at a time, to see which individual was responsible for the paranormal activity. One by one, each of them took their hands away but the table only stopped rocking when the last of the sitters lifted her hands. Dr. Crandon had solved the mystery: the medium was his wife!

At first, the idea of being a medium seemed like a lark to the fun-loving Mina. Throughout the summer of 1923, the Crandons held one séance after another at their home at 10 Lime Street. Each time, Mina seemed to exhibit some new ability. It seemed that Dr. Crandon only had to read about some new spirit manifestation before his wife could duplicate it.

Within a month of her first official séance, Dr. Crandon announced a plan to place his wife under hypnosis so that they could try and make contact with the psychic control who would serve as her spirit guide. At first, Mina resisted this idea, claiming that she didn't want to miss any of the "fun" while she was under hypnosis. Eventually, however, she gave in to her husband's wishes and soon, a deep male voice made itself heard to the Crandon home circle.

The voice turned out to belong to Mina's brother, Walter Stinson, who had been crushed to death in a railroad accident in 1911. From this point on, Walter's spirit was a regular presence in the Crandon séance room. He proved to have a strong personality, a quick wit and was given to using salty language. Many visitors to the séance room became convinced of what they heard simply because they could not imagine that such coarse and vulgar language would come from the mouth of the pretty doctor's wife. A number of observers noted that Walter's voice did not seem to come from Mina at all. The sound seemed to emanate from another part of the room and would continue even when Mina was in a trance or had her mouth filled with water. The effect seemed so remarkable that one skeptic, searching for a plausible explanation for what he had experienced, wondered if perhaps Mina was able to speak through her ears! Walter became well known as Mina's spirit guide and, along with his sister, began to find fame all over the world.

But Mina hardly needed Walter's help to become a popular medium, especially among her male sitters. Mina resembled nothing so much as a light-hearted flapper. Even Houdini conceded that she was an exceedingly attractive woman, and one psychic researcher warned his colleagues to "avoid falling in love with the medium." She usually greeted her sitters wearing only a flimsy dressing gown, bedroom slippers and silk stockings. This attire, leaving almost nothing to the imagination, was supposedly intended to rule out the possibility of trickery or concealment, but it also tended to distract male visitors. Mina's slender figure, fashionably bobbed hair and merry light blue eyes made her, in the words of one admirer, "too attractive for her own good." To make matters more titillating, it was rumored that it was not uncommon for her to hold sessions in the nude and, according to some, she was especially adept at manifesting ectoplasm from her vagina.

Dr. Crandon believed that his lovely wife was a "remarkable psychic instrument" and he took her abroad to build up a consensus of favorable opinion from European experts. One of these was Sir Arthur Conan Doyle, who declared her to be a "very powerful medium" and, he said, "the validity of her gifts was beyond all question." J. Malcolm Bird, from *Scientific American*, shared Doyle's opinion and wrote a series of articles extolling her virtues. It was Bird who gave her the name "Margery" in an effort to protect the Crandons' privacy. Under this name, her fame steadily grew.

By bringing Margery to the attention of *Scientific American*, Conan Doyle had inadvertently started the most controversial portion of her career. The panel was deadlocked over whether or not genuine phenomena were occurring in Margery's presence. No one would commit to anything without Houdini's opinion, which was why Orson Munn brought him back into the investigation. Not everyone was happy about this. J. Malcolm Bird who unbelievably, given his opinions about Margery to start with had been assigned to observe, organize and record the investigations. Bird wanted Houdini disqualified from the panel and for this reason, started the investigations without him.

Meanwhile, Houdini traveled to Boston, anxious to see Margery for himself.

On July 23, Houdini called at the Crandon home. He wanted to see Mina perform under the same circumstances that his colleagues had experienced. The medium, meanwhile, relished the idea of converting the notorious debunker to her cause. Some observers saw the séance as an acid test, not just of Margery's authenticity but of Spiritualism itself.

Houdini and Munn booked rooms at the Copley Plaza Hotel, ignoring the offer that the Crandons had made for the two men to join the other members of the committee who were staying at their home. They did accept a dinner invitation from the couple, and found Dr. Crandon to be a gracious host and a fascinating conversationalist. Margery, as they had heard, was a beautiful woman -- attractive, sensuous and confident.

It was so hot that evening that the men -- Crandon, Houdini, Munn, Bird, and R.W. Conant, who worked in the committeeman Comstock's laboratory -- removed their coats in the upstairs séance room. Bird confessed to Houdini that the room itself had never been thoroughly examined. Harry immediately went to work to remedy this sloppy oversight. There was no door to be locked between the room and the hallway leading to the stairs. He inspected the séance props: a megaphone, a three-sided cabinet, a phonograph, which usually played Margery's favorite song "Souvenir" and a bell box. This fourteen-inch-long wooden box contained batteries and a bell. A slight tap on a lever on the top would complete an electrical circuit and the bell would ring.

Margery and the four men sat in chairs forming a circle. She asked them to link hands with one another. The medium was seated between Houdini and her husband. Bird sat outside of the circle, his right hand clasped around the linked hands of Margery and the doctor. Margery's right foot was pressed against her husband's left foot and her left foot was pressed against Houdini's right foot. These body contacts were meant to prove that the medium's hands and feet were "under control" when the manifestations began.

Houdini watched as a spirit bell rang, a voice called out in the darkness, and a megaphone crashed to the floor at his feet. If these manifestations impressed him, he gave no sign of it. When the lights came back on, Houdini politely thanked his hosts and left.

On the drive back to the hotel, he finally spoke about what he was feeling. "I've got her," he said. "All fraud, every bit of it. One more sitting and I will be ready to expose everything."

Houdini was impressed by what he had seen at the Crandon home and very impressed with the famous Margery --- though not by her supernatural powers, he quickly assured Orson Munn. At his hotel that night, he explained how and why his conclusions about Margery differed from those of some members of the panel. One feat that had puzzled the panel was the ringing of the "spirit bell box." Although sitters on either side of her held Margery's hands, and her feet were in contact with theirs, the bell box rang many times during the séance, a happening that she attributed to Walter.

Usually, the bell box sat on the floor between Margery's legs, but Houdini had insisted that it be placed on the floor at his own feet. Regardless, the bell rang repeatedly. Houdini had a ready answer for this: "I had rolled my right trouser leg up above my knee. All that day, I had worn a silk rubber bandage around that leg, just below the knee. By night, the part of the leg below the bandage had become swollen and painfully tender, thus giving me a much keener sense of feeling and making it easier to notice the slightest sliding of Mrs. Crandon's ankle or flexing of her muscles... I could distinctly feel her ankle slowly and spasmodically sliding as it pressed against mine while she gained space to raise her foot off the floor and touch the top of the box." In other words, Margery's foot, and not the spirit of her dead brother, had been responsible for ringing the bell.

Another of the evening's mysteries had involved a megaphone that, according to the spectral voice of Walter, had levitated in the air above the sitter's heads. Walter commanded that Houdini tell him where to throw the object and the magician instructed him to toss it in his direction. Moments later, the megaphone crashed to the floor in front of him. Houdini had an explanation for this, too. Earlier in the evening, when one of Margery's hands was free, she had snatched up the megaphone and had placed it on her head like a dunce cap. In the total darkness of the séance room, no one could have seen her do this. She later made the megaphone fly across the room by simply snapping her head forward. Houdini said: "This is the slickest ruse that I have ever seen..."

The next day, Houdini and Munn returned to Lime Street. In the séance room, alone with the publisher, he demonstrated that his explanations were practical.

In the wake of the first séance, Houdini refused to speak publicly about Margery. He did not reveal his opinions over what had occurred that night. Instead, he asked that more stringent tests be performed. It was rumored that Margery had somehow outwitted Houdini. Rumors also flew that perhaps her powers were genuine after all. Houdini ignored the rumors. He was convinced that he knew the truth.

That night, the tests were resumed in Dr. Comstock's apartment at the Charlesgate Hotel. His secretary, Gladys Wood, searched Margery before the séance and made a statement: "She removed most of her clothes and I examined her and them carefully. She wore a loose green linen dress into the séance room and I examined this carefully before she put it on. She also removed her shoes, and I examined her feet and shoes carefully. She then put her shoes on again. She also took down her hair, which I searched."

Dr. Comstock sat outside the circle recording his observations with a Dictaphone. The events began at 8:45 p.m. Walter's voice called for a card table to be substituted for the heavy table around which the circle had been formed. The card table was put into place with the bell box on top of it.

Background music was supplied by a phonograph and Dr. Comstock noted when it was started and stopped. The first manifestation in the darkened room was the movement of the threefold screen that had been set up behind Margery. At the end of the séance, it was found closed and flat, but still standing upright.

The card table eerily tipped in the dark and swung toward Houdini, but it never fell completely over. At 9:45 p.m., it lurched over sideways, spilling the bell box to the floor. At 10:07, the bell box was put, at Walter's suggestion, between Houdini's feet. At 10:12, the bell rang shrilly three times. Walter shouted for Munn to straighten up. The publisher admitted that he had been bending over. Walter instructed Munn to tell the bell how many times it should ring and it chimed five times at his suggestion. Walter bid the sitters good night and the séance was abruptly over.

Dr. Comstock, Houdini, Munn and Bird went to another room to discuss what had taken place. Houdini said that he had released his grip on Munn's hand in the dark and had reached under the table when it was tilting. He felt Margery's hand, lifting it. He had quickly pulled his hand away and reached for Munn's ear in the dark. He leaned over and whispered, "Shall I denounce and expose her now?" The publisher whispered that he should wait.

Houdini, who had rolled up his trouser leg again, revealed that Margery's stocking had caught on the garter of his right stocking. When she complained that the buckle was hurting her, he had unfastened it. After that, he could feel her leg moving as it extended toward the bell box.

Harry was all for calling the newspapers immediately and exposing Margery as a fraud. The other men voted him down.

Munn and Houdini took the night train to New York. Bird stayed on as the Crandons' guest. During the trip, Munn told Harry that the September issue of the magazine had already gone to press, carrying an article by Bird praising Margery's mediumship. Houdini advised him to stop the presses. When the public learned that Margery was a fraud, the article would be embarrassing to the prestigious magazine. At first, Munn objected to the cost of remaking the issue, but he finally agreed to do it and the Bird article was removed.

Houdini was not the only member of the committee bothered by Bird's actions and writings. Dr. Walter Franklin Prince was also disturbed by Bird's early articles in *Scientific American* lauding Margery's gifts. He and Houdini were even more annoyed by his statements to the press. Bird was not a committee member; he was an employee of the magazine. Both men believed that the committee should be independent of the publication. They met with Munn and voiced their complaints.

Munn said that if Margery was using trickery, as Houdini claimed, the committee had to prove this to the public. Houdini was given the assignment of constructing a device that would prevent the medium from using her head, hands, and feet in the manner that he described.

Harry set about making plans for additional séances. To assure proper control at future sittings, Houdini designed a special "fraud preventer" cabinet, a crate with a slanted top that had openings at the top and sides for the medium's head and arms. Once inside, Margery's movements --- and her chances for deception --- would be severely limited. Reluctantly, Margery agreed to conduct a séance from inside the cabinet, but not before Houdini and her husband exchanged such harsh words that they nearly came to blows. Dr. Crandon had earlier boasted to Sir Arthur Conan Doyle that he was willing to "crucify" any investigator who doubted his wife. Needless to say, Houdini was high on his list of potential victims.

J. Malcolm Bird offered to take Houdini's "fraud-preventer" to Boston in his car, but Harry, trusting no one, replied that he would transport it himself. He and Collins, his assistant, lugged it to Dr. Comstock's apartment early on the morning of August 25, 1924. It was an odd-shaped box that might have been a storage crate for an old-style roll top desk. There was ample room inside for the medium to sit comfortably on a chair. Semicircular holes were cut out of the hinged front and top panel so that when the cabinet was closed, a hole was created to circle the occupant's neck. Her hands were extended through holes in the cabinet sides so that committeemen could "control" them. Provision was also made for panels of wood to be nailed over the side openings should the committee wish to test her with her hands inside the box.

After the Crandons inspected the box, they withdrew and held a hasty conference. When they returned, the doctor insisted that Margery be allowed to try out in the device with her friends before she submitted to the committee's test. Reluctantly, the committee agreed.

The first séance with the cabinet was held behind closed doors as the investigators waited in another room. In thirty minutes, Dr. Crandon ushered his friends out and allowed the committee into the room. Bird, who was not present at the séance, wrote one version of what happened. Houdini, who was actually present, offered another. Both agreed that the sloped front of the box broke open in the dark. Dr. Crandon stated that Walter was responsible. Houdini said that Margery forced it open with her shoulders as it had only been held in place by two narrow strips of brass. With the front open, Margery could have leaned forward and reached the bell box, which was on a table in front of her, with her head.

The argument between Houdini and the Crandons became so heated that Walter's voice called out for peace and quiet. Margery's friends rushed into the room to replace the investigators and "psychic harmony" was temporarily restored. When the committee members were invited to return, Walter demanded to know how much Harry was being paid to stop the phenomena in the séance room. Houdini replied that he was actually losing money since he had to pass up a theater date in Buffalo to come to Boston for the séance. The séance then continued, but no manifestations were produced.

Eventually, Walter told Dr. Comstock to take the bell box under a light and examine it. Walter insisted that Houdini had done something to the bell so that it would not ring. An examination of the bell revealed that a piece of rubber had been wedged against the clapper, rendering it inoperable. Outraged, Dr. Crandon accused the magician of trying to sabotage the proceedings, a charge that Houdini repeatedly denied.

The committee members were angry. Even if he had not tampered with the bell box, they stated that Houdini had not managed to build a "fraud-proof box" as he claimed he would do. Harry replied that he hadn't expected Margery to break out of it. He vowed that he would have the box in proper condition for the séance the next night.

As for the rubber wedge, he said Margery or her friends must have put it there to try and discredit him.

For the second séance, the box was heavily reinforced. Four staples, hasps and padlocks had been added. Unexpectedly, J. Malcolm Bird showed up for the session. Munn had told him to stay away from the hotel and Bird wanted to know why. Houdini and Dr. Prince were more than happy to enlighten him: Bird had given the Crandons information about the committee's findings in July and had also released unauthorized statements to the press. Before he was escorted from the hotel suite, he was allowed to formally resign as secretary for the committee.

Once again, Bird and Houdini told different stories about what occurred at the August 26 séance. Bird, who still believed in the authenticity of Margery's mediumship, but who was not present, said Houdini was satisfied by a search conducted by a woman of Margery's body and clothing. Houdini, on the other hand, wrote that he had objected to the superficial examination that was carried out. But Dr. Crandon would not permit a physician to be called for a more thorough inspection of his wife's anatomy.

The record of the séance was lacking in some important details. Apparently a pillow was placed under Margery's feet in the box, but it was not known who suggested this to be done or who actually put the pillow there.

Houdini held Margery's left hand as it was extended from the box. On the other side, Dr. Prince took her right hand. This was an important change as prior to this, Dr. Crandon had always controlled his wife's right hand. Harry repeatedly cautioned Dr. Prince not to release Margery's hand, not even for a moment.

Margery asked why he made such an issue of this. Harry replied, "I'll tell you, in case you have smuggled anything into the cabinet box you cannot conceal it as both your hands are secured and as far as they are concerned, you are helpless."

"Do you want to search me?" Margery asked.

"No, never mind, let it go," he replied. "I am not a physician."

Walter's voice sounded in the room. "Houdini, you are clever indeed, but it won't work."

Walter claimed that there was collapsible carpenter's ruler under the pillow on which Margery rested her feet. While Houdini had not been in the room just prior to the sitting, Walter said that Collins, Houdini's assistant had been, insinuating that Houdini arranged to have it hidden there. His voice became loud and abusive, "Houdini, you God damned bastard, get the hell out of here and never come back! If you don't, I will!"

The box was unlocked and a carpenter's ruler, two feet long and folded into six-inch sections, was found tucked under the pillow. Dr. Comstock suggested that it had been left there when the box was being repaired. Orson Munn brought Collins into the room to be questioned. Collins said that his ruler was still in his pocket and he pulled it out to show them.

Houdini dictated a statement to the stenographer who was present: "I wish it recorded that I demanded Collins to take a sacred oath on the life of his mother that he did not put the ruler in the box and knew positively nothing about it. I also pledge my sacred word of honor as a man that the first I knew of the ruler in the box was when I was informed so by Walter."

In Houdini's opinion, the folding ruler had been planted in the box in order to make him look bad. He swore that he had not put it there and the Crandons denied they were responsible. They blamed Houdini and he blamed them. He resented anyone that would take their word --- and especially the word of Walter, the spirit guide --- over his.

No one knows how the ruler ended up in the box. In his biography of Houdini, author William Lindsay Gresham quoted Collins as admitting, years later, that he had hidden the ruler in the box on Houdini's instructions. The source of the story, although not given by Gresham, was Fred Keating, a magician who had been a guest of the Crandons in the house on Lime Street at the time Hereward Carrington was investigating Margery. Keating, however, was biased against Houdini. Several days before Gresham interviewed him, Keating had seen an unpublished manuscript in which Houdini, while praising Keating as a magician, commented in unflattering terms about Keating's skills as a psychical investigator. Author Milbourne Christopher believed that the story of Collins' so-called "confession" was sheer fiction.

Unfortunately, the investigators did not thoroughly rule out all possibilities of fraud. If the ruler had been taken to a laboratory for analysis, fingerprints might have been found to show who had last handled it. The *Scientific American* committee, however, was not that scientific.

On the day of the third and final August séance, Munn, Prince, Houdini and the Crandons had dinner together. Houdini later wrote that Margery said she had heard he planned to denounce her from the stage of Keith's Theater. If he did, she said, her friends would give him a thrashing. She didn't want her son to read someday that his mother was a fraud.

Houdini, who usually had a soft spot for mothers, was unmoved by her words. "Then don't be a fraud," he coldly told her.

Dr. Comstock brought a medium-control device of his own that night. It was a shallow wooden box into which Margery and an investigator, sitting face-to-face, put their feet. A board was locked in place over their knees. The sides of the box were open, except at the bottom and top so the restraint wouldn't interfere with a "psychic structure." When the medium's hands were held, and the bell box was on the floor by the box, she was under excellent control.

According to Houdini's account, while the committee waited for the bell to ring and other manifestations to occur, Dr. Crandon turned to him and spoke, "Someday, Houdini, you will see the light, and if it were to occur this evening, I would gladly give $10,000 to charity."

Harry replied, "It may happen, but I doubt it."

The doctor repeated. "If you were converted this evening I would willingly give $10,000 to charity."

Dr. Comstock's fraud control was effective. When Margery's hands were held by someone other than her husband, and while her hands and feet were immobilized, no spirit phenomena were produced. Nothing of interest occurred that night.

Houdini had not been converted and Dr. Crandon still had his $10,000.

The aftermath of the Margery séances was troubling for everyone involved. There were many, including some of the committee, who believed that Houdini had been the one who was caught cheating this time. He was widely discredited for it, leading some to doubt the integrity of some of his earlier investigations. In any case, *Scientific American* finally declined to grant the prize to Margery, in large part because of Houdini's exposure. The confrontational magician had quarreled, often violently, with every member of the committee. J. Malcolm Bird, whom Houdini suspected of active collusion with the Crandons, was angry with the magician and he continued to insist Harry should have been disqualified at the very beginning.

Houdini further outraged Bird, the Crandons and their supporters when he published a small book called "Houdini Exposes the Tricks Used by the Boston Medium Margery." He was adamant about the fact that Margery was doing nothing more than offering clever tricks. In his final verdict, he wrote: "My decision is, that everything which took place at the séances which I attended was a deliberate and conscious fraud..."

From the other side, Walter chimed in his final disparaging words about Houdini. He ended them with a prediction: the magician would be dead within a year. Houdini managed to defy this prophecy, but not by much. He died in 1926 and in an interview with the press, Margery had only good things to say about the magician, praising him for his virile personality and great determination.

Despite Houdini's exposure, Margery emerged from the debacle relatively unscathed. She continued her séances and by the end of 1924, she had begun to produce even greater manifestations, including "spirit arms" that rang the bell box and caused objects to fly about in the séance room.

In 1925, J. Malcolm Bird published a book that supported Margery and as the research officer of the American Society for Psychical Research, he was able to sway many other ASPR members to her side. They became her greatest supporters and devoted hundreds of pages in the ASPR journal to her séances.

Eric J. Dingwall, an officer of the Society for Psychical Research in England, read of his American colleagues' support, and decided to investigate the medium for himself. He wanted to see the ectoplasm that Margery was manifesting and Dr. Crandon allowed him to view it by the light of a red lamp, which Crandon flashed on and off to reveal quick glimpses of the substance. Too much light, Dr. Crandon said, would have an inhibiting effect on the mysterious material, said to be the manifestation of spirit emanations. Dingwall wrote to a friend: "The materialized hands are connected by an umbilical cord to the medium. They seize upon objects and displace them. Later, when he was permitted to grasp one of the "ghost hands," he described it as feeling like "a piece of cold raw beef or possibly a piece of soft, wet rubber."

Halfway through his investigations, Dingwall began having doubts. Dr. Crandon's red lamp never allowed him to see the ectoplasm actually emanating from Margery's body. He had only seen it after the fact. Odder still, many of the photographs revealed that a large number of the emanations seemed to be hanging from slender, almost invisible threads. Others who looked at the photos said that the "hands" looked suspiciously like animal lung tissue, a substance that Dr. Crandon could have obtained through his work at Boston hospitals. Dingwall's final report on the case was inconclusive.

As usual, Margery was unconcerned. Sitters continued to file into the séance room at the Crandons' Lime Street home. One investigation after another raised allegations of fraud but no one was ever able to make the accusations stick. Even J.B. Rhine, who would later become one the foremost personalities in paranormal research, was intrigued by Margery but was unimpressed with what he saw. As always, though, Conan Doyle defended the medium and when Rhine published an unflattering account of his experiences with Margery, Sir Arthur bought space in several Boston newspapers to run a reply. The black-bordered message read simply: "J.B. Rhine is an ass."

In 1928, Margery began to develop a highly unusual manifestation that made her even more widely known in Spiritualist circles. On the table in front of her during a séance would be placed two dishes containing water, one hot and the other cold. In the first dish was a piece of dental wax. When the wax was softened, it was claimed that Margery's spirit guide, Walter, would make an impression of his thumb on it. Then, the thumbprint was put into cold water to harden. The prints appeared mysteriously on the same night that Margery obtained the wax from her dentist. A so-called fingerprint expert called in by the Crandons stated that the thumbprint matched one that was taken from an old razor that once belonged to Walter Stinson.

Margery had confounded the skeptics and believers were enthralled by this new manifestation. It was as if the spirit was leaving a calling card, but better. The excitement soon came to a crashing end, however.

Psychic researcher E.E. Dudley set out to compare Walter's wax thumbprint with those belonging to regulars at the Crandon séances and made a surprising discovery: Walter's thumbprint was identical to that of Margery's dentist, Dr. Frederick Caldwell. Someone had apparently used a sample thumbprint that Dr. Caldwell made for Margery to create a metal die-stamp that was suitable for making impressions in wax.

This was the end of the ruse. Many of Margery's most devoted followers drifted away. J. Malcolm Bird, once her staunchest defender, admitted that, at times, he had been guilty of elaborations and half-truths about Margery's so-called "wonders." Even Conan Doyle was strangely quiet. The scientific community let it be known that Margery's séances were no longer of interest.

Margery's decline was quick and tragic. After the death of Dr. Crandon in 1939, Mina grew depressed and turned to alcohol for consolation. She began to look older than her years, gained weight and saw her beauty fade away. She continued to hold séances, finding people who still believed in her, and during one sitting, she grew so distraught that she climbed to the roof of her home and threatened to throw herself off. She died at the age of fifty-four in 1941.

Many researchers today believe that some elements of the paranormal were present in Crandon's séances, but just what was genuine and what was not remain unknown. Mina and her husband were known for baiting investigators and trying to fool them if possible. The Crandons never seemed to care who believed them and who did not. Just what secrets did Mina Crandon hold? We'll never know; she took them with her to her grave.

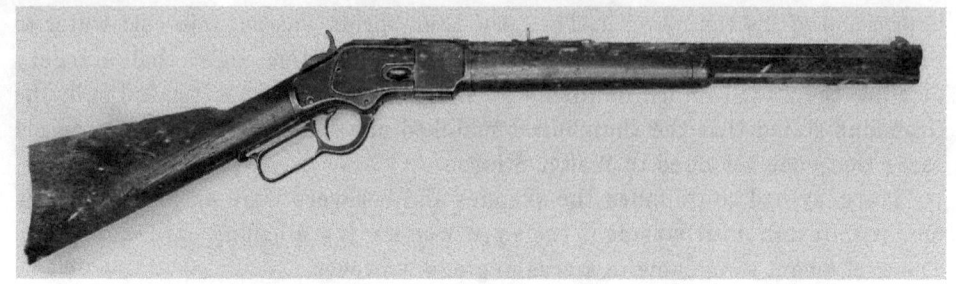

WINCHESTER RIFLE
An Heir to a Fortune Builds a House for the Spirits

A Winchester repeating rifle seems like an odd addition to a collection of objects intended to create a timeline of supernatural history, but in reality, it must have a place of honor. The rifle has a direct connection to a house --- a house that is no ordinary home. It is a place with a richer haunted history, a more mysterious origin and a great connection to the spirit world that anywhere else that I can think of.

The place is known as the Winchester Mystery House in San Jose, California. Most ghost enthusiasts are familiar with the house, but not everyone knows the story behind the story. The house is an enigma. It is a massive structure of which no accurate room count has ever been taken. Doors open to brick walls, staircases lead to nowhere, hallways end at blank walls, secret passages honeycomb parts of the building and all this combines to create a carnival funhouse of gigantic proportions. But why? Who built this fantastic place and for what reason? Why was an ordinary farmhouse turned into a labyrinth? And why did construction here never cease, continuing twenty-four hours a day without letup, for decades?

The story of the mysterious mansion began in September 1839 with the birth of a baby girl to Leonard and Sarah Pardee of New Haven, Connecticut. The baby was named Sarah and as she reached maturity, she became the belle of the city. She was the center of attention at all social events, thanks to her musical skills, her fluency in foreign languages and her sparkling charm. Her petite beauty was also much admired by the young men about town. At four feet, ten inches, she resembled a lovely doll.

At the same time that Sarah was growing up, a young man was also maturing in another prominent New Haven family. The young man's name was William Wirt Winchester and he was the son of Oliver Winchester, a shirt manufacturer and businessman. In 1857, he took over the assets of a bankrupt firm that made the Volcanic Repeater, a rifle that used a lever mechanism to load bullets into the breech.

Obviously, this type of firearm was a vast improvement over the muzzle-loading rifles of recent times, but Winchester still saw room for improvement. In 1860, the company developed the Henry Rifle, which had a tubular magazine located under the barrel. Because it was easy to reload and could fire rapidly, the Henry was said to average one shot every three seconds. It became the first true repeating rifle and a favorite among the Northern troops at the outbreak of the Civil War.

Money began to pour in and Oliver Winchester soon amassed a large fortune from government contracts and private sales. He re-organized the company and changed its name to the Winchester Repeating Arms Company. They soon began producing a new rifle, simply known as the Winchester, which improved on the earlier models. Cartridges were fed into the magazine through a small opening in the breech. It was easy to load and to fire and it became an immediate success, thanks to its fast action and the fact that its ammunition was interchangeable with that of a number of Colt revolvers. In that way, only one supply of ammo was needed for both rifle and pistol.

The family prospered and on September 30, 1862, at the height of the Civil War, William Wirt Winchester and Sarah Pardee were married in an elaborate ceremony in New Haven.

Four years later, on July 15, 1866, Sarah gave birth to a daughter named Annie Pardee Winchester. Just a short time later, the first disaster struck for Sarah, as her baby contracted an illness known as "marasmus," a form of protein deficiency in which the body wastes away. The infant died on July 24. Sarah was so shattered by this event that she teetered on the edge of madness for some time. In the end, it would be nearly a decade before she returned to her normal self. Sadly, she and William would never have another child.

Then, another tragedy struck. William, now heir to the Winchester empire, was struck down with pulmonary tuberculosis. He died on March 7, 1881. As a result of his death, Sarah inherited over $20 million, an incredible sum, especially in those days. She also received 48.9 percent of the Winchester Repeating Arms Company and an income of about $1,000 per day, which was not taxable until 1913, when income taxation went into effect.

But her newfound wealth could do nothing to ease her pain. Sarah grieved deeply, not only for her husband, but also for her lost child. The wound of the infant's death had been opened once more. She locked herself in her room, refused to leave the house, eat properly or take care of herself in any way. Her health began to deteriorate. Friends urged her to leave New England and seek a warmer climate, which would ease the severe arthritis that she had developed.

Sarah refused to go. She did not want to leave the place where her loved ones were buried.

A short time later, a friend suggested that Sarah might wish to speak to a Spiritualist medium. The well-meaning friend suggested that perhaps the medium might be able to ease her suffering and perhaps put her into contact with her late husband. This finally lured Sarah from her home. She attended a service conducted by a Boston medium named Adam Coons.

"Your husband is here," the medium told her and then went on to provide a description of William Winchester. "He says for me to tell you that there is a curse on your family, which took the life of himself and your child. It will soon take you, too. It is a curse that has resulted from the terrible weapon created by the Winchester family. Thousands of persons have died because of it and their spirits are now seeking vengeance."

Sarah was then told that she must sell her property in New Haven and head towards the setting sun. Her husband would guide her and when she found her new home in the West, she would recognize it. "You must start a new life," said the medium, "and build a home for yourself and for the spirits who have fallen from this terrible weapon, too. You can never stop building the house. If you continue building, you will live. Stop and you will die."

Shortly after the séance, Sarah sold her home in New Haven and with a vast fortune at her disposal, moved west to California. She believed that she was guided by the hand of her dead husband and she did not stop traveling until she reached the Santa Clara Valley in 1884. Here, she found a six-room home under construction that belonged to a Dr. Caldwell. She entered into negotiations with him and soon convinced him to sell her the house, along with the 162 acres that surrounded it. She tossed away any previous plans for the house and started building something much more ambitious - and much stranger - than a simple farmhouse. She had her pick of local workers and craftsmen and for the next thirty-six years, they built and rebuilt, altered and changed and constructed and demolished one section of the house after another. She kept twenty-two carpenters at work nonstop. They worked like busy elves, year round, twenty-four hours a day. The sounds of hammering and sawing were heard throughout the day and night.

As the house grew to include twenty-six rooms, railroad cars were switched onto a nearby line to bring building materials and imported furnishings to the house. The structure was rapidly growing and expanding and while Sarah claimed to have no master plan, she met each morning with her foreman and they would go over her hand-sketched plans for the day's work. The plans were often chaotic but showed a real flair for building. Sometimes, though, they would not work out the right way, but Sarah always had a quick solution. If this happened, they would just build another room around an existing one. The foreman could never figure out where his employer got her ideas, but to Sarah, they came quite easily.

One of the first rooms that had been added to the house had been a "séance room." It was located on the second floor in the center of the house and was painted dark blue. It had been designed with no windows and with a single entrance. There was only one key to the room. No one ever entered it but Sarah. She would go into this room and attempt to "commune with the spirits," sitting quietly in meditation until the spirits divulged their structural ideas for the house. She would then ponder these ideas and place them on paper.

Sarah also had a bell tower installed. The tower was very high and virtually unreachable. The bell rope hung down through the inside of the tower to a secret room in the cellar. The room was only accessible through an underground tunnel that was known only to a Japanese servant and his apprentice. The bell ringer carried a finely tuned pocket watch and, in his quarters, was a very expensive chronometer. Each day, he telephoned an astronomical observatory in order to check the accuracy of his timepieces. Sarah believed that time was very important to the ringing of this bell, which she used to contact the spirits.

It was said that the bell tolled each night at midnight, one hour later and then finally at two o'clock in the morning. It remained silent the rest of the time. From her studies of the occult, or perhaps from the spirits themselves, Sarah learned that the element of time was very important in regard to the arrival of visitors from the other world.

As the days, weeks and months passed, the house continued to grow. Rooms were added to rooms and then turned into entire wings, doors were joined to windows, levels turned into towers and peaks and the place eventually grew to a height of seven stories. Inside the house, three elevators were installed, as were forty-seven fireplaces. There were countless staircases that led nowhere; a blind chimney that stopped short of the ceiling; closets that opened to blank walls; trap doors; hallways that doubled back on themselves; skylights that were stacked one atop another; doors that opened to steep drops to the lawn below; and dozens of other oddities. All of the stair posts were installed upside-down and many of the bathrooms had glass doors.

It was also obvious that Sarah was intrigued by the number thirteen. Nearly all of the windows contained thirteen panes of glass; the walls had thirteen panels; the greenhouse had thirteen cupolas; many of the wood floors contained thirteen sections; some of the rooms had thirteen windows and every staircase but one had thirteen steps. This exception is unique in its own right. It is a winding staircase with forty-two steps, which would normally be enough to take a climber up three stories. In this case, however, the stairs only rise nine feet because each step is only two inches high.

While all of this seems like madness to us, it made sense to Sarah. In this way, she could thwart the spirits who came to the house for evil purposes, or who were outlaws or vengeful people in their past life. These bad men, killed by Winchester rifles, could wreak havoc on Sarah. The house had been designed as a maze to confuse and discourage the malevolent spirits.

Each night, at midnight, when the bell summoned Sarah and her spirit guides to the séance room, she would travel down the hallways in a circuitous course that would be sure to confuse any ghost who was following her. Besides the twisting corridors, Sarah also had access to secret panels that opened at the push of a button, windows through which to climb between one room to the next, and staircases that led both up and down to the same level in different parts of the house. She could have easily lost any pursuer, earthly or otherwise.

In addition to trying to confuse the vengeful spirits killed by Winchester rifles, Sarah also made an effort to appease the friendly ones. The house was richly furnished and decorated with gold and silver chandeliers, art glass windows, Belgian crystal, art-molded bronze bathtubs, exquisite marble and wonderful Tiffany glass windows that were said to have cost more than $1,000 each. Two of these windows are located in Sarah's ballroom and are engraved with two quotes from Shakespeare: "Wide unclasp the tables of their thoughts" and "These same thoughts people this little world." The significance of these two quotations was known only to Sarah and remains a mystery today.

After her death, vast warehouses were discovered on the property that were found to contain supplies and fixtures that would have later been incorporated into the house. Among the pieces were elaborate light fixtures, ornate hardware, art glass windows and doors, wooden doors of cedar, oak, walnut, maple and mahogany, floor tiles, plumbing; and much more. Sarah had carefully cataloged all of it.

In addition to its eccentricity and the rich decor, the house also had a number of innovations that were far ahead of their time. In the laundry room, the wash trays had fitted washboards and center tubs to make laundering easier. The house was fitted with a hot water heater that warmed the water for all of the indoor plumbing. A thermostatically controlled shower was fitted into one bathroom that sprayed water from all directions. Sarah invented a crank that would open and close windows from the inside, like that used in several top-end brands of windows today. The house had electricity and its own private gas plant, along with an extensive burglar alarm system and a heated spa that was designed to ease the pain of Sarah's arthritis. This room was designed with several fireplaces, large windows to let in the sun and numerous radiator vents. The heat generated here was her greatest remedy for aching joints.

Needless to say, the frenzied building that was going on at the house did not exactly earn Sarah a good reputation in town. The stories carried home by the workmen about their eccentric employer would have been enough to raise many eyebrows. She went out of her way to have her groundskeepers plant large bushes along the property line, hoping to keep out the stares of the curious. In all of the years she lived in the house, she was observed in town only one time.

Because she never went calling on her neighbors, she did not expect people to call on her. In fact, she did not want anyone, save for the workmen, to enter her home. Any curiosity-seeker, or even well-meaning local, who approached the house was quickly turned away by one of the servants. Eventually, the front door was ordered locked and boarded up and was never used again.

And Sarah did not discriminate when it came to turning away visitors, whether they were famous or not. One such caller was President Theodore Roosevelt, a Winchester rifle and hunting enthusiast. He came to the house while on a Western tour, but it is unknown whether he ever spoke with Sarah. His entourage was conducted to the rear carriage house, which had been designed so that Sarah's horse and buggy could actually drive into the mansion. There were several doors from the carriage area that led into various passageways, although one of them was only five feet high, a private entrance for the diminutive Sarah. Roosevelt managed to get into the house, but no record remains as to whether he met Sarah. Some visitors were not even that lucky. Christian Science founder Mary Baker Eddy was turned away at the gate.

The house continued to grow and by 1906, it had reached a towering seven stories tall. Sarah continued her occupancy, and expansion, of the house, living in melancholy solitude with no one other than her servants, the workmen and, of course, the spirits. It was said that on sleepless nights, when she was not communing with the spirit world, Sarah would play her grand piano into the early hours of the morning. According to legend, the music would be admired by passersby on the street outside, despite the fact that two of the keys were badly out of tune.

Because of the number of bedrooms in the house, Sarah would often sleep in a different one each night. She did have a particular favorite, though, and it became a place where she often spent the daylight hours also. She called it the "Daisy Room," because of the daisies that had been cast into the stained glass windows. It was located on the second floor and here, Sarah would often sit and watch the horse-drawn traffic pass by on the street outside. She often slept here at night, napping in the hours before midnight and returning here after her sessions with the spirit architects were completed. She loved this room very much -- or at least she did until the early morning of April 18, 1906.

Shortly after 5 a.m., Sarah was dozing when she was suddenly awakened by the bed shaking. In the dim light of the gas lamp, she saw the walls of the room begin to crack. The furniture began to shake and books and glass ornaments fell to the floor from shelves and tables. Then, with horror, she saw the plaster ceiling start to crumble and collapse. She was certain that the spirits of those killed by the Winchester rifles had finally come to claim her soul!

The house began to collapse, sending wood and plaster down into the room. Sarah struggled to get to the door and escape into the corridor, but her path was blocked by debris. Terrified, she ran to the internal communication system that she had installed in the maze-like house. She would call on her servants to save her. The intercom recorded her call, but not where she was. Finally, frightened and hysterical, Sarah fainted, sure that the vengeful spirits had come for her.

The great San Francisco Earthquake of 1906 had struck. When it was all over, portions of the Winchester Mansion were nearly in ruins. The top three floors of the house had collapsed into the gardens and would never be rebuilt.

Hours passed before the servants and workmen were able to free Sarah from the Daisy Room. When they found her, she was a trembling wreck. She would never set foot in that bedroom again. She ordered it boarded up and sealed off. The room would never be used again during Sarah's lifetime and her private belongings, bedding and furniture were left just as they were.

For the next several months, the workmen toiled to repair the damage done by the earthquake, although surprisingly, the mammoth structure had fared far better than most of the buildings in the area. Only a few of the rooms had been badly damaged, although it had lost the highest floors and several cupolas and towers had toppled over.

Expansion on the house began once more. The number of bedrooms increased from fifteen to twenty and then to twenty-five. Chimneys were installed all over the place, although strangely, they served no purpose. Some believe that perhaps they were added because the old stories say that ghosts like to appear and disappear through them. On a related note, it has also been documented that only two mirrors were installed in the house. Sarah believed that ghosts were afraid of their own reflection.

Throughout the construction of the house, Sarah was always concerned about security. Besides having a burglar alarm, she had locks installed so that every door required a key to open it. It was said that the number of keys needed for the house filled three large buckets. One has to wonder if so many locks were really necessary. Rumors claimed that the Winchester Mansion was filled with treasure, gold and cash, yet no one ever attempted to rob the place. Imagine a bandit who slipped inside one night and entered the bizarre labyrinth of Sarah's mansion! In this case, the house's reputation as an impenetrable maze served a very useful purpose.

In addition to the vast expanse of the house, Sarah also had a wonderful wine cellar constructed. She enjoyed sipping imported wines and liqueurs and it was said that her cellar was unequalled on the West Coast.

One afternoon, she went down to the wine cellar and moments later, came running back upstairs, screaming all the way. On the cellar wall, she had discovered the black imprint of a large hand that she was sure had been left there as a warning from the spirit world. The servants tried to explain to her that the handprint had been there for years and had been left by one of the workmen but Sarah refused to listen. Leaving the cellar exactly as it was, she had the entrance bricked over and then hidden by so many other structures that the treasure trove of wine has never been found.

On September 4, 1922, after a conference session with the spirits in the séance room, Sarah went to her bedroom for the night. At some point in the early morning hours, she died in her sleep at the age of 83. She left all of her possessions to her niece, France Marriott, who had been handling most of Sarah's business affairs for some time. In her will, Sarah had a couple of unusual requests. She asked that her casket be carried out of the house through the back door, consistent with her refusal to use the front entrance. She also requested that all subsequent owners of the house allow the ghosts to be welcome there and that they keep the property in good repair and tell all visitors about Sarah's project.

Little did anyone know, but by this time, Sarah's formerly large bank account had dwindled considerably. Rumor had it that somewhere in the house was hidden a safe containing a fortune in jewelry and a solid-gold dinner service with which Sarah had entertained her ghostly guests. Her relatives forced open a number of safes but found only old fishing lines, socks, newspaper clippings about her daughter's and her husband's deaths, a lock of baby hair, and a suit of woolen underwear. No solid gold dinner service was ever discovered.

The furnishings, personal belongings and surplus construction and decorative materials were removed from the house and the structure itself was sold to a group of investors who planned to run it as a tourist attraction. One of the first to see the place when it opened to the public was Robert L. Ripley, who featured the house in his syndicated newspaper column, "Believe it or Not."

The house was initially advertised as having 148 rooms, but so confusing was the floor plan that every time a room count was taken, a different total came up. The place was so puzzling that it was said that workmen took more than six weeks just to get the furniture out of it. The moving men became lost because it was a "labyrinth," they told the magazine, *American Weekly*, in 1928. It was a house "where downstairs leads neither to the cellar nor upstairs to the roof." The rooms of the house were counted over and over again and five years later, it was estimated that 160 existed, although no one is really sure if that is correct.

Today, the house has been declared a California Historical Landmark and is registered with the National Park Service as "a large, odd dwelling with an unknown number of rooms."

Most would say that such a place must still harbor at least a few of the ghosts who came to reside there at the invitation of Sarah Winchester. The question is, do they really haunt the place? Some would say that perhaps no ghosts ever walked there at all, that the Winchester Mansion is nothing more than the product of a bereaved woman's unstable mind and too much wealth being allowed into the wrong hands. Others feel differently, believing wholeheartedly that the house remains haunted.

In 1975, just one year after the house was placed on the National Register of Historic Places, Keith Kittle, who was the manager of the property, invited Jeanne Borgen to visit. She was, at that time, a well-respected psychic and Kittle thought that her visit would make a great publicity stunt for the Halloween season. He really didn't expect anything to come of it, but it would garner a lot of attention for the house. Shortly after arriving, the psychic held a press conference and when asked if there were ghosts in the house, she said that she had already seen one that morning. She also planned to hold a late night séance two evenings later.

When the time came for the séance, she chose one of Sarah's bedrooms for the event. A table was set up and another psychic, Joy Adams, sat down while Borgen paced back and forth, trying to locate cold spots. She said that all questions for the spirits should be directed to Adams, who by this time, had entered a trance-like state.

One of the reporters spoke up and asked if she liked living in the house. When the answer came from the mouth of Joy Adam's, it was in the voice of a much older woman. "Yes, I love it very much," she said and began to laugh, explaining that she had just remembered some of the wonderful things that had happened while staying in the house with her spirit friends. Then, she suddenly stopped laughing and said, rather sharply, "The townspeople. They always talk about me."

While Joy Adams was talking, Jeanne Borgen was walking about the room with her hands outstretched, hoping to encounter patches of frigid air that would indicate the presence of spirits. She suddenly stopped and pointed at one of the reporters. According to witnesses, the previously clean-shaven man suddenly sported a spectral beard. He complained of being cold, while another reporter cried out that he felt hands pushing downward on his shoulders.

The witnesses also said that Borgen's face suddenly appeared to age before their eyes. Her hair appeared to turn gray and her face became etched with lines.

In moments, she was unable to stand and appeared to be suffering a heart attack. It only lasted for a moment and then was gone.

When it was over, Borgen stated that Sarah Winchester had graced them with her presence and that the discomfort that she had felt was due to the fact that there were so many people in the room. After all, Sarah had closely guarded her privacy.

In 1979, authors Richard Winer and Nancy Osborn visited the Winchester House while doing research for a book about haunted places. They got permission to spend the night there from Keith Kittle. They originally planned to sleep in the séance room, but were pointed to another room by one of the tour guides.

"It's the Daisy Room in the front that frightens me," the guide told them. "That's the room where Sarah Winchester was trapped during the 1906 earthquake." The guide really couldn't pinpoint any particular thing about the room which disconcerted her, but she did say that sometimes the room would get very cold, but only in certain places.

With that in mind, Winer and Osborn decided to bed down on mats in what was once Sarah's favorite bedroom. They had not been there very long when Winer discovered an area of the room that was much colder than the surrounding atmosphere. Thinking that it might be a draft, he searched for a place where the wind might be coming from but could find nothing. He realized too that the cold air was not moving. It was perfectly still and it was occupying an area that would roughly be the size of a human body.

Convinced they were not alone in the room, they eventually laid down and went to sleep, but they wouldn't stay that way for long. Just after two in the morning, Nancy shook Winer awake. "Wake up! Do you hear it?"

It was the sound of piano music, being played quite beautifully, except for the fact that two of the keys were flat. "Sarah Winchester's piano was supposed to have two flat keys," Winer said.

A short time later, they heard the sound of footsteps walking down the hallway outside the bedroom. They looked to see who was there but found nothing. After that, neither one of them slept for the rest of the night.

The strange events at the Winchester House continued for many years and still continue today. Dozens of psychics have visited the house over the years and most have come away convinced, or they claim to be convinced, that spirits still wander the place. In addition to the ghost of Sarah Winchester, there have also been many other sightings throughout the years.

But more compelling than the claims of psychics are the strange stories passed on by staff members who work in the house. A number of years ago, a woman named Sue Sales took a tour through the house and encountered a small, gray-haired lady seated in the kitchen. At the end of the tour, she asked the guide about the lady dressed as Sarah Winchester and why this cleverly costumed woman had not been pointed out. The guide told her that there had been no one dressed in costume that day.

One night in 1979, several employees were buffing the floors on the second level of the house when they heard footsteps on the floor above them. They were the only ones in the building at the time.

In January 1981, Allen Weitzel was locking up the house for the night and as he walked the entire route of the tour, he shut down the lights as he went. He then locked the doors and walked out to the parking lot to get into his car. When he turned and looked back at the house, all of the lights on the third floor had been turned on again.

A security guard once admitted that they often have a lot of false alarms at the house, with the security system being tripped, even though no one is ever found inside. Strangely, when they go to investigate, the alarms are usually found to have been triggered from the inside, even though the exterior alarms have not gone off. In other words, someone, or something, is moving about inside the mansion, even though there is no way that they could have gotten inside.

One summer afternoon, a tour guide named Gina Anging was on the third floor when the door to the servant's call station somehow slammed shut. There was no wind that could have closed the door and no one else was on that floor at that time. Gina could offer no explanation for what happened.

One evening, a tour supervisor named Mike Bray was closing the house for the night. He was walking down an upstairs hallway when he heard the distinct sound of someone whispering his name. He searched all over for someone else in the house, but this occurred at the end of the day and the rest of the staff members had already left.

Another tour guide, Amy Kinsch, was sweeping the floor in the front kitchen when she caught the overpowering scent of chicken soup. She realized quickly that this wasn't possible, for she was certainly not cooking soup, and she went in search of where the odor was coming from. The closest possible source was the caretaker's rooms, but once she walked toward them, she could no longer smell the soup. The event remained mysterious, even after another guide had an identical experience about six months later.

There have been a number of strange events reported at the Winchester House for many years and they continue to be reported today. In addition to the ghost of Sarah Winchester, there have also been many other sightings, as well.

In the years that the house has been open to the public, employees and visitors alike have had unusual encounters here. There have been footsteps; banging doors; mysterious voices; windows that bang shut so hard they shatter; cold spots; strange moving lights; doorknobs that turn by themselves and don't forget the scores of psychics who have their own claims of phenomena to report.

Obviously, these are all of the standard reports of a haunted house, but are the stories merely wishful thinking, reports of ghosts and spirits to continue the tradition of Sarah Winchester's bizarre legacy? Or could the stories be true? Was the house really built as a monument to the dead? Do phantoms still lurk in the maze-like corridors of the Winchester Mystery House?

I urge you to visit the house if you should ever get the chance. I can promise that you will find not another piece of American architecture like the Winchester Mansion - and who knows what else you might find while you're there?

A SMALL BELL
The Making of the Modern Ghost Hunter

During the latter part of the nineteenth century, as Spiritualism was becoming more and more a part of the mainstream in American culture, the need grew for psychical investigation. Science, skeptics and even ordinary people demanded methods by which the claims of the spirit mediums could be tested. Were they truly making contact with the dead?

Scientific and amateur groups were formed, like the Society for Psychical Research SPR and its American counterpart, to look into the activity that was allegedly being manifested by mediums. Soon, though, investigations began to focus less on mediums and Spiritualists and more on hauntings, setting the standard for the ghost hunters to come. The early investigators established the need to question the evidence of ghosts, ruling out all possible natural explanations for the activity before accepting that it might possibly be real.

It was during this period, in the early twentieth century, that a man emerged whom I like to refer to as the "original ghost hunter." He was not the first to examine the possibilities of ghosts but he was probably the most influential person in the field of paranormal investigation, as we know it today. This man's name was Harry Price and although disliked and distrusted by many, there is no denying that he was one of the most influential figures in the formative years of ghost research. He was a highly charismatic personality whose energy and enthusiasm for the paranormal made him the first "celebrity ghost hunter." Price was instrumental in bringing ghost research to the general public, realizing that only by making the research entertaining could he attract the attention of the masses. Because of this, after his death in 1948, jealous "colleagues" would attack not only Price's research, but also the man himself, staining his reputation for years to come.

Price was regarded as an embarrassment during his time and effects of the criticisms heaped on him still linger today. Despite more recent work supporting his claims and methods, many British researchers still regard Price as something of an enigma. Because of his flamboyant manner and continuous self-promotion, Price made a number of enemies within the psychical research field. Much of the resentment revolved around that fact that Price had no real scientific training but was still so skillful at what he did. Price was a deft magician and an expert at detecting fraud, so he was not taken in by many of the fraudulent mediums that plagued paranormal research of the time. His success was a slap in the face to many of the established psychical researchers with scientific credentials.

Regardless of this, his work is considered groundbreaking for many today and his investigations at the house known as Borley Rectory became some of the first documented attempts to track down the ghosts of a single haunted location. Price first emerged in the volatile climate of the 1920s, when men like Harry Houdini were also investigating the claims of mediums in the midst of great controversy. When Price came on the scene, he also began making a name for himself -- and began to make many enemies as well.

Harry Price was born in London in 1881, the son of a grocer and traveling salesman. His interest in the paranormal began in 1889 when he saw his first performance by a stage magician. From that point on, he became an amateur conjurer and began collecting what would become an immense library of books on magic.

Price had his first encounter with the supernatural at age fifteen, when he and a friend locked themselves overnight in a reportedly haunted house. After hearing noises in an upstairs room that they could not explain, and listening to what appeared to be footsteps on the staircase, they set up an old-fashioned powder-flash camera at the bottom of the stairs. About an hour later, they clearly heard the footsteps descending the stairs again and fired the camera. When the plate was developed, it showed nothing but an empty staircase. Price would always consider this his first encounter with a ghost.

After graduating from school, Price worked at a number of jobs, including as a journalist. In 1908, he met and married a wealthy heiress named Constance

Mary Knight. He then settled down to become an independently wealthy ghost hunter, which would allow him to pursue his interests around the world.

By the time that Price joined the Society for Psychical Research in 1920, he had already begun his career as Britain's most famous ghost investigator. He had spent many hours at alleged haunted houses and in the investigation of Spiritualist mediums. He was by then an expert magician and soon distinguished himself within the SPR for using his magic skills to debunk fraudulent psychics, which was in keeping with the main thrust of the SPR's investigations at the time.

One of Price's first efforts exposed the work of spirit photographer William Hope, who was making a fortune taking portraits of people that always seemed to include the sitter's dead relatives. Price was sent to investigate and soon published his findings. He claimed that Hope used pre-exposed plates in his camera, which Price found out by secretly switching the plates the photographer was using with plates of his own.

It was only chance that led Price into another aspect of his career. One afternoon, while taking the train from London to his West Sussex country home near Pulborough, Price met Dorothy Cranshaw, a twenty-two-year-old hospital nurse who went by her middle name of Stella. The two happened to strike up a conversation about psychic anomalies during which Stella told the investigator that she had been experiencing strange phenomena for years. She said that rapping noises, cold chills and household objects inexplicably taking flight had been bothering her for some time. Price, excited at the prospect of a new test subject, told her that he was a psychic investigator and asked if she would submit to being tested as a medium. Stella agreed and a series of séances were scheduled at the London Spiritualist Alliance, where Price had offices. Stella was given a modest payment for her time since she was required to take off work in the afternoons to come to the sittings.

The first séance brought some surprises: namely that Stella, who had never considered herself a medium, had a spirit control that came through to the sitters. The spirit guide, "Palma," communicated by rapping and would follow requests, like moving a heavy oak table in various directions around the room. At the same séance, thermometers recorded rapid temperature drops. These swift temperature changes would become a staple of Stella's séances.

Price brought a number of devices into the séance room in an effort to study the phenomena scientifically. One of the regular sitters, H.W. Pugh, built a special double table with the inner portion made of a wire mesh cage where items that were to be manipulated could be placed without the possibility of being tampered with. The first time that the table was used, several musical instruments were placed inside and a rattle was somehow thrown out of the closed cage.

Price, being an amateur inventor, designed new equipment of his own to test the young woman's abilities. One of them was the "telekinetoscope," a clever device that used a telegraph key that, when depressed, would cause a red light to turn on. A glass dome covered the key so that it could not be physically manipulated. The intention was that only psychic powers could operate it. During the séances, the red light occasionally turned on.

During the sittings, always conducted in front of witnesses, Stella managed to produce all sorts of strange, physical phenomena. During one séance, she managed to levitate a table so high that the sitters had to rise out of their chairs to keep their hands upon it. Suddenly, three of the table legs broke away and the table folded and collapsed! Needless to say, this ended the sitting.

The first series of séances ran for eleven sittings and was finally stopped by Stella, who was exhausted by the weekly trials. She often grew very tired during the séances, her pulse would race and the sudden drops in temperature caused her to shake uncontrollably. She saw a doctor about her exhaustion and he recommended that she rest. Her exhaustion, and her frequent absences from work, caused her to lose her job at the hospital where she was employed.

Price also suffered because of the séances with Stella. He had a background in conjuring and had only recently entered into psychical research. His fellow magicians criticized him for taking Stella's phenomena seriously. In addition, he was criticized from the other side of his research, as well. The SPR was uncomfortable with Price's affiliation with the London Spiritualist Alliance, feeling that it was too closely aligned with the Spiritualist community. Even though an SPR officer had attended Stella's sittings, SPR leaders convinced Price that any further séances should be held at their headquarters.

It was with some difficulty that Price was able to convince Stella to continue the experiments. She had found a secretarial job with a manufacturing company and was reluctant to jeopardize her new employment. Finally, she agreed to two more séances in late 1923. After this, she ended her association with Price. Their relationship, which had been warm, now turned chilly, for reasons that are not altogether clear. Stella publicly pleaded fatigue but different reasons are suggested in a letter that she wrote to Price in 1926. By this time, whatever had occurred was forgotten and Stella began working with Price again after an absence of three years. In her letter, she apologized and stated that she had "badly misjudged" him in 1923.

The 1926 sittings were held at Price's National Laboratory for Psychical Research, which had just been established at the London Spiritualist Alliance. The phenomena surrounding Stella were similar to what they had been, although weaker than a few years before. She offered fourteen séances before bringing things to an end in August. She returned to work with Price again in 1927, so that he could study the anomalous temperature drops, and participated in a series of nine final sittings with him in 1928, shortly before she was married.

Stella married Leslie Deacon in August 1928, at which point she brought her career as a medium to an end. She never worked professionally and all of her sittings were conducted with Harry Price. What became of her later in life is unknown but she is believed to have lived into her sixties, spending the remainder of her life in London.

In the end, Stella's career as a medium turned out to be short-lived but the careful research into her abilities earned her great respect in psychical circles and also earned prestige and respectability for Price.

During a break between sessions with Stella, Price began searching for other mediums to investigate. He traveled to Munich for a series of sittings with Willi Schneider at the laboratory of Baron Albert von Schreck-Notzing. Price was so impressed with what he saw during the séances that he invited Willi to his own laboratories. He was also impressed with the publicity-seeking methods of von Schreck-Notzing and decided to emulate him in his own career.

Soon, Price began testing additional mediums and set about trying to measure some aspects of the séances in a scientific manner. He managed to record strange temperature drops and other phenomena that finally convinced him of the reality of the paranormal. From this point on, he devoted more of his time to pursuing genuine phenomena rather than debunking mediums. This did not sit well with the SPR.

The relationship between Price and the society had always been strained. Eventually, in 1923, he formed the National Laboratory for Psychical Research. It would take three additional years for the laboratory to get up and running and would be located in the London Spiritualist Alliance. This was the final straw for the SPR and, in 1927, they returned Price's donation of a massive book collection. To make matters worse, after Price's death, it would be three members of the SPR who would attempt to discredit him.

Most of the members of the SPR treated Price with something verging on contempt. In those days, the main officers of the society were made up of members of the British upper class and most were related to one another by marriage. Price was most definitely not of their class and breeding, as his father had been a salesman for a paper manufacturer, and Price himself had worked as a salesman and journalist before his marriage. This in itself seemed to make his research suspect in many of their eyes. He was simply, in the dismissive words of one of the members of the society's governing council, "not a gentleman." He was also looked down upon for the fact that he was not as well educated as other members and had no formal scientific training. He remained a member of the organization until his death in 1948 but he was not always a welcomed one.

In 1926, Price came across the case of a Romanian peasant girl, Eleonora Zugan, who was apparently experiencing violent poltergeist phenomena, including flying objects, slapping, biting and pinching. The girl had been rescued from an insane asylum by a psychic investigator whom Price had met in Vienna. Price brought the girl to London and began a series of laboratory tests that were only partially successful. Testimony and reports from the testing claimed that "stigmata" physical marks without explanation appeared on the girl's body under conditions that precluded the possibility of her producing them by natural means. It was also stated that she was able to move objects with her mind. No cause could be discovered for her abilities outside of the fact that she had been severely abused as a young child. Eleonora's abilities ceased abruptly at the age of fourteen when she entered puberty.

In 1929, Rudi Schneider, whose abilities were said to surpass those of his brother, Willi, traveled to England to be tested by Price. The investigator was still adding new scientific technology to his array of gadgets and one device wired Rudi's hands and feet, and those of everyone else seated around the séance table, to a display board. A light would signal if anyone moved enough to break the electrical circuit. Despite these controls, Rudi was said to have produced an array of effects, including ectoplasm, rappings and table levitations. Lord Charles Hope, a leading SPR investigator, was astounded, as was Price himself. At the end of the sessions, Price declared that the phenomena produced by Rudi was "absolutely genuine" and "not the slightest suspicious action was witnessed by any controller or sitter."

In the spring of 1932, Price began testing Rudi again. In these sessions, he planned to photograph Rudi's manifestations as further evidence of his psychic abilities. Although Price obtained some favorable results, the sittings were not as successful as before for Rudi's talents seemed to have diminished with age. In the fall, Hope conducted more tests of the young man and he, too, noticed a decline in his abilities. Still, he maintained that Rudi's powers were genuine.

And then, as Hope was preparing his report, Price rocked the paranormal community with the announcement that Rudi was a fraud. As evidence, he produced a photograph taken during a séance showing Rudi reaching for a table. The camera had been set to go off if there was any movement by the medium. The resulting image was grainy and shadowed, but it managed to destroy Rudi's reputation and embarrass the investigators who had declared him to be genuine, including Harry Price. Those who claimed that Price was simply a publicity-seeking fraud were and still are hard-pressed to explain why he would have made himself look ridiculous in this matter.

By the time of Rudi Schneider's downfall, the appearance of credible new mediums had all but ceased. Soon, Price had turned his attention from investigating mediums and psychics to investigating haunted houses and bizarre phenomena.

Occasionally, Price's cases took a decidedly weird turn as he traveled the globe looking for examples of the paranormal at work. One trip took him to Germany where he went to test an ancient spell that was said to have the power to convert a mountain goat into a handsome young man. Needless to say, the spell failed and Price was the subject of much ridicule.

Another of Price's strangest cases was that of Gef, the talking mongoose. The case began in 1931 with a disembodied voice claiming to be that of a mongoose, a weasel-like creature native to India. It began at an isolated place called Cashen's Gap on the Isle of Man and, according to the Irving family, who owned the remote farmhouse where the mysterious creature appeared, Gef killed rabbits, spoke in various languages, imitated other animals and even recited nursery rhymes.

Price personally investigated the case in the company of Richard S. Lambert, who wrote material for a popular radio show called "The Listener." To their disappointment, Gef refused to manifest until after they had left. Price failed to detect any evidence of outright fraud. The case may have been related to poltergeist phenomena as Voirrey Irving, the thirteen-year-old daughter in the family, was closely associated with the manifestations of the talking mongoose. For some unknown reason, poltergeists tend to emerge in the vicinity of troubled adolescents, usually girls.

Lambert, who investigated other supernatural cases with Price, almost lost his job over the Cashen's Gap affair. The publicity around the case caught the attention of his employers at the BBC and one of his supervisors concluded that Lambert's interest in the supernatural reflected poorly on the broadcaster's competence. Lambert sued him for defamation of character and kept his job.

The Cashen's Gap case was also investigated by Nandor Fodor, a psychiatrist and a pioneer in the field of poltergeist phenomenon related to human subjects. Fodor interviewed a number of witnesses to the phenomena, many of them hostile to the haunting, but he couldn't shake any of the testimony to say that it was not real. Fodor did not accept the explanation of a poltergeist, and he half-seriously suggested that Gef might have actually been a mongoose that learned to talk. Voirrey Irving, who died in 2005, insisted to the end of her life that Gef was not a hoax. The case remains a mystery today.

During this period, Price also made some serious contributions to psychic research, although they were not as widely publicized. In 1933, he persuaded the University of London to open a library and set up the University Council for Psychical Investigation. The library still exists today at the university and consists mainly of Price's enormous occult collection.

The year 1929 marked a turning point in Price's career, although the case would not be made public for several years. In was in that year that he became involved in an investigation that would take over his life and make him famous. The case involved a huge, deteriorating Essex house called Borley Rectory, which will be discussed in more detail later in this chapter.

It would be during Price's investigations of Borley Rectory that he would become the best known and most accomplished of the early ghost hunters, setting the standard for those who would follow. He carefully documented both his findings and his methods and established a blueprint for paranormal investigations.

Many of Price's accounts from Borley would be first-hand, as he claimed to see and hear much of the reported phenomena, including hearing bells and rapping noises and seeing objects that had been inexplicably moved from one place to another. In addition, he also collected accounts from scores of witnesses and previous tenants of the house, and from neighbors and local people who had their own uncanny experiences with the rectory.

Price even leased the house for an extended one-year investigation. He ran an advertisement seeking open-minded researchers to literally camp out at the rectory and record any phenomena that took place in their presence. After choosing more than forty people, he then printed the first-ever handbook on how to conduct a paranormal investigation. A copy given to each investigator explained what to do when investigating the house, along with what equipment they would need.

Price turned the Borley investigations into two books entitled *The Most Haunted House in England* 1940 and *The End of Borley Rectory* 1946 . Both books became very popular and entrenched Price solidly as the premier organizer of well-run paranormal investigations. Despite what his detractors would claim, the books would set the standard for future investigations and would mark the first time that detailed accounts of paranormal research had been exposed to the general public. While his critics saw this only as further grandstanding, future investigators were able to use Price's books when researching their own cases.

Regardless of what some may think of his methods and research, Harry Price must be remembered today as a pioneer in paranormal investigation. He is the one person who so many modern researchers even unknowingly emulate today with their investigations. Price managed to give ghost research a place in the public eye and opened it up to those who don't fit into the categories of professional scientists, hardheaded skeptics, or fall into the realm of gullible "true believer." If for no other reason than this, we owe him a debt of gratitude.

BORLEY RECTORY

One of the most famous haunted houses of all time, and unquestionably the most famous case in Harry Price's career, was that of Borley Rectory. The last ten years or more of Price's life were dominated by the long, complex and rewarding investigation of this house and its hauntings. None of his earlier cases had ever involved so many people, aroused so much interest or caused him so many problems. His two books that were written about the case became bestsellers and captured the imagination of the public. At the time of his death, he was in the final preparations for a third book on Borley Rectory. More than sixty years later, interest in the story has yet to cease.

There have been critics and attention-seekers who have maintained that the whole thing was a hoax, a publicity stunt that was created by Price. One journalist accused him after his death, of course of deliberately lying about the phenomena and producing some of the activity with a "pocketful of pebbles and bricks," which he supposedly tossed when his companions' backs were turned. On the other hand, there are those who were actually present when the strange activity occurred who could assure the doubters that the house was truly as haunted as Price claimed.

It would be impossible to retell the entire story of Borley Rectory here and give it the space that it deserves. Price needed two entire books to do it and was forced to leave out several hundred pages of his notes. What I will present here is an outline of events and theories about Borley and offer it as a groundbreaking case in the history of paranormal research. To some ghost hunters, a case from the 1930s will seem impossibly old-fashioned and out of date but I submit it to you here as one of the first in-depth and documented accounts of haunted house investigations, one that still has the power to fascinate and has helped to set the standards that we attempt to imitate today.

The tiny parish of Borley is located in a desolate, sparsely populated area in Essex, near the east coast of England. It is a lonely place and would be largely forgotten if not for the fact that it is the location of what came to be known as "The Most Haunted House in England."

Harry Price would begin the chronicle of Borley in 1362, when Edward III bestowed the manor of Borley upon Benedictine monks, but as much of this history is shrouded in mystery, we will state with more certainty that the manor was in the possession of the powerful Waldegrave family for three hundred years. Between 1862 and 1892, the Reverend Henry Dawson Ellis Bull, an Oxford-educated "sporting parson" who was a relative of the Waldegraves, was the rector of Borley Church. A year after his appointment, he built Borley Rectory, an enormous ugly, brick building with enough rooms to house his large family. Bull and his wife, Caroline, had twelve living children by 1881, according to the census of that year. Despite warnings, he had built the house on a site believed by locals to be haunted. Bull was succeeded as rector by his son, the Rev. Harry F. Bull, who remained at the post until his death in 1927. After that, the rectory was vacant for over a year until October 1928, when the Rev. Guy Eric Smith was appointed as Borley's rector. However, he and his wife, Mabel, fled just one year after moving in, plagued by both the ghosts and the house's deteriorating condition. Smith had accepted the position sight unseen, without being aware that it had been offered to twelve other clergymen, all of whom had turned it down. The rectory had no electricity or running water at the time; the roof leaked and the place was much too big for two people.

There had been many strange happenings in and around the rectory for many years before the residency of the Smiths, but they had been kept quiet by all concerned. In 1886, Elizabeth Byford quit her position as a nursemaid at the rectory when she heard "ghostly footsteps" walking down a passage. More than fourteen years later, two daughters of the Rev. Henry Bull were the first to spot what would become the famous "phantom nun" on the rectory's lawn. The sighting occurred in the middle of the afternoon and would coincide with other strange happenings that were reported by the family, including phantom knocks, unexplained footsteps and more. The young women were repeatedly unnerved by these events but their father seemed to regard them as splendid entertainment. He and his son, Harry, even constructed a gazebo where they could smoke their after-dinner cigars and watch for the appearance of the phantom nun on a nearby path that they christened the "Nun's Walk."

Rev. Harry Bull often discussed the spirits with his friend J. Hartley, who later supplied information to Harry Price. Hartley said that in 1922, Bull told him it was his opinion that, "The only way for a spirit, if ignored, to get into touch with a living person, was by means of a manifestation causing some violent physical reaction, such as the breaking of glass or the shattering of other and similar material elements."

Hartley added that the rector declared that on his death, "If he were discontented, he would adopt this method of communicating with the inhabitants of the Rectory."

The members of the Bull family were not the only ones to see the ghostly nun on the grounds or outside the gates of Borley Rectory. Fred Cartwright, a local carpenter, saw her four times in two weeks, according to the account he gave to Price. Up until 1939, fourteen people were reported to have seen the nun. Three others said they had seen a phantom coach and horses with "glittering harness" sweep across the grounds and two others said they had seen the apparition of a headless man.

In June 1929, two years after the death of Harry Bull and nine months after Rev. Smith came to the rectory, the story of ghostly occurrences at Borley was mentioned in the *Daily Mirror*. The next day, Harry Price received a telephone call from Alexander Campbell, an editor at the newspaper, asking to investigate. He was told about various types of phenomena that had been reported there: the phantom footsteps; strange lights; ghostly whispers; a headless man; a girl in white; the sounds of a phantom coach outside; the apparition of the home's builder, Henry Bull; and of course, the spirit of the nun. This spectral figure was said to drift through the garden with her head bent in sorrow.

Local legend had it that a monastery was once located on the site and that a thirteenth-century monk and a beautiful young novice were killed while trying to elope from the place. As punishment, the monk was hanged and his would-be bride was bricked up alive within the walls of her convent. Price scoffed at the idea of such a fanciful tale but was intrigued by the phenomena associated with the house.

Price was accompanied on his first visit to Borley by his secretary, Lucie Kay, and Vernon C. Wall, a reporter from the *Daily Mirror*. Together, they listened to the experiences of Rev. Smith and his wife and even observed some minor examples of poltergeist phenomenon for themselves. Price also conducted a long interview with Mary Pearson, the Smiths' maid, who claimed to have seen the ghostly coach and horses twice and was firmly convinced the house was genuinely haunted. Later that night, the group held a séance in the "Blue Room" on the second floor the house, where much of the manifestations had allegedly occurred, and where both Rectors Bull had breathed their last. They were purported to make contact with Harry Bull. Whether they did or not, they were startled when a bar of soap jumped up off the floor and slammed into a basin. The following day, Price held more interviews and spoke with two of the Rev. Henry Bull's daughters and the Coopers, a married couple who formerly lived in a cottage on the rectory grounds. The Coopers had moved out in 1920, blaming uncomfortable feelings caused by the ghosts.

The events that occurred, and the witness interviews, were enough to convince Price that something strange was going on at the rectory. That June day would begin more than eighteen years of intensive paranormal investigation. It would be during his investigations of Borley Rectory that he would become the best known and most accomplished of the early ghost hunters, setting the standard for those who would follow. Price coined the idea of the "ghost hunter's kit;" used tape measures to check the thickness of walls and to search for hidden chambers; perfected the use of still cameras for indoor and outdoor photography; brought in a remote-control motion picture camera; put to use a finger-printing kit; and even used portable telephones for contact between investigators. He was quite impressed by the house and believed that it represented one of the most exciting and fascinating puzzles of his career.

His second visit to Borley came two weeks after the first. This time, he documented the appearance of a religious medal and some other items that seemed to show there was a Roman Catholic element to the haunting. There were also times when bells once used to summon the servants rang throughout the house, although the wires had been cut many years before. The constant ringing was a source of great worry for Reverend Smith and his wife and this, along with other manifestations, convinced the couple to abandon the house on July 14, 1929.

Over the course of the next fourteen months, the rectory remained empty while the happenings reportedly continued. According to local accounts, a window was opened from the inside, even though the rectory was deserted and the doors were securely locked. The main staircase was found covered with lumps of stone and small pieces of glass. People who lived nearby reported seeing lights in the house and hearing what were described as "horrible sounds" around the time of the full moon.

Even though Rev. Smith and his wife moved out of the house because of the ghosts, things had been rather peaceful up until that point. All that would change in October 1930, when Reverend Smith was replaced by the elderly Reverend Lionel Foyster, a cousin of the Bulls, who moved into the rectory with his young wife, Marianne, and Adelaide, their adopted daughter. Their time in the house would see a marked increase in paranormal activity. People were locked out of rooms, household items vanished and reappeared, windows were broken, furniture was moved, odd sounds were heard and much more. The worst of the incidents seemed to involve Mrs. Foyster, as she was thrown from her bed at night, slapped by invisible hands, forced to dodge heavy objects which flew at her day and night, and was once almost suffocated under a mattress.

The activity during this period was more varied and far more violent than ever before. Rev. Foyster kept a diary and later compiled a manuscript that was never published called "Fifteen Months in a Haunted House." Harry Price would later use excerpts from the manuscript in his books about Borley Rectory. There is no question that Rev. Foyster, Marianne, Adelaide then a toddler and later, a young boy who stayed with them as a guest, went through some strange and often terrifying experiences, including the mysterious messages that appeared inexplicably, scrawled in pencil on the walls of the house by an unknown hand.

They seemed to be pleading with Mrs. Foyster, using phrases like "Marianne, please help get" and "Get light mass prayers here."

Things became so bad by May 1931 that the Foysters left the rectory so that they could get a few days of peace and quiet. In June, Dom Richard Whitehouse, a friend of the Foysters, began an investigation. He found things scattered all over the unoccupied house and when the family returned, the violent phenomenon began again. At one point, Mrs. Foyster was hurled from her bed three times in a row.

In September of that year, Harry Price learned of these new and more violent manifestations. A short time later, he and several of his friends paid a visit to the rectory and saw some of it for themselves, including mysterious locking and unlocking doors and bottles that were tossed about. Because nearly all of the poltergeist-like activity occurred when Mrs. Foyster was present, Price was inclined to attribute it to her unknowing manipulations. He also considered the idea that some of it might be trickery. However, he did believe in the possibility of the ghostly nun and some of the other reported phenomenon. The rectory did not fit into pre-conceived notions of a haunted house, which was one of the reasons that it would gain such a reputation.

Despite the implications of the violent phenomena centering on Marianne, Price maintained that at least one of the spirits in the house had found the rector's wife to be sympathetic. This was the only explanation he could find for the mysterious messages. He believed the writings had come from another young woman, one who seemed to be from her references, a Catholic. These clues would later fit well with Price's theory that the Borley mystery was a terrible tale of murder and betrayal, in which the central character was a young nun, although not the one of legend who was said to have attempted to elope with a priest.

A short time after Price's visit, Mrs. Foyster, Dom Richard Whitehouse and the Foysters' maid, Katie, were seated in the kitchen with all of the doors and windows closed, when bottles began to appear, seemingly from nowhere, only to shatter on the floor. At the same time, the disconnected bells in the house suddenly began ringing once again.

The months that followed brought more ringing bells and door locking but after a séance was held, things quieted down considerably. The bells still rang occasionally and objects flew about but there was what Price described as a "different atmosphere" after the sittings. The remainder of 1934 was quiet but in 1935, the manifestations returned and became more violent. Things frequently vanished or were broken and by October of that year, the Foysters had reached the limits of their endurance. They left the house and the church decided to sell the place, as it was now believed to be unfit for any clergyman to occupy.

The church offered the house to Harry Price -- for about one-sixth of its value -- but after some hesitation, he decided not to buy the place but to rent it for a year. The house was in need of extensive repairs, the grounds were so badly overgrown that they needed the attention of a corps of gardeners. What's more, Borley was 150 miles from Price's home in Pulborough. Overall, purchasing Borley would be an expensive and time-consuming endeavor. Price planned to conduct an extended, around-the-clock investigation, using scores of volunteers to track and document anything out of the ordinary that occurred there. As it turned out, the investigation was never that well-organized. Even so, in spite of often-poor record keeping and periods when the house was unoccupied, the year-long investigation remains a landmark in the annals of the paranormal.

Price's first step was to run an advertisement in the personal column of the *Times* of London on May 25, 1937, looking for open-minded researchers to literally "camp out" at the rectory. They were to record any phenomena that took place. The advertisement read:

"HAUNTED HOUSE: Responsible persons of leisure and intelligence, intrepid, critical, and unbiased, are invited to join rota of observers in a year's night and day investigation of alleged haunted house in Home Counties. Printed instructions supplied. Scientific training or ability to operate simple instruments an advantage. House situated in lonely hamlet, so own car is essential. Write Box H.989, The Times, E.C.4"

Price was deluged with over 200 applicants, most of whom were unsuitable. After choosing 48 people who seemed to fit the criteria for suitable ghost-hunters, he then printed the first-ever handbook on how to conduct a paranormal investigation. It became known as the "Blue Book" and a copy was given to each investigator. It explained what to do when investigating the house, along with what equipment they would need. Although it now seems dated, much of the information remains relevant to investigators today.

During the investigations, the researchers were allowed wide latitude when it came to searching for facts. Some of them brought their own equipment, others kept precise journals and others turned to séances, which would prove interesting during the period between 1935 and 1939. The greatest aid to Price in the Borley investigations was Sidney H. Glanville. It was Glanville who compiled with great zeal the famous "locked box," which contained a detailed record of the Borley story from its beginning to the night of the devastating fire that destroyed the rectory in 1939. Some of the material was eventually published in Price's books and Glanville was completely in charge of the investigations when Price was not present.

The observers that Price recruited came from many different walks of life, but all of them contributed to the pile of data that began to accumulate. Many of them spent nights in the empty rectory. The former library, where the Reverend Henry Bull used to lie on the floor and take pot shots at rabbits on the lawn outside, had been set up as the "base room," where various instruments had been installed. There was also a supply of canned goods, a cot, and a telephone that Price had left strict orders was to be used only for "reporting phenomena to the person or persons whose names have been given me, or to request assistance from those persons." Some came alone and others came in groups. All had signed an agreement to pay their own expenses and keep the location of the investigation a secret. They were skeptics, believers and debunkers alike. A good many of them neither saw nor heard anything but quite a few of them had strange experiences. These experiences varied from unexplained sounds to moving objects, weird lights and even full-blown apparitions. Most of the events were witnessed by more than one person and the nun was seen by the majority of them.

The corps of observers established beyond doubt that Borley Rectory was the center of some major paranormal disturbances. The number of the disturbances, their variety and the length of their duration supplied an answer to any accusations that Harry Price staged the phenomenon for publicity or some other purpose. The vast majority of the activity was not witnessed by Price at all. Instead, the reports came from independent observers who often had no idea that others were experiencing the same events.

There were two important developments during Price's tenancy of the house. One was the previously mentioned wall writings. These frantic pleas for help looked like they had been hurriedly scrawled and were often hard to decipher. They had first started to appear during the Foysters' occupancy. Most of them were addressed to "Marianne" and some non-believers suggested that Mrs. Foyster had written them, although no one could provide a motive for such a pointless hoax. Strangely, the scrawls continued to appear on the walls long after Mrs. Foyster had left the Rectory. Price believed that they provided vital clues to the mystery behind the haunting. The observers who noted the new messages circled and dated them so that there would be no mistake as to which were old and which appeared later on.

The other important development of 1937 - 1938 was the series of séances that was held by Sidney Glanville, some of his family and several friends. During a sitting with a planchette, an alleged spirit calling itself "Marie Lairre" related that she had been a nun in France but had left her convent to marry Henry Waldegrave, a member of the illustrious family whose manor home once stood on the site of Borley Rectory. While living at the manor, "Marie" wrote that her husband had strangled her and had buried her remains in the cellar. The story went well with the most interesting of the Borley phenomena, namely the reported phantom nun and the written messages pleading for a mass. Price theorized that the former nun had been buried in unconsecrated ground and was now doomed to haunt the property seeking rest.

In March of 1938, five months after Marie's first appearance, another piece of automatic writing came from a spirit calling itself "Sunex Amures." The message promised that the rectory would burn down that night and that the proof of the nun's murder would be found in the ruins. Borley Rectory did not burn that night, but exactly eleven months later, on February 27, 1939, a new owner, Captain W.H. Gregson, was unpacking boxes of books when an oil lamp overturned and started a fire. The blaze quickly spread and the rectory was gutted. The fire started where the spirit had predicted it would and local people who came to watch reported seeing figures walking in a second-floor bedroom where the floor had been burned away. It happened to be the "Blue Room," where both the Reverend Bulls had died.

The ruins of the rectory were finally demolished in 1944 but the story was far from over.

The publication of Price's first book on Borley, *The Most Haunted House in England*, brought a deluge of letters. The wall-writings, the planchette messages and the various reports from the observers who had answered Price's classified ad led to arguments, new theories and new facts. Price was able to point out the parallels and similarities in a dozen other hauntings. The rectory was in ruins but this did not keep people away. Throughout the years of World War II, visitors explored the rubble and occasionally spent the night in the eerie remains of the building. In 1941, a businessman named H.F. Russell paid a visit to the Borley grounds with two of his Royal Air Force officer sons. While there, he claimed that he was seized by an invisible presence and dashed to the ground. Two years later, some Polish officers spent the night in the ruins and they claimed to see and hear a number of chilling sights and sounds. In particular, they saw a shadow on the Nun's Walk and a man's figure in one of the rooms. The Polish officers rebuilt the floor in the Blue Room and set up chairs and a table where séances could continue to be held.

Other visitors included a commission from Cambridge University, which was formed by A.J.B. Robertson of St. Johns College. He would go on to contribute a long essay to Price's second book on Borley. Robertson and his colleagues were interested in the inexplicable "cold patches" in the house. They investigated the house from 1939 until its demolition in 1944. The report that Robertson wrote at the end of the investigation was cautious but stated that: "There appears, in fact, to be something at the rectory which cannot all be explained away. It must be remembered that the investigations described here form only part of a much wider survey which has brought to light very many mysterious phenomena."

Some of the most fascinating and ultimately relevant investigations into the rectory were conducted by Rev. W.J. Phythian-Adams, Canon of Carlisle. After reading Price's book, studying plans of the house and photographs of the wall writings and doing a detailed analysis of Borley's history, Canon Phythian-Adams prepared a detailed and convincing account of events leading up to the haunting. To put together his report, he used the history of the Waldegrave family, as well as statements from a medium that Price had contacted to try and use psychometric powers on an apport an object that appears seemingly out of nowhere by paranormal means that had been found by an observer in the Borley sewing room. He combined all of the pieces of the Borley story into a speculative account. He collated the wall writings with the séance messages and extracted the symbolic and literal meanings of the information that had been gathered. There had been many other attempts at interpreting the messages, especially the wall writings, and all had concentrated on the desperate attempts the nun had made to try and get the living to do something to help her. But no one else tried to what Canon Phythian-Adams did: create a consecutive narrative that sounded convincing.

There would be those who would say that his story was nothing more than clever guesswork but Canon Phythian-Adams told Harry Price to dig for the nun's remains and he told him exactly where. In August 1943, in the company of Rev. A.C. Henning; Dr. Eric H. Bailey, senior assistant pathologist of the Ashford County Hospital; Roland F. Bailey, his brother; Flying Officer A. A. Creamer; Captain W.H. Gregson and his two nieces, Georgina Dawson and Mrs. Alex English, Price began to dig in the cellars of the ruined rectory.

On the exact spot where Canon Phythian-Adams had indicated having never visited the site , they found a large antique brass preserving pan, a silver cream jug and a jawbone with five teeth. Dr. Bailey declared it to be a left mandible, probably from a woman. They also found part of a skull. The next day, they found two religious medals, one of which was made of gold. Price took the bone fragments from Borley to the studios of A. C. Cooper, Ltd., well-known art photographers, who would then document the finds. At the studio, another strange act in the Borley haunting was played out. While setting up the skull to have it photographed, it slipped and broke into four pieces. Moments later a valuable oil painting fell off its easel and crashed to the floor. A clock that had not worked in more than ten years suddenly started back up again, functioning for just twenty minutes before stopping, this time for good. Five months later, the Cooper studios were destroyed in an air raid. Coincidence? Perhaps, but based on all of the other strange happenings connected to Borley, it is worthy of mention.

In May 1945, a Christian burial for the bones appeared to provide the ghost with the rest she had long sought. The service was conducted by the Rev. Henning in the small village of Liston, less than two miles from Borley.

The nun was never seen at the rectory again but weird events continued to occur there. They were frequent enough that Price made plans for a third book about the site, although it was never completed. As his research progressed, Price lined up fifty new witnesses to more recent phenomena, including Rev. Henning, officials from the BBC, local residents and strangers. It seemed that after the ruins of the rectory were demolished, the ghosts moved across the road to Borley Church, where a great many manifestations began to occur in the vestry and throughout the building. Many reliable people heard the organ being played when the church doors were locked and no one could possibly enter. Rev. Henning, then rector of the church, was one of the witnesses. He contributed his accounts to Price for the third book.

Perhaps this was just one of the reasons that the story of Borley Rectory has never really died. Its legacy remains today and it has gone done in history as one of the world's most haunted houses.

And as for Harry Price, his legacy continues, as well. Price died from a heart attack at his home in Pulborough on March 29, 1948. He was 67 years old. His tremendous labors and volumes of research remain today. He is still regarded as highly controversial but he is not without devoted fans. One of those who spoke most highly of Price, Sir Albion Richardson, Recorder of Nottingham, stated that: "Borley Rectory stands by itself in the literature of psychical manifestation. The large numbers of the public who are interested in these things are under a debt of gratitude to Mr. Harry Price, for without his untiring energy and skilled experience as an investigator, the story of Borley Rectory would have remained unrevealed. The manifestations are proved by the evidence, to the point of moral certainty."

ZENER CARDS
During the Waning Days of Spiritualism, a True Psychic Emerges

With the days of séances, floating tambourines and ectoplasm on the decline, researchers began to search for other evidence of the paranormal. Mediums, now usually referred to as "psychics," began to be tested by methods other than tying them to a chair and waiting for objects to fly around the room. One method of testing was the deck of Zener cards that were used to conduct experiments into extra-sensory perception ESP . They were designed by psychologist Karl Zener in the early 1930s and were used during his experiments with his colleague, parapsychologist J.B. Rhine.

The new cards replaced standard playing cards, which had previously been used for ESP tests. There were many problems with using regular cards, largely in that the participant was only credited with a correct prediction when he or she guessed both the number and suit of the card. This meant that the chance for correctly guessing a card was greatly reduced. This, along with other issues, led to the development of Zener's cards.

There are just five different Zener cards: a hollow circle one curve , a Greek cross two lines , three vertical wavy lines or "waves" , a hollow square four lines , and a hollow five-pointed star. There are twenty-five cards in a pack, five of each design.

During the tests, the person conducting it would pick up a card in the shuffled pack, observe the symbol on the card and then record the answer of the person being tested for extra-sensory perception. The subject had to correctly determine which of the five designs was on each card in question.

It wasn't as exciting as a séance, but it was more in keeping with the low-key sensibilities of psychic testing at the time. Researchers were hoping to get away from some of the recent embarrassments that had occurred in England.

What must have surely been one of the low points in the history of Spiritualism involved the career of a British medium named Helen Duncan. Some continue to maintain to this day that she was a "martyr" to the movement but most see her as one of the frauds that helped to sound the death knell for the Spiritualist movement as it existed up until that time.

Helen Duncan was born in Scotland in 1898. She married at the age of twenty and began to develop psychic talents that were much in demand by the 1920s. She traveled the country during this period and held séances in private homes and Spiritualist churches. She convinced thousands of people that the dead could return in various forms but most often, through ectoplasm, that slimy, white substance said to be manifested by spirits. In reality, Helen's "ectoplasm" was found to be nothing more than a mixture of paper, cloth, egg white and surgical gauze. She was able to regurgitate the substances on demand. Any lingering doubts about this were dispelled by the medium's husband, who gave an interview late in life that admitted he had seen his wife swallowing various things before her séances.

In addition to her ectoplasmic forms, Duncan also worked with spirit guides. One in particular was a child named "Peggy," who played an important role during the séances. However, in 1933, at a sitting in Edinburgh, a policewoman grabbed at "Peggy" as she passed by her and discovered that the ghostly girl was actually a torn piece of white underwear. Duncan was arrested, charged with fraud and fined £10. Less than two months later, though, she was back at work.

Undaunted by her exposure, Duncan proceeded to give a series of test sittings for the National Laboratory of Psychical Research, under the direction of its founder, Harry Price. Price had already exposed a number of fraudulent mediums by this time, but he believed in the possibility of psychic phenomena. He was of the opinion that some mediums did manage to produce genuine mental and physical phenomena. Price soon found that Duncan did not fit into this category. Photographs taken during her sessions revealed that the "ectoplasm" she produced was a length of cheesecloth whose bound edges, texture and creases were clearly visible.

None of what should have been embarrassing exposures made any difference to Helen's public. Outside of the laboratories, her fame continued to grow and sitters continued to insist that they recognized departed friends and loved ones in the ectoplasmic faces that she materialized. During World War II, her mediumistic powers were much in demand by relatives of those who had died in the service. She held a number of séances in Portsmouth, Hampshire, the home port of the Royal Navy, and one of these, held on January 19, 1944, was raided by the police. A plainclothes policeman who was present blew a whistle to give a signal and other officers burst in. A grab was made for the ectoplasm issuing from the medium and the séance was abruptly brought to an end. Although nothing incriminating was found, Duncan, along with three others who arranged the séance, Ernest and Elizabeth Homer and Francis Brown, was taken to the Portsmouth magistrate's court and arraigned on charges of conspiracy.

At the preliminary hearing, the court was told how Lieutenant R.H. Worth of the Royal Navy had attended one of Duncan's séances and suspected fraud. He bought two tickets for 25 shillings each for the night of January 19 and took a policeman named Cross with him. Cross grabbed the "ectoplasm" that floated past him which he believed was a piece of white sheet, although no sheet was found when the séance was raided but he was unable to hang onto it. After the hearing, bail was refused and as a result, Duncan was remanded to Holloway Prison in London for four days before the case was resumed in Portsmouth.

The prosecution seemed to be unsure of what to charge the mediums with. On their first appearance at Portsmouth, they were charged under the Vagrancy Act of 1824, but the charge was then amended to one of conspiracy. When the case was eventually transferred to the central criminal courts, the Witchcraft Act of 1735 was cited. Under this dusty and long-unused law, the defendants were accused of pretending "to exercise or use a kind of conjuration that through the agency of Helen Duncan spirits of deceased persons should appear to be present." Other charges were brought under the Larceny Act and they were accused of taking money "by falsely pretending they were in a position to bring about appearances of the spirits of deceased persons."

Needless to say, the Witchcraft Act of 1735 was hopelessly outdated, regardless of the guilt or innocence of the defendant. Spiritualists were dismayed by the use of the act to bring about prosecution of the famous medium. They believed that she would be found guilty whether or not her powers were genuine. They were angry because they believed that Duncan was an authentic medium and was being persecuted for her genuine gifts. The prosecution, however, clearly believed that Duncan was a fraud, which was why they charged her with larceny. The use of the Witchcraft Act remains a bit of an enigma but it certainly gained the trial a lot of publicity.

The trial took place in later winter of 1944 and lasted for seven days. Numerous witnesses testified to events they had seen at Duncan's séances. One of them, Kathleen McNeill, claimed that she had attended a séance where her sister had appeared. This sister had died just a few hours before, after an operation, and news of her death could not have been known to Duncan at the time. At another séance, McNeill claimed that her father strode out of the spirit cabinet, looking just as he had when he was alive.

Two journalists, H. Swaffer and J.W. Herries, were also called by the defense. The flamboyant Swaffer told the court that not only was ectoplasm real, it could not have been regurgitated by the medium. Herries claimed that he had seen Sir Arthur Conan Doyle materialize at one of Duncan's séances. He saw the author's well-known features and recognized his voice, he said.

The prosecution had to make little effort to convince the jury that Duncan was a fraud. They made liberal use of photographs taken at Duncan's séances showing blatantly fake "ectoplasm" emerging from the medium's mouth and nose. One particular favorite was a photo of the spirit child "Peggy" slithering out of Duncan's nostrils. In the photo, the "ectoplasm" had a face that was obviously that of a child's doll!

Prosecuting counsel John Maude produced a long piece of butter muslin and referred to the report by Harry Price, who stated that he believed Duncan swallowed the material and then regurgitated it. The jury seemed convinced that she was a fraud. At the start of the trial, the defense offered the jury an actual demonstration of Duncan's mediumship but the judge declined the offer and stated that perhaps Mrs. Duncan should testify as a witness instead. The defense replied that Helen could not testify, as she was in a trance during the séances and unable to discuss what transpired. On the final day, the judge changed his mind and asked the jury if they wanted to see Helen Duncan perform. After a couple of minutes of discussion, they declined the offer.

It took just twenty-five minutes for the jury to return their verdict: they found the four defendants guilty of conspiracy to disregard the Witchcraft Act. They were discharged from giving verdicts on the other counts. The judge deferred pronouncing sentence until after the weekend but when he court did reconvene, he stated that the verdict had not been concerned with whether "genuine manifestations of the kind are possible... this court has nothing to do with such abstract questions. The jury has found this to be a case of plain dishonesty." He sentenced Duncan to nine months in prison and she was led away moaning and crying. Of the other defendants, Mrs. Brown was given four months she had previous convictions for larceny and shop-lifting and the Homers were each given a small fine and placed on probation for the next two years.

Helen Duncan served her sentence at Holloway Prison. The Spiritualist movement, shocked by the verdict, called for a change in the law to prevent such prosecutions in the future. They felt that Duncan had been unfairly treated but they did cool their enthusiasm for her after the trial. Public perception was that a fraud had been exposed and officials in the movement decided to put some distance between themselves and the medium.

When she was released from prison on September 22, 1944, Duncan announced that she was retiring from séances, but thanks to the large number of faithful followers that she still had, she soon changed her mind. She continued to offer private séances for years afterward.

In 1951, the Witchcraft Act of 1735 was repealed and replaced with the Fraudulent Mediums Act. Helen Duncan's trial had certainly prompted this change in the law but the Spiritualists' hopes that they would no longer be subjected to police harassment were short-lived. In November 1956, police raided a séance taking place in Nottingham. They grabbed the medium, searched her and photographed her. They shouted that they were looking for beards, a mask and a shroud but found nothing.

The medium conducting the séance was Helen Duncan.

Duncan became ill after the raid, possibly from shock, and died five weeks later. The doctors listed the cause of death as diabetes and heart failure, but a certain segment of the Spiritualist community thought otherwise. Some complained of "police brutality" and even "murder," mostly because the medium had been interrupted during a trance, which all agreed could be extremely dangerous. Even today, Helen Duncan is still seen by some as a martyr to the cause of Spiritualism, a victim of the world's intolerance.

To most, though, she is seen as another fraudulent medium that, unlike most in the same circumstances, actually got her day in court. Those who point to the egg white and muslin "ectoplasm," the phony photographs and the "spirit guides" formed out of torn underwear would say that in this case, justice prevailed.

But it would be a mistake to conclude from the story of Helen Duncan that this time period produced no worthy successors to the mysterious mediums of the past who were never revealed to practice fraud. Puzzling manifestations and strange happenings were by no means dead, so to speak. One of the most dramatic and unusual events in the history of the entire Spiritualist movement occurred in October 1930.

Just two days after the huge British airship, the R101, had gone down in flames on a hillside in northern France while on a voyage from England to India --- killing 48 of its 54 passengers --- the halting voice of a man claiming to be its captain spoke through the lips of a medium in London. In short and disjointed sentences, he described his horrifying last moments before the airship burned. His account of the crash included a wealth of technical information that was not only confirmed six months later by an official inquiry but was well beyond the knowledge of the medium delivering the message. The disaster, which occurred on October 5, 1930, claimed the lives of dozens of British citizens, including two high-ranking aviation officials. It shook the government's confidence in airships and ended the British efforts to develop these types of craft for commercial use. In short, the disaster had a devastating effect on England as a whole.

The séance at which this dramatic communication took place occurred at the National Laboratory of Psychical Research, which had been founded by Harry Price four years earlier. Price, his secretary, and journalist Ian D. Coster, had arranged a sitting with a reportedly talented young medium named Eileen Garrett. The purpose of it was to try and make contact with the spirit of Sir Arthur Conan Doyle, who had recently passed away. The report of the séance was to be published in an upcoming magazine.

Eileen Garrett was born in March 1893 in County Meath, Ireland. Her parents both committed suicide and she went to live with an aunt and uncle. When she began to exhibit paranormal abilities at an early age, her aunt dismissed her visions and contact with the spirits as the products of an overactive imagination. Nevertheless, when she was a young girl, she claimed to see her favorite aunt Leone, who lived twenty miles away, walking up a path carrying a baby. She claimed that Leone approached and told her, "I am going away now, and I must take the baby with me." Eileen told her adoptive mother what had happened, and she was punished for lying. The following day, she learned that Leone had died in childbirth, along with the baby.

Eileen later said that her childhood was a very unhappy one. She married three times. Her first marriage, to Clive Barry, produced three sons, all of whom died young, and one daughter, Eileen, who succeeded her mother as the president of the Parapsychology Foundation, which Garrett later founded in New York.

Following her divorce from Barry, Eileen ran a hostel for soldiers who were wounded in the Great War. Many of the men who recovered from their wounds returned to the front and Eileen often experienced precognitive visions of their deaths there. Needless to say, this often disturbed her, which is likely why she accepted a last-minute marriage proposal from one such man just before he returned to the battlefield. One month after the wedding, he was reported to be missing in action. Eileen sensed that he and several others had been killed in an explosion, which was soon confirmed. In 1918, just before the end of the war, she married J.W. Garrett, another wounded soldier. The marriage to Garrett ended in 1927. She was engaged to marry a third time, but tragedy struck once again when she and her fiancée both became ill. He died of pneumonia and Eileen almost died following a mastoid operation. After that, she remained single for the rest of her life.

In 1919, a frequent visitor to Garrett's hostel began to tell her of messages that he had purportedly received through a spirit medium from his dead daughter. Although skeptical, Eileen recalled the strange experiences from her childhood and decided to listen to the man. She later accompanied him to the London Spiritualist Alliance, where she witnessed a clairvoyant during a séance. Curious, she began to attend regular meetings at the Alliance and at one of them, she experienced her first involuntary trance, during which she spoke of seeing the deceased family members of a number of sitters who were present.

The bizarre experience left her feeling both physically ill and emotionally drained. She was so upset when she came home that her husband forbid her to have anything more to do with the group. She went along with his wishes but couldn't help but try and find out more about what had happened to her. At the suggestion of a friend, she consulted a hypnotist. During the first session, Eileen again fell into a trance, this time under the control of a spirit named Uvani. The hypnotist tried to convince her that Uvani was a spirit that was independent of her own personality but the idea was so totally opposed to Eileen's views that she broke off work with the hypnotist with the intention of abandoning her burgeoning mediumship.

Before long, though, Eileen found herself back at the London Spiritualist Alliance, where she was introduced to more advanced mediums and then got involved with Harry Price's National Laboratory of Psychical Research. She soon began to make quite a reputation for herself as a talented medium and worked with a number of well-known researchers in the growing field. She was later tested by J.B. Rhine at Duke University and Rhine considered her to be one of the finest mediums of the day.

Eileen happened to be in southern France when war broke out again in 1939 and she stayed there until 1941, when she was able to make it to Portugal and then on to the United States. She became a U.S. citizen in 1947, established a publishing house called Creative Age Press, started a monthly magazine called *Tomorrow* and then founded the Parapsychology Foundation in 1951. She remained a popular and respected medium throughout the 1950s and 1960s, frequently working with parapsychologist Hans Holzer to investigate haunted houses throughout the eastern United States, before passing away in September 1970. In addition to the history she left behind with the Parapsychology Foundation, she also published seven nonfiction books and a number of novels that she wrote under the name of Jean Lyttle.

The event that established Eileen Garrett as a medium to be reckoned with was undeniably the séance that occurred in October 1930 with Harry Price. Shortly after the sitters gathered in the séance room, Eileen went into a trance.

Instead of making contact with Conan Doyle, as they had planned, the sitters heard a voice that announced himself as Flight Lieutenant Herbert Carmichael Irwin. In jerking, staccato phrases, the voice spoke:

I must do something about it... The whole bulk of the dirigible was entirely and absolutely too much for her engine's capacity. Engines too heavy. It was this that made me on five occasions have to scuttle to safety. Useful lift too small. Gross lift computed badly --- inform control panel. And this idea of new elevators totally mad. Elevator jammed. Oil pipe plugged ... Flying too low altitude and never could rise. Disposable lift could not be utilized. Load too great for long flight... Cruising speed bad and ship badly swinging. Severe tension on the fabric, which is chafing... Engines wrong - too heavy --- cannot rise. Never reached cruising altitude - same in trials. Too short trials. No one knew the ship properly. Weather bad for long flight. Fabric all waterlogged and ship's nose is down. Impossible to rise. Cannot trim. Almost scraped the roofs of Achy. Kept to railway. An inquiry to be held later it will be found that the superstructure of the envelope contained no resilience and had far too much weight in envelope. The added middle section was entirely wrong... too heavy, too much over weighted for the capacity of the engines...

The reporter who took down this strange and frightening communication in shorthand at first resented the intrusion of Irwin, when he had expected the voice of Sir Arthur Conan Doyle. But he soon realized that he had unwittingly been part of a dramatic moment in psychical history. He published the story and it was read by, among others, Will Charlton, a supply officer at Cardington, where the R101 was built and tested and from where it departed on its final journey. Charlton asked Harry Price for a copy of the séance report. After studying it, he and his colleagues pronounced it an "amazing document," containing more than forty highly technical --- and highly classified--- details of what occurred during the airship's final flight. Charlton added: "It appeared very evident that for anyone present at the séance to have obtained this information beforehand was grotesquely absurd."

Charlton was so impressed by the evidence that he began his own psychic investigation and ultimately became a Spiritualist. The only theory that he could put forth to explain everything that happened was that "Irwin did actually communicate with those present at the séance, after his physical death."

Before the official inquiry into the disaster, Major Oliver Villiers of the Ministry of Civil Aviation participated in a séance with Eileen Garrett. Through the medium, he heard the voices of others who had lost their lives in the crash. The following is a portion of a conversation that took place during the séance between Villiers and Major George Herbert "Lucky Breeze" Scott, one of the victims, speaking through Eileen:

Villiers: "What was the trouble? Irwin mentioned the nose."

Garrett: "Yes. Girder trouble and engine."

Villiers: "I must get this right. Can you describe exactly where? We have the long struts labeled from A to G."

Garrett: The top one is O and then A,B,C, and so on downward. Look at your drawing. It was starboard of 5C. On our second flight after we had finished we found the girder had been strained, not cracked, and this cause trouble to the cover...

Later, Villiers asked Scott if the girder had broken and gone through the airship's covering.

Garrett: "No, not broke, but cracked badly and it split the outer cover... The bad rent in the cover on the starboard side of 5C brought about an unnatural pressure, forced us into our first dive. The second was even worse. The pressure on the gas bags was terrific, and the gusts of wind were tremendous. This external pressure, coupled with the fact that the valve was weak, blew the valve right off, and at the same time the released gas was ignited by a backfire from the engine."

The Court of Inquiry report later showed that practically every one of these statements was correct. Not a single one of them was incorrect.

Eileen Garrett's death in 1970, Archie Jarman, a researcher and writer who had known her for nearly forty years, revealed that she had asked him in the early 1960s to "dig into the famous R101 airship case as deep as I could delve." Jarman agreed to do so and refused to accept any fees or expenses for Eileen, so that whatever his investigation disclosed, it would be seen that he worked "without fear or favor." He later wrote:

The completed saga, so often briefly mentioned, turned out to be a pretty massive affair. It took nearly six months and finally filled 455 pages of typescript and blueprints. It involved two trips to France, seeking the few remaining witnesses at Beauvais, where the R101 crashed. There were conferences with aeronautical experts, such as the designers of the R101's heavy diesel engines which were partly responsible for the fatal crash , and with the aging but still-active captain of its sister ship, the R100.

It was the technical aspects of this case that makes it unique in psychic history. It would be harder to believe that Eileen Garrett obtained her obscure and specialized data by mundane means than to accept that, in some paranormal manner, she had contact with the psyche of the dead Captain Irwin.

Eileen Garrett is remembered today as one of the greatest mediums who ever lived. And interestingly, she was one of the most "low-key" mediums in Spiritualist history. No spirit forms ever manifested in her presence, no tables tipped, no rapping sounds were heard and yet, without any fanfare, she managed to obtain some of the greatest evidence of life after death that has ever been recorded. Many saw her work as a turning point. They dismissed séance phantoms as proof of the next world and began to see mental mediumship as genuine evidence of a life beyond this one.

A RADIO
Communication with the Spirit World Goes Beyond the Ouija Board

As interest in the more theatrical trappings of Spiritualism continued to wane, modern believers and researchers began looking for other methods to communicate with the dead. New kinds of apparatus, like radios and recording devices, soon captured the attention of investigators and even today, recorders are considered essential pieces of equipment in paranormal investigations.

The practice of attempting to record ghosts is called Electronic Voice Phenomena EVP . The sounds that make up EVP are apparently sonic events of unknown origin, which can be heard, and sometimes captured in recordings, on various types of electronic apparatus, including tape recorders and even radio equipment.

The voices on the tapes - alleged to be the voices of the dead -- take on diverse forms, sometimes seeming to sing or to speak in gibberish. The messages often make a sort of backward sense, as though communication is difficult. They can also apparently speak directly to researchers and call them by name. They can be heard over telephones and as anomalous interference on tape recordings. Some of them seen to enjoy engaging in dialogue, answering questions or supplying personal information about the researchers, possibly as a way of establishing credibility.

Of course, with all science both conventional and paranormal , there are those investigators who are so keen on finding evidence to support the validity of their beliefs that they will impose meaning on what might be simply random sounds. This tendency seems especially prevalent when it comes to the recording and research of EVP.

But simple recorders are not the only instruments used to try and communicate with the spirit world. Instrumental Transcommunication ITC is defined as using technical means to receive meaningful messages from the other side. The ITC method originated as a form of EVP but encompasses a myriad of techniques to try and make contact with the spirit world using television, radios, telephones, computers and the popular "ghost boxes."

Communicating with the dead through electronic means has been around since the beginning of audio devices. The first known recording of spirit voices occurred in 1901 when Russian ethnologist Waldemar Bogoras went to Siberia to visit the shaman of a local tribe. Using a gramophone recorder during a spirit conjuring ritual, he recorded purported ghostly voices speaking in English and Russian. These are considered the first spirit voices ever recorded by a modern instrument.

The first recordings of what were alleged to be ghosts were made during a séance in the 1940s, when the Rev. Drayton Thomas was investigating spirit medium Gladys Osborne Leonard. During a sitting, he captured an audible disembodied voice that he later came to believe was that of his deceased father.

The psychic Attila von Szalay, who often claimed to hear disembodied voices in the air around him, started researching EVP with Raymond Bayless in the early 1950s. Their initial attempts with a 78-rpm record cutter and player were disappointing. Regardless, they continued their efforts using a device that Bayless invented. It consisted of a box with an interior microphone resting inside of an old-fashioned speaking trumpet. The microphone cord led out of the box and connected to a reel-to-reel tape recorder. Almost immediately, the researchers began to hear whispers originating from inside of the box, which they managed to record. Some of the messages that they recorded were very strange indeed. Among them was a female voice saying what sounded like, "Hot dog, Art!" Von Szalay carried on taping for many years using an open microphone connected to a reel-to-reel recorder.

Around 1959, Friederich Jurgenson, a retired Swedish opera singer, film producer and bird watcher, was recording bird songs in the woods near his home. When he played back his tapes, he discovered to his amazement that strange and garbled fragments of human speech had somehow made their way onto the recording. This was in spite of the fact that he was sure that he had been completely alone when the recording was made. He allegedly recognized two of the voices as those of his dead mother, who called him by her pet name for him, and his deceased wife. As he listened to the tapes, he found that the voices spoke in different languages. Also, he noted that longer phrases spoken by the mysterious voices often had improper structure and bad grammar and in some cases, the syllables were stretched or compressed in a way that made it difficult to understand what was being said. The strangest aspect of all was the eerie way that the voices seemed to reply to comments that Jurgenson inadvertently made. He began to hold conversations with the voices by recording questions and then later searching the tapes for answers. After four years of recording, he gave a press conference about his findings in 1963 and published a book called *Roesterna Fraen Rymden* Voices from the Universe . His conclusion was that the tape recorder acted as a form of electronic communication link to the realm of the dead.

In the later part of the 1960s, a student of Jurgenson named Dr. Konstantin Raudive began cataloguing thousands of EVP recordings. Some of the recordings were made available in book and record form and were later released as *Breakthrough: An Amazing Experiment in Electronic Communication with the Dead.*

There was resurgence in interest in EVP starting in the 1970s and 1980s, especially after the publication of the book *Voices of Eternity* by Sarah Estep. In addition to her more than fifteen years of research in the field, Estep also founded the American Association of Electronic Voice Phenomena, which still exists today. It was Estep who came up with a classification system for EVP:

Class A: The message can be heard without headphones and listeners generally agree on what words were spoken.

Class B: This classification usually requires careful listening through headphones to be able to discern the message content and not everyone will always agree on what words are spoken.

Class C: Requires headphones and often amplification and filtering to be able to understand this classification and the words may not still be completely discernable.

But merely recording the voices proved to not be enough for some researchers - they wanted to interact with whoever was speaking. In the 1950s, some researchers began developing theories concerning radio waves as a way to contact the dead. Short-lived projects like the "Psychfon" and others began trying to use radio technology, but with mixed results.

In the 1970s, a retired inventor and entrepreneur named George W. Meek embarked on the quest to develop a technology-based approach for communicating with the dead. He had followed the trends in EVP experimentation with great interest and wanted to try and invent something that was more advanced and less subject to controversy than the rudimentary tape-recorded methods that were popular at the time. Meek wanted to devise a system that would consistently allow clear two-way communication with the spirit world.

Meek and several interested colleagues formed the Meta Science Foundation and set to work. In the early stages of their trans-dimensional engineering work the group was guided by communications received in trance channeling sessions with psychic mediums in Philadelphia. During those Philadelphia séances, contact was reportedly made with several deceased but still very communicative scientists. One such contact was said to be with the spirit of Dr. William Francis Gray Swann. Swann was a university physics professor and a leader in cosmic ray research who had lived and died in Philadelphia. Swann had been the first director of the Bartol Research Foundation of the Franklin Institute. The Swann crater on the moon is named after him. His discarnate spirit was said to have provided Meek's group with the theoretical background and technical foundation upon which to begin construction of a new type of spirit communication device. The "Spiricom," as it soon came to be called, was born.

The name "Spiricom" was used to refer to an evolving series Mark I - IV, etc. of experimental devices that were built and tested over a period of several years. Initial results from the Spiricom experiments were mixed. Some interesting effects were observed but the desired quality of communication remained elusive. Then, in 1977, one of Meek's associates, an electronics technician named Bill O'Neil, reported that he had achieved voice contact with a spirit entity called "Doc Nick" while using the Mark III version of the Spiricom. Doc Nick was said to have been a former medical doctor and HAM radio operator who was able to assist O'Neil, Meek, and the Meta Science group by making technical suggestions for improving the Spiricom. Soon, contact with another deceased scientist was reported as having come to Bill O'Neil through the Mark IV version of the Spiricom. This new contact identified himself as Dr. George Jeffries Mueller, a university professor and electronics specialist who had died fourteen years earlier. Over the next few years, Dr. Mueller's Spiricom-empowered voice suggested further technical improvements to the system. In particular, Mueller was credited with suggesting a combination of thirteen specific audio frequency tones, which were to be used as the optimum background sound source by which a spirit could make itself heard by the researchers.

The Mark IV device was housed in a number of cumbersome radio devices, reminiscent of early HAM radio gear. It was neither portable nor easy to operate and the voices that were obtained were very mechanical and robotic, as if coming through an electronic larynx device used by someone whose vocal chords no longer work. In addition, some of the "spirits" that came through raised doubts among skeptical researchers. For example, in one recording of a dialogue with a spirit of someone who allegedly died in the 1830s, the "spirit" uses the word "okay." This was a problem since the word did not exist in the historical lexicon of the period when they supposedly lived. The word "okay" was a term coined by early railroad telegraph operators several decades later. Either the spirit had picked it up by listening to the researchers which was possible , or the contact was not as legitimate as it seemed. But while we can nit-pick about these communications, the concept was clear: Some experimenters were communicating with the unknown using new, modern and non-traditional methods.

Around 2001, a licensed HAM radio operator and electronic technician named Frank Sumption began experimenting with EVP and created a device that used a white noise generator, an amplifier, a small sound chamber, a microphone and a radio receiver to purportedly communicate with the dead. The device was designed to tune through radio stations along the dial, catching them for a few seconds, and with those words and regular static provide a method for spirits to speak. Sumption made the plans available on the Internet for anyone to build and thanks to this, scores of imitation boxes have come along, all of which are supposed to do the same thing.

Basically, the boxes receive little snippets of speech from various radio stations as they scan through the AM or FM band. At any given moment, the device may spew forth some words from a passing station, which believers will put together as a message, allegedly from beyond. Needless to say, many researchers are very skeptical about the whole thing, seeing the "messages" as nothing more than wishful thinking - much like opening a dictionary, pointing to words with your eyes closed and then making a "message" from them. They believe that messages received from such boxes are random words that are interpreted to mean whatever the listener wants to hear.

But is that the case every time? I don't believe that it is. Aside from the instances of pure fraud that exist in regards to such boxes and fraud DOES exist , there are also documented accounts of solid information and unexplainable contact that has been made, as well. I've seen such instances for myself!

But of all of the accounts of modern spirit communication that have been passed along, there is none more compelling that the alleged "Telephone to the Dead" that was invented by the famous American genius, Thomas Edison. The inventor of the light bulb - along with countless other amazing advances in technology - at one time expressed in interest in creating an electronic method of communicating with the dead. Unfortunately for the legend, though, no device was ever created, nor were the plans for one ever discovered among Edison's voluminous paperwork.

But, of course, that hasn't stopped the frauds who claim that it was!

A self-taught genius, Edison began experimenting with scientific theories as a child. His vision and incredible curiosity led to inventions like the light bulb, the phonograph, storage batteries, the film projector and much more. He worked tirelessly Edison was a notorious insomniac to create ways to make the world work better, communicate better and to be better entertained. Throughout his life, he maintained that it was possible to build anything if the right components were available. This idea would later be applied to a machine that he believed could communicate with the spirit world.

In spite of his theories about the possibility of such a machine, Edison was not a believer in the supernatural, nor was he a proponent of the popular Spiritualist movement. He had always been an agnostic and although he did not dispute the philosophies of religion, he didn't necessarily believe in their validity. He believed that when a person died, his body decayed but his intelligence lived on. He thought that the so-called "spirit world" was simply a limbo for disembodied intelligence.

He took these theories a step further by announcing that it might be possible to devise a machine that could communicate with the inhabitants of this limbo. An article in the October 1920 issue of *American* magazine, was entitled "Edison Working to Communicate with the Next World. The news of the invention made headlines around the world. In an essay that Edison wrote in 1920, he stated:

Now what I propose to do is furnish psychic investigators with an apparatus which will give a scientific aspect to their work. This apparatus, let me explain, is in the nature of a valve, so to speak. That is to say, the slightest conceivable effort is made to exert many times its initial power for indicative purposes. It is similar to a modern power house, where man, with his relatively puny one-eighth horse power, turns a valve which starts a 50,000 horse-power steam turbine. My apparatus is along those lines, in that the slightest effort will be magnified many times so as to give us whatever form of record we desire for the purpose of investigation. Beyond that I don't care to say anything further regarding its nature. I have been working out the details for some time; indeed a collaborator in this work died only the other day. In that he knew exactly what I am after in this work, I believe he ought to be the first to use it if he is able to do so. Of course, don't forget that I am making no claims for the survival of the personality; I am not promising communication with those who have passed out of this life. I merely state that I am giving psychic investigators an apparatus which may help them in their work, just as optical experts have given the microscope to the medical world. And if this apparatus fails to reveal anything of exceptional interest, I am afraid that I shall have lost all faith in the survival of the personality as we know it in this existence.

According to journals and newspapers, Edison began working on the apparatus - even though no plans of prototypes for it were ever found. Regardless, he continued to talk about its possibilities. He mentioned the machine again in 1920: "I have been at work for some time building an apparatus to see if it is possible for personalities which have left this earth to communicate with us and I hope to be able to finish it before very many months pass."

But apparently he never did. In recent times, this mysterious instrument has been dubbed the "Telephone to the Dead," but it's never turned up. Edison never referred to his proposed device by this name. It was given to the device by charlatans who attempt to cash in on a machine that never really existed.

But Edison may have built... well, something. In his essays, the item he was working on was likened to a valve that would amplify the ability for the spirits to manipulate the object so that "it does not matter how slight is the effort, it will be sufficient to record whatever there is to be recorded." That doesn't sound much like a "telephone." Could Edison have turned his energies to something else entirely? In a 1933 issue of *Modern Mechanix* magazine, there is an article that claims a secret meeting took place in Edison's lab in 1920 where he tried to communicate with the dead. Complete with illustrations, the article describes how Edison set up a beam projector and photoelectric receiver with delicate instruments that would register anything including smoke that would cross the beam's path. A group of scientists sat in the room for hours, but nothing happened.

If the story is true, then Edison did maintain an interest in the spirit world up until the time of his death, but he almost certainly gave up on plans for any kind of "telephone." The article about this "experiment" was published about in 1933, two years after Edison's death and thirteen years after the experiment and never addressed what happened to the device. What happened to it? Were there plans that still existed somewhere? Apparently not because, like the plans for the "telephone," they were never found. The Edison estate has stated that he was never involved in work with a device to communicate with the dead because no plans, or instruments, have ever been found.

So, how has such a story stayed alive over the years?

Legend has it that Edison continued to work on the "Telephone to the Dead" until he became comatose in 1931 and died shortly thereafter. But did it really exist? If it did, would it have worked? In the years following his death, curators at both of the Edison museums in Florida and New Jersey searched extensively for the components or the prototype for the machine to communicate with the dead. No trace of it was discovered but the accounts of the mysterious machine did not end with the inventor's death. The famous magician and friend of Edison's, Joseph Dunninger, claimed that he was shown a prototype of the machine but few others ever said they saw it.

In 1941, two of Edison's associates allegedly made contact with him during a séance that took place in New York. During the sitting, Edison's spirit allegedly claimed that plans and schematics for his apparatus were in the care of three of his assistants. Edison said that his "valve" machine had been completed, but had never worked. Then, in a second alleged séance, Edison made some suggestions about altering the apparatus so that it might work. Inventor J. Gilbert Wright was present at this séance and claimed that he made the changes that Edison told him about. Wright reportedly worked on the apparatus until his death in 1959 but that was the last that anyone ever heard of it.

Since that time, the machine to communicate with the dead has never resurfaced, making the device the greatest mystery of Edison's complex and intriguing life.

Unfortunately - especially for gullible members of the public - there are those who claim to possess Edison's machine, having obtained working plans for it from the spirit of its inventor. As of this writing, there are several people making such claims and charging members of the general public a hefty price for exhibitions of this "astonishing" technology.

The era of Spiritualism may have been filled with incidents of fraud, but sadly, taking advantage of believers in the spirit world did not end when the golden years of Spiritualism came to an end.

A HOSPITAL DESK AND CHAIR
A True Story of Possession that Shaped America's Belief in Evil

In 1949, the Devil came to St. Louis.... Or at least, if you believe the stories that have been told for the last sixty-odd years, a reasonable facsimile of him did.

This is a story that has been told for three generations. It is a terrifying story that has inspired books, films and documentaries. It is, without question, one of the great unsolved mysteries of the supernatural. It is a story that has been confused by theories and legends and even after sorting through all of them, it's difficult to separate fact from fantasy. What really happened to bring a young Lutheran boy and his frightened family from Maryland to St. Louis, where they pleaded for help from the Catholic Church? What happened at the old Alexian Brothers hospital that still has former staff members whispering about it in fear today? Did inaminate objects in the boy's hospital room truly manifest a residual feeling of evil from the events that took place around them? And, most of all, was this boy really demonically possessed?

The story began not in St. Louis, but in the small Washington, D.C. suburb of Cottage City, Maryland. As many readers already know, what has come to be known as the "St. Louis Exorcism Case" would go on to inspire William Peter Blatty's 1971 best-selling book and the movie based on it, *The Exorcist.* In the novel, a young girl is possessed by a demon and is subjected to an exorcism by Catholic priests. In the true story, though, the subject of the alleged possession was not a girl but a boy who has been identified in various accounts as "Roland" or "Robbie Doe." Robbie as we will call him here was born in 1935 and grew up in Cottage City. He was the only child of a dysfunctional family and had a troubled childhood.

In January 1949, the family of thirteen-year-old Robbie began to be disturbed by scratching sounds that came from inside the walls and ceilings of the house. Believing that the house was infested with mice, the parents called an exterminator but he could find no sign of rodents. To make matters worse, his efforts seemed to exacerbate the problem. Noises that sounded like someone walking in the hallway could be heard and dishes and objects were often found to be moved without anyone admitting to have moved them.

The noises were disturbing, but they weren't nearly as frightening as when Robbie began to be attacked. His bed shook so hard that he couldn't sleep at night. His blankets and sheets were torn off. When he tried to hold onto them, he was reportedly pulled off the bed and onto the floor with the sheets still gripped in his hands.

Those who have come to believe the boy was genuinely possessed feel that he may have been invaded by an invisible entity after experimenting with a Ouija board. He had been taught to use the device by his "Aunt Tillie," a relative who took an active interest in Spiritualism and the occult. Tillie had passed away a short time before the events began. She had lived in St. Louis and had died of multiple sclerosis on January 26, 1949. In the written accounts of the exorcism, it was noted that the family believed there was a connection between the woman's death and the problems with Robbie.

Many of the early events in the case were chronicled by the Jesuit priests who later performed the exorcism. Apparently, a diary was kept and it was the same diary that author William Peter Blatty heard about when he was a student at Georgetown University in 1949. He first became interested in the story after reading about in newspaper articles and discussed it with his instructor, the Rev. Thomas Bermingham, S.J. The "diary" of the Robbie Doe case came to light in the fall of 1949 under rather odd circumstances. Fr. Eugene B. Gallagher, S.J., who was on the faculty of Georgetown, was lecturing on the topic of exorcisms when one of his students, the son of a psychiatrist at St. Elizabeth's Hospital in Washington, spoke of a diary that had been kept by the Jesuits involved in the Robbie Doe exorcism. Father Gallagher asked the psychiatrist, who may have been one of the professionals involved in the early stages of the case, for a copy of the diary and eventually received a 16-page document that had the rather mundane title of "Case Study by Jesuit Priests." Its contents, however, were far from mundane. It had apparently been intended for use as a guide for future exorcisms. Blatty asked to see a copy of the diary, but his request was refused.

He later turned back to newspapers for information about the case and discovered that one article listed the name of the priest involved. His name was Rev. William S. Bowdern, S.J. of St. Louis. Bowdern refused to comment on the case for the newspaper reports, as priests who perform exorcisms are said to be sworn to secrecy. Blatty tried contacting him anyway but the priest refused to cooperate. Out of respect, Blatty changed the identity of the possession victim in his book to a young girl, but the exorcist in the novel remains a thinly veiled characterization of Father Bowdern. Father Bowdern passed away in 1983, never publicly acknowledging the fact that he was involved in the sensational St. Louis case.

But the diary remained and revealed a series of bizarre occurrences reaching from Maryland to St. Louis.

The strange knocking, scratching and attacks on Robbie continued and soon, the family was desperate. They turned to the Lutheran Church for help and the Rev. Luther Schulze, the pastor of the family's church, tried praying with Robbie and his parents in their home and then with Robbie alone. Nothing seemed to help and Schulze questioned whether the house was haunted - or if the boy was. He offered to let Robbie spend the night in his home and his parents quickly agreed. They were anxious to try anything that might help by this time.

That night, Mrs. Schulze went to the guest room and Robbie and the minister retired to the twin beds in the master bedroom. About ten minutes later, Schulze reported that he heard the sound of Robbie's bed creaking and shaking. He also heard strange scratching noises inside of the walls, just like the ones that had been heard at Robbie's own house. Schulze quickly switched on the lights and saw Robbie's bed was vibrating. When he prayed for it to stop, the vibration grew even more violent. He stated that Robbie was wide awake but he was not moving in a way that would cause the bed to shake.

Schulze then suggested that Robbie try and sleep in a heavy armchair that was located across the room. While Schulze watched him closely, the chair began to move. First, it scooted backward several inches and its legs jolted forward and back. It slammed against the wall and then it tipped over and deposited the boy unhurt onto the floor.

Trying not to be frightened or discouraged, Rev. Schulze made a pallet of blankets on the floor for Robbie to sleep on. As soon as the boy fell asleep though, the pallet began to slide across the floor and slipped under one of the beds. When Robbie was startled awake by the movement, he sat up and struck his head on one of the bedposts. Again, the minister made up the pallet, only to this time have it whip across the floor and slide under the other bed. Robbie's hands were visible the entire time and his body was taut with tension. He was not making the blankets move.

Schulze was now puzzled and a little afraid. He suggested that Robbie's parents take the boy to see a medical doctor and a psychologist to rule out any kind of physical or mental problems that might be causing the phenomena to take place. The minister also contacted J.B. Rhine, the famed founder of the parapsychology laboratory at Duke University. He explained what was going on and Rhine and his partner and wife, Louisa Rhine, drove from North Carolina to Cottage City to see the boy. Unfortunately, no activity took place while the investigators were present, but Rhine did deduce that it sounded like a classic poltergeist case in which the boy's unconscious abilities were influencing the objects around him. The details fit well with other experimental results that Rhine had been obtaining.

And while the explanation suggested by Rhine must have appealed to the minister, he did an abrupt about-face a short time later when the phenomena took another turn. A week or so after the incident at Schulze's home, bloody scratches began to appear on the boy's body. Perhaps startled by this new turn of events, Schulze suggested that the family contact a Catholic priest, telling the family that "Catholics know about these kinds of things."

After that, things get more confusing. According to some sources, Robbie's father went to the nearby St. James Church in Mount Rainier, Maryland. There, he met with a young priest named Edward Albert Hughes who was the assistant pastor of the church at the time. Hughes was skeptical and reluctant to get involved in the matter, but he did agree to go and see Robbie. During the visit, Robbie allegedly addressed the priest in Latin, a language that he did not know. Shaken, Hughes was said to have applied to his archbishop for permission to conduct an exorcism. The sources go on to say that the ritual was performed at Georgetown University Hospital in February. Robbie seemed to go into a trance and he thrashed about and spoke in tongues. Hughes ordered the boy to be put into restraints but Robbie somehow managed to work a piece of metal bedspring loose and he slashed the priest with it. The stories say that Hughes subsequently left St. James, suffered a nervous breakdown and during masses that he held later in life, he could only hold the consecrated host aloft in one hand.

This story turned out not to be true. Father Hughes became assistant pastor of St. James Church under Rev. William Canning in June 1948 and he served without a break until June 1960. He was later reassigned to St. James in 1973 and stayed there until his death in 1980. Church records do not indicate that he ever suffered a breakdown, or that he ever made an attempt to exorcize Robbie at Georgetown University Hospital. However, Robbie was checked into the hospital under his real name for several days during the period when the alleged exorcism attempt took place. Records say that he underwent extensive medical and psychological evaluations, but there was no mention of an exorcism.

Father Hughes also never visited Robbie in his home. In truth, his mother brought him to St. James only once for a consultation. There is nothing to suggest that Robbie spoke to the priest in Latin and no evidence to say that Father Hughes was ever slashed with a bedspring. Those who knew Hughes personally remember him suffering no injuries during this period and the fact is, the church social calendar showed him to be quite busy during the weeks after Robbie's release from the hospital.

But strange things continued to occur. Robbie's hospital stay was documented as occurring between February 28, 1949 and March 2, 1949 but according to the priest's "diary," strange things began to happen on February 26. The statement records that "there appeared scratches on the boy's body for about four successive nights. After the fourth night words were written in printed form. These letters were clear but seemed to have been scratched on the body by claws."

At about this same time, Robbie's mother began to suggest that perhaps a trip away from Maryland might free the boy from the strange happenings. She thought that perhaps they could leave their troubles behind by visiting St. Louis. Robbie's mother was a native of that city and still had many relatives there. The more she considered this, the better the idea seemed. And apparently, "something" agreed because the word "Louis" inexplicably appeared on Robbie's rib cage. When this "skin branding" occurred, Robbie's hands were visible and his mother specifically noted that he could not have scratched the words himself. He had been under observation at the time and the words, according to witnesses, had simply appeared.

The priest's diary even noted that the mysterious writing also appeared on Robbie's back. Later on, while in St. Louis, there was some discussion about sending Robbie to school while in the city but the message NO appeared on his wrists. A large letter "N" also appeared on each of his legs and his mother feared disobeying what she saw as a supernatural order. It has been suggested that perhaps Robbie created the writing himself with his mind, either consciously or unconsciously. With that in question, it should be noted that before his parents consulted a priest, they also had him examined by a psychiatrist. He reported that the boy was quite normal, as did a medical doctor who gave him a complete physical examination.

At this point, records do indicate that Robbie's mother took him to consult with Father Hughes at St. James Church. During this one documented visit, he suggested that the family use blessed candles, holy water and special prayers to perhaps rid the boy of his problems. Robbie's mother began the use of the blessed candles and on one occasion, a comb flew violently through the air and struck them, snuffing out the flames. The kitchen table once overturned in the boy's presence and milk and food flew off of counters and onto the floor. Another time, a coat jerked from a hanger and a book landed at Robbie's feet. A chair that the boy was sitting in spun around so fast that he was unable to stop it. He eventually had to stop attending school because his desk refused to remain in the same place.

The priest's diary went on to add that "the mother took the bottle of holy water and sprinkled all of the rooms." She then took the bottle and placed it on a shelf but it snapped into the air and flew onto the floor, although it did not break.

A 1975 report stated that attempts were also made to baptize Robbie into the Catholic faith in order to help him. The press mentioned that one of these attempts was made during Robbie's hospital stay not an exorcism, as was later reported and then later in St. Louis. Another baptism attempt was allegedly made in February 1949. It was said that as Robbie's uncle was driving him to the rectory for the ceremony, the boy suddenly glared at him, grabbed him by the throat and shouted, "You son of a bitch, you think I'm going to be baptized but you are going to be fooled!"

The Catholic baptism ritual usually only takes about fifteen minutes but for Robbie, it reportedly lasted for several hours. It was said that when the priest asked, "Do you renounce the devil and all his works?" Robbie would go into such a thrashing rage that he had to be restrained.

In early March, after being released from the hospital and found physically and mentally normal, Robbie boarded a train to St. Louis with his parents. The family was taken in by relatives who lived in a brick, two-story house on Roanoke Drive in Bel Nor, a north side suburb. It was there, the boy's mother hoped, that he might be freed from the strange and horrifying events that were plaguing him. For those readers who are convinced that nothing was occurring in this case aside from overactive imaginations and silly superstition, they may want to consider the trip to St. Louis itself as evidence that *something* supernatural or not was taking place. The fact that Robbie's parents would take the boy out of school, his father would abandon his employment and they would all travel halfway across the county in a last-ditch effort to find help is suggestive -- if not downright convincing-- that terrible things were indeed happening.

Unfortunately, Robbie did not improve in St. Louis. His aunt and uncle, as well as various other relatives, witnessed more of the "skin brandings" and also saw his bed shaking on many occasions. On March 8, 1949, the shaking of the mattress and scratching continued. Robbie's cousin saw a stool that was sitting near the bed fly across the room. The boy was so concerned about Robbie that he even tried lying down on the bed beside him to stop the mattress from moving. To his dismay, it didn't work. Finally, another of Robbie's cousins, who had attended St. Louis University, went to see her old teacher there, Rev. Raymond J. Bishop, S.J. She asked him if he might be able to assist Robbie. He agreed to look into the situation and it was Father Bishop who brought William Bowdern into the case.

Father Bowdern was not on the faculty of St. Louis University. In 1949, he was the pastor of St. Francis Xavier College Church, located at the corner of Grand and Lindell Boulevards in St. Louis. He was a native of the city and had served as a chaplain during World War II. He had many years of experience dealing with people and their problems and he listened carefully to the story that Father Bishop told him. Then, he and Bishop went to see Paul Reinert, S.J., the president of the university. All of them were skeptical about the case and were concerned with bringing embarrassment to the church and the college, but they decided that it might be well to have the boy say some prayers and to give him a priestly blessing.

Apparently, Father Bishop first went to see the family alone. He came to bless the house and the room in which Robbie slept. A second-class holy relic of St. Margaret Mary was pinned on the boy's bed. But even after the blessing and in spite of the relic, the bed still shook and swayed and the scratches still appeared all over the boy's body. Bishop then sprinkled holy water on the bed in the form of a cross and the movement suddenly ceased. It started up again after the priest stepped out of the room. Then, a sharp pain allegedly struck Robbie in the stomach and he cried out. His mother pulled back the bed covers and lifted the boy's pajama top to reveal angry red lines that zigzagged across the boy's abdomen. During this entire time, Robbie was in clear view of at least six witnesses.

The next two nights passed in the same way, with a shaking mattress, scratching noises and objects being thrown about. On March 11, Father Bishop returned to the home and this time, he brought Father Bowdern with him. The Jesuits were still skeptical about the case but were open-minded enough to observe the boy and also to study the literature available about demonic attacks on humans. The priests came and prayed again and this time, the activity did not respond. However, as soon as the two priests left, a loud noise was reportedly heard in Robbie's room and several family members rushed in to see what had happened. They discovered that a seventy-five- pound bookcase had swiveled in a complete circle, a bench had turned over and a crucifix that one of the priests had left under Robbie's pillow had moved to the end of the bed. As they rushed into the room, the mattress was violently shaking and bouncing once more. Needless to say, the family was terrified.

Unfortunately, there is no reliable, clear-cut information about how the decision was reached by the Jesuits to perform an exorcism. According to Church doctrine, there are a number of different conditions that have to be met to show that someone is truly possessed. Whether or not these conditions were met is unknown, but Bowdern and Bishop went to Archbishop Joseph E. Ritter for permission to perform an exorcism on March 16. Ritter had a reputation as a down-to-earth progressive and earlier in the decade, he had campaigned hard to integrate the St. Louis schools and parishes. Later, he would also play a large role in the sweeping reforms that came to the Church that were known as Vatican II. The Jesuits, who already have a tense history with the Catholic Church as a whole, had no idea how Ritter would respond to the request. Surprisingly, he prompted agreed.

And the exorcism began...

The chronology throughout the remainder of the case is extremely confusing. It is not clear how long Robbie stayed at his relatives' house where portions of the exorcism took place , but it is known that he was taken to the Alexian Brothers Hospital in south St. Louis, possibly for as long as a month, and that portions of the exorcism were also carried out in the rectory of St. Francis Xavier College Church. That rectory has since been demolished and replaced by a newer one.

It also isn't clear how many people were actually actively involved in the exorcism. The names of the exorcists given out in St. Louis were Father Bowdern, Father Bishop and Father Lawrence Kenny. Father Charles O'Hara of Marquette University in Milwaukee was also present as a witness he later passed on information about what he saw there to Father Eugene Gallagher at Georgetown University and there were undoubtedly several hospital staff members and seminary students who were also in attendance.

One of these students was Walter Halloran, who I was able to personally interview before his death in 2005. At that time, he was a strapping young former football player who had been asked along to hold Robbie down. Exorcisms were known for being often violent rituals and the Jesuits must have felt that the young man would prove to be very useful. After the exorcism, Halloran finished his studies and later became a Jesuit priest.

The exorcism started at the home of Robbie's family. The priests came late in the evening and after Robbie went to bed, the ritual began. The boy was said to go into a trance, his bed shook and welts and scratches appeared on his body. Bishop was said to have wiped away blood that welled up in the scratches while Halloran attempted to hold the boy down. An exorcism is said to be a dire spiritual and physical struggle. The demon that takes control of the person also tries to break the faith of the exorcist involved. Father Bowdern had prepared himself for the exhausting events through a religious fast of prayer, bread and water. It is said that from the time he first learned of Robbie's plight until the exorcism had run its course, Bowdern lost nearly forty pounds.

As the prayers commanding the departure of the evil spirit began, Robbie winced and rolled in a sudden seizure of pain. Over the next two hours, the boy was branded and scratched thirty times on his stomach, chest, throat, thighs, calves and back. All the while, he reportedly cursed and screamed obscenities in a voice that "ranged from deep bass to falsetto." The ritual came to an end that night near dawn, but little progress had been made.

The ordeal continued for many weeks and through many readings of the exorcism ritual. According to the witnesses, the boy's responses became more violent and repulsive as time went on. He allegedly spoke in Latin, in a variety of voices, in between bouts of screams and curses. He spat in the faces of the priests who knelt and stood by his bed and his spittle and vomit struck them with uncanny accuracy and over great distances. He punched and slapped the priests and the witnesses. He constantly urinated, belched and passed gas that was said to have an unbelievably foul stench. His body thrashed and contorted into seemingly impossible shapes all through the night. Each morning, though, he would appear to be quite normal and would profess to have no memory of the events that took place after dark. He usually spent the day reading comics or playing board games with the student assistants.

The ritual continued with the prayers being recited every day, despite Robbie's rabid reaction to them. The exorcism seemed virtually useless and so the priests requested permission to instruct Robbie in the Catholic faith. They felt that his conversion would help to strengthen their fight against the entity controlling the boy. His parents consented and he was prepared for his first communion. During this time of instruction, Robbie seemed to quiet somewhat and he was moved to the church rectory. He seemed to enjoy his lessons in the Catholic faith, but this time of peace would not last. As Robbie prepared to receive communion, the priests literally had to drag him into the church. He broke out in a rage that was worse than anything the exorcists could remember.

By this time, the family was exhausted and was ready to give up. Father Bowdern began searching for a new approach and so he made arrangements to return Robbie to Maryland and continue the ritual. It was said that during the train ride, Robbie became maniacal and attacked Father Bowdern. He and the others present wrestled with Robbie until he finally fell asleep.

Bowdern found no accommodations to continue the exorcism with Robbie in Maryland. No one would have anything to do with the boy and so he returned with him to St. Louis. Robbie's instructions in the Catholic faith continued. It was now Holy Week, the week before Easter, and Robbie was taken to White House, a Jesuit retreat that overlooked the Mississippi River. It was there where the exorcism was continued.

Events now seemed to be at an impasse. Seeking a solution, Bowdern again plunged into the literature regarding possession. He learned of an 1870 case that took place in Wisconsin that seemed similar to Robbie's plight and he devised a new strategy. On the night of April 18, the ritual resumed. Bowdern forced Robbie to wear a chain of religious medals and to hold a crucifix in his hands. Suddenly, Robbie became strangely contrite and he began to ask questions about the meaning of certain Latin prayers. Bowdern ignored him, though, refusing to engage in conversation. Instead, he demanded to know the name of the demon that possessed the boy and when he would depart. Robbie exploded in a rage.

Five witnesses held him down while he screamed that he was a "fallen angel" but Bowdern continued on with the ritual. He recited it incessantly for hours until Robbie suddenly interrupted in a loud, masculine voice, identifying himself as "St. Michael the Archangel." The voice ordered the demon to depart. Robbie's body went into violent contortions and spasms. Then, he fell quiet. A moment later, he sat up, smiled and then spoke in a normal voice. "He's gone," Robbie said and then told the priests of a vision that he had of St. Michael holding a flaming sword.

The exorcism was finally over.

Robbie left St. Louis with his parents twelve days later and returned to Maryland. He wrote to Father Bowdern in May 1949 and told him that he was happy and that he had a new dog. He was, by last report, still living in Maryland and is a devout Catholic with three children. He has only dim recollections of what happened in 1949.

Father Bowdern believed until the end of his life that he and his fellow priests had been battling a demonic entity. His supporters in this maintain that there were many witnesses to the supernatural events that took place and that no other explanations existed for what they had seen. A full report that was filed by the Catholic Church stated that the case of Robbie Doe was a "genuine demonic possession." According to Father John Nicola, who had the opportunity to review the report, he noted that forty-one persons had signed a document attesting to the fact that they had witnessed paranormal phenomena in the case.

Was Robbie really possessed? Many people don't believe that he was. Some have stated that they think Robbie's troubled childhood was to blame. The "possession" started as a way to get attention, or to get out of school, and then it snowballed into the mess that it became. Most of the debunkings of the case only deal with the inconsistencies of some reports; they never delve into the possible supernatural events that were witnessed and only address the incidents in Maryland, never those that took place in St. Louis.

And there are other theories. Some would agree that while Robbie was not possessed, he was afflicted with another unexplainable paranormal disturbance. They point to psychokinetic events, when physical objects move about, because of some sort of magnetic power that is generated by disturbed people, especially adolescents. While medical doctors have no interest in this, a few more adventurous scientists have grudgingly speculated that perhaps the human mind has abilities and energies that are still unrecognized. These energies just might be able to make objects move, writing to appear and beds to shake. If it can really happen, it just might explain what happened to Robbie Doe.

Others feel that Robbie suffered from a mental illness. He may have been hallucinating or suffering from some weird psychosomatic illness that caused him to curse and scream and to thrash about so violently.

It should be noted, however, that people who have suggested that all of this was nothing more than a hoax or a mental illness are all people who were in no way involved in the case. Even Father Walter Halloran, later stated that while he was not an expert in exorcisms and could not make an official determination about whether the possession was genuine or not, he did feel that it was real. "I have always thought in my mind that it was," he said. He described seeing objects move, witnessing Robbie's bed lift off the floor and other strange events. Since he was present during the events of 1949, his opinion has to be considered and acknowledged far beyond those who speculate and yet were not even born when the exorcism occurred.

Skeptics aside, there are many who believe the events in St. Louis were real. They believe that Robbie truly was possessed and accept no other explanation for what happened in 1949. And perhaps they are right because there is no question that memories of the exorcism remain vivid today in a variety of eerie ways.

After the exorcism at the old Alexian Brothers Hospital concluded, Brother Rector Cornelius, the monk in charge of the institution, went to the fifth floor corridor of the old wing, turned a key in the lock on the door of the room that had been used for Robbie's exorcism and stated that it was to be kept permanently locked. From that day on, the Alexian Brothers in St. Louis maintained the secrets of the exorcism. The existence of Father Bishop's diary also remained a secret for many years and a copy of it was placed inside the locked hospital room. Everyone who worked in the hospital, though, knew why the room was kept locked.

For years after the exorcism, people who were involved in the case, or who worked at the hospital, shared stories of things they heard and saw during the ordeal that occurred in the psychiatric wing. Orderlies spoke of cleaning up pools of vomit and urine in the boy's room. Staff members and nurses claimed to hear the sounds of someone screaming and the echoes of demonic laughter coming from Robbie's room. More than anything, though, they spoke of the cold air that seemed to emanate from the room. No matter how warm the rest of the hospital was, the area around the door to the boy's room was always ice cold.

And even after the exorcism ended, something apparently remained behind. Was it some remnant of the entity that possessed Robbie or perhaps the impression of the horrific events that occurred in the room? Whatever it was, the room was never re-opened. Electrical problems plagued the surrounding rooms and it was always cold in the hallway outside the door to this particular room. The entire section of the hospital was eventually closed but whether or not this was because of the "exorcism room" is unknown.

As the years passed, tales about the locked room were passed on to new monks who came to serve at the hospital. They knew that the room was located in a wing for extremely ill mental patients but did not understand why the room was kept sealed -- until they heard about what had happened there. The Alexians who had been on the staff in 1949 would not soon forget what they had seen and heard.

In the early 1950s, one of the Alexian brothers was working at a summer camp for boys that was operated by the St. Louis archdiocese near Hillsboro, Missouri. He was a gentle, friendly man who was well liked by the boys. One afternoon, the burly monk was sitting at a table in the mess hall with several of the boys. They were talking and laughing and paying little attention to a radio that was playing in the background.

Then, a song by Kay Kyser came on the radio. It was about the cartoon character Woody Woodpecker and it featured Woody's jangling and rather maniacal laugh. The large Alexian lunged across the table and roughly yanked the radio's electrical cord out of the socket. Trembling and breaking out in a cold sweat, he simply told his companions that he couldn't stand the song. Later on, though, he told them about the nights in the spring of 1949, when he and the other monks were kept awake by wild, chilling laughter - laughter that sounded a lot like Woody Woodpecker's -- coming from one of the rooms in the old wing of the Alexian Brothers Hospital.

Other Alexians had their own stories to tell. They spoke of banging sounds on their doors at night, voices calling in the darkened corridors, and more. Staff members would continue to tell the stories in the years to come and I have personally spoken to more than a dozen nurses, maintenance people, orderlies and doctors who have dark and distinct memories of the old wing and the locked room on the psychiatric floor. Some of them have told me that sometimes, even after all of these years, they still dream about that wing and that locked door.

The stories about the "St. Louis Exorcism" have continued to circulate over the years, and many of the stories have involved the physical locations that were connected to the case. One of them, the old rectory of the St. Francis Xavier Church, was torn down many years ago and in 1978, the old Alexian Brothers Hospital became a memory as well. But stories about the hospital are still told today.

In May 1976, work began on a new Alexian Brothers Hospital and in the first phase of the construction, some of the old outbuildings were torn down and a new six-story tower with two-story wings was built. In October 1978, the patients were moved out of the original hospital building and the contractor ordered the structure to be razed. It was done, but not without difficulty. Workers on the demolition crew claimed to be unable to control the wrecking ball when that floor was taken off. The ball swung around and hit a portion of a new building but luckily, it did no damage. This incident seemed to further enhance the legend of the locked room.

Before the demolition was started, workers first combed through the building for old furniture that was to be taken out and sold. One of them found a locked room in the psychiatric wing and broke in. The room was fully furnished with a dust-covered bed, nightstand, a chair and a desk table with a single drawer. Before removing the table, the worker curiously opened the drawer to see what was inside. He found a small stack of papers inside, which would turn out to be the priest's diary of the exorcism.

The furniture, including all of the items in the locked room, was sold to a company that owned a nursing home that was located a short distance from the hospital. All of the furniture that was salvaged from the hospital was locked in a room on the fourth floor of the nursing home and was never used. The nursing home was later torn down and many of the demolition workers, like the staff people and the city inspectors who had come through, refused to go on the fourth floor -- but were never able to explain why. What became of the furniture from the locked room is unknown.

Or at least that's one version of the story...

In recent years, another, far stranger story about the fate of the items within the room has come to light. According to sources, the furniture was removed from the locked room at the time of the demolition but was never sold to the nursing home with the rest of hospital funiture. The bed, nightstand, chair and desk table were instead moved and locked away in the basement of a rectory in St. Louis. A number of years later, the rectory was scheduled to be torn down and movers were brought to haul away a number of items that were left in the basement. According to one of them, he arrived at the rectory with some other workers and they were taken down into the basement by a priest, who unlocked a door to one of the rooms in the rear of the basement and then stood back to let the men inside. The worker distinctly remembered that the priest refused to set foot inside. Within the room, they found several pieces of furniture that they were directed to remove and then seal up into a wooden crate. After that, the crate was to be placed in a locked storage facility. The movers completed the task and then moved the crate to a storage warehouse across the river in Illinois. According to the story, the furniture from the "Exorcism Room," as it became known, is still there, sealed in a crate and largely forgotten.

In closing, I can only say that the St. Louis Exorcism case, whether you believe in demonic possession and exorcisms or not, remains unsolved. There is simply no way to adequately dismiss every unusual thing that was reported in this case without just saying that everyone involved was either a liar, drunk or insane. For myself, I can't say whether young Robbie Doe was possessed, or not possessed, but what I can say is that this is one of the few cases of alleged "possession" that has left me with many lingering questions.

The reader, of course, is advised to judge for himself but as for myself, I think there are certainly more things in heaven and earth than are dreamt of in our philosophies and I'll just leave it at that.

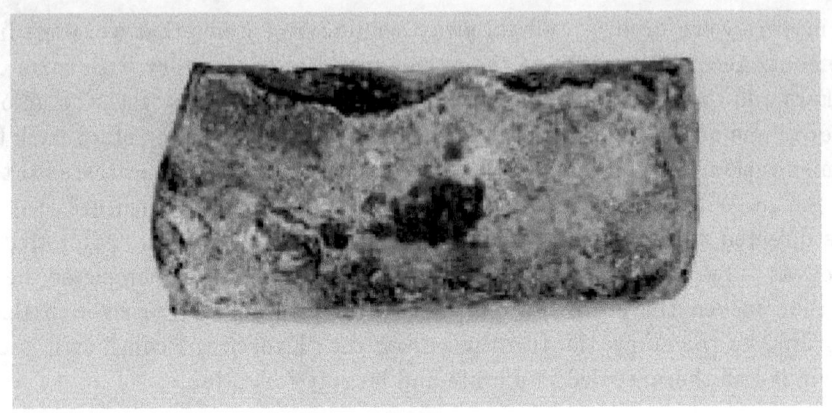

A BRICK
Lingering Energies of the St. Valentine's Day Massacre

The story of the infamous St. Valentine's Day Massacre is not only one of the best-known tales in the annals of organized crime, but it's also one that is very familiar to paranormal enthusiasts, as well. Many know the stories of lingering spirits that are believed to still be found at the site where the massacre occurred, but do readers also know that the lingering energy of the event was said to have actually spread all over the country in the late 1960s? It was at that time when bricks from the demolished garage on Chicago's North Clark Street - where seven men met their deaths - began wreaking havoc on anyone who possessed them.
Or so the stories go.

The rise of organized crime in Chicago began with the advent of Prohibition. The law that banned the sale and production of liquor went into effect in 1920 and vast fortunes began to be made by lawless elements in the city. The decline of these criminal empires began almost a decade later in February 1929. It was on St. Valentine's Day of that year that the general public no longer saw the mob as "public benefactors," offering alcohol to a thirsty city, but as the collection of cold-blooded killers and thugs that it truly was. The massacre changed the face of Chicago crime forever and led to the end of Al Capone's role as mob boss of the city.
Capone, who had started out as a gun for hire for an old benefactor named John Torrio, quickly rose through the ranks of the underworld to become Torrio's second in command. After his boss had a brush with death when friends of

murdered mobster Dean O'Banion tried to kill him, Capone took over the operations of the South Side Outfit, eventually creating a multi-million-dollar crime empire at the age of only twenty-six. By 1929, Capone had wiped out most of his rivals, with the exception of the remnants of O'Banion's old gang, now run by George "Bugs" Moran. Moran spent a good part of his time purposely antagonizing Capone and made several attempts to kill him in revenge for the murder of Dean O'Banion in 1924.

In December 1928, Capone left Chicago for Miami Beach, where he kept a second home. In early February, one of his closest confidantes from Chicago, Jack McGurn, arrived for a short visit. After his departure, Capone spoke as telephone records would later show at length every day with Jake Guzik, the Outfit's collector and another confidante of Capone, who lived at Chicago's Congress Hotel. The telephone conversations between the two men stopped on February 11. Then, a single call was placed to Capone's Palm Island winter home three days later.

That call came on February 14 - St. Valentine's Day.

A light snow was falling on North Clark Street that morning of February 14. Traffic was moving slowly as a black 1927 Cadillac touring car edged onto the street from Webster Avenue. There was a police alarm on the running board and fastened to the back of the driver's seat was a gun rack like the one used in squad cars. The driver of the Cadillac, who had on horn-rimmed glasses, was wearing a policeman's uniform, which included a cap and brass star. A man sitting next to him in the passenger's seat also wore a police uniform. The three men in the back seat were wearing long trench coats and fedoras.

As the Cadillac turned the corner onto Clark Street, a truck sideswiped it, forcing it to stop. The truck driver, Elmer Lewis, horrified at having hit what he assumed was a police car, scrambled out of his cab and, filled with remorse and nervous fear, hurried toward the Cadillac. The blue-uniformed man behind the wheel smiled at him, a gap showing where one of his upper front teeth was missing, and waved, reassuring him that no real damage was done and that he could return to his truck as if nothing had happened. Baffled but relieved, Lewis watched the black Cadillac drive on for about half a block, then stop in front of a shipping and packing company at 2122 North Clark. Four men got out of the car and went inside.

Meanwhile, North Side gang leader George Moran was on his way to the garage on North Clark Street. The night before, a man had called Moran and offered him a truckload of hijacked Old Log Cabin whiskey from Detroit that could be his for $57 per case. Moran had told him to deliver the shipment around 10:30 a.m. to the garage, which was used as a distribution point for the gang. He told the hijacker that he would have men on hand to help unload the truck. Moran had been suffering from a head cold and got a late start for the rendezvous. In his Parkway Hotel apartment, he kissed his wife Alice goodbye and took the elevator to the lobby, where his met up with his gambler friend Ted Newberry. It was a little after 10:30, and they had several blocks to walk to the garage. The temperature was a biting 15 degrees and a bone-chilling wind was blowing from the west. Hunched against the cold, their coat collars pulled up to their ears, Moran and Newberry took a shortcut through an alley behind the garage. Willie Marks, one of the gang's specialists in business racketeering, was also running late. He arrived on Clark Street by trolley car at almost the same time.

The garage was a one-story building, constructed from red brick. It was sixty feet wide and one hundred and twenty feet long, framed by four-story buildings on either side. Both the plate-glass window and the glass-paneled door to the right of it had been painted black to hide the interior from the view of passersby. A white sign with black lettering was displayed in the lower half of the window. It read:

S-M-C CARTAGE CO.
Shipping - Packing
Phone Diversey 1471
Long Distance Hauling

Behind the window, running the width of the building, was a narrow office that was separated from the warehouse by a wooden partition. The warehouse had a concrete floor and brick walls. The original whitewash that had covered the brick walls had turned grimy and yellow with age. Tall, wide doors at the rear opened onto the loading area in the alley.

On the morning of February 14, three empty trucks were parked in the warehouse. A fourth was jacked up in the center of the floor and lying under it, wearing oil-spattered coveralls and putting in a new oil pan, was Johnny May, a 35-year-old failed safecracker that Moran hired as a mechanic for $50 a week. May lived in an apartment at 1249 West Madison Street with his wife, Hattie, their six children and a German Shepherd named Highball. The dog had accompanied his master to work and was tied by his leash to the front bumper of the truck. May had brought some scraps of meat for him in a paper bag.

Six other men were in the warehouse that morning, gathered around a coffee pot that percolated on a hot plate, giving out a tempting aroma. A small iron space heater in the corner gave out a little warmth, but not enough for the men to remove their hats and overcoats.

The men included the Gusenberg brothers, Frank and Pete, who had a long day ahead of them. As soon as the hijacked liquor was delivered, they were supposed to drive two empty trucks to Detroit to pick up some smuggled Canadian whiskey. Pete "Goosey" Gusenberg was a forty-year-old career criminal who first started showing up in police files in 1902. He spent several years in Joliet prison for burglary, earning his parole in 1911, only to end up in Leavenworth in 1923, sentenced along with "Big Tim" Murphy and others after a mail freight car robbery. After his release, he became a gunman for Moran. Pete's common-law wife was a woman named Myrtle Coppleman. As far as Myrtle knew, her husband was a travelling salesman named Peter Gorman.

Frank Gusenberg was four years younger than his brother and despite having a police record that dated back to 1909, his only prison sentence was for ninety days for disorderly conduct. Frank was a bigamist, married to two women named Lucille and Ruth at the same time. Neither woman knew of the other's existence. Like his brother, Frank posed as a travelling salesman, using his alleged career as a front for his real profession of robbery, burglary and murder for hire.

Adam Heyer was also present that morning. A business college graduate and certified accountant before doing prison time for embezzlement, he handled all of the gang's finances and also managed the Fairview Kennel Club, the North Side gang's dog-racing enterprise. Little else is known about Heyer. Even his wife of seven months, Mame, did not know his birth date, although he was believed to be around forty years old.

Al "Gorilla" Weinshank or Weinshenker , the newest member of the gang, had helped Moran muscle into the cleaning and dyeing rackets and was the owner of a speakeasy called the Alcazar. Heavyset and round-faced, he bore a resemblance to Moran, which was enhanced on February 14 by the fact that both men happened to be wearing tan fedoras and gray overcoats. It is believed that he may have been mistaken for Moran by a lookout that morning.

The sixth man was Albert Kachellek, who was better known as James Clark, an alias that he had adopted to spare his mother grief over his frequent brushes with the law. Clark was forty-two years old and had first been arrested in 1905 for robbery. He spent the next nine years in and out of the Pontiac Reformatory and Joliet Penitentiary. With a string of murders under his belt, he was known as Moran's chief gunmen, often wreaking havoc alongside the Gusenbergs. Oddly, Clark was identified as George Moran's brother-in-law by newspaper reporters after the massacre. This mistake was hotly denied by his sister, Marie Neubauer, at the coroner's inquest but writers copying previous writers have kept this error alive after all of these years.

The seventh man in the garage that day was the anomaly of the group. His name was Reinhart Schwimmer and he was an optometrist although today he would be considered an optician since he had no formal training. Schwimmer was a wanna-be who spent most of his time with gangsters. He was twenty-nine years old and had started associating with members of the North Side gang after his divorce in 1923. He spent much of his time in the company of O'Banion and other members of the gang, to the detriment of his legitimate business. Even after marrying a rich widow, he couldn't stay away from them. He liked to pretend that he was in the bootlegging business and often boasted that he could have people killed if he wanted to. After his second wife divorced him in 1928, he moved into the Parkway Hotel and befriended George Moran. Schwimmer was considered part of the gang, although he never got involved in crime - he simply liked the rush of being in the company of gangsters. On the morning of February 14, he had dropped into the garage, as he frequently did on the way to work, to see what the gang was up to. He had stayed behind to chat - a decision that he would live to regret, but not for very long.

Elmer Lewis, the truck driver, was not the only person to see the Cadillac stop at the S-M-C Cartage Co. and four men go inside, the ones in uniform leading the way. On the second floor of the rooming house next door, the landlady, Jeanette Landesman, was ironing a shirt when she heard the car and the truck collide at the corner. She went to the window to take a look and then saw the Cadillac move off, only to stop in front of the warehouse. Mrs. Landesman watched as four men from the Cadillac went into the building.

When Moran and Newberry saw the car parked out front, they assumed that a police raid or a shakedown was taking place and hurried down the street to a coffee shop. They decided to sit there and wait things out until the cops left. Willie Marks, approaching from the south, reached the same conclusion. He ducked into a doorway and avoided the garage altogether.

On the second floor of the rooming house, Mrs. Landesman heard a peculiar banging sound outside, almost like someone furiously beating a drum. The sound lasted for more than a minute and then it was followed by two thunderous blasts, like two cars backfiring. The silence that followed was broken by the anguished sound of a howling dog. Disturbed, Mrs. Landesman went back to the window and looked out at the snowy, windy street. Her friend across the way, Mrs. Alphonse Morin, looked out of her third-floor window at the same time and they both saw the same four men reappear. The first two, in civilian clothes, had their hands raised. The two men behind them, wearing police uniforms, held guns to their backs and prodded them toward the car. It was a police raid and two men had been arrested, the two women assumed; the fifth man driving the car must have been a plain-clothes detective. They climbed into the Cadillac and drove away, continuing south on Clark Street and turning right onto Ogden Avenue.

Next door in the garage, the dog continued to howl mournfully and Mrs. Landesman's uneasiness grew. Finally, she asked one of her tenants, a man named McAllister, to see what was going on next door and find out why the dog was howling. He went next door to the warehouse but he didn't stay inside for long. His face was a ghostly pale when he hurried back up the steps into the rooming house. "The place is full of dead men," he cried.

We will never know for certain what took place inside the S-M-C Cartage Co. on the cold morning of February 14, 1929. Only one man survived the initial slaughter and he never talked. However, historians and crime enthusiasts have spent many years trying to put together the pieces of one of the greatest technically unsolved crimes in history.

Here's what most think happened that day:

The massacre was set in motion by a telephone call from a rooming house across the street from the garage, signaling the killers that everything was in place for an assault on the North Side gang. It is believed that Weinshank was mistaken for George Moran, who had gotten up late and had not arrived.

At 10:30 a.m., a Cadillac touring car, painted and outfitted to look like a police car, pulled up in front of the warehouse and four men got out, two of them dressed in police uniforms and two in plain clothes. A fifth man, also in plain clothes, stayed behind the wheel of the car.

The Moran gang members inside were likely puzzled when the two uniformed officers walked into the garage. Protection money was undoubtedly being paid to avoid problems from the police but the gangsters probably assumed that it was a raid being carried out to appease the reformers. It was likely that they would be out of jail almost as quickly as they were taken in. The uniformed officers took weapons from five of the men in the garage. Reinhart Schwimmer was unarmed and so was Johnny May, who was pulled from under the truck protesting that he was only a mechanic and not part of the gang. He was a failed criminal and had promised his wife that he would stay on the straight and narrow. As he promised her, he carried a St. Christopher medal in a metal case in his back pocket. All of the men felt harassed and only Schwimmer was likely excited to be arrested. Now he would be able to prove to his friends that he really did have gangster connections.

After removing the weapons from the North Side men, the police signaled the two men in plain clothes who were waiting on the other side of the front office partition. The two men walked into the warehouse, Thompson machine guns in their hands. The North Side men were lined up against the wall and shot to death with the Tommy guns. Only one of them survived - Frank Gusenberg. With fourteen slugs in his body, he managed to crawl about twenty feet from the rear wall. The others laid dead where they had fallen at the foot of the wall, Clark on his face, Weinshank, Heyer, May and Schwimmer on their backs. Pete Gusenberg had died kneeling; his upper body slumped against a chair. Schwimmer was still wearing his hat and Weinshank's tan fedora rested on his chest. Where the seven men had been standing against the wall, the bricks were now covered with blood. Darker crimson stains ran across the oily floor. Highball, howling and snapping, pulled at his leash, trying in vain to get to the executioners.

The murders had been carried out with precision. The Tommy guns were swung back and forth three times, first at the level of the victim's heads, then down to their chests and then down once again to their abdomens. Some of the corpses on the floor were only held together by bits of gristle, flesh and bone. In spite of this, life must have still flickered in Johnny May and James Clark after the machine gun fire, for they had also been blasted with shotguns at such close range that their faces had almost been obliterated.

Then, leaving pools of blood, seventy shell casings and the mutilated bodies of seven men behind, the plain clothes killers walked out with the phony cops, whose hands were raised, pretending that they were being arrested. The driver was waiting for them in the car outside, and they drove away and out of sight.

After the discovery of the massacre, the police were summoned and the investigation began. It wasn't long before crowds began to gather in front and in back of 2122 North Clark Street, all hoping to get a look at the dead men inside.

When the police arrived, Sergeant Tom Loftus was the first on the scene. Oddly, a detective named Clarence J. Sweeney would later place himself at the scene and would also claim that he was at the side of Frank Gusenberg when he died from his wounds three hours later. Sweeny kept the myth going over the years, involving himself more and more in the story, but Loftus was actually the first policeman to arrive and he questioned Gusenberg before the ambulance got there. Frank had managed to crawl almost twenty feet, leaving a bloody trail behind him, before collapsing on the floor.

Loftus asked him: "Do you know me Frank?"
Gusenberg: "Yes, you are Tom Loftus."
Loftus: "Who did it or what happened?"
Gusenberg: "I won't talk."
Loftus: "You're in bad shape."
Gusenberg: "Pete is here, too."

Loftus then asked him if they were lined up at the wall and Gusenberg again told him that he wasn't going to talk. Gusenberg's legendary statements of "Nobody shot me" and "I ain't no copper" turned out to be fabrications of

Detective Sweeney and the newspapers. Sweeney claimed to be at Frank's bedside, yet Loftus detailed Officer James Mikes to be near Gusenberg at all times with no mention of Sweeney ever being there.

Loftus visited Gusenberg at Alexian Brothers Hospital and tried to question him again. Once more, Frank refused to talk. Before he died, though, Loftus asked him if the killers wore police uniforms and this time Frank whispered "Yes" before he finally succumbed to his wounds.

One newspaper quote that was printed correctly, though, came from George Moran. When he learned of the massacre that he had only escaped by a few minutes, he told reporters: "Only Capone kills like that."

News of the massacre quickly spread throughout the city and across the country - even to as far away as Miami Beach, where Al Capone was conveniently hosting guests who were in town for the impending world championship heavyweight fight between Jack Sharkey, known as the Boston Gob, and Georgia's William "Young" Stribling, known as the King of the Canebrakes. Capone had invited more than 100 guests to Palm Island, including sportswriters, gamblers, show business people, racketeers and politicians. Capone was a boxing enthusiast himself and he bet on Sharkey to win the title. He frequently visited his training camp and was photographed by news cameramen standing between Sharkey and Bill Cunningham, a sportscaster and former All-American center.

On the night of February 14, Capone hosted an elaborate party at his estate. They feasted on a huge buffet and drank champagne served by a half-dozen of Capone's bodyguards. Mae Capone, Al's wife, stayed quietly in the background, seeing that everybody had everything they needed. When it came to be his son's bedtime, his father took Sonny by the hand and led him from group to group to say goodnight. Albert Francis Capone had turned ten two months before. The small boy with the hearing aid, a shy, withdrawn little figure with big eyes and a bashful small, was a sharp contrast to his bombastic father.

The guests at the party that night whispered among themselves about the gangland massacre that was being reported in the evening papers and on radio broadcasts. Tact prevented them from speaking about it too loudly. Capone never mentioned it at all.

The next morning, when additional details had been published, among them Moran's comment about the massacre, Jack Kofoed, the sports editor for the *New York Post*, who had brought his wife, Marie, to the party, called on his host. "Al, I feel silly asking you this," he said, "but my boss wants me to. Al, did you have anything to do with it?"

"Jack," Capone said solemnly, "the only man who kills like that is Bugs Moran."

In the minds of many in Chicago, the St. Valentine's Day Massacre was the final blow to the city's already bloody reputation. Mortified and angry, the Chicago Association of Commerce which had founded the Chicago Crime Commission in 1919 posted a reward of $50,000 for the arrest and conviction of the killers. Finally having had enough of the mobsters in their midst, the angry public collected another $10,000 for the reward. The city council and the state's attorney's office each added $20,000, bringing the total to $100,000, the biggest price ever put on the heads of gangsters.

But no agency wanted a swifter solution to the case than the police department because many people believed just what the killers wanted them to believe: that police officers had carried out the murders. This was the kind of reputation that the Chicago Police Department had earned by the end of the 1920s: that it was a corrupt, scandal-ridden, lawbreaking organization. Even the local Prohibition administrator, Frederick D. Silloway, spoke out against the department. "The murderers were not gangsters," he said. "They were Chicago policemen. I believe the killing was the aftermath to the hijacking of 500 cases of whiskey belonging to the Moran gang by five policemen six weeks ago on Indianapolis Boulevard. I expect to have the names of these five policemen in a short time. It is my theory that in trying to recover the liquor the Moran gang threatened to expose the policemen and the massacre was to prevent the exposure."

Chief of Police William F. Russell, likely unsure about what illicit activities many of his men were involved in, joined in: "If it is true that coppers did this, I'd just as soon convict coppers as anybody else." Chief of Detectives John Egan added, "I'll arrest them myself, toss them by the throat into a cell and do my best to send them to the gallows."

The next day, Silloway retracted the accusation that he made against the department, claiming that he had been misquoted. To ease tensions with the police, his bosses in Washington transferred him to another district. By then, however, the damage was done and suspicions lingered for many years.

The investigation proceeded under John Egan, the state's attorney's staff and Cook County Coroner Dr. Herman N. Bundeson, each working different angles of the case. Egan and his men searched the S-M-C Cartage Co. and recovered the empty .45-caliber machine-gun cartridges.

Assistant State's Attorney Walker Butler and his detectives canvassed the neighborhood and found two corroborating stories at 2119 and 2125 North Clark Street, rooming houses run by Mrs. Michael Doody and Mrs. Frank Orvidson. Ten days before the massacre, three young men showed up, looking for rooms to rent along North Clark Street. Mrs. Doody was able to accommodate two of them and Mrs. Orvidson took in the third. They said that they were cab drivers who worked the night shift and they insisted on rooms in the front, overlooking Clark Street. The three men rarely left their rooms. When either landlady went in to clean, the tenant was almost always at the window, looking down at the street outside. All three of them vanished on the morning of the massacre. Butler suspected that the Purple Gang was somehow involved in the murders and he showed the landladies photographs of sixteen members. They identified three of them as the mysterious lodgers. But when questioned, at Butler's request, by the Detroit police, all three of the men produced unshakable alibis from people who swore they had been nowhere near Chicago.

On February 22, a fire broke out in a garage behind a house at 1723 North Wood Street, about three miles west of the crime scene. The firemen who answered the call discovered a black Cadillac touring car that had been partially demolished by an acetylene torch, axes and hacksaws. The torch, it was believed, had accidentally started the blaze and the men wrecking the vehicle had fled before its destruction was complete. Egan examined the remains of the Cadillac and the still-legible engine number allowed him to trace the car to a Cook County Commissioner named Frank Wilson, who had sold the car to an auto dealership on Irving Park Road. The car dealer stated that he had then sold the car to a man identifying himself as "James Morton of Los Angeles" in December.

From the owner of the Wood Street property, a neighborhood grocer, Egan learned that a man named "Frank Rogers" had rented the garage on February 7. He gave his address as 1859 West North Avenue, which was right around the corner. The house was now deserted but, significantly, it adjoined the Circus Café, the headquarters of Claude Maddox and the Circus gang, whose ties to Capone, the Purple Gang and Egan's Rats of St. Louis were well known. Even more significant was the fact that one of Maddox's gang members, "Tough" Tony Capezio, had recently been badly burned in a fire. It has been suggested that Capezio had been cutting up the car to get rid of evidence and had accidentally started the fire using the acetylene torch too close to a can of gasoline. The police could never prove it, however.

Another member of the Circus gang at the time was Tony Accardo, who, according to a police theory formed later, helped plan the massacre. Soon after, he became a Capone gunman and was often seen seated in the lobby of Capone's Lexington Hotel headquarters with a Tommy gun across his knees. Most likely, however, Accardo was not directly involved in the murders. He was a small-time member of the gang in those days and was liked tasked with disposing of evidence with Capezio and others.

Unable to pin anything on Maddox and his men, the police continued searching for "James Morton" or "Frank Rogers" but no trace of them were ever found. As for George Moran, he refused to disclose anything about the liquor truck hijacker who had telephoned him on the night before the massacre, other than that he had known him for a long time and planned to "pay him back" for his treachery.

The police only had theories, but they developed one that they believed was accurate:

Al Capone ordered the massacre, leaving the planning to others. Jack McGurn certainly took part in the planning, as did Jake Guzik, who spoke frequently with Capone by telephone from the Congress Hotel. The plan that was conceived called for two men who could persuade their victims to surrender their weapons without a fight, which was the reason behind the police uniforms. These men had to be total strangers to the Moran men, which meant that they had to be imported likely by Maddox from either Detroit or St. Louis. They were kept hidden until needed and then provided with the phony police car.

The function of the three Clark Street lodgers was to watch for Moran in exactly the same way that earlier Capone gang ambushes had been carried out. The killers were then informed by telephone when Moran entered the warehouse. What saved Moran's life was his resemblance to Al Weinshank. Believing that Moran had already arrived, the lookouts gave the word to the killers.

The collision with the truck on Clark Street suggested the route that the killers took: north along Wood Street for a mile to Webster Avenue, then east for two miles on Webster to Clark, which would have taken about fifteen minutes. The men wearing civilian clothes probably waited in the garage's front office while their uniformed companions relieved the Moran gang of their weapons. After that, they emerged with Tommy guns and ordered the seven men to face the wall. Even though the killers may have realized by then that Moran was not there, they didn't dare let the others live since it's possible that they recognized the men in civilian clothing. The killers then staged their final scene to confuse any witnesses as they reappeared on the street posing as policemen after a raid with their prisoners.

The investigators may have figured out the methods of the massacre, but debate raged as to the reasons behind it and just who might have been involved - a debate that continues to this day.

Crime historians have named the most likely suspects even though they number more than the actual number of killers as Fred "Killer" Burke, a former Egan's Rats and Purple Gang mobster who had joined up with Capone; Fred Goetz, a longtime mobster and friend of Burke's; Robert Carey, another Egan's Rats member who worked bank jobs with Burke; Ray Nugent, another St. Louis man associated with Burke and the others; Gus Winkler, believed to be fifth, wheel man at the massacre; Claude Maddox, founder of the Circus gang and an associate of many of Capone's men, and then there were others.

While Fred "Killer" Burke became a leading suspect in the massacre case, he was far from the only one. Almost immediately after the murders, the Chicago Police began "rounding up the usual suspects" and one of the first arrested was Jack McGurn. The warrant sworn out for the arrest of McGurn was based on the testimony of a young man named George Brichet who was on the street in front of the Clark Street warehouse on February 14. As he was passing by, he saw the killers enter and he heard one of them say "C'mon, mac." He picked out McGurn's photograph from a rogue's gallery and said that he recognized him. Many historians have questioned the identification, although they don't doubt that Brichet heard what the man said correctly. Referring to someone as "mac" in those days was almost as common as calling them "pal," "buddy" or "mister." It didn't necessarily have to be someone's actual name. Brichet heard it and repeated it to the cops, who saw it as a perfect excuse to roust McGurn, who they felt was undoubtedly tied into the massacre somehow.

When the police showed up for McGurn, they found him at the Hotel Stevens with a pretty blonde named Louise Rolfe. He was indicted for seven murders and his bail was set at $50,000. He raised that amount using a hotel that he owned for collateral. It was valued at over $1 million. McGurn's alibi before the grand jury was Louise Rolfe, dubbed the "Blonde Alibi" by newspapermen. He swore that he had never left her side at the Hotel Stevens between 9:00 p.m. on February 13 and 3:00 p.m. on February 14. The state's attorney had him indicted for perjury but before McGurn could be tried on that charge, he married Louise. A wife cannot be forced to testify against her husband.

As the investigation into the massacre dragged on, McGurn's lawyer began calling for his client to be brought to trial. Under Illinois law, if the accused demanded trial at four separate terms of court and the state was not prepared to prosecute him, the state had to dismiss the case. Between the spring and winter of 1929, McGurn made four demands for trial. None of them were met and on December 2, he walked out of the courtroom a free man. By then, the authorities had revised their version of his role in the massacre and concluded that although he did not take part in the murders, he definitely had a role in their planning. They had no evidence of this, however, and McGurn was never charged with anything relating to the crime.

Later, he and Louise were late convicted of conspiring to violate the Mann Act, which prohibited interstate transport of women for "immoral purposes" when visiting Capone in Florida. The convictions were later overturned by the U.S. Supreme Court.

So, who really carried out the St. Valentine's Day Massacre? Thanks to the ballistics that tied Fred Burke to the crime, it seems likely that he and his former Egan's Rats companions performed the hit at the behest of Al Capone. But for whatever reasons - indifference, corruption, or lack of hard evidence - the murders were never officially solved.

The theories about who was actually involved in the St. Valentine's Day Massacre are as numerous as the theories as to why the massacre actually took place. There have been scores of theories put forth by crime historians over the years and just about any of them can make sense if they are presented in just the right way. Many of them are preposterous and impossible and others seem to make a cunning bit of sense. Logically, the massacre was ordered by Capone but planned by his henchmen in an effort to eliminate George Moran and bring an end to the harassment by the North Side gang once and for all.

There were a number of reasons why Capone would want Moran and his gang out of the way, not the least of which was the constant hijacking of Capone's liquor trucks and the undercutting of his business interests in the city. It could have also been retribution for the murders of Tony Lombardo and Pasqual Lolordo, Capone's presidents of the Unione Siciliane, which the North Side gang had carried out. Moran's backing of Joe Aiello, a hated Capone enemy, would have also increased Capone's emnity for the man. Capone was also being hampered by Moran in his takeover of the Cleaners and Dyers Association, which was a powerful racket that Capone wanted to expand into. There was also the matter of revenge for a murder attempt on Jack McGurn by the Gusenbergs, something that likely figured into McGurn's thoughts as he was helping to plan the massacre.

The massacre was a simple, cold-bloodedly efficient assassination that was meant to kill George Moran and break the back of the North Side gang, opening up their territories and operations to Al Capone. While the definite identities of the killers will always remain a mystery, the reason behind the massacre has never seemed very puzzling.

The St. Valentine's Day Massacre marked the end of any significant gang opposition to Capone, but it was also the event that finally began the decline of Capone's criminal empire. The massacre had simply taken things too far and the authorities - once content to let gangsters kill gangsters - and even Capone's once-adoring public, were ready to put an end to the bootleg wars. The massacre started a wave of reform that would eventually send Capone out of power for good.

Chicago, in its own way, memorialized the warehouse on Clark Street where the massacre took place. It became a tourist attraction and the newspapers even helpfully printed the photos of the corpses upside-down so that readers would not have to turn their papers around to identify the bodies.

Right after the massacre, the S-M-C Cartage Co. was temporarily boarded up. The building had been leased by Moran gang associate Adam Heyer but was owned by Frank C. Brusky, who moved his own trucking firm Brusky Overland Movers into the space in 1930. When he did, he renovated the building, added two windows and added space for storage on the second floor.

During the renovations, Brusky discovered a trap door in the corrugated ceiling of the garage, right above the spot where the Moran gangsters were killed. The door led to a concrete chamber that was nestled against the second floor wall and which was undetectable from below. The chamber contained funnels, a stool, an alcohol hydrometer, a crate that could contain a five-gallon bottle of liquor and a block and tackle system that could lower the crate to the floor of the garage. Brusky called the police, who searched the premises again. They first believed the secret room to be torture chamber for rival gangsters, but Police Captain Thomas Condon concluded that it was merely an alcohol cache.

By 1935, the building was occupied by Red Ball Movers, Inc., a moving company that also did telephone directory pick-ups and exchanges each year. In 1936, it was purchased by Anaconda Van Lines, which was owned by Samuel J. McArthur.

In 1949, the building was taken over by Charles and Alma Werner, who turned it into a moving, packing, shipping and storage office for antique furniture. At the time, they had no idea of the buildings' bloody past. They soon found that tourists, curiosity-seekers and crime buffs visited the place much more often than customers, all of them asking to see the infamous wall in back. Depending on her mood, Mrs. Werner either turned them away or allowed them to take a look. She once stated that she wished she and her husband had never bought the building. The Werners were later bought out by the city of Chicago, who wanted the place torn down and replaced with apartments for the elderly.

In 1967, the building was demolished. However, the bricks from the bullet-marked rear wall were preserved and purchased by a Canadian businessman named George Patey. The bricks were packed and shipped across the border and then put together as a moveable crime show for shopping centers, museums and galleries with the massacre wall as the main attraction. The traveling show was only a moderate success so, in 1971, Patey opened a Roaring Twenties' themed nightclub called the Banjo Palace and rebuilt the wall, for some strange reason, in the men's restroom. Three nights each week, women were allowed to peek inside at this macabre attraction. To add to the entertainment value of going to the bathroom next to a wall where seven people were murdered, Patey had Plexiglass placed in front of the wall so that patrons could urinate and try and hit targets that were painted on the glass. The club closed down in 1976 and the 417 bricks that made up the back wall were placed into storage until 1997.

Patey began offering the wall for sale, along with a written account of the massacre but had trouble selling the thing in one large piece. Patey, along with a friend named Guy Whitford who contacted me about the wall in 2002 tried to sell the single piece for some time. The original lot came with a diagram that explained how to restore the wall to its original form. The bricks were even numbered for reassembly. They remained on the market for several years, but there were no buyers. Eventually, Patey broke up the set and began selling them one brick at a time for $1,000 each. Patey died in December 2004 and had sold many bricks by the time he died. The remainder of the wall has since been purchased and rebuilt in a mob museum located in Las Vegas, Nevada.

The rest of the bricks are in the hands of private owners, who bought them from Patey. Oddly, though, legend has it that Patey actually sold some of the same bricks more than one time. The stories say that some of the bricks were returned to him after they had been sold. It seemed that anyone who bought one was suddenly stricken with bad luck in the form of illness, financial ruin, divorce and even death. According to the stories, the bricks themselves had somehow been infested with the powerful negative energy of the massacre. Many have called this story a "journalistic embellishment," but there are many who maintain that it's the truth - and that the lingering energy didn't effect just the bricks from the blood-spattered wall.

The entire warehouse had been built from brick and many of them were carried from the site by workmen and curiosity-seekers during the demolition of the building. It was said that from these bricks, too, come tales of misfortune and bad luck. Many will vouch for the dire events that plagued them after carrying away one of the "massacre" bricks. Are such stories true? The reader will have to decide what they believe.

Whatever the legend of the bricks, and whether or not they were somehow "haunted" by what happened, there is little doubt that the site on Clark Street was haunted - at least for a while.

For many years, people walking along the street, or who lived nearby, reported hearing the sounds of screams, moans, muffled voices and even the thump-thump-thump of Tommy gun fire. The garage is long gone now, demolished in a misguided attempt by city officials to erase all vestiges of Chicago's gangster past. A portion of the block was taken over by the Chicago Housing Authority and a fenced-in lawn that belongs to a senior citizen development now marks the area where the garage once stood. Five trees are scattered about the area and the one in the center actually marks the point where the rear wall once stood, where Moran's men were lined up and gunned down.

The apartment building, where Mrs. Landesman lived and heard the sound of Highball barking in the garage, still stands but all remnants of the S-M-C Cartage Co. have vanished.

Or have they?

According to reports, residents of the senior housing complex built on one end of the old lot have had strange encounters in the building, especially those who live on the side that faces the former massacre site. A television reporter from Canada interviewed a woman who once lived in an apartment that overlooked the small park and she often complained that, at night, she would hear strange voices, unusual sounds and knocking on her door and her window. She complained to the management, who dismissed her claims as imagination but assigned her another apartment. A new tenant moved into the rooms and she also complained of odd happenings, including knocking sounds on her door at night. When she opened the door to see who was there, she never found anyone nearby. One night, the tenant even stated that she saw a dark figure that was wearing an old-style hat. He remained in place for a few moments and then faded away. Most of the strange phenomena experienced by the new tenant also faded away and soon eerie events either stopped completely or she got so used to them that they no longer bothered her anymore.

Outside, along Clark Street, passersby and the curious occasionally reported strange sounds, like weeping and moaning, and the indescribable feeling of fear as they walked past the former site of the garage. Skeptics tried to laugh this off, saying that the sounds were nothing more than the overactive imaginations of those who knew what once occurred on the site but based on the reports of those who had no idea of the history of the place, something strange was apparently occurring.

And those who were accompanied by their dogs also reported their share of weirdness, too. The animals seemed to be especially bothered by this piece of lawn, sometimes barking and howling, sometimes whining in fear. Their sense of what happened here many years ago seemed to be much greater than our own.

However, many believe that what dogs were sensing was not the human trauma experienced at the massacre site, but rather the trauma that must have been experienced by Johnny May's German Shepherd, Highball. The poor animal must have been terrified by what occurred that morning, from the deafening sounds of the Tommy guns to the bloody slaying of his beloved owner. Tied to the front bumper of the truck, Highball had nowhere to run. It should be noted again that it was not the sound of machine-gun fire that alerted Mrs. Landesman to the horror inside the garage; it was the howling and barking of the terrified dog.

Tragically, Highball was so traumatized by the events of that morning that he had to be put down after the massacre. *Chicago Sun* reporter Russell V. Hamm, who was one of the first newsmen on the scene, said that the dog was never the same again and his bizarre behavior left the police no choice but to euthanize him.

Could the animals that subsequently passed by this empty lot have sensed the trauma suffered by Highball so many years ago? As any ghost buff can tell you, it's the events of yesterday that create the hauntings of today and sometimes, those who lived in the past can leave a little piece of themselves behind to be experienced in the present over and over again.

While the site of the St. Valentine's Day Massacre seems to be quiet today, the violent events of the city's gangster era still reverberate over time. Men like Al Capone, whether city officials want to admit it or not, left an indelible mark on Chicago. It seems that the events of St. Valentine's Day 1929 left one, too.

AIRPLANE PARTS
How the Ghosts of Flight 401 Sent Chills Through the Airline Industry

On the cold winter's night of December 29, 1972, Eastern Airlines aircraft number 310 waited in a dimly lit jet runway outside of New York's John F. Kennedy International Airport's Terminal One. It was set to take off at 9:00 p.m., bound for Miami. But unknown to the crew and passengers on board, the plane would never arrive.

When it departed that night, it was designated Flight 401 - a name that has since become one of the most famous aircraft flights in the annals of the supernatural. It was a haunting that affected dozens of airplanes as the ghosts of the fatal flight became attached to the salvaged parts that were taken from the downed plane.

The plane that became Flight 401 was a new Lockheed L-1011 Tristar, the pride of Eastern's fleet. It stood as tall as a five-story building and Eastern's version of the aircraft was designed to carry two hundred and twenty-nine passengers. As far as the company was concerned, the new Tristars were the most comfortable aircraft ever built. They boasted eight-foot ceilings, indirect lighting, individual temperature control, music headsets and the kind of comfort that could only be found in most living rooms. A chandelier decorated the front of the airplane and there was a stand-up, padded bar in the back. Perhaps the most interesting feature of the L-1011 was the kitchen, which was equipped to serve dinner for more than three hundred people. It was tucked away below decks, accessible by two elevators from the main cabin.

Aircraft 310 was one of a dozen L-1011s that Lockheed had delivered to Eastern Airlines that year. They were excellent aircraft but their design, manufacture and maintenance were not without problems. While the fleet was being built by Lockheed, Rolls Royce, the manufacturer of the engines, faltered under the pressure of the development costs and went bankrupt. This forced the project behind schedule and it went into financial disarray. When the new airplanes were finally delivered to Eastern in the spring of 1972, they were plagued with problems, particularly in the new advanced engines. The L-1011s were constantly taken out of service for maintenance that winter but Aircraft 310 seemed to have fewer issues than the other planes. Lockheed delivered it on August 18 and it was put into service three days later. By December 29, it had been flying for only a little over four months. It had been regularly maintained and the current flight log showed only minor issues. There had been no entries for more than sixty days complaining of trouble with the landing gear. The aircraft had made five hundred and two landings, including the one that had brought it into JFK earlier that evening when it had flown in from Tampa. Routine service was carried out on the plane at 7:43 p.m. and the flight dispatcher cleared it for a 9:00 p.m. departure to Miami as Flight 401.

The engineer and second officer for Flight 401 was Donald Luis Repo, a fifty-one-year-old pilot who had worked for Eastern Airlines for twenty-five years. He was a native of Massachusetts who was now living in Miami. He had gone to sleep early the night before because he was trying to shake off a cold. When he awoke, he flew to Tampa, where he boarded Aircraft 310 for the flight to New York. He would be flying back to Florida with the same crew.

One of the duties of the flight engineer was to board the plane early, before the captain and first officer, and go through a checklist that made sure the plane was equipped with various items like spare light bulbs, a first aid kit, rain repellant, smoke goggles, a hand ax, and other things. Repo would also fill out the takeoff data card, which had to match the weight limits on the manifest. The manifest listed nine passengers in the forward cabin and one hundred and forty-four in the rear, with a total of one hundred and fifty-three in all. As it turned out, there would actually be one hundred and sixty passengers on board. For balancing purposes, it was estimated that each passenger weighed an average of one hundred and seventy pounds, which figured out to be a total payload, with luggage and freight of almost thirty-five thousand pounds. The manifest, despite the fact that there was a miscount on the passenger number, was meticulously detailed. Four hundred pounds were also added for the additional men who would occupy the flight deck jump seats during the trip. Warren Terry, a co-pilot, and Angelo Donadeo, a maintenance specialist, were off-duty airline employees who were "dead-heading" - airline slang for employees hitching a ride as they returned from a duty assignment.

Flight 401 was in the very capable hands of Captain Robert Loft, a tall, trim fifty-five-year-old who had been working for Eastern Airlines for thirty-two years. He was comfortable and relaxed before takeoff, having flown the route many times before. He was in good health and had spent the morning working in his yard in Plantation, Florida.

First Officer Albert Stockstill occupied the co-pilot seat on the right side of the cockpit during takeoff. He was a former Air Force pilot and a native of Louisiana who now lived in Miami. Stockstill had even more flying time in the L-1011 than Loft. He had slept late that morning and after getting up, had spent a couple of hours in his home workshop building a light airplane.

The crew started the engines and at 9:20 p.m., word came from the tower that it was their turn to take off. Once on the runway, Stockstill released the brakes, applied thrust and Aircraft 310 rolled forward and gathered speed for nearly a mile down the runway. Loft rested his hands on the thrust levers with all of the assurance of a man who carried out this task many, many times before. As captain, he was the final authority on whether the takeoff was aborted, or the plane left the runway. Everything was fine with the flight, he decided, and the jet soared upward into the night sky.

Flight 410 flew south over Norfolk, Virginia, over Wilmington, North Carolina, and then out over the Atlantic. When the airplane passed east of Jacksonville, Florida, it would be one hundred and fifty-five miles out to sea. A computer-stored flight plan would bring Flight 401 inland over West Palm Beach, and then south to Miami.

The flight attendants on board Aircraft 310 was a close-knit, fun-loving group of young women. Their uniforms in the winter of 1972 were dark brown, beige and powder blue. Flight attendants had the option of wearing skirts, slacks or shorts with boots that zipped to the knee. The senior flight attendant on Flight 401 wore blue shorts with her brown boots. Her name was Adrienne Hamilton, age twenty-seven. The pretty, slender Texan had been flying with Eastern for five years.

The day's trip was a quick turnaround for the flight attendants: Miami to New York and then back to Miami. The crew had checked into Eastern's in-flight office at Miami International at 3:35 p.m., and by 11:50 p.m., they were schedule to be off-duty. From Miami to New York, the ten female flight attendants few on Flight 26, a dinner flight. At JFK, they changed planes to work Flight 410.

Flight 26 had arrived late into JFK and Adrienne and her crew had only twenty-three minutes to get from one plane to another. They almost missed Flight 401.

Immediately after takeoff, Warren Terry, the dead-heading pilot who occupied one of the jump seats in the cockpit, moved to an empty seat in first class. This left four crew members on the flight deck for the remainder of the trip. The first officer and co-pilot, Bert Stockstill, flew the plane. Bob Loft, the captain, operated the radio. This was normal operating procedure for Eastern Airlines with the pilot and co-pilot alternating turns flying the plane. The other man was then in charge of radio traffic. Behind Stockstill sat Don Repo, the flight engineer. The fourth man in the cockpit was Angelo Donadeo, who was not there in a working capacity. He was also no stranger to the L-1011. He had been Eastern's maintenance manager in Miami and since September, had been working as a technical supervisor specializing in troubleshooting the new L-1011 fleet. On Friday morning, he had been in New York examining an L-1011 that was having engine trouble. With this job completed, he was anxious to return to Miami in order to close on a new house.

For the most part, the flight was uneventful. Once the plane was out of the New York area, the weather was good and Stockstill put the aircraft on autopilot and dimmed the cockpit lights to allow for better visibility outside. The cockpit speakers were turned on, so even without headphones, it was possible to listen to the conversations between Loft and the air traffic controllers, as well as conversations between various planes that were also in the sky.

For most of the trip, a DC-10, National Airlines Flight 607, was flying ahead of the L-1011. But as it approached the Miami International Airport, Flight 607 began experiencing difficulties with its landing gear. At 11:19 p.m., the north arrival radio operator gave Flight 607 its final approach course. The National pilot, however, asked for an extended pattern because they were going to have to crank down their landing gear. One minute later, National 607, with a light indicating a hydraulic leak radioed the controller and asked for fire trucks to be out on the runway when they arrived.

The men on Flight 401's flight deck listened to the pilot on the National plane as he dealt with the troubled gear. With the emergency equipment rolling onto the field near runway Nine Right, in anticipation of National 607, Eastern 401 was assigned the other parallel runway, Nine Left.

At 11:32 p.m., the north approach controller instructed Flight 401 to change radio frequencies and initiate contact with the local controller. Loft contacted the Miami tower and advised them that Flight 401 was on its final approach. He instructed Stockstill to lower the landing gear when a message came back from the tower to continue their approach to runway Nine left. Loft acknowledged the controller and then began a series of practiced, terse, checklist exchanges with the rest of the flight crew in preparation for landing.

From his jump seat behind the captain, Angelo Donadeo looked out a side window and noticed that they were making a west to east approach. The plane was crossing the Palmetto Expressway, a major highway just west of the airport. It was at that moment that Donadeo realized they had a problem.

Stockstill was landing the plane and he announced that they had no nose gear. The flap position warning horn began to sound and from that point on the cockpit was periodically filled with the clang of various warning signals, as well as voices coming from the radio speakers. Captain Loft spoke, "I gotta... I gotta raise it back up," he said. "Goddamn it. Now I'm gonna try it down one more time."

For a moment, the two horns sounded in the cockpit and then the flap position warning horn became silent. Stockstill spoke in a calm voice. "Want to tell them we'll take it around and circle around and fart around?"

At 11:34 p.m., Loft spoke to the Miami control tower. "Well, ah, tower, this is Eastern 401, it looks like we're gonna have to circle; we don't have a light on our nose gear yet." The light, located on the lower right side of the center instrument panel, indicated when the nose gear was down and locked in position for a landing. However, it was still dark at this point. The local controller advised them to climb back to two thousand feet. They had lowered to less than one thousand feet in preparation to land. Stockstill reached for the landing gear handle as he prepared to take them out of their descent. However, Loft stopped him. He suggested, "Put the power on first, Bert. Thataboy. Leave the goddamn gear down until we find out what we got." Donadeo saw that while Stockstill was still flying the plane, Loft applied power to the throttles and the plane began to pull out of its descent.

From behind Loft and Stockstill, Repo offered to check the lights but his test still failed to illuminate the small, square light for the nose gear. Stockstill suggested that perhaps the light assembly was not properly seated in the fixture and asked Loft to jiggle it. Loft was unable to reach the light since it was on the co-pilot's side of the panel. He was using the radio and Stockstill was still flying the plane. Repo came forward and attempted to make the light work, but nothing happened.

At 11:35 p.m., Loft radioed the approach tower and reported their position. They were instructed to remain at two thousand feet and maintain a route that would take them in a wide U-turn, swinging first to the north and slowly around and away from the airport and out toward the Everglades. Loft told Stockstill to put the plane on autopilot and see if he could get the light to work. Stockstill managed to extract the light fixture from the instrument panel. Inside of the plastic square were two small light bulbs. Donadeo glanced around the flight deck and saw Repo examining the fixture. He did not see the flight engineer remove the old bulbs and put in two new ones, even though there were spare bulbs on board. Then the fixture was replaced in the socket - sideways. Loft noticed and pointed out the error to Repo. Unfortunately, inserted sideways, the fixture had jammed and the light was still off.

There were other ways to confirm that the landing gear was down and Loft chose one of them. He turned to Repo and told him to climb down into the forward avionics bay, a space beneath the flight deck that was often referred to as the "hell hole." The bay was accessible through a trap door in the floor of the cockpit and inside was an optical sighting device that could be used to see the landing gear.

Meanwhile, Stockstill was still trying to remove the jammed light assembly. He was considering using pliers, cushioned with a tissue, to try and pull it out. Loft told him that it would break if he tried to do that. Stockstill continued his efforts, which Loft quickly lost patience with. Again, he ordered Repo down into the avionics bay. "To hell with this," he said, "Go down and see if it's lined up...that's all we care. Then fuck around with that goddamned twenty-cent piece of light equipment we got on this bastard!"

The cockpit voice recorder picked up the sound of laughter. It was clear that the crew viewed the malfunction as more of an annoyance than any sort of emergency. At 11:38 p.m., Loft calmly spoke into the microphone to the Miami tower and told them that Flight 401 would go out a little farther west and see if they could get the light to come on. The controller responded that they had them now traveling westbound.

While Flight 401 was flying over the Everglades, the skies above Miami were busy with other flights. At the airport, National 607, the plane that had experienced landing gear problems, was finally given clearance to land on runway Nine Right. Fire trucks were standing by. Unlike the problem with Flight 401's faulty light, National 607's issue was seen as a real emergency. At the same time, Avianca 781 took off from runway Nine Left, followed by Eastern 470. Eastern Flight 111 landed on runway Nine Left. West Indian Flight 790 entered a final approach and immediately behind it was Lan-Chile 451. Backed up and waiting to land was National Flight 437. In the midst of all of this traffic, National Flight 607 landed without incident.

On Flight 401, Stockstill was still fighting with the light. "I don't know what the hell is holding that son of a bitch in," he said. "Always something - we could have made schedule."

They turned their attention back to the problem with the landing gear and decided that it was probably down. A test on the light showed that it was not working anyway and they were convinced that Repo would discover the gear was in place when he returned from the avionics bay. Unfortunately, when he came back up, he was unable to confirm it. It was too dark, he said, even with a little light shining in the right direction, he was unable to tell if the landing gear was down. Loft threw a switch on the overhead panel and told him to look again.

Repo went back down the ladder and this time, Donadeo followed him down. When Donadeo left the flight deck, he noticed that Stockstill had his right hand on the yoke and was pushing or pulling on the jammed light assembly with his left. Loft had loosened or unfastened his seat belt and was reaching across the center control pedestal, trying to help with the irritating light. The captain's left arm was braced against the top of the glare shield a fixture that shades the control panel from outside light through the windshield and he was reaching for the light with his right hand, crossing just forward of the throttles.

At the airport, the approach controller looked at the altitude reading for the blip on his radar screen that represented Eastern 401. The plane was supposed to be at two thousand feet, but the green numerals read nine hundred. The controller radioed the plane. "Eastern 401, how are things coming along out there?"

Loft replied. "Okay, we'd like to turn around and come back in."

The controller radioed back. "Eastern 401, turn left heading one-eight-zero."

Loft acknowledged and the L-1011 began a gradual left turn. On the radio speakers, the approach controller could be heard telling Lan-Chile 451 to descend to fifteen hundred feet. The Lan-Chile pilot acknowledged the instructions.

The next voices on the flight recorder were the last ever heard from Loft and Stockstill.

"We did something to the altitude," Stockstill said.

Loft: "What?"

Stockstill: "We're still at two thousand, right?"

Loft: "Hey, what's happening here?"

At the airport, the approach controller handled another plane and then looked again at the radar screen. In the data block next to Flight 401, the words read "CST" - for "coast," which is shown when a beacon target is lost or becomes too weak for three sweeps of the radar antenna.

He quickly radioed the plane. "Ah, Eastern 401, are you requesting equipment?"

There was only the whisper of static over the line.

He tried once more. "Eastern, ah, 401, I've lost you, ah, on the radar there, your transponder. What's your altitude now? Eastern 401, Miami."

There was no reply from Flight 401.

The airplane crashed northwest of Miami, almost nineteen miles from the end of runway Nine Left, into the heart of the Everglades, a vast swamp region of water, sawgrass, marshland and alligators. The L-1011 was traveling two hundred and twenty-seven miles an hour when it hit the ground. The left wingtip hit first, then the left engine and the left landing gear. Together, they slashed three long trails through the heavy sawgrass. Each trail was five feet wide and more than one hundred feet long.

When the main part of the fuselage hit the ground, it continued to move through the grass and water, coming apart as it went. It hit once, lifted into the air and then slammed back down again with a hard, grinding sound. About halfway along its path, the nose of the plane spun clockwise and careened around until it was sliding backwards. As the plane was skidding through the swamp, a fireball rushed through the cabin, from front to rear. Passengers felt a blast of cold air and then a wet wave of fuel as the plane broke apart. The huge white fuselage crumpled and tore into five large sections and countless smaller pieces. From the first impact to the point that it came to a shuddering halt, the plane traveled more than one-third of a mile.

Passengers drowned in the murky water. Others were thrown from the plane, suffering broken bones, paralyzing injuries and death. As the plane broke apart, an apparently random pattern of death and survival was repeated throughout the aircraft. Some died, while people seated next to them survived. One woman was thrown out of the plane, her seat intact, and died from multiple injuries, while the poodle she brought with her in a pet carrier under her seat survived. Two passengers in first class were thrown out of the plane and ended up fifty yards away from one another. Both lived. A two-year-old boy was hurled three hundred feet from the plane. He was unmarked except for two small cuts on his face. He died. A young mother was killed on impact but her six month-old daughter survived.

At 11:42 p.m., a private plane that had just taken off from Miami International Airport radioed the tower. The pilot reported seeing a "tremendous flame" in the Everglades. One minute later, at 11:43 p.m. National Airlines Flight 661 reported a "big explosion out west."

Earlier that same evening, a local man named Robert Marquis and a friend, Rayburn Dickinson, were out in the Everglades in an airboat, gigging frogs. By 11:40 p.m., Marquis and Dickinson had caught about thirty pounds of frogs and were working their way east, toward the glow of lights from Miami. Suddenly, Marquis noticed the lights of a large jet. The plane was flying west and seemed very low. Although he couldn't hear it over the sound of the airboat's motor, he knew it was very close and could see the strobe lights flashing on the ends of its wings. Moments later, he saw "a ball of fire, an orange, orange glow that just lit up and spread out for about eight thousand feet across the Glades; looked like maybe it went up a hundred foot high, just for a short duration of eight or ten seconds."

He yelled to Dickinson, "That was a plane crash, wasn't it?"

Marquis pushed forward on the throttle and started darting across the swamp toward where he had seen the flash.

Two minutes after Flight 401 disappeared from the radar screen at Miami International, the telephone rang at the U.S. Coast Guard station at Opa-Locka operations center and an alarm was sounded. By 11:45 p.m., the ready crew was airborne in a Sikorsky Sea Guard helicopter. Allan Pell, a lieutenant commander, was the senior office on board. At this point, it was only known that the plane had disappeared from radar. Pell had doubts about a crash. The L-1011 was a brand new plane and it was a clear night. It seemed unlikely that the plane had gone down.

Meanwhile, Robert Marquis was racing to the scene in his airboat. He drove through the dark swamp for almost fifteen minutes and then cut the engine to listen. He heard screams in the distance that sent chills down his spine. He continued in the direction of the screams and stopped again. Now, the cries were coming from behind him. He ran the airboat around a thick stand of sawgrass and suddenly saw a huge piece of wreckage right in front of him. He literally ran right into it, had to stop the boat, get out and turn it around. He soon discovered the path where the plane had hit the ground. It was about fifty to a hundred yards wide and filled with trash and debris.

Marquis later recalled, "When I first started working into the wreckage, I began seeing people - some of them laying in the water, some of them wandering around, walking, but very slowly. I got as close as I could without running over anybody, and then I got out. There were dead people everywhere. And everywhere I looked were half-naked people. Some completely naked. I felt so helpless. The first one I came to was a man who looked like he was about to drown. Looked like both his legs were broken. Couldn't move. The only thing he could move was his head, and it kept falling into the water. He said, 'Help me; I can't hold my head up much longer.' So I pulled him up and rested his back and propped his head up out of the water. There were lots of people in turned-over seats, their heads in the water. I tried to help the ones that possibly were drowning."

After a few minutes of struggling to assist the survivors that he could find, Marquis noticed a helicopter in the sky. It was obviously searching for the crash, but it was looking in the wrong area. Marquis waded back to his airboat, grabbed a helmet light that he had made himself and began wildly waving it in the direction of the helicopter.

The Coast Guard chopper crew saw the faint light flashing in the distance and the pilot swooped toward it. As the wreckage came into sight, Lieutenant Commander Pell saw bodies, a few people stumbling through the water and the tall grass and the looming tail of the plane, one of the few distinguishable pieces of wreckage. The helicopter made one full sweep of the area and then climbed back up to three hundred feet to establish radio contact. Pell called the air station. "We've got one hell of a mess out here," he reported.

Pell landed the helicopter and took on survivors, three men and a woman, and then lifted off into the night sky. They would be the first four of one hundred and seventy-six victims - dead and alive - who would be transported from the horrific scene. The chopper lifted off at 12:46 a.m., one hour and four minutes after the crash.

When the helicopter took off, it left Coast Guard Petty Officer Don Schneck behind. Carrying only a small flashlight, he climbed aboard Marquis' airboat for a ride to the main sections of the wreckage. He was dropped off about fifty feet from a large section that still had the right wing of the airplane attached to it. After wandering in the darkness for about twenty-five yards, he came upon a man standing in the water, calling for help. The man told Schenck that his wife was hurt. In the blackness of the swamp, the Coast Guard officer had not seen a woman sitting next to the man. She was bleeding from the thigh. Schneck used the man's belt to apply a tourniquet and then continued on.

He soon came upon the cockpit section, jutting from the water at a forty-five degree angle. The roof was smashed and it was cluttered with wreckage. He was stunned when he heard voices coming from the debris. He later wrote, "I could not imagine anyone surviving inside the twisted remains of the cockpit. I heard two voices yelling that they could see my light. I peered into a few small holes in the side of the wreckage and could see someone, who was moaning slightly."

Schenck went around to the other side of the wreckage and found senior flight attendant Adrienne Hamilton and another crew member, Sue Tebbs. After checking their injuries and providing what little help he could, Schneck began to move some pieces of debris away from Hamilton. As he did, he discovered the co-pilot, Stockstill, suspended off the ground, wrapped in a tangle of wall wires that were the remains of the cockpit's wall. He could only see the man's head and shoulders but Schenck checked his eyes and knew that he was dead. He then worked his way into the ruins of the flight deck and found Captain Loft sprawled across the control panel under the windshield. He was alive and moving around and Schenck told him to remain still. Loft, however, told him that he was going to die and tried to get out of the cockpit. After Schenck calmed him down, he went below to try and help the two men trapped in the avionics bay. Loft died before he could be rescued.

By now, ambulances were speeding west from Miami on US Highway 41. The nearest road was eight miles from the crash site but it was eventually determined that rescue vehicles could proceed single file along the top of a flood control levee to within one hundred yards of the scene. The levee was also used as a helicopter landing pad.

Rescue workers soon began to arrive on the scene, finally coming to assist Schenck, Marquis and Dickinson, who, up until that time, were the only people helping the survivors. The rescuers found a scene of carnage and horror. One man was still alive under the center fuselage section with just his head and feet sticking out of the mud. His hips and pelvis were obviously broken since both his legs were perpendicular to his torso with each foot next to his head. It took six men more than thirty minutes to dig around him and pull him out. They were only able to do so by rocking the huge section back and forth and causing the man even more agony. Victims were scattered throughout the swamp in various states of injury. Far too many were dead.

Survivors were taken to several hospitals around Miami that were closest to the crash site. Palmetto was the most convenient and had a helipad. Hialeah Hospital was also close and when the helicopter pilots complained that it was a difficult place to land because of the numerous power lines around it, police cars marked an alternate site in the parking lot of the Hialeah Race Track. Both hospitals received six chopper loads of survivors - thirty-two people in all.

Mercy Hospital also received four flights. The first survivor handed from a helicopter at Mercy Hospital was the white poodle that had managed to live through the crash under her owner's seat. The first human victims were received by a veteran nurse named Ferne Pletchan, who came out to the helipad to help with the unloading. She was struck by their silence. None screamed. A few moaned. Others wept softly. A little boy cried for his mother. Most of the victims seemed to be in a daze and yet were touchingly grateful for blankets and caring hands that wiped away the mud from the faces. Over and over again, they said only two words: "Thank you."

The first light of dawn brought a swarm of chartered helicopters to the crash site, each of them filled with television cameramen and reporters. They hovered over the remains of Flight 401 for a few minutes and then flew back to Miami. The images of the crash would soon shock the American public.

In the swamp, Jimmy Duckworth, a police sergeant, supervised the recovery of bodies from the wreck. Duckworth and his team waited while Dr. Joe Davis, the medical examiner, attended a meeting in Miami with the National Transportation Safety Board investigators who had arrived during the night from Washington. When Davis and the NTSB team made it to the crash site, the recovery teams were finally allowed to leave the levee where they had been gathered and wade out into the murky water. Behind them waited airboats piloted by wildlife officers from the state Game Commission. They would be in charge of ferrying the dead out of the Everglades.

The search began at a spot they designated as point zero; a spot that was distant enough from the wreckage that all agreed no bodies would have been thrown beyond. From that point, the searchers spread out in a long line and slowly advanced toward the remains of the plane. When a body was found, the team was to mark it with an indelible number, photograph it, tag the body, plant a small yellow flag near the head with the same number on it, and place the corpse in a body bag. The airboats would then come and pick up the body.

After dredging through the muck for thirty minutes, Duckworth's team found the first body at 12:30 p.m. It was the naked body of a young woman. A second corpse, a naked man, was found fifteen minutes later. The body of a young boy was discovered about four hundred yards away. He was lying in two inches of water, fully dressed, and had no apparent signs of injury. Another young woman was found next. She was lying on her back, eyes open, her right hand extended as though reaching out for something or someone.

And the search continued. The grueling, heart-breaking work continued for several days until the sun was shining down on a forest of bright yellow flags, each with a number scrawled on it.

On New Year's Day, a passenger named Braulio Corretjer, died in the hospital from his injuries. Searchers also found the body of a flight attendant named Stephanie Stanich in the Everglades. She was still strapped in her seat. On Tuesday, the medical examiner and the airline agreed for the first time about the number of survivors and casualties; seventy-seven people had lived through the crash and ninety-nine bodies had been found in the swamp. But by then, two of the original survivors - Don Repo and Corretjer - had died in the hospital. Two more would die later. In the end, Flight 401 had carried one hundred and seventy-six passengers and within a month of the crash, the death toll stood at one hundred and three victims.

In the days that followed, the National Transportation Safety Board NTSB conducted an investigation into the crash. They searched through the wreckage, interviewed survivors and witnesses and studied the flight data. When investigators climbed into the crushed cockpit, they found the control panel virtually intact. The clock had stopped at the moment of the crash. The airspeed needle on Loft's side of the flight deck read one hundred and ninety-eight knots. The altitude select panel was set at two thousand feet. The nose gear light assembly was found jammed on its side and protruding one-quarter inch from its normal position. It contained two burned-out light bulbs. All three throttles were in the full forward position, an indication that the pilots discovered the problem at the last moment and tried to pull out of it.

Angelo Donadeo, whose spot in the cockpit jump seat made him a crucial observer of what occurred on the flight deck, was interviewed on January 8. He was under heavy sedation at the time in a Miami hospital and he reluctantly signed the transcript of his interview, believing that his medical condition may have altered his version of the events.

But Donadeo's testimony wasn't needed to discover a peculiarity in the forward avionics bay - two autopilot computers, which controlled the plane's nose up and down attitude, were mismatched. One of the computers was a model 1-7 and the other a model 1-8. The difference between the two was that while one required fifteen pounds of pressure on the column to disengage the system, the other needed twenty pounds of pressure. Although the two computers were slightly different, both worked properly when tested, along with the five other computers that survived the crash. Regardless, it was a troubling anomaly.

Eventually, all of the evidence that was gathered - investigations, flight data recorder printouts, and voice recordings of the pilots - and presented in a public hearing on March 5, 1973. Investigators now had a clear picture of what had occurred.

The flight had been normal until the final approach into Miami. When Stockstill had looked at the landing gear indicator, the green light that stated that the gear was properly locked into the "down" position did not illuminate. This failure had two possible explanations: either the gear had not come down, or the light was not working. The pilots recycled the gear. When the light still failed to come on, they aborted the landing to examine the situation. The tower instructed the L-1011 to pull out of its descent, climb to two thousand feet, and circle out over the Everglades. The cockpit crew removed the malfunctioning light assembly and the flight engineer was sent down into the avionics bay to visually check the landing gear. Fifty seconds after they reached their assigned altitude, and when the plane was halfway through its U-turn, the captain instructed the co-pilot to put the L-1011 on autopilot. For the next eighty seconds, the plane maintained level flight. Then it dropped one hundred feet, flew level for the next two minutes, and then began a descent that was so gradual that it was not perceived by the crew. In the next seventy seconds, the plane lost only two hundred and fifty more feet but this was enough to cause the altitude warning alarm to go off, which was clearly heard on the cockpit recordings. During the NTSB investigation, one Eastern captain stated that modern aircraft like the L-1011 have so many "clickers and clackers and bells" that the cockpit becomes overwhelmingly filled with alarm tones. Perhaps so much so, he theorized, that pilots begin to stop hearing them, to simply tune them out. For whatever reason, there was no indication on Flight 401's voice recordings that pilots heard the alarm.

Meanwhile, the crew continued to attempt to reinstall the light assembly, which had been taken out to see if it was working or not and then had been incorrectly pushed back into the panel, causing it to become jammed. During the NTSB investigation, an Eastern L-1011 captain noted that after the accident, he and a mechanic tried to remove and replace the gear lamp only to find that, although it is square in shape, it has a small track and groove which only line up when the lamp is positioned correctly. He testified that the track started halfway in, so if you started to push it in incorrectly, you wouldn't realize the mistake until it was wedged in the housing.

Within fifty seconds, the plane was at half of its assigned altitude and was slowly continuing to drop. At the moment when Stockstill's radio altimeter beeped, the plane was dropping at fifty feet per second. This time, the crew heard the warning, but it was too late.

The question remained however - why did the airplane that was locked on autopilot dive into the Everglades?

The answer came in small pieces. One of the first clues came from the testimony of Eastern pilot Captain Daniel Gellert, who stated that he had noticed that the altitude hold function could be disengaged by bumping the control column. Many pilots doubted Gellert's testimony, but the incident was strikingly similar to a situation encountered by Thomas Oakes, another Eastern pilot. Oakes had been one of the first captains qualified to fly the L-1011. He had the altitude hold function disengage on a flight on January 8, ten days after the crash of Flight 401. Oakes testified that he and the co-pilot noticed the malfunction and then proceeded to re-set the autopilot and then trip it off by bumping the control column several times. They noted the problem in their log book. Although these may have been freak occurrences, Eastern took it seriously and sent a printed notice about the malfunction to their L-1011 pilots on January 15.

Given this information, the NTSB hypothesized that Loft had probably bumped the control column when he turned to tell flight engineer Repo to go down into the avionics bay and check on the landing gear. The NTSB reported noted: "If the captain had applied a force to the control wheel while turning to talk to the second officer, the altitude hold function might have been accidentally disengaged." The autopilot had apparently not turned off completely, but rather had switched into the "Control Wheel Steering" mode. The plane was no longer locked at two thousand feet, but would fly steadily at whatever level the pilots selected, purposefully or accidentally, by pressure on their control wheels. From this point on, even a slight nudge would be enough to edge the plane up or down.

A part of the mystery that was never solved, though, was whether the altitude hold light extinguished when the function disengaged. In both Gellert's and Oakes' cases, they noted the autopilot light went out when they bumped the columns. But Stockstill might have been deceived by the mismatched autopilot computers on the plane. Because the computers were mismatched, Loft's side required fifteen pounds of pressure to disengage, and Stockstill's side required twenty pounds of pressure. If Loft bumped the column with more than fifteen, but less than twenty pounds of pressure, Loft's altitude hold light would have gone out, and Stockstill's light would remain on, giving him the erroneous impression that the autopilot was still engaged and holding the plane at two thousand feet. No one could know for sure what happened, but either way, the NTSB did not believe this was a crucial factor in the accident.

The final report cited the cause of the crash as pilot error, specifically, "the failure of the flight crew to monitor the flight instruments during the final four minutes of flight, and to detect an unexpected descent soon enough to prevent impact with the ground. Preoccupation with a malfunction of the nose landing gear position indicating system distracted the crew's attention from the instruments and allowed the descent to go unnoticed."

In the tragic ending, one hundred and three people died - all because of two burned-out light bulbs that would have cost $12 to replace. And ironically, the plane's landing gear was found to be in the down and locked position, which meant that the disaster should have never happened at all.

As it happened, the crash of Flight 401 was not the end of the story.

Captain Bob Loft and flight engineer Dan Repo were among the one hundred and three people who lost their lives when Flight 401 crashed into the Everglades on that December night in 1972. Initially, both men were among the survivors but Loft succumbed to his wounds about an hour after the crash, before rescuers could get him to the hospital. Repo, critically injured, was reportedly angry when he was pulled from the wreckage. He survived about thirty hours before he also died.

Both of the men would be found to be at fault by the NTSB investigation, although most of the blame fell on Loft's shoulders. They were accused of being preoccupied with finding a source for the indicator light problem and ignoring the fact that the plane was steadily losing altitude. When they discovered what was wrong it was too late - a fact that apparently haunted both men after their deaths for their ghosts soon began to be encountered aboard other Eastern L-1011 jets.

Apparently, to save costs, Eastern ordered the salvageable parts of the aircraft Number 310 to be removed and incorporated into other Eastern planes.

Soon after, reports of the ghosts of Repo, Loft and even some unidentified flight attendants were encountered on various Eastern flights. For the next year or so, they were most often seen on Eastern's aircraft Number 318, or on other L-1011s, all of which contained salvaged parts from Flight 401. Eastern crew members and passengers saw the ghosts or heard them speak on the plane's intercom systems or received verbal messages and warnings from them. Witnesses also experienced cold sensations and invisible presences, aircraft power turning on by its own volition and a tool inexplicably appearing in a mechanics hand when no one was in the area.

Substantiation of the sightings was difficult, however. Eyewitness reports made to Eastern's management were met with skepticism and a fear of further damaging the airline's reputation and causing a further loss of business. The crash had done enough damage and for the public to hear that the ghosts of some of the lost plane's crew were visiting other flights could make for a public relations disaster. For the most part, eyewitness crew members were told that perhaps seeing a psychiatrist would be in order - which most took as a precursor to being fired. After that, most were reluctant to talk to anyone investigating the hauntings and the sightings that did occur were often covered up. Log sheets that contained the sighting reports, as well as the names of witnesses, mysteriously disappeared from the planes where they occurred. Normally, a logbook would contain entries for several months, but these pages vanished. To this day, many hotly deny the stories of the ghosts from Flight 401, despite the scores of credible witnesses that eventually came forward.

Of course, denying the existence of the ghosts did not stop them from being seen. The eyewitness reports continued and were so widely circulated throughout the aviation community that Eastern finally removed the salvaged parts associated with Flight 401. Many believe the reports were so numerous because the ghosts allegedly visited different planes at various times of the day and night, thereby exposing themselves to a wide range of people. In addition, Repo and Loft were often recognized by people who had once worked with them. Both men, especially Loft, had been with Eastern for many years and had worked with hundreds of different crew members.

Repo was seen more often that Loft and was often seen in aircraft Number 318's galley, where flight attendants claimed to see his face reflected in the door to an oven. The attendants also reported that the galley felt unusually cold and clammy, or that there was the strong presence of someone in the room with them. During one incident, Repo's ghost allegedly repaired an oven that had an overloaded circuit. It wasn't until another engineer came to fix the oven, and told a flight attendant that he was the only engineer on the plane, that she realized something was strange. She looked up Repo's photograph and realized that he was the man who had first come to make the repairs.

But Repo's ghost seemed to be especially concerned about the safety and operation of the plane. When his ghost appeared, he often made suggestions or gave warnings to crew members who only realized that he was an apparition after he had vanished. Repo's ghost was seen on the flight deck, either sitting at the engineer's instrument panel or with just his face reflected in it. During one visit, a flight engineer was making a pre-flight inspection when he recognized Repo's ghost. Before vanishing, the spirit told the engineer that he had already made the inspection.

Repo's ghost once warned a flight engineer that there would be an electrical failure on the plane and a check revealed that there was a faulty circuit. Another time, his ghost warned an attendant about a fire on the plane and on still another occasion, the phantom pointed out a problem in the plane's hydraulic system. Repo's ghost even told a captain that there would never be another crash on an L-1011, because "we will not let it happen."

On several occasions, Captain Loft's ghost was seen sitting in the plane's first class section. During one incident, a flight attendant asked the uniformed man why his name was not on the passenger list. When he did not respond, she called her supervisor over, along with a flight captain. It was the captain who recognized Loft sitting in the seat and moments later, the ghost disappeared. Loft's ghost also appeared in the crew compartment and it was suspected that his voice was heard during one flight, warning passengers about seat belts and smoking rules. No one else claimed to have made the announcements.

Eventually, once the parts from Flight 401 were removed from the various planes, the hauntings came to an end. Eastern Airlines ceased operations in January 1991, leaving behind a mystery of what actually happened in the planes they were said to have been visited by ghosts.

A TELEPHONE
How the Photograph of a Flying Telephone Made Headlines in a Mysterious Poltergeist Case

The tragic story of Tina Resch is one of the most intriguing and controversial cases in the modern annals of the paranormal. In 1984, a young girl in Columbus, Ohio, began apparently manifesting psychokinetic activity in her parents' home. Thanks to a hasty photograph of a telephone that seemingly took flight under its own power, the case captured the attention of the American public, believers and skeptics alike, and it went on to become one of the most famous paranormal happenings of the late twentieth century - and a horrific portrait of a young woman's shattered life.

In March 1984, the John and Joan Resch family living in the house on Blue Ash Road included their son, Craig, their adopted daughter, Tina, and four foster children. That month, fourteen-year-old Tina became the focus for a strange and very frightening series of events. On a Saturday morning, all of the lights in the Resch home suddenly went on at once, even though no one had touched any of the switches. John and Joan assumed the incident had been triggered by a power surge and they telephoned the local utility company. It was suggested that they call an electrician, which they did. An electrical contractor named Bruce Claggett came to the house and he assumed, as did John and Joan, that it was simply a problem with the circuit breaker. However, he soon learned differently. He was unable to make the lights stay off and even went as far as taping the switches in the off position. As fast as he could tape them, however, the lights would turn back on again. Closet lights that operated with a pull string would be turned out, but seconds later the bulbs would be glowing again. Claggett finally gave up, unable to explain what was going on.

By that evening, stranger things were being reported like lamps, brass candlesticks and clocks flying through the air; wine glasses shattering; the shower running on its own; eggs rising out of the carton by themselves and then smashing against the kitchen ceiling; knives flying from drawers; and more. A rattling wall picture was placed behind the couch, only to slide back out again three different times.

As the weekend wore on, a pattern began to develop. The intensity and focus of the activity seemed to be Tina, who was even struck by a number of flying objects. A chair was seen tumbling across the floor in Tina's direction and it was only stopped from hitting her when it became wedged in a doorway. Family members, neighbors and unrelated witnesses saw Tina being hit by flying objects, which came from opposite sides of the room from where she was standing.

Near midnight on Saturday, the Columbus police were summoned to the house, but there was nothing they could do. The only respite from the strange events came on Sunday, when Tina left the house for church, and then again in the afternoon when she went out to visit a friend.

By Monday morning, the house was a wreck and literally dozens of reliable witnesses, including reporters, police officers, church officials and neighbors, had seen the unexplained phenomena in the Resch home for themselves. Desperate for help, the family turned to the news media for an explanation. When reporters for the *Columbus Dispatch* arrived, they also witnessed the strange happenings. One of the reporters, Mike Harden, knew of Dr. William G. Roll's work on similar cases and suggested to Joan Resch that she contact him immediately.

Roll arrived in Columbus on March 11. As the project director of the Psychical Research Foundation in Chapel Hill, North Carolina, he had long been considered the country's leading expert on poltergeist phenomena. Roll was born in Bremen, Germany, in 1926, where his father was the American vice-counsel. He graduated from the University of California at Berkeley in 1949, where he studied philosophy and psychology, the closest fields he could find to psychical research. In 1950, he went to England to study at Oxford, and with the support of the Society for Psychical Research and famous psychic Eileen Garrett, he set up a small research laboratory, where he worked from 1952 to 1957.

While at Oxford, Roll got in touch with J.B. Rhine at Duke University in North Carolina. In 1957, Rhine invited Roll to come to Duke and a year later, he was sent, along with fellow parapsychologist J.G. Pratt, to investigate a poltergeist that was plaguing a house in Seaford, Long Island. Their report concluded that the disturbances were most likely the result of unconscious manipulations by a young boy in the family. Roll and Pratt coined the term "recurrent spontaneous psychokinesis" RSPK to explain these types of cases. It is in general use today as another name for poltergeist activity.

Since that time, Roll had investigated well over one hundred cases of poltergeists, both modern and historical. From his reports and personal observations, Roll determined that there were patterns of RSPK effects in the reportedly "haunted" locations. These inexplicable, spontaneous physical effects repeatedly occurred when a particular person was present. He believed that the activities were expressions of unconscious PK carried out by the individual acting as the agent.

Roll's past research certainly made him qualified to study the events in Columbus but even so, he had little idea of what to expect from the case. He had come at the invitation of Joan Resch, after seeing the case widely reported in the newspapers. He and an assistant ended up spending a week in the house and while the poltergeist activity seemed to calm down just after the pair arrived, it made a noisy return by the end of the week.

The most impressive events occurred on March 15, when Roll observed a brief flurry of activity first hand. The incidents that he witnessed took place when he and Tina were alone on the second floor of the house. As things began to happen, Roll stayed very close to her and left his tape recorder running so that he would have an accurate account of the events. A slamming sound came from the bathroom when what Roll believed to be a bar of soap was thrown from a dish on the sink. He and Tina walked into the bathroom and then emerged again. As they did so, a picture on the wall to their left suddenly fell to the floor. Roll had the girl under observation the entire time and saw no movement on her part. Tina became upset because the picture was one of her mother's favorites. Fortunately, it was not broken, but the nail had been ripped out of the wall. Roll offered to nail it back up again and began to do so when the poltergeist once again began to react.

"I was keeping Tina under close watch throughout this period," Roll later reported. "So when I hammered in the nail, she was standing right next to me and I was very aware of her exact position and what she was doing. Before I proceeded, I placed my tape recorder on the dresser, which was behind us and to our left. As I was hammering in the nail, we heard a sound like something falling to the floor. We turned around and my tape recorder was on the ground." The recorder had somehow managed to travel about nine feet, seemingly without assistance. Roll could see no way that Tina could have touched it.

Roll had been hammering the nail back in with a pair of pliers that he had found on the dresser. When he was finished, he had laid them back down again. During the few moments that his attention was focused on the traveling tape recorder, the pliers had also been flung from the top of the dresser and had landed about six feet away. Tina had been nowhere near them at the time.

Not surprisingly, as the case made national news, cries of fraud began to be raised by the debunking community. Three representatives of the Committee for the Scientific Investigation of Claims of the Paranormal CSICOP showed up at the Resch house unannounced on March 13, while Roll was still investigating. One of the group members was the debunker and magician James Randi, who had already publicly attacked the case in the press. The CSICOP investigators became more skeptical when Joan Resch refused to allow Randi into the house. She had no objection to the other two investigators, both scientists, but would have nothing to do with Randi. Because of this, the entire CSICOP team decided to withdraw for reasons that remain unclear and began to issue negative statements about the case, even though they had never actually investigated it.

One of the strangest twists in the saga of the Columbus poltergeist came about when *Columbus Dispatch* reporter Mile Harden and photographer Fred Shannon, a thirty-year veteran of the *Dispatch*, visited the house. The newsmen would make national news themselves with their involvement in the case and would release a series of photographs that would shock the world.

Shannon received the first call from Harden on March 5, 1984. He phoned him directly from the Resch home and asked him to come to the house immediately. Shannon packed up his gear, never realizing that he was about to embark on one of the most bizarre assignments in his career. Even Harden's words of warning over the telephone did not prepare him for what he was about to experience. What he actually came into contact with in the Resch home happened in a short amount of time, but his later testimony about what he saw would become compelling evidence of the paranormal.

Shannon was met at the door by Harden. He was introduced to the Reschs and they began to explain to him about the strange happenings that had been taking place. The "force," as they were calling it, was hurling household objects all about the place and the majority of the disturbances seemed to be aimed at Tina. They began to show him around the house, starting in the dining room, where the chandelier had been damaged by flying wine glasses, as well as by other objects that had crashed into it. The force had almost completely destroyed the fragile long-stemmed glasses that the Reschs kept in the room. When Shannon arrived, only one wine glass remained on the portable bar in the corner.

After looking over the damage for a few minutes, John and Joan Resch went into the adjoining kitchen, leaving the photographer alone in the dining room with Mike Harden and Tina. Moments later, they followed the girl's parents into the other room and, within seconds, they heard the sound of glass shattering in the dining room. "Uh-oh," Joan Resch groaned, "there goes the last wineglass." They raced back into the dining room and found the splintered remains of the glass in the opposite corner from where it had been.

The now-perplexed photographer followed the rest of the group back into the kitchen a few minutes later and to his surprise, he found that the force again chose that moment to react. A tremendous clatter was heard in the dining room and when they returned, they found that six metal coasters which had also been sitting on the portable bar had sailed through the air in the same direction as the wineglass. They now lay in a scattered pile near the broken shards of glass.

According to Shannon, they re-entered the kitchen and the Reschs filled him in about all of the things that had happened in the room. For example, "all hell broke loose" whenever Tina opened the door to the refrigerator. Eggs would fly out and splatter on the ceiling, jars would overturn, and containers of leftovers would burst open and expel their contents onto the floor. On one occasion, a stick of butter had erupted from the icebox and had sailed across the room to become lodged between two cabinet doors. Instead of slowly sliding to the floor, though, the butter inexplicably began moving upwards toward the ceiling.

The Reschs then took Shannon into the living room. They explained about the time that a large, overstuffed chair chased Tina out of the room, cartwheeling until it slammed into the wall and dislodged a picture. Shannon was intrigued by the story, so he decided to take a photo of the chair and the picture, the frame of which was still intact although the glass was shattered. He asked Tina to pose next to the chair and to hold the picture so that he could see it through his camera lens. At that same instant, when he shot the photo and the flash went off, Shannon heard a loud crash. Tina claimed that something knocked the picture out of her hand. Shannon was thinking that she had just dropped the picture and the crash when it hit the floor was what had startled him but he soon had second thoughts about this. He noticed that Tina was still holding a corner of the picture frame in her hands, as if something had struck the picture and had knocked it out of her hands, leaving her holding one small, broken corner of it.

Unnerved and upset, Tina sat down on a couch in the family room. As Shannon and Harden turned to go back into the kitchen, they heard a tremendous booming sound. Without thinking, Shannon immediately turned and snapped a photo. The developed image would later show Tina covering her head because the lamp on the stand next to her had crashed to the floor. Since his eyes were not on her at the time, Shannon was unable to say for sure whether or not Tina knocked over the lamp herself, but he was confident that she had not. "I had swung around so rapidly," he later said, "that I don't see how she would have had time to knock over the lamp and so completely cover her head. She was covering her head because she had been attacked by so many various objects. She was a badly frightened girl and her fear never left her all during the time these things were going on. At this point, I had been in the house for fifteen minutes!"

Tina sat down on the arm of a chair across the room from the couch where she had been sitting. Shannon took up a position in the doorway near a love seat, with his back to the kitchen. Suddenly, the love seat that was next to him began to move towards Tina. It pivoted on one leg and shuffled toward her about eighteen inches. Needless to say, the skeptical photographer was startled --- but not so much so that he was unable to snap a photo of the shocked expression on Tina's face. "I knew the photo wouldn't mean much to someone who wasn't there, as I was, to see what had happened," Shannon explained. "Anybody who chose to think that way would say it was just a setup. So I was looking for other things to happen. I didn't have long to wait."

Shannon and Harden decided to observe the girl more closely and took a seat on the couch, with Tina on the loveseat, facing them. On the floor in front of her was a colorful afghan, which Joan Resch had earlier explained had once risen off the floor and had covered Tina. Within a few moments of the journalists sitting down, they saw this repeated and Shannon took a photo of her with the afghan draped over her body. He had no explanation for how it could have lifted from the floor and could find no method by which Tina could have accomplished this on her own.

Later, the three of them went into the kitchen and were talking with John and Joan, when they all heard a loud sound in the unoccupied family room. Shannon stated that it sounded, "like a cannon had gone off --- it had that much force." They went to investigate and learned that a heavy bronze candlestick which had been on the floor to the immediate left of the loveseat and near the back door had taken flight a short distance and had banged into the door. The door, which was made of metal, was hit with such force that two dents were left on it. The Reschs had taken to placing heavy objects like the candlestick on the floor because it seemed that items left on walls and tables had a habit of flying in Tina's direction. Once, a wrought-iron clock had flown from the wall and had hit her in the back of the head, leaving a lump.

A few moments later, another bronze candlestick took flight from the other side of the loveseat, near the kitchen. Tina was sitting in a chair in the family room and Shannon and Harden were watching her from a couch across the room. No one was anywhere near the candlestick and yet somehow, it moved. According to Tina, who had been at an angle to see the candlestick, it had flown four or five feet into the kitchen before making a ninety-degree turn and shooting down the hallway. She said that it had been turning end over end through the air. Shannon admitted that he had not seen the candlestick move, but he had certainly heard it. As it propelled itself, the object made a roaring sound, an incredible noise that he said sounded "something like a locomotive."

Everyone was shocked and when they recovered, they all got to their feet and hurried into the hallway. The first thing they saw was the hanging lamp at the entrance to the doorway. The lamp was swinging back and forth quite rapidly from what Shannon believed was wind left behind by the fast-moving candlestick. The lamp, he later reported, was swinging as if it were in a hurricane.

The incident with the candlestick was only one of the strange things that happened while Harden and Shannon were watching Tina in the family room. Most of the other incidents involved telephones that were located on a stand next to Tina's chair. Usually, two telephones were kept on the stand. The reason for this was that when the outbreak began, the house was plagued with all sorts of electrical problems, including malfunctions with the telephone in the family room. Because of this, the Reschs bought a second, cheap phone and installed it next to the sturdier, original phone. Both sat on the stand next to the chair in the family room but it was the second phone that was most affected by the "force" in the house.

According to Fred Shannon, he was present on seven different occasions when one or the other of the phones flew in Tina's direction. The first two times, they hit her on the left side and fell next to her on the couch. During the other incidents, the phones flew over Tina's lap in the direction of the loveseat. The events occurred unexpectedly, usually minutes apart, but happened in seconds. This made it nearly impossible for Shannon to get a photograph. At one point, he sat for more than twenty minutes with the camera up to his eye, waiting for something to happen, but nothing did. Each time that he would lower the camera so that he wasn't immediately ready to take a photo --- the phone would go flying through the air!

That caused him to wonder if he was dealing with a blind force after all. Could it be aware of his presence? If this was true, he decided to devise a strategy.

He brought the camera to his eye, his finger poised on the trigger, and waited, watching Tina for about five minutes. Then, without taking his eyes off her, he lowered the camera to the level of his waist, still keeping it pointed in her direction and his finger on the shutter. As he did this, he turned his head in the direction of the kitchen, where the Reschs were talking with some visitors. He waited patiently for something to happen, pretending that his attention was somewhere else.

A few seconds later, he saw a white blur out of the corner of his eye and by the time that he pressed the shutter of the camera, a phone had streaked through the air and had sailed all the way across the chair in which Tina was sitting! The resulting photo captured not only the flying telephone but also the frightened expression on Tina's face as she jerked backwards to keep from being hit. In all, Shannon was able to get three different photos of the telephone in flight but this first one was the one that got the most attention. The day after it appeared in the local newspaper, it was picked up by the Associated Press and made front pages all over the country.

The photo was immediately attacked by the debunkers, who began savaging the entire case, but Shannon was adamant about what he had seen. He emphasized in writing: "I am damned sure that she did not throw those phones. From what Mike and I observed, I would say that she couldn't possibly have thrown them -- absolutely no way. We were sitting in a well-lighted room; we were looking right at her. When one of us was looking away for a moment, the other had his eyes on Tina all the time. And of course, there were some objects that took flight while she was nowhere near them --- the candlesticks, for example."

Shannon also witnessed an incident with the telephones that did not involve Tina. It occurred just a few minutes after he took the astounding photo of the phone in flight. A Franklin County Children Services caseworker and an associate arrived at the house on business and the caseworker sat down in the loveseat. Shannon warned her not to sit there, as he knew that she would be in the direct path of the telephone. She didn't take him seriously and made several comments to assure him that she thought the whole thing was a joke, but she humored him anyway by moving to the other cushion on the loveseat. She stood up, shuffled sideways and sat back down again. Just as she was lowering herself to the seat, the phone shot through the air and landed hard on the cushion where she had been sitting. If she had not moved, the phone would have struck her in the chest. The incident startled her so much that she and her co-worker quickly finished their business and left.

A little while later, Harden, Shannon and Tina were standing in the middle of the family room when a box of tissues which was also on the phone table suddenly leapt into the air. It zipped past Shannon's leg and landed on a small table next to the couch. When it hit the table, it did not skip or bounce even though it had been moving at tremendous speed. Instead, it stopped in place as if it had been caught by a magnet or glued into position.

This was the last activity that Shannon witnessed in the family room but his experiences at the Resch house were not yet over. He decided to take some photos in the kitchen and hoped that if he got Tina to open the refrigerator door, something would fly out of it, as had been allegedly happening over the last few days. The kitchen was already a mess from these past incidents and in fact, the Reschs had been cleaning the room during most of the time that Shannon and Harden had been in the house.

Tina waited in the kitchen as he set up his camera in the corner, directly across the room from the refrigerator. Shannon ducked low to avoid being hit by any flying food and asked Tina to open the door, but nothing happened. She repeated it three times but everything inside remained where it was. Tina decided to use the moments of inactivity to make a sandwich and Harden and Shannon decided to pack up and leave, having spent nearly four hours in the house.

As soon as the story of the baffling activity in the Resch house, and Shannon's accompanying photo, began to appear in newspapers, self-appointed critics of the paranormal immediately began an attack on the reality of the events that were being reported. In spite of the fact that none of them had investigated the case, nor had been to Columbus, they were convinced that the whole thing was a hoax. The debunkers managed to obtain the negatives of the photos that Fred Shannon had shot in the house. Because there were three photos of a phone in the air above Tina's lap not just the one that appeared in AP wire stories , Shannon was immediately accused of faking the photos and having Tina throw the phone so that he could photograph it. Although Shannon explained how he managed to capture three photos, he was dismissed as a fraud. This was done without investigation of the scene, assessment of the evidence and with no regard to Shannon's thirty-year career and outstanding reputation.

The debunkers also dismissed the entire case based on the fact that Roll admitted that he believed that Tina had faked some of the less impressive activity in the house. However, he did believe that genuine activity was taking place, even when conceding there was some limited fraud involved as well. "It is certain that Tina threw a lamp down on one occasion," he said. "That's obvious. She told me that she did the same thing on two other occasions. So there's no doubt there were some fraudulent occurrences."

Roll stated that it was not uncommon for victims of poltergeists to get into the act themselves as part of the mischief making. He had been able to formulate many of the poltergeist patterns into a profile through his research. Usually at the center of the activity was a child or teenager who possessed a great deal of internal anger, usually caused by a stressful situation in the household or a mental disturbance. The PK was an unconscious, and unknowing, way of venting that hostility without fear of punishment. Because of the mental states of the agents in many of his cases, genuine phenomena and trickery often went hand in hand.

In such cases, the PK effects of the unstable person will actually cause genuine phenomena to occur. However, as the events are recorded and gain the attention of others in the household and sometimes even the authorities and media , the agent in the case begins to receive the much-needed attention they desired. As this begins to occur, the phenomena will cease. To continue the attention, the agent will often fake phenomena. Unfortunately, as the agent is often caught in the act of doing this, debunkers will claim the entire case was a hoax and are able to discredit any research material gathered in the early stages. Because of this, many authentic cases are never brought to public record.

Roll felt that the minor fraudulent episodes that occurred did not discredit the Resch case. "I can only say that when I was present, I couldn't find any ordinary explanation for the incidents I witnessed," he stated. "In my opinion, it is very unlikely that they were caused normally. And of course there are a number of witnesses we interviewed in Columbus who had seen things under conditions where no family members could have caused them."

Later that month, Roll took Tina back to North Carolina where he and other scientists conducted computer-based ESP and PK tests on her. The results of the tests were in no way striking, leading most to believe that she did not possess any long-term psychic abilities. As in other poltergeist cases, the mysterious happenings seemed to be confined to a short period of time. And while there were some minor poltergeist incidents in Roll's home and at the home of a counselor where Tina was staying, the researchers believed that her aggressive manipulations were short-lived.

What caused the manifestations? No one knows for sure and the story behind the Columbus poltergeist remains a mystery. Poltergeists in general tend to focus on disturbed children who are suppressing hostility and anger. The displacement of energy acts as a safety valve for the pent-up emotions. In Tina's case, there had been recent problems at home over the fact that Tina, against the wishes of John and Joan, had begun searching for her biological parents. Also, Tina's best friend of two years had ended their friendship just two days before the events began. To make matters worse, the Reschs had recently taken Tina out of school because she was having trouble getting along with other students. She was apparently unpopular with most of her classmates and was having difficulty with one of her teachers. Because of this, she was being tutored at home and was seemingly "cut off" from the outside world. All of this apparently combined to create an outward transference of energy.

Eventually, the activity ended and after Tina's return from North Carolina, only a few minor incidents were reported in her home. Roll was never sure of the cause of the case, but his studies pointed to the theory that poltergeist agents seemed to suffer from disturbances in the central nervous system. This may have been the case with Tina Resch, for even though the bizarre incidents ended in her home, her story was not quite over.

Many poltergeist agents have been documented to be in poor mental health, which deteriorated further in stressful situations. This might explain the findings of many standard psychologists and mental health professionals. They often discover that patients with unresolved emotional issues are associated with, or have lived in, houses where poltergeist activity has been reported. In addition, while studying the personalities of those thought to be poltergeist agents, psychologists have found anxiety issues, phobias, mania, obsessions, dissociative disorders and even schizophrenia. In some cases, psychotherapy may eliminate the poltergeist phenomena but apparently, not in all of them.

For despite counseling, Tina Resch went from being an unhappy child to being a disturbed adult. She went from one disastrous situation to another, finally to two marriages, the first at age sixteen, and two divorces and then to a sentence of life in prison for the felony murder and aggrevated battery of her three-year-old daughter, which occurred when the child was being watched by Tina's boyfriend. She claimed to be innocent of the crime, and witnesses confirmed that she not present when it was committed. There was no trial. Instead, Tina accepted a plea bargain of life imprisonment rather than face the possibility of a death penalty. She was sent to a Georgia prison in 1994 and remains there today.

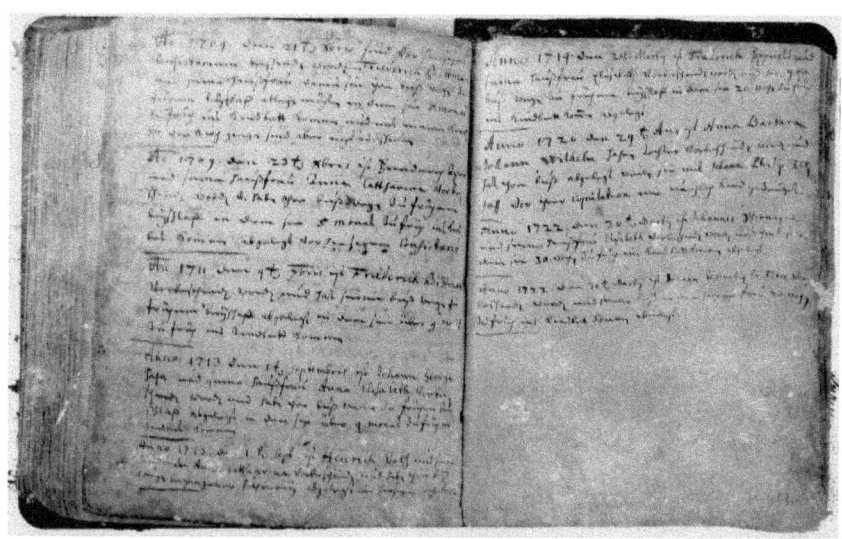

HISTORICAL RECORDS FILE
How Uncovering History Revealed the True Story of One of "America's Most Haunted Houses"

Handprints in the mirrors, footsteps on the stairs, mysterious smells, vanishing objects, death by poison, hangings, murder and gunfire -- the Myrtles Plantation in the West Feliciana town of St. Francisville, Louisiana, holds the rather dubious record of hosting more ghostly phenomena than just about any other house in the country. But what could be more dubious than the honor itself? That would be the questionable history that has been presented to "explain" why the house is so haunted in the first place.

Long acclaimed as one of the most haunted houses in America, the Myrtles attracts an almost endless stream of visitors each year and many of them come in search of ghosts. There seems to be little doubt about the fact that the house is haunted - it's the reason that it's haunted that has been called into question. For several generations, owners and guides at the plantation have been presenting "facts and history" that they know is blatantly false. The Myrtles, according to hundreds of people who have encountered the resident spirits, is indeed haunted, but not for the reasons that we have been told.

It was a simple check of historical records that revealed the real story. The true story of the Myrtles may not be as glamorous as the story presented by the staff at the plantation, but it is certainly strange. The history of the plantation is filled with death, tragedy and despair, leading us to wonder why a fanciful history was created in its place.

The Myrtles Plantation was constructed by David Bradford in 1794, and since that time, has allegedly been the scene of at least ten murders. In truth, though, only one person was ever murdered there but, as has been stated already, some of the people who have owned the house have never let the truth stand in the way of a good story. But as the reader will soon discover, the plantation has an unusual history that genuinely did occur, one that may, and likely has, left its own real ghosts behind.

David Bradford was one of five children born in America to Irish immigrants. In 1777, he purchased a tract of land and a small stone house near Washington County, Pennsylvania. He became a successful attorney, businessman and Deputy Attorney General for the county. His first attempt to marry ended only days before his wedding no details are known about this but he later met and married Elizabeth Porter in 1785 and started a family.

As his family and business grew, Bradford needed a larger home and he built a new one in the town of Washington. The house became well known in the region for its size and remarkable craftsmanship, with a mahogany staircase and woodwork imported from England. Many of the items had to be transported from the East Coast and over the Pennsylvania mountains at great expense. Bradford would use the parlor of the house as an office, where he would meet with his clients.

Unfortunately, he was not able to enjoy his splendid new house for long. In October 1794, he was forced to flee, leaving his family behind. Bradford became involved in the infamous Whiskey Rebellion and legend has it that George Washington placed a price on the man's head for his role in the affair. The Whiskey Rebellion took place in western Pennsylvania and began as a series of grievances over high prices and taxes forced on those living along the frontier at that time. The complaints eventually erupted into violence when a mob attacked and burned down the home of a local tax collector. In the months that followed, residents resisted a tax that had been placed on whiskey, and while most of the protests were nonviolent, Washington mobilized a militia and sent it in to suppress the rebellion. Once the protests were brought under control, Bradford left the region on the advice of some of the other principals in the affair.

After leaving Washington, Bradford first went to Pittsburgh. Leaving his family in safety, he traveled down the Ohio River to the Mississippi. He eventually settled at Bayou Sara, near what is now St. Francisville, Louisiana. Bradford was no stranger to this area. He had originally traveled here in 1792 to try and obtain a land grant from Spain. When he returned in 1796, he purchased six hundred acres of land and a year later, built a modest, eight-room home near Baton Rouge that he named "Laurel Grove." He lived there alone until 1799, when he received a pardon for his role in the Whiskey Rebellion from newly elected President John Adams. He was given the pardon for his assistance in establishing a boundary line, known historically as "Ellicott's Line," between Spain and the United States.

After receiving the pardon, Bradford returned to Pennsylvania to bring his wife and five children back to Louisiana. He brought them to live at Bayou Sarah and they settled into a comfortable life there. Bradford occasionally took in students who wanted to study the law. One of them, Clark Woodrooff, not only earned a law degree but also married his teacher's daughter, Sarah Mathilda.

Clark Woodrooff was born in Litchfield County, Connecticut, in August 1791. Having no desire to follow in his father's footsteps as a farmer, he left Connecticut at the age of nineteen and sought his fortune on the Mississippi River, ending up in Bayou Sarah. He arrived in 1810, the same year that citizens of the Feliciana Parish rose up in revolt against the Spanish garrison at Baton Rouge. They overthrew the Spanish and then set up a new territory with its capital being St. Francisville. The territory extended from the Mississippi River as far east as the Perdido River, near Mobile, Alabama.

Still seeking to make his fortune, Woodrooff placed an advertisement in the St. Francisville newspaper, the *Time Piece*, in the summer of 1811. He informed the public that "an academy would be opening on the first Monday in September for the reception of students." He planned to offer English, grammar, astronomy, geography, elocution, composition, penmanship and Greek and Latin. The academy was apparently short-lived for in 1814, he joined Colonel Hide's cavalry regiment from the Feliciana Parish to fight alongside Andrew Jackson at the Battle of New Orleans. When the War of 1812 had ended, Woodrooff returned to St. Francisville with the intention of studying law.

He began his studies with Judge David Bradford and soon earned his degree. He also succumbed to the charms of the Bradford daughter, the lovely Sarah Mathilda. Their romance blossomed under the shade of the crape myrtle trees that reportedly gave the home its lasting name. The young couple was married on November 19, 1817 and for their honeymoon, Woodrooff took his new bride to The Hermitage, the Tennessee home of his friend, Andrew Jackson.

After the death of David Bradford, Woodrooff managed Laurel Grove for his mother-in-law, Elizabeth. He expanded the holdings of the plantation and planted about six hundred and fifty acres of indigo and cotton. Together, he and Sarah Mathilda had three children, Cornelia Gale, James, and Mary Octavia. Tragically, their happiness would not last.

On July 21, 1823, Sarah Mathilda died after contracting yellow fever. The disease was spread through a number of epidemics that swept through Louisiana in those days. Hardly a family in the region went untouched by tragedy and despair. Although heartbroken, Woodrooff continued to manage the plantation and to care for his children with help from Elizabeth. But the dark days were not yet over. On July 15, 1824, his only son, James, also died from yellow fever and two months later, in September, Cornelia Gale was also felled by the dreaded disease.

Woodrooff's life would never be the same but he managed to purchase the farm outright from his mother-in-law. She was quite elderly by this time and was happy to see the place in good hands. She continued to live at Laurel Grove with her son-in-law and granddaughter, Octavia, until her death in 1830.

After Elizabeth died, Woodrooff turned his attentions away from farming to the practice of law. He and Octavia moved away from Laurel Grove and he left the plantation under the management of a caretaker. He was appointed to a judge's position over District D in Covington, Louisiana, and he served in this capacity until April 1835. On January 1, 1834, he sold Laurel Grove to Ruffin Grey Stirling.

By this time, Woodrooff was living on Rampart Street in New Orleans and had changed the spelling of his last name to "Woodruff." He had also been elected as the president of public works for the city. During this period, Octavia was sent to a finishing school in New Haven, Connecticut, but she returned home to live with her father in 1836. Two years later, she married Colonel Lorenzo Augustus Besancon and moved to his plantation, Oaklawn, five miles north of New Orleans.

In 1840, the Louisiana governor, Isaac Johnson, appointed Woodruff to the newly created office of Auditor of Public Works and he served for one term. Then, at sixty years of age, he retired and moved to Oaklawn to live with Octavia and her husband. He devoted the remainder of his life to the study of chemistry and physics and died on November 25, 1851. He was buried in the Girod Street Cemetery in New Orleans.

In 1834, Laurel Grove was purchased by Ruffin Grey Stirling. The Stirlings were a wealthy family who owned several plantations on both sides of the Mississippi River. On January 1, Ruffin Grey Stirling and his wife, Mary Catherine Cobb, took over the house, land, buildings and all of the slaves that had been bought from Elizabeth Bradford by her son-in-law.

Since the Stirlings were leaders in the community, they needed a house befitting their social status. They decided to remodel Laurel Grove. Stirling added a broad central hallway and the entire southern section. The walls of the original house were removed and repositioned to create four large rooms that were used as separate ladies' and gentlemen's parlors, a formal dining room and a game room. Trips to Europe to purchase fine furnishings resulted in the importation of skilled craftsmen, as well. Elaborate plaster cornices were created for many of the rooms, made from a mixture of clay, Spanish moss and cattle hair. On the outside of the house, Stirling added a 107-foot-long front gallery that was supported by cast-iron posts and railings. The original roof was extended to encompass the new addition, copying the existing dormers to maintain a smooth line. The addition had higher ceilings than the original house, so the second story floor was raised one foot. The completed project nearby doubled the size of David Bradford's house and in keeping with the renovations, the name of the plantation was officially changed to "the Myrtles."

Four years after the completion of the project, Stirling died on July 17, 1854 of consumption, as tuberculosis was called at the time. He left his vast holdings in the care of his wife, Mary Cobb, who most referred to as a remarkable woman. Many other plantation owners stated rather patronizingly from a twenty-first century point of view that she "had the business acumen of a man," which was high praise for a woman in those days, and she managed to run all of her farms almost single-handedly for many years.

In spite of this, the family was often visited by tragedy. Of nine children, only four of them lived to be old enough to marry. The oldest son, Lewis, died in the same year as his father. Daughter Sarah Mulford's husband was murdered on the front porch of the house after the Civil War. The war itself wreaked havoc on the Myrtles and on the Stirling family. Many of the family's personal belongings were looted and destroyed by Union soldiers and the wealth that they had accumulated was ultimately in worthless Confederate currency. To make matters worse, Mary Cobb had invested heavily in sugar plantations that had been ravaged by the war. She eventually lost all of her property. She never let the tragedies of the war, and the others that followed, overcome her, however, and she held onto the Myrtles until her death in August 1880. She was buried next to her husband in the family plot at Grace Church in St. Francisville.

On December 5, 1865, Mary Cobb hired William Drew Winter, the husband of her daughter, Sarah Mulford, to act as her agent and attorney and to help her manage the plantation lands. As part of the deal, she gave Sarah and William the Myrtles as their home.

William had been born to Captain Samuel Winter and Sarah Bowman on October 28, 1820 in Bath, Maine. Little is known about his early life or how he managed to meet Sarah Mulford Stirling. However, they were married on June 3, 1852 at The Myrtles and together, they had six children, Mary, Sarah, Kate, Ruffin, William and Francis. Kate died from typhoid at the age of three. The Winters first lived at Gantmore plantation, near Clinton, Louisiana, and then bought a plantation on the west side of the Mississippi known as Arbroath.

Twelve years after the death of Ruffin Stirling, and after the Civil War, William was named as agent and attorney by Mary Stirling to help her with her remaining lands, including Ingleside, Crescent Park, Botany Bay and the Myrtles. In return, Mary gave William the use of The Myrtles as his home. Times were terrible and Winter was unable to hold onto it. By December 1867, he was completely bankrupt and the Myrtles was sold by the U.S. Marshal to the New York Warehouse & Security Company on April 15, 1868. Two years later, however, on April 23, the property was sold back to Mrs. Sarah M. Winter as the heir of her late father, Ruffin G. Stirling. It is unknown just what occurred to cause this reversal of fortune but it seemed as though things were improving for the family once again.

But soon after, tragedy struck the Myrtles once more. According to the January 1871 issue of the *Point Coupee Democrat* newspaper, Winter was teaching a Sunday school lesson in the gentlemen's parlor of the house when he heard someone approach the house on horseback. After the stranger called out to him, saying that he had some business with him, Winter went out onto the side gallery of the house and was shot. He collapsed onto the porch and died. Those inside of the house, stunned by the sound of gunfire and retreating hoofbeats, hurried outside to find the fallen man. Winter died on January 26, 1871 and was buried the following day in the cemetery at Grace Church. The newspaper reported that a man named E.S. Webber was to stand trial for Winter's murder but no outcome of the case was ever recorded. As far as is known, Winter's killer remains unidentified and unpunished.

Sarah was devastated by the incident and never remarried. She remained at The Myrtles with her mother and brothers until her death in April 1878 at the age of forty-four.

After the death of Mary Cobb Stirling in 1880, the Myrtles was purchased by Stephen Stirling, one of her sons. He bought out his brothers but only maintained ownership of the house until March 1886. There are some who say that he squandered what was left of his fortune and lost the plantation in a game of chance but most likely, the place was just too deep in debt for him to hold on to. He sold the Myrtles to Oran D. Brooks, ending his family's ownership. Brooks kept it until January 1889 when, after a series of transfers, it was purchased by Harrison Milton Williams, a Mississippi widower who brought his young son and second wife, Fannie Lintot Haralson, to the house in 1891.

Injured during the Civil War, in which he served as a fifteen-year-old Confederate cavalry courier, Williams planted cotton and gained a reputation as a hard-working and industrious man. He and his family, which grew to include seven children, kept the Myrtles going during the hard times of the post-war South. But tragedy was soon to strike the Myrtles again.

During a storm, the Williams' oldest son, Harry, was trying to gather up some stray cattle and fell into the Mississippi and drowned. Shattered with grief, Harrison and Fannie turned over management of the property to their son, Surget Minor Williams. He later married a local girl named Jessie Folkes and provided a home at the Myrtles for his spinster sister and maiden aunt, Katie. Secretly called "the Colonel" behind her back, Katie was a true Southern character. Eccentric and kind, but with a gruff exterior, she kept life interesting at the house for years.

By the 1950s, the property surrounding the house had been divided among the Williams heirs and the house itself was sold to Marjorie Munson, an Oklahoma widow who had been made wealthy by chicken farms. It was at this point, they say, that the ghost stories of the house began. They started innocently enough but soon, what may have been real-life ghostly occurrences took on a "life" of their own.

There is no question that the most famous ghostly tale of the Myrtles is that of Chloe, the vengeful slave who murdered the wife and two daughters of Clark Woodruff in a fit of jealous anger. Those who have been reading this chapter so far have already guessed that there are some serious flaws in this story but for the sake of being complete, I included the tale here since it has long been told by owners and guides at the house.

According to the story, the troubles that led to the haunting at the Myrtles began in 1817 when Sarah Mathilda married Clark Woodruff. Sara Matilda had given birth to two daughters and was carrying a third child, when an event took place that still haunts the Myrtles today.

Woodruff had a reputation in the region for integrity with men and with the law, but was also known for being promiscuous. While his wife was pregnant with their third child, he started an intimate relationship with one of his slaves. This particular girl, whose name was Chloe, was a household servant who, while she hated being forced to give in to Woodruff's sexual demands, realized that if she didn't comply, she could be sent to work in the fields, which was the most brutal of the slaves' work.

Eventually, Woodruff tired of Chloe and chose another girl with whom to carry on. Chloe feared the worst, sure that she was going to be sent to the fields, and she began eavesdropping on the Woodruff family's private conversations, dreading hearing the mention of her name. One day, the Judge caught her at this and ordered that one of her ears be cut off to teach her a lesson and to put her in her place. After that time, she always wore a green turban around her head to hide the ugly scar that the knife had left behind.

What actually happened next is still unclear. Some claim that what occurred was done so that the family would just get sick and then Chloe could nurse them back to health and earn the judge's gratitude. In this way, she would be safe from ever being sent to the fields. Others say that her motives were not so pure and that what she did was for one reason only: revenge.

For whatever reason, Chloe put a small amount of poison into a birthday cake that was made in honor of the Woodruff's oldest daughter. Mixed in with the flour and sugar was a handful of crushed oleander flowers. The two children, and Sarah Mathilda, each had slices of the poisoned cake but Woodruff didn't eat any of it. Before the end of the day, all of them were very sick. Chloe patiently attended to their needs, never realizing if it was an accident that she had given them too much poison. In a matter of hours, all three of them were dead.

The other slaves, perhaps afraid that their owner would punish them also, dragged Chloe from her room and hanged her from a nearby tree. Her body was later cut down, weighted with rocks and thrown into the river. Woodruff closed off the children's dining room, where the party was held, and never allowed it to be used again as long as he lived. Tragically, his life was cut short a few years later by a murderer. To this day, the room where the children were poisoned has never again been used for dining. It is called the game room today.

Since her death, the ghost of Chloe has been reported at the Myrtles and was even accidentally photographed by a past owner. The plantation still sells picture postcards today with the cloudy image of what is purported to be Chloe standing between two of the buildings. The former slave is thought to be the most frequently encountered ghost at the Myrtles. She has often been seen in her green turban, wandering the place at night. Sometimes the cries of children accompany her appearances and at other times, those who are sleeping are startled awake by her face, peering at them from the side of the bed.

I am sure that after reading this story, even the most non-discerning readers have discovered a number of errors and problems with the tale. In fact, there are so many errors that it's difficult to know where to begin. However, to start, it's a shame that the character of Clark Woodruff has been so thoroughly damaged over the years with stories about his adulterous affairs with his slaves and claims that he had one of his lovers mutilated. Sadly, these stories have been accepted as fact, even though no evidence whatsoever exists to say that they are true. In fact, history seems to show that Woodruff was very devoted to his wife and was so distraught over her death that he never remarried.

Before we get to the problem of Chloe's existence, we should also examine the alleged murders of Sarah Mathilda and her two daughters. In this case, the legend has twisted the truth so far that it is unrecognizable. Sarah Mathilda was not murdered. She died tragically from yellow fever according to historical record in 1823. Her children, a son and a daughter ---- not two daughters ----- died more than a year after she did. They certainly did not die from the result of a poisoned birthday cake. Also, with this legend, Octavia would not have existed at all her mother was supposed to have been pregnant when murdered but we know that she lived with her father, got married and lived to a ripe old age. In addition, Woodruff was not killed. He died peacefully at his daughter and son-in-law's plantation in 1851.

The key to the legend is, of course, Chloe, the murderous slave. The problem with this is that as far as we can tell, Chloe never existed at all. Not only did she not murder members of the Woodruff family but it's unlikely that the family ever had a slave by this name. Countless hours have been spent looking through the property records of the Woodruff family, which are still available and on file as public record in St. Francisville, searching for any evidence that Chloe existed. It was a great disappointment to learn that the Woodruffs had never owned a slave, or had any record of a slave, named Chloe, or Cleo, as she appears in some versions of the story. The records list all of the other slaves owned by the Woodruff family but Chloe simply did not exist.

So how did such a story get started?

In the 1950s, the Myrtles was owned by wealthy widow Marjorie Munson, who heard some of the local stories that had gotten started about odd things happening at the house. Wondering if perhaps the old mansion might be haunted, she asked around and that's when the legend of "Chloe" got its start. According to the granddaughter of Harrison and Fannie Williams, Lucile Lawrason, her aunts used to talk about the ghost of an old woman who haunted the Myrtles and who wore a green bonnet. They often laughed about it and it became a family story. She was never given a name and in fact, the "ghost" with the green bonnet from the story was described as an older woman, never as a young slave who might have been involved in an affair with the owner of the house. Regardless, someone repeated this story of the Williams' family ghost to Marjorie Munson and she soon penned a song about the ghost of the Myrtles, a woman in a green beret.

As time wore on, the story grew and changed. The Myrtles changed hands several more times and in the 1970s, it was restored again under the ownership of Arlin Dease and Mr. and Mrs. Robert F. Ward. During this period, the story was greatly embellished to include the poison murders and the severed ear. Up until this point, it was largely just a story that was passed on by word of mouth and it received little attention outside of the area. All of that changed when James and Frances Kermeen Myers passed through on a riverboat and decided to purchase the Myrtles. The house came furnished with period antiques and enough ghost stories to attract people from all over the country.

Soon, the story of the Myrtles was appearing in magazines and books and receiving a warm reception from ghost enthusiasts, who had no idea that what they were hearing was a badly skewed version of the truth. The house appeared in a November 1980 issue of *LIFE* magazine but the first book that I have found that mentioned the house was by author Richard Winer. Both the magazine article and the Winer book mentioned the poison deaths of Sarah Mathilda and her daughters.

As time went on and more authors and television crews came calling at the Myrtles, the story changed again and this time, took on even more murders. In addition to the deaths of Sarah Mathilda, her daughters and Chloe, it was alleged that as many as six other people had been killed in the house. One of them, Lewis Stirling, the oldest son of Ruffin Grey Stirling, was claimed to have been stabbed to death in the house over a gambling debt. However, burial records in St. Francisville state that he died in October 1854 from yellow fever.

According to legend, three Union soldiers were killed in the house after they broke in and attempted to loot the place. They were allegedly shot to death in the gentlemen's parlor, leaving bloodstains on the floor that refused to be wiped away. One fanciful account has it that years later, after the Myrtles was opened as an inn, a maid was mopping the floor and came to a spot that, no matter how hard she pushed, she was unable to reach. Supposedly, the spot was the same size as a human body and this was said to have been where one of the Union soldiers fell. The strange phenomenon was said to have lasted for a month and has not occurred since. The only problem with this story is that no soldiers were ever killed in the house. There are no records or evidence to say that there were and in fact, surviving family members denied the story was true. If the ghostly incident occurred, then it must have been caused by something else.

Another murder allegedly occurred in 1927, when a caretaker at the house was supposedly killed during a robbery. Once again, no record exists of this crime and an incident as recent as this would have been widely reported. The only event even close to this, which may have spawned the story, occurred when the brother of Fannie Williams, Eddie Haralson, was living in a small house on the property. He was killed while being robbed but this did not occur in the main house, as the story states.

The only verifiable murder to occur at the Myrtles was that of William Drew Winter and it differs wildly from the legends that have been told. As described previously, Winter was lured out of the house by a rider, who shot him to death on the porch. It is here where the stories take a turn for the worse. In the legend, Winter was shot and then, mortally wounded, staggered back into the house, passed through the gentlemen's parlor and the ladies' parlor and onto the staircase that rises from the central hallway. He then managed to climb just high enough to die in his beloved's arms on the seventeenth step. It has since been claimed that ghostly footsteps have been heard coming into the house, walking to the stairs and then climbing to the seventeenth step where they, of course, come to an end.

While dramatic, this event never happened either. Winter was indeed murdered on the front porch by an unknown assailant but after being shot, he immediately fell down and died. His bloody trip through the house never took place --- information that was easily found in historical records.

So, is the Myrtles really haunted?

There is nothing to say that the Myrtles is *not* haunted. In fact, there is no denying that the sheer number of accounts that have been reported and collected here would cause the house to qualify as one of the most haunted sites in the country. However, as you can see from the preceding pages, the house may be haunted, just not for the reasons that have been claimed for so many years.

In all likelihood, the infamous Chloe never existed and even if she did, historical records prove that Sarah Mathilda and her children were never murdered but died from disease. Instead of ten murders in the house, only one occurred and when William Winter died, he certainly did not stagger up the staircase to die on the seventeenth step, as the stories of his phantom footsteps allegedly bear out. Such tales belong in the realm of fiction, not in the chronicle of one of the alleged "most haunted houses in America."

The house may really be haunted by the ghost of a woman in a green turban or bonnet. The Williams family had an ongoing tale about her and while it may have been a story that was never meant to be told outside the family, the story spread nonetheless. They admit that while the ghost apparently did exist, no identity was ever given to her. It's also very likely that something unusual was going on at the Myrtles when Marjorie Munson lived there, which led to her seeking answers and to her first introduction to the ghost in the green headdress. Did she see the ghost? Who knows? But many others have claimed that they have.

Frances Myers claimed that she encountered the ghost in the green turban in 1987. She was asleep in one of the downstairs bedrooms when she was awakened suddenly by a black woman wearing a green turban and a long dress. She was standing silently beside the bed, holding a candlestick in her hand. She was so real that the candle even gave off a soft glow. Knowing nothing about ghosts, Myers was terrified and pulled the covers over her head and started screaming. Then she slowly peeked out and reached out a hand to touch the woman, who had never moved, and to her amazement, the apparition vanished.

Others claim that they have also seen the ghost and in fact, she was purportedly photographed a number of years ago. The resulting image seems to show a woman but it does not fit the description of a young woman like Chloe would have been. In fact, it looks more like the older woman that was described by the Williams family. Could this be the real ghost of the Myrtles?

Even after leaving out the ridiculous stories of the poisonings and Winter's dramatic death on the staircase, the history of the Myrtles is still filled with more than enough trauma and tragedy to cause the place to become haunted. There were a number of deaths in the house from yellow fever alone, and it's certainly possible that any of the deceased might have stayed behind after death. If ghosts stay behind in this world because of unfinished business, there are a number of candidates to be the restless ghosts of the plantation's stories.

And, if we believe the stories, the place truly is infested by spirits from different periods in the history of the house. There have been many reports of children who are seen playing on the wide verandah, in the hallways and in the rooms. The small boy and girl may be the Woodruff children who, while not poisoned, died within months of each other during one of the many yellow fever epidemics that brought tragedy to the Myrtles. A young girl, with long curly hair and wearing an ankle-length dress, has been seen floating outside the window of the game room, cupping her hands and trying to peer inside through the glass. Is she Cornelia Gale Woodruff or perhaps one of the Stirling children who did not survive until adulthood?

The grand piano on the first floor plays by itself, usually repeating the same chord over and over again. Sometimes it continues on through the night. When someone comes into the room to investigate the sound, the music stops and will only start again when they leave.

Scores of people have filed strange reports about the house. In recent times, various owners have taken advantage of the Myrtles' infamous reputation and the place is now open to guests for tours and as a haunted bed and breakfast. Rooms are rented in the house and in cottages on the grounds. The plantation has played host to a wide variety of guests, from curiosity-seekers to historians to ghost hunters. Over the years, a number of films and documentaries have also been shot on the ground and many of them have been paranormal in nature.

One film, which was decidedly not paranormal, was a television mini-series remake of *The Long Hot Summer,* starring Don Johnson, Cybill Shepherd, Ava Gardner and Jason Robards. A portion of the film was shot at the Myrtles and it was an experience that the cast and crew would not soon forget. One day, the crew moved the furniture in the game room and the dining room for filming and then left. When they returned, they reported that the furniture had all been moved back to its original position. No one was inside either room while the crew was absent. This happened several times, to the crew's dismay, although they did manage to get the shots they needed. They added that the cast was happy to move on to another set once the filming at the Myrtles was completed.

Employees at the house often get the worst of the events that happen here. They are often exposed, first-hand, to happenings that would have weaker folks running from the place in terror. And some of them do! One employee was hired to greet guests at the front gate each day. One day while he was at work, a woman in a white, old-fashioned dress walked through the gate without speaking to him. She strolled up to the house and vanished through the front door without ever opening it. The gateman quit his job and never returned to the house.

The Myrtles can be a perplexing place. History has shown that many of the stories that have been told about the place, mostly to explain the hauntings, never actually occurred. In spite of this, the house seems to be haunted anyway. The truth seems to be an elusive thing at this grand old plantation house but there seems to be no question for those who have stayed or visited here that it is a spirited place. At the Myrtles Plantation, the ghosts of the past - whoever they might be -- are never very far away from the living.

THE UNBROKEN DOOR
How an Investigation into What Really Happened at A Notorious Haunted House Revealed it to Be One of America's Greatest Hoaxes

I was barely a teenager when the sensational book by Jay Anson, *The Amityville Horror*, was released. I will never forget snatching up a copy from a local bookstore, only to read it and then re-read it again. Could such things really happen? Could ghosts destroy a family the way that evil spirits did George and Kathy Lutz? Could a ghost force someone to kill, as demonic entities caused young Ronald DeFeo to murder his entire family?

And most terrifying of all -- could the American public be so easily deceived into believing the events chronicled in the book were actually real? The answer to that question is a resounding "yes," as is proven by the fact that many people still believe in the veracity of "The Amityville Horror," one of the greatest paranormal hoaxes of all time.

But how did it all begin? How could we all be fooled so easily? And what events led up to the release of the book? To answer those inquiries, we have to go back to November 1974 and understand the true events that occurred in the house on Ocean Avenue in the placid, upscale village of Amityville on Long Island.

The horrific carnage that prefaced the story of the "Amityville Horror" began one night in November 1974. The DeFeo family, Ronald, Sr. and Louise, their two young sons, Marc and John, and two daughters, Dawn and Allison, were sleeping peacefully in their comfortable, three-story, waterfront home. The silence of the house was shattered when Ronald DeFeo, Jr., nicknamed "Butch," murdered his parents and his siblings with a high-powered rifle. One by one, he killed them as they slept, beginning a tale of terror that has endured for more than three decades.

On the surface, the DeFeos seemed to be a happy all-American family. Ronald, Sr. had been born and raised in Brooklyn and had worked hard at his father-in-law's Buick dealership until he finally became successful. In 1965, he moved his family to Long Island's Suffolk County and into the sprawling Dutch Colonial with the distinctive quarter-moon windows at 112 Ocean Avenue. It was perfect for the family, with two stories, plus an attic, and a boathouse on Amityville Creek. When the family moved there in 1965 they erected a signpost in the front yard that read "High Hopes," a physical reminder of what the house meant to them.

Beneath the illusion of success and happiness, though, Ronald was an angry man, given to bouts of rage and violence. He and Louise often fought and he was a threatening figure to his children. As the oldest child, Butch often bore the brunt of his father's high expectations and ill temper. He was an overweight, sullen boy who was often picked on in school. His father harassed him to stand up for himself -- but never at home. Ronald, Sr. had no room for backtalk or disobedience.

As Butch grew older, he grew stronger and larger and was no longer as tolerant of his father's abuse. Their shouting matches turned into physical battles and even Ronald, Sr., with his own anger issues, began to realize that his son's temper and violent behavior were not normal. He and Louise arranged for Butch to visit a psychiatrist but it did no good. The young man insisted there was nothing wrong with him and refused to work with the counselor. In the absence of any other solution, the DeFeos began simply buying Butch whatever he wanted in order to placate him. At the age of fourteen, his father gave him a $14,000 speedboat to cruise the Great South Bay, an arm of the Atlantic Ocean. Whenever Butch needed money, he only had to ask and it was handed to him.

By the time that he was seventeen, Butch had been kicked out of the parochial school that he had been attending because of drug use. His behavior had also become more erratic and his violent outbursts more psychotic. The altercations with his father grew more frequent and more dangerous. One night, when Butch was eighteen, a fight started between his mother and father. To settle the matter, Butch grabbed a 12-gauge shotgun from his room, loaded a shell into the chamber and went downstairs. Without hesitation, he pointed the gun at his father and pulled the trigger. Mysteriously, though, it did not go off. Ronald, Sr. froze in place and watched as his son lowered the gun and walked out of the room. He was completely unconcerned that he had nearly killed his father in cold blood. The fight was over but Butch's reaction was a foreshadowing of events to come.

In the weeks before the murders, the relationship between Butch and his father reached a breaking point. He was unhappy with the money that he "earned" from his father he had an easy job at the Buick dealership and a weekly allowance that he used on drugs and alcohol and so he arranged to be "robbed" one day on the way to make a business deposit at the bank.

Ronald, Sr. was at the dealership when his son returned from being "robbed at gunpoint" and exploded into a rage when he heard Butch's story, berating the staff member who had entrusted him with the money in the first place. The police were called and when they arrived, they naturally wanted to speak with Butch. Instead of devising a fictional story about the robbery, he became tense and irritable with them. He soon became outright violent when they began to suspect that he was lying. Butch began to curse at the startled officers, banging on the hood of a car in his grandfather's lot to emphasize his rage. The police backed off for the moment, but Ronald, Sr. had already come to his own conclusion about the motive for his son's behavior -- he knew that he had stolen the money.

On the Friday before the murders, Butch was asked by the police to look at some mug shots on the chance that he might be able to identify the thief who had allegedly robbed him. He initially agreed to do it but then backed out at the last minute. When his father heard this, he confronted Butch and demanded to know why he would not cooperate with the authorities. The two began shouting at each another and then Butch ran to his car and drove away. This fight had not turned into a violent one -- but violence was coming.

The night of Wednesday, November 14, was a cool one in Amityville. The streets were quiet and so was the house at 112 Ocean Avenue. Everyone had gone to sleep with the exception of Butch, who was brooding in his attic room. The more he simmered, the more determined he became to solve his problems once and for all. He took out a .35-caliber Marlin rifle from the storage space where he kept several weapons and started, silently but purposefully, downstairs, toward his parents' bedroom. He opened the door and walked in, raising the rifle to his shoulder and without hesitation, opened fire on his father's prone body. The first shot ripped into Ronald, Sr.'s back, to the left of his spine. The second shot struck him in the upper back, shattering his heart.

Louise DeFeo had now awakened but before she had time to do more than clutch the crucifix she wore on a gold chain around her neck, Butch fired at her, too. He shot her twice, shattering her rib cage and collapsing her right lung, and then left her to die in the spreading pool of blood on the bed.

Despite the crack of the rifle shots, no one else in the house stirred. Butch left his parents' room to continue the massacre, making his two young brothers, John, age nine, and Marc, twelve, his next victims. He entered the second-floor bedroom the two boys shared and fired one shot into each of them as they lay sleeping. Marc was killed instantly, while John, whose spinal cord was severed by his brother's attack, twitched for a few moments and then lay still. Again, the shots had not roused the remaining members of the family and Butch went unchallenged into his sister Allison's bedroom next door.

As Butch walked into the room, Allison, age thirteen, stirred and looked up just as he pointed the rifle at her face and pulled the trigger. His youngest sister was killed instantly. Butch then walked upstairs to the third floor and entered the attic bedroom where his eighteen-year-old sister, Dawn, a secretarial school student, slept. The shotgun blast literally blew the left side of her face off.

It was just after 3:00 a.m. In a span of less than fifteen minutes, Ronald "Butch" DeFeo, Jr., had brutally slain every member of his family in cold blood. Butch calmly showered, trimmed his beard, and dressed in his customary jeans and work boots. He then grabbed a pillowcase into which he stuffed his bloody clothing, a bloody towel, eight shell casings that had carefully collected from the rooms where his family lay dead, a rifle scabbard, a pistol holder, one full box of .35-caliber Marlin ammunition and one empty box, and headed out to his car. The rifle he tossed into the water at the foot of Ocean Avenue but fearing that the other items would float, he drove into Brooklyn and disposed of the pillowcase and its gruesome contents by tossing it into a storm drain. He then had breakfast at a luncheonette before reporting to work at his grandfather's Buick dealership.

From work, Butch called home several times and when his father failed to show up, he acted bored with nothing to do and left around noon. He called his girlfriend, Sherry Klein, and told her that he had left work early and planned to come over. On the way to Amityville, he ran into his friend, Bobby Kelske, and stopped to talk. After that, Butch went to Sherry's house and casually mentioned that he had tried to call home several times but there had been no answer. He tried again in her presence just to show her what he meant. Acting puzzled, but unworried, he and Sherry spent the afternoon shopping and then met up with

Bobby Kelske later at a local bar. He was now feigning concern about being unable to reach anyone at home and he told everyone who would listen that he planned to go there and to see what was going on. He returned a few minutes later in a state of apparent agitation. "Bob, you gotta help me," he told his Kelske, "Someone shot my mother and father!"

The two friends were joined by a small group of patrons from the bar and they all piled into Butch's car. When they arrived at the house, Kelske ran upstairs to the master bedroom and found Ronald, Sr. and Louise in the blood-soaked bed. He returned outside to find Butch apparently beside himself with grief. One of Butch's bar acquaintances, Joey Yeswit, had found the telephone in the kitchen, and called the police. Within ten minutes, Officer Kenneth Geguski was at the scene. As he arrived, he found a group of men gathered on the DeFeos' front lawn. Butch was now sobbing uncontrollably. The officer went inside and then called headquarters from the kitchen. Butch was now at the kitchen table, still crying. As he listened to Geguski's call about his murdered parents and brothers, he told the officer that he also had two sisters. Geguski put the receiver down and hurried back upstairs. By this time another village patrolman had arrived, Officer Edwin Tyndall. The two of them found Dawn and Allison. There was too much blood for them to even guess what kind of gun had killed the DeFeos.

Shortly after 7:00 p.m., the neighborhood was buzzing with word of what had transpired in the house called High Hopes. The house itself was filled with police personnel, while neighbors and curiosity-seekers gathered on the front lawn. Suffolk County detective Gaspar Randazzo was the first to question Butch, the massacre's sole survivor. Butch claimed that the family might have been killed by a notorious mafia hitman who had long had a grudge against his family. Detective Gerard Gozaloff joined in the questioning and suggested that if the murders were indeed linked to organized crime, that Butch might still be a target. Any further questioning should take place at police headquarters. It was there that they were joined by a third detective, Joseph Napolitano.

At the station, Butch gave the police his written statement. He claimed to have been home the night before, and said he stayed up until 2:00 a.m. watching a World War II thriller on television. At 4:00 a.m., he reported hearing the toilet flush in the bathroom that his brothers and youngest sister shared. Since he couldn't go back to sleep, he decided to head to work early. He described the rest of his day, leaving work early, visiting with Sherry and Bobby, drinking at the bar, and trying to reach his family by telephone.

After Butch submitted his statement, the detectives continued to question him about his family, and about his suggestion that a hitman, Louis Falini, might be the killer. Butch explained that Falini had lived with them for a period of time, and that he had helped Butch and his father carve out a hiding space in the master bedroom closet where Ronald, Sr., kept a stash of gems and cash. The argument with Falini had stemmed from an incident where Falini criticized some work Butch had done at the auto dealership. Around 3:00 a.m., the detectives had finished their questioning and Butch went to sleep on a cot in a back filing room. He gave every appearance of being a cooperative witness, and so far the detectives had no reason to hold him under suspicion of anything.

That soon began to change as investigators continued examining the evidence. Butch had been careless enough to leave a box that had contained a shotgun as well as boxes of Marlin .35-caliber ammunition in his room, which detectives learned matched the murder weapon. Subsequent questioning of Bobby Kelske led to the discovery that Butch was a gun fanatic, and that he had recently staged the robbery of the receipts from the Buick dealership.

The detectives began to seriously consider the possibility that Butch had been playing them, that he may be their suspect, and that he at least knew much more about the killings than what he had told them so far. At 8:45 a.m., Detective George Harrison shook Butch awake. When roused, he asked if the detectives had found the killer yet but Harrison had not come with news of Falini -- he was there to read Butch his rights. DeFeo protested that he had been cooperative all along and he went so far as to waive his right to counsel, seemingly to prove that he was an innocent witness with nothing to hide.

By this time, Gozaloff and Napolitano were exhausted. Two other officers, Lieutenant Robert Dunn, and Detective Dennis Rafferty took over. Rafferty re-read Butch his rights, and proceeded to question him about the prior two days. Rafferty focused on the time of the murders. Butch had written in his statement that he was up as early as 4:00 a.m., and that he heard his brother in the bathroom at that time. Rafferty continued to press Butch until he was able to pry him away from his earlier version of when the crime took place Butch claimed that it had been after he had gone to work , establishing that the crime actually took place between 2:00 and 4:00 a.m.

Butch's story began to crumble. Dunn and Rafferty hammered at the discrepancies in Butch's version of events and what the evidence led police to believe actually happened. Butch was physically linked to the scene once the time of the murders was established. At first, he tried desperately to make the best out of a deteriorating situation, trying to make the detectives believe that while he had indeed been present in the home during the murders, he had been hiding in fear of being discovered and killed. He insisted that he had only been in each bedroom after the murders had taken place. But Rafferty continued on, telling Butch about the ammunition that had been found in his room.

More desperate than ever, Butch continued to lie. He claimed that he had been awakened at 3:30 a.m. and that Louis Falini had been there with a gun pointed at his head. He had forced Butch to accompany him as he went from room to room, methodically killing each member of the DeFeo family. The police let Butch keep talking, and he eventually implicated himself as he described how he gathered and then discarded evidence from the crime scene. They kept him talking, shouting more questions at him and then finally one of them asked him if it had really happened that way Butch claimed.

"No," Butch finally confessed. "It all started so fast. Once I started, I just couldn't stop. It went so fast."

The trial of Ronald DeFeo, Jr., for the murder of his family, began on October 14, 1975, nearly a year after the murders took place. The prosecution of DeFeo was the responsibility of Gerald Sullivan, an assistant district attorney of Suffolk County. Despite DeFeo's confession, despite the fact that he had been able to lead investigators to the exact spot where he had disposed of the evidence, and despite the fact that Butch's rifle was positively identified as the murder weapon, Sullivan took no chances in his approach to prosecuting the case.

During the period of pre-trial interviews and jury selection, Sullivan had studied DeFeo and had questioned him and he knew that Butch was a pathological liar. He had retained well-known area attorney William Weber for his defense and his pattern of behavior before the murders would afford Weber the opportunity to plead innocence by reason of insanity on his client's behalf. But Sullivan knew that Butch DeFeo was not crazy, but a violent, cold-blooded killer. His opening statement said as much and asked the jury to consider all of the facts and to not provide DeFeo with an excuse for his actions.

The question of DeFeo's mental state at the time of the murders would remain the defining piece of evidence upon which his acquittal or conviction would rest. Prior to the trial, Weber had attempted to have the case dismissed, alleging that Butch had been refused access to counsel right before the police took his confession. He also claimed that the confession was obtained under duress, but neither of these claims was accepted by the judge and Weber was left to defend his client's actions on the grounds that he was legally insane at the time the murders took place.

Sullivan knew that he could not argue only that DeFeo was not insane. He needed to present a full portrait of a man who was capable of murdering six defenseless members of his own family. He called a number of witnesses, including police officers and detectives who worked the case, as well as relatives and friends of Butch. He used their testimony to get his point across but no witness was as damning as DeFeo himself.

Weber called Butch to testify and attempted to lead his client to supply responses that would enhance his claim of insanity. On the stand, DeFeo failed to identify photos of his mother and then when asked if he killed his father and other family members, he admitted that he did but said that it was in self-defense. The district attorney refused to react to this, even when some of the members of the jury gasped aloud. Weber continued on unfazed and he asked Butch why he had done such a thing.

Butch quickly replied: "As far as I'm concerned, if I didn't kill my family, they were going to kill me. And as far as I'm concerned, what I did was self-defense and there was nothing wrong with it. When I got a gun in my hand, there's no doubt in my mind who I am. I am God."

To the jury, Sullivan feared that DeFeo's testimony might seem to be that of a deranged lunatic and so he assaulted his diatribes during cross-examination. He ridiculed Butch's seeming inability to identify his mother's photograph and worked to expose the inconsistencies between his testimony and the statement he gave police on the night of the crime. His questions then began to center around the murders themselves and DeFeo's conflicting accounts of his actions. Sullivan knew that he would not get a straight accounting from Butch in regard to what had happened but he wanted to goad him into anger and perhaps into revealing the twisted sense of pleasure that he had gotten from killing his entire family.

He was able to make Butch so angry that he actually threatened the prosecutor's life. "You think I'm playing," the bearded young man shouted from the stand. "If I had any sense, which I don't, I'd come down there and kill you now."

The ability to prove or disprove DeFeo's alleged mental condition was crucial to the success of both sides and leaving nothing to chance, each retained the services of two highly reputable psychiatrists. Dr. Daniel Schwartz was retained for the defense and was experienced in the criminal field. He had interviewed a number of defendants and had testified in hundreds of cases. He would later gain widespread national notoriety as the psychiatrist who found David Berkowitz to be criminally insane in the wake of the "Son of Sam" slayings.

Sullivan knew that what he did at this point in the trial was crucial to his case. Despite the fact that he had his own expert witness, he had to rely on his skills to keep the trial on track. As he later wrote about the case: "The jurors had been learning about DeFeo and his murders for almost two months. They had listened to his lies and vituperation for days. Dr. Schwartz had only talked to him for hours. I would show that the psychiatrist didn't know the real Butch DeFeo."

As it happened, Sullivan caught a fortunate break in the form of Weber's questioning of his own witness. In a move that could clearly be interpreted as overconfidence in Schwartz's ability on the stand, Weber posed only a few preliminary questions to his witness, and then proceeded to let Schwartz deliver a lecture on psychosis, disassociation, and criminal insanity. However, Sullivan noticed a number of key points that Weber let go and did not challenge and he would soon focus on those.

Sullivan opened his line of questioning by referring to Schwartz's prior experience as an expert witness, attempting to rattle him by demonstrating the extent to which he had researched the witness. He then moved to the case at hand and began questioning Schwartz about why DeFeo would have removed evidence from the crime scene. If he were truly insane, why bother with this?

Schwartz offered several opinions but Sullivan continued to press him. Hotly, Schwartz finally retorted that DeFeo was "not hiding this crime from anybody by picking up the shell. The bodies are there. The bullets are in the people."

"Everything that he could get that would connect him with the crime, he removed from the house, didn't he?" pressed Sullivan.

"What you are talking about is trivia compared to the six bodies," Schwartz responded flatly.

His indifferent response angered the prosecutor. "Trivia that he removed the evidence out of that house that would connect him to the crime, trivia that has nothing to do with whether he thought that the crime was wrong?" thundered Sullivan.

Sullivan next took aim at Schwartz's actual diagnosis of DeFeo as a neurotic.

"So it's your testimony, as I understand it, Dr. Schwartz, that the fact that it wasn't too bright to throw everything in that sewer drain all together in one location is significant of the fact that it was neurotic that he did this?" Schwartz responded that this was the case, noting that DeFeo appeared to be acting without any clear purpose in mind, someone distracted by paranoid, neurotic delusions. This would become Schwartz's greatest mistake in his testimony.

"Did he tell you about not wanting to leave clues for the police?" asked Sullivan.

"I asked him about the casings, and he said he didn't want to leave the police any clues as to what kind of gun it had been. He was not a friend of the cops, and he didn't want to help them."

Schwartz had just contradicted himself. Sullivan knew it and it's likely that the psychiatrist knew it, as well. The district attorney almost laughed. "Okay, now you know why he removed the casings, don't you?" he asked derisively.

Dr. Harold Zolan testified for the prosecution. Sullivan devised an elaborate question-and-answer exchange with Zolan, making a deliberate effort to give the jury access to Zolan's thought process, so that they might come to understand how Zolan had reached his assessment. Unlike Schwartz, Zolan attributed DeFeo's behavior to an antisocial personality, a form of personality disorder that he distinguished from any form of mental illness. Essentially, those with such a personality disorder are fully aware of their actions, are fully able to comprehend the difference between right and wrong, but are motivated by an imperious, self-centered attitude. When finished, Sullivan was confident that between his methodical questioning and Zolan's well-thought-out responses, the jury was finally in possession of clinical evidence that Butch was guilty of murder.

On Wednesday, November 19, 1975, the judge sent the jury into deliberations. Despite Sullivan's painstaking efforts, the prosecutor knew that a guilty verdict was not a sure bet. He was rewarded for his skepticism when the jury's first vote came back 10-2, with two holdouts who were still uncertain about DeFeo's mental state at the time of the murders. After reviewing transcripts of DeFeo's testimony, however, the vote came back at a unanimous 12-0.

On Friday, November 21, 1975, Ronald DeFeo, Jr., was found guilty of six counts of second-degree murder. Two weeks later, he was sentenced to twenty-five years to life in prison on all six counts. He remains incarcerated today at Green Haven Correctional Facility in Dutchess County, New York.

The tragedy in Amityville made grim local news but few outside of New York ever heard about the house until later, when the other news starting making the papers. Those events began on December 18, 1975, when a young couple named George and Kathy Lutz bought the house on Ocean Avenue for $80,000. Just a week before Christmas, they moved into their new "dream home" with Kathy's three children from a previous marriage. They would later claim that the dream home soon became a nightmare.

Almost from the moment that they moved into the house, the Lutz family would insist they were aware of an unearthly presence in the place. They began to hear mysterious noises that they could not account for. Locked windows and doors would inexplicably open and close. George Lutz, a sturdy former Marine, claimed to be plagued by the sound of a phantom brass band that would march back and forth through the downstairs. When a Catholic priest entered the house, after agreeing to bless it, an eerie, disembodied voice allegedly told him to "get out."

The events began to intensify. The thumping and scratching sounds grew worse, a devilish creature was seen outside the windows at night, George Lutz was seemingly "possessed" by an evil spirit and green slime oozed from the walls and ceiling. The family was further terrified by ghostly apparitions of hooded figures, clouds of flies that appeared from nowhere, cold chills, personality changes, sickly odors, objects moving about on their own, the repeated disconnection of their telephone service and communication between the youngest Lutz child and a devilish pig with glowing red eyes that she called "Jodie." Kathy Lutz reported that she was often beaten and scratched by unseen hands and that one night, she was levitated up off the bed.

The family managed to hold out for twenty-eight days before they gathered up some of their possessions and fled from the house. According to their story, they left so quickly that they didn't take their furniture with them. The demonic spirits, they said, had driven them from their home!

And then, things started to get really scary...

In February 1976, not long after the Lutz family left the house, local residents were stunned to see New York Channel 5's news team doing a live news feed from the house on Ocean Avenue. The news crew filmed a séance and a dramatic "investigation" of the place conducted by Ed and Lorraine Warren, two of America's most famous "demonologists."

For those unfamiliar with the Warrens, Lorraine claims to be a clairvoyant and a trance medium who is said to have the uncanny ability to contact the spirit world. On the other hand, her late husband, Ed, claimed to be a demonologist who was an expert on hauntings. From the 1950s through the 1980s, the Warrens, who were based in Connecticut, were recognized as authorities when it came to ghosts and demons. While they were still active until the death of Ed Warren a few years ago, their methods have been repeatedly questioned in recent years - along with the authenticity of many of their cases. Regardless, in 1976, their stamp of approval on the events reported at Amityville caught the nation's attention.

The Warrens went to the house for the first time in February and while George Lutz allegedly refused to accompany them, he did loan them a key. The Warrens stated that they found old newspapers around the house and that the refrigerator was still stocked with food. It was obvious to them, they said, that the Lutz family had left in a hurry. The Warrens brought two other psychics with them to the house to conduct their séance. They later reported that they "sensed" an "unearthly presence" in the house and Ed Warren also claimed to experience heart palpitations that he blamed on the occult forces. The house was haunted, they said, by the angry spirits of Native Americans who had once inhabited the area and by "inhuman spirits." The story was that the Shinnecock Indians had used the land where the house was later built as a place where sick and insane members of the tribe were isolated until they died. They did not bury the dead there, however, because they supposedly believed the land was "infested with demons."

Not long after, George and Kathy Lutz teamed up with a writer named Jay Anson and together, they produced what would become a best-selling book called *The Amityville Horror*. The book would go on to spawn a bad movie and a number of even worse sequels and not surprisingly, the Warrens were hired by producer Dino de Laurentis and the production company to serve as consultants about the supernatural occurrences portrayed in the film. They also made the rounds of the talk show circuit, solemnly discussing the horrifying events in Amityville.

The "Amityville Horror" grew from news reports and newspaper articles to books, magazines and television reports. The story would become internationally known, until around the world, people recognized the name of Amityville. Most amazing was the fact that this terrifying story was absolutely true --- or so it read in bold print on the cover of the best-selling book. But not everyone was convinced, even in paranormal circles. In fact, a few of them smelled something bad in Amityville.

One of those was a paranormal investigator from New York named Dr. Stephen Kaplan. George Lutz had approached him on February 16, 1976 about conducting an investigation of the house on Ocean Avenue. This was shortly before Lutz turned to the Warrens instead. At that time, Kaplan was the executive director of the Parapsychology Institute of America, based on Long Island, and he was a frequent guest on the popular WBAB radio program "Spectrum with Joel Martin." He received a phone call from Lutz, who wanted the Parapsychology Institute to investigate the house for supernatural activity. Lutz asked about a fee for the group's services and Kaplan told him that they did not charge for investigations but that "if the story is a hoax...the public will know." A few days later, Lutz called and cancelled the investigation. He claimed that he and his wife did not want any publicity about the house. This may have been why the Channel 5 news story came as such a surprise to Kaplan and his colleagues a few days later.

Kaplan would later claim to have been suspicious of the call, and the Lutz's motives, from the very beginning. When he began asking questions, he asked what specifically had happened to the family in the house. Lutz said that he was unable to describe the phenomena but that there were demons in the house that he knew by name. When asked to name them, Lutz refused, claiming that they would appear if he mentioned their names aloud. Kaplan asked who told him that and Lutz said that he had read it in a book. He could not remember the title, he said, but it had been one of many about demonology, ghosts and psychic phenomena that he had read since buying the house on Ocean Avenue.

As the story of the "Amityville Horror" became an international sensation, Kaplan was at work collecting evidence and materials about the house and the claims made by the Lutz family, Jay Anson, the Warrens and the media. Although convinced of the validity of the paranormal and a believer in supernatural activity, Kaplan was not convinced of the truth behind the Amityville case. While it was possible that a haunting could have occurred at the house, especially in light of the violent events that had taken place there, there was something not quite right about the accounts of the Lutz family. After some initial investigation, Kaplan became sure that a hoax was being perpetrated on the public and such a hoax could prove to be damaging for legitimate paranormal cases in the future. With that in mind, he became determined to show that the entire story was a farce.

Little did he know that he would face an uphill battle, not only against the Warrens, but against the general public, too. By this time, the Warrens had become too firmly entrenched to back out of the case. They continued to resolutely support the Lutzes' claims of the house being haunted, or possessed, by evil forces. They began their own campaign to try and discredit Stephen Kaplan, especially after his untimely death a number of years later. To this day, in spite of confessions and in the face of overwhelming evidence to the contrary, Lorraine Warren still maintains that the house was haunted.

The general public had been so force-fed the story by the media, that Kaplan's evidence against the house being haunted seemed to fall on deaf ears. Thanks to the fact that the truth was not as glamorous or as dramatic as the original story, the new story was scarcely reported and was barely noticed at first. In fact, Kaplan's diaries of the investigations were turned into a book that did not get published for many years after the events took place. The problem remained that the public loved the story and the Dutch Colonial on Ocean Avenue became a Long Island landmark. People traveled from all over the country to drive past and gape at it. Tourists made it their first stop on Long Island and locals soon became fed up, calling the sightseers the "Amityville Horribles." The trouble with curiosity seekers and complaints from locals were so bad in the late 1970s that they drove one Amityville police chief into early retirement.

Kaplan had discovered that the "Amityville Horror" was pure invention. In 1979, attorney William Weber confessed to his part in the hoax during a paranormal radio show hosted by author Joel Martin. Weber admitted that he and George Lutz had concocted the story of the haunting over a few bottles of wine. Weber's motive was to get a new trial for DeFeo, using a "Devil made him do it" defense. According to Weber, Lutz merely wanted to get out from under a mortgage that he couldn't afford. His contracting business was in trouble and he needed a scheme to bail him out. Weber later filed a $2 million lawsuit against the Lutzes, charging them with reneging on their book deal.

Kaplan found ample proof, outside of this glaring confession, that the story was a hoax. He gained access to the house on many occasions and found that the so-called "Red Room," where the book claimed occult ceremonies took place, was nothing more than a small basement room that gave access to plumbing pipes. A girl who had been friends with Allison DeFeo later said that the DeFeo children used to store toys there. No "demonic face" had ever appeared on the bricks inside the fireplace. He also noted that the original front door of the house said to have been blown off its hinges and broken, according the book was still in place and undamaged. In fact, the extensive damage to doors and windows that was recounted in the book never happened at all. All of the old hardware -- hinges, locks and doorknobs -- was still in place and there were no disturbances to the paint or the varnish.

In addition, Kaplan found a writer for the local newspaper who had also been suspicious of the story. After some searching, the columnist discovered that the Lutzes had returned the day after "fleeing" from the house to hold a garage sale. He also charged that during their "28-day nightmare" they never once called the police for assistance, something that would have been commonly done under the circumstances. He also found that there had been no snowfall when the Lutzes claimed that they found "cloven hoof prints" in the snow.

He also learned that the role of the priest was completely exaggerated in the drama. In the book, the priest character named Father Mancuso is terrorized by a demon while trying to bless the new home. He is then stalked by the demon back to the rectory, where he is afflicted with boils, bleeding palms, a fever, and the smell of excrement. In real life, the house was blessed but the man who performed the ceremony was not a priest and he was never plagued by demonic activity after visiting the house.

More recently, author Ric Osuna has stated that George Lutz, who died of heart disease in 2006 after divorcing Kathy in the 1980s and having been criticized by his former stepsons, informed him that, "setting the record straight is not as important as making money off fictional sequels."

Kathy Lutz died in 2004 of emphysema.

The list of things that did not happen in the house went on and on and to most researchers, like Kaplan and many others, the evidence for an "Amityville Hoax" was overwhelming.

Even George Lutz backtracked years later when he described the events in the house. His new account of cold spots, odd noises, smells and a slamming door or two, were a far cry from the allegedly "true" events that had been recounted for the book. In fact, he no longer claimed to "flee" from the house but said that the family moved out because the place was so oppressive that he fell into a deep depression. A haunting? Perhaps - but it wasn't even close to the hoax that had been perpetrated on the public.

Jim and Barbara Cromarty, who later moved into the house, also maintained that it was not haunted. Because of the problems they had experienced with the curiosity-seekers, they sued the hardcover and paperback publishers of *The Amityville Horror*, as well as Jay Anson and George and Kathy Lutz. They stated that the entire case had been a put-on from the beginning and it had "blighted their lives." The suit was later settled for an undisclosed amount.

This, along with the publication of *The Amityville Horror Conspiracy* by Stephen Kaplan, should have put an end to the case, but it did not. In fact, decades later, people still often question the facts behind the case and the real events that may, or may not, have occurred in Amityville. Today, most researchers concede that the story was mostly, if not entirely, fabricated. To the general public, though, the truth remains much more uncertain and some theorists believe that there are still things about the story that do not add up.

All of the weak utterances of "truth" in this story continue to be arranged to look like something they are not. To this author, they are a perfect example of this entire case as a whole --- a blending of fact with fiction in an attempt to titillate and terrify the American public.

A LEATHER BALL
Despite Questionable History and Exaggerated Claims, Spirits Stalk the Halls of America's Most Infamous Former Hospital

One of the first questions that people ask when they learn that I write about the supernatural for a living is whether or not I have ever seen a ghost. Since I confess to being as psychic as a fence post, I don't go around seeing dead people. I have had some pretty strange experiences, but there have only been a handful of occasions when I actually believe saw ghosts. Could they have been tricks of the light or the products of an overactive imagination? It's possible, at least in a couple of instances, but there is no question about what I saw at the Waverly Hills Sanatorium in 2002. I saw a ghost.

And that should come as no surprise, since Waverly Hills is one of the most haunted places that I have ever visited.

During the 1800s and early 1900s, America was ravaged by a deadly disease known to many as the "white death": tuberculosis. This terrifying and very contagious plague, for which no cure existed before antibiotics were discovered, claimed entire families and occasionally, entire towns. In 1900, Louisville, Kentucky, had the highest tuberculosis death rate in America. Built on low swampland, Louisville was the perfect breeding ground for disease. In 1910, construction was started on a two-story frame hospital on a windswept hill in southern Jefferson County. The building was designed to accommodate forty or fifty patients, and as the number of patients increased, it became clear that a new hospital was needed.

The new structure, known as Waverly Hills, opened in 1926. Built in the collegiate gothic style, it was considered the most advanced tuberculosis sanatorium in the country. Even so, most of the patients succumbed to the disease. There was no medicine available at that time to treat tuberculosis and so patients were offered rest, fresh air and lots of nutritious food. Sadly, the main use for the hospital was to isolate those who had come down with the disease to keep them away from those who were still healthy. Families were tragically divided with parents, and even children, forced into the sanatorium with little contact with their loved ones.

Treatments for tuberculosis were sometimes as bad as the disease itself. Some of the experiments that were conducted in search of a cure seem barbaric by today's standards but others are now common practice. Patient's lungs were exposed to ultraviolet light to try and stop the spread of bacteria. This was done in "sun rooms," using artificial light in place of sunlight, or on the roof or in the hospital's open porches. Since fresh air was thought to be a possible cure, patients were often placed in front of huge windows or on the open porches, no matter what the season. Old photographs show patients lounging in chairs, taking in the fresh air, while literally covered with snow.

Other treatments were less pleasant --- and much bloodier. Balloons would be surgically implanted in the lungs and then filled with air to expand them. Needless to say, this often had disastrous results, as did an operation where muscles and ribs were removed from a patient's chest to allow the lungs to expand further and let in more oxygen. This blood-soaked procedure was seen as a "last resort" and many patients did not survive it.

While the patients who survived both the disease and the treatments left Waverly Hills through the front door, many others left through what came to be known as the "body chute." This enclosed tunnel for the dead led from the hospital to the railroad tracks at the bottom of the hill. Using a motorized rail and cable system, bodies were lowered in secret to the waiting trains. This was done so that patients would not see how many were leaving the hospital as corpses.

There are many inaccurate reports as to how many people died during Waverly Hills' decades of operation. Some claim that tens of thousands died within the walls of the hospital but this number is greatly exaggerated. According to Dr. J. Frank Stewart, a former assistant medical director at the hospital, the highest number of deaths to occur at Waverly Hills in a single year was one hundred and fifty-two. By 1955, those numbers had dropped to as low as forty-two deaths and it's been estimated based on death certificates that were filed that approximately six thousand people died there, dating all of the way back to the original hospital records from 1911. While far short of the numbers being tossed about in the legends, it's still a tremendous number of deaths to have occurred in a single structure.

By the late 1930s, tuberculosis had begun to decline worldwide and by 1943, new medicines had largely eradicated the disease in the United States. A small jump in new cases did occur after World War II and many soldiers returning from the war were housed at Waverly Hills. Dr. Stewart noted in his autobiography that many of the soldiers had cases that were so advanced that they did not live for more than a week after arriving at the hospital.

In 1961, Waverly Hills was closed only to re-open a year later as Woodhaven Geriatrics Sanitarium. There have been many stories told about patient mistreatment and unusual experiments during the years that the building was used an old age home. Some of them have been proven to be false but others have unfortunately turned out to be true. Electroshock therapy, which was considered to be highly effective in those days, was widely used for a variety of ailments. Budget cuts in the 1960s and 1970s led to both horrible conditions and patient mistreatment and in 1982 the state closed the facility for good.

Is any wonder, after all of the death, pain and agony within these walls, that Waverly Hills is considered to be one of the most haunted places in America?

The buildings and land were auctioned off and changed hands many times over the course of the next two decades. In 1983, a developer purchased the property with plans to turn it into a minimum-security prison for the state of Kentucky. Plans were dropped after neighbors protested and a new idea to turn the former hospital into apartments was devised. A lack of financing caused this plan to be abandoned.

In March 1996, Waverly Hills and the surrounding land was bought by Robert Alberhasky, who ran Christ the Redeemer Foundation, Inc. He had plans to construct the world's tallest statue of Jesus on the Waverly site, along with an art and worship center. The statue, which was inspired by the famed Christ the Redeemer statue in Rio de Janeiro, was to be situated on the roof of the hospital at a cost of about $4 million. The next phase of his plan was to convert the sanatorium into a chapel, theater and gift shop for another $8 million. Not surprisingly, donations to the project fell far short of what was expected. During the first year, only $3,000 was raised towards the effort and the project was scrapped in December 1997.

Alberhasky abandoned the Waverly Hills property and then, in order to recoup some of his costs, tried to have the property condemned so that the buildings could be torn down and the land redeveloped. This plan was blocked by the county and according to rumor, demolition work was then done around the southern edge of the building in order to undermine the structural foundations and collect insurance money. This scheme also failed and in 2001, Waverly Hills was sold to Charlie and Tina Mattingly, the current owners of the property.

By 2001, the once-stately building had been nearly destroyed by time, the elements and vandals who came looking for a thrill. Waverly Hills had become the local "haunted house" and it became a magnet for the homeless looking for shelter, and teenagers, who broke in looking for ghosts. The hospital soon gained a reputation for being haunted and stories began to circulate of resident ghosts like the little girl who was seen running up and down the third floor solarium, the little boy who was spotted playing with a leather ball in the corridors, the hearse that appeared in the back of the building dropping off coffins, the woman with the bleeding wrists who cried for help and others. Visitors told of slamming doors, lights in the windows when no power was running through the building, strange sounds and eerie footsteps in empty rooms.

Other legends told of a man in a white coat who was seen walking in the kitchen and the smell of cooking food that sometimes wafted through the room. The kitchen was a disaster, a ruin of broken windows, fallen plaster, broken tables and chairs and puddles of water and debris that resulted from a leaking roof. The cafeteria had not fared much better. Even so, a number of people reported hearing footsteps in the room, seeing a door swinging shut under its own power and the smell of fresh baked bread.

Perhaps the greatest - and most controversial - legend of Waverly Hills was connected to the fifth floor of the building. This area of the old hospital consisted of two nurses' stations, a pantry, a linen room, a medicine room and two medium-sized rooms on both sides of the two nurses' stations. One of these, Room 502, is the subject of many rumors and legends and just about every curiosity-seeker that had broken into Waverly Hills over the years wanted to see it. This is where, according to the stories, people have seen shapes moving in the windows, have heard disembodied voices and, if the legends are to be believed, some have even jumped to their deaths.

There are a lot of legends about what went on in this part of the hospital but perhaps the biggest misconception was that this was a floor used to house mentally ill tuberculosis patients. This was not the case. The patients here were not insane, nor were they confined to their rooms. They were free to move about, just like patients on all of the other floors of the hospital. This floor, thanks to its design, allowed patients to still benefit from the fresh air and sunshine that was believed to cure tuberculosis, or at least extend the lives of those with the disease. It was centered in the middle of the hospital and the two wards, extending out from the nurses' station, were glassed in on all sides and opened out onto a patio-type roof.

According to the stories, a nurse was found dead in Room 502 in 1928. She had committed suicide by hanging herself from the light fixture. She was said to have been twenty-nine years old at the time of her death, unmarried and pregnant. According to the legend, her body hung there for hours before she was discovered. No records exist that prove this story, but it's still widely told. And this would not be the only tragedy said to be connected to Room 502.

In 1932, stories say, another nurse who worked in the same room jumped from the roof patio and plunged to her death. No one seems to know why she would have done this but many have speculated that she may have been pushed over the edge. Again, there are no records to confirm this but the rumors continue to persist.

Those are the stories anyway. As with so many legends, no records exist to say that any of these things actually happened. There are also conflicting accounts as to how the pregnant nurse managed to hang herself. Some say that she did it from the light fixture, others from a pipe over the door and some say from the rafters. There are no rafters, the pipe over the door was part of a sprinkler system installed in 1972 and the light fixture is suspended from a decorative chain that would not hold the weight of a person. There is no actual documentation of either death, although some claim the stories were verified by a former staff member named John Thornberry, who died in 2006. According to his obituary, Thornberry was born in 1922, which would have made him six and ten years old at the time of the alleged deaths in Room 502. This makes his "verification" more than a little problematic.

So, what happened in Room 502 that could cause so many people to claim paranormal experiences there? Is it overactive imaginations, or is it something real? It's hard to say, but it seems likely that something occurred in that room to cause the legend to take root in the first place. What that might have been, no one knows. The story of Room 502 may have been loosely based on some forgotten facts but the truth remains buried under speculation and rumor.

In spite of this, strange things continued to be reported. Over the course of the next year, volunteers working toward the restoration of the building experienced ghostly sounds, heard slamming doors, saw lights appear in the building when there should have been none, had objects thrown at them, were struck by unseen hands, saw apparitions in doorways and corridors and more. But none of the stories that I had been told could have prepared me for my first visit to Waverly Hills.

The first time that I visited the hospital was in September 2002. I was in town for a convention and a friend of mine, who had been working with the owners at Waverly Hills, offered to take me to see the place that I had been hearing so much about. At that point, the old hospital had been opened for tours but had not reached the level of "infamy" that it has today. There were yet to be any television shows, books or websites dedicated to it.

It was literally a dark and stormy night when we arrived at the hospital and it had been raining all day. I was looking forward to seeing the place, no matter what the weather, and not because I was convinced that I would meet one of the former patients face to face - I simply wanted to experience the place for myself. By this time, I had traveled all over the country and had been to hundreds of places that were alleged to be haunted. I had felt just this same way before exploring all of them, so Waverly Hills was no different. To me, it was just an old, spooky building with a fascinating history. The fact that it was alleged to be haunted simply added to the experience. I had long since abandoned the idea of expecting too much.

After meeting with the owners, we went inside and started our exploration of the building. It was almost silent. All I could hear was the sound of our own footsteps, our hushed voices and the drip of rain as it slipped through the cracks in the roof and splashed down onto the floor. I was given the full guided tour and saw various rooms: the treatment areas, the kitchen, the morgue and on and on. We climbed the stairs to the top floor and I saw the legendary Room 502, as well as the lights of Louisville as they reflected off the low and ominous-looking clouds that had gathered above the city.

The only floor that we skipped over was the fourth. My friend explained that this was the only floor in the building to which the entrance was kept locked and he had saved it for last. When we finally arrived on the fourth floor, I got the distinct feeling that something strange was in the air. I make absolutely no claims of any psychic ability whatsoever but there was just something about this floor of the hospital that felt different than any of the others. What had been nothing more than an old, broken-down building suddenly seemed different. I can't really put into words what felt so strange about it but there almost seemed to be a tangible "presence" that I had not encountered anywhere else in the place. And right away, eerie things started to happen.

We had entered the floor in what I believe was the center of the building. Behind us was a wing that I was told was not safe to enter. Sections of the floor had collapsed and this area was off-limits to tours and visitors. The strange thing about it was that both of us clearly heard the sounds of doors slamming from this part of the building. I can assure you that it was not the wind. The wind was not strong enough that night to have moved those heavy doors and it clearly sounded as though someone was closing them very hard. When I questioned my friend about who else could be up there with us, he said we were the only ones because the floors were unsafe in that section. I investigated on my own and determined that he was correct; there was no one walking around on that part of the fourth floor.

I switched off my flashlight and we walked down the corridor using only the dim, ambient light from outside. The hallway runs through the center of the building and on either side are former patient rooms. Beyond the rooms is the porch area that opens to the outside. It was there where the patients were placed to take in the fresh air. There was never any glass in the huge outer windows, which has left the interior of the floor open to the elements. On this night, the windows also illuminated the corridor, thanks to the low-hanging clouds that glowed with the lights of Louisville. We walked down through the dark and murky corridor and I began to see shadows that flickered back and forth. I was sure that this was trick of the eye, likely caused by the lights or the wind moving something outside. But it was where the corridor angled to the right that I got a look at something that was definitely not a trick of the eye!

In order for the reader to understand what I saw, I have to explain that the hallway ahead of us continued straight for a short distance and then turned sharply to the right. In the early 1900s, most institutions of this type were designed in this manner. It was what was dubbed the "bat-wing" design, which meant that there was a main center in each building and then the wings extended right and left, then angled again so that they ran slightly backward like a bird, or bat, wings. Directly at the angle ahead of us was a doorway that led into a treatment room. I only noticed the doorway in the darkness because the dim light from the windows beyond it had caused it to glow slightly. This made it impossible to miss since it was straight ahead of us.

We took a few more steps and then, without warning, the clear and distinct silhouette of a man crossed the lighted doorway, passed into the hall and then vanished into a room on the other side of the corridor. I got a distinct look at the figure and I know that it was a man and that he was wearing something long and white that could have been a doctor's coat. The sighting only lasted a few seconds but I knew what I had seen.

And for some reason, it shocked and startled me so badly that I let out a yell and grabbed hold of my friend's jacket. I am not sure why it affected me in that way; perhaps it was the setting, the figure's sudden appearance, my own anxiety --- or likely all of these things. Regardless, after my yell, I demanded that my friend turn on a light and help me examine the room that the man had vanished into. After my initial fright, I became convinced that someone else was on the floor with us. My friend assured me we were the only ones there but he did help me search for the intruder - in an empty room with only one way in or out. There was no one there. Whoever that figure had been he had utterly and completely vanished.

I doubt that I was the first person to see this mysterious apparition on the fourth floor and it's unlikely that I will be the last. However, this sighting convinced me that Waverly Hills is haunted. Usually, for me to declare a place to be haunted, I must have my own unexplainable experience that goes beyond a mere "bump in the night" or spooky photograph. In this case, I had actually seen a ghost and at the time, I could count my personal ghost sightings on two fingers.

Waverly Hills is haunted and for me, seeing was believing.

HANDPRINTS IN A METAL GATE
How a So-Called "Vanishing Hitchhiker" Left Real Physical Evidence of Her Presence Behind

For many who know me, my endless fascination with the famous Chicago ghost known as "Resurrection Mary" is often a source of amusement. I include her in as many lectures that I give as I can and even wrote an entire book about her and the hauntings along Archer Avenue, that spellbinding highway on which she can always often be found.

But what created my obsession with this elusive spirit? Believe it or not, I can trace it back to a cereal box -- a box of Honeycombs cereal that my mother purchased one Halloween season in the late 1970s. That October, the cereal maker decided to manufacture boxes with three different 45-rpm records pressed into the cardboard. Each of the records had a different story on it and once you finished eating all of the cereal, you could cut it out of the box and play it on your record player. I don't remember what one of the stories "The Miser's Gold" was about, but I do remember that one of them was a dramatized version of "The Legend of Sleepy Hollow" and the other was "The Vanishing Hitchhiker."

I remember sitting transfixed in front of the record player in our basement, listening to the scratchy sounds of the story on the record. The quality was not great what do you want from a record that used be part of a cereal box? but I can remember my hair standing on end when the narrator went out to the cemetery the next morning and found….. Well, I won't ruin the story for you, but let me just say that this record probably had a greater impact on me than years of wandering around so-called haunted houses and sitting for hours in dark graveyards at night. It would still be a few more years before my life's occupation would be discovered after reading a copy of Richard Winer's book *Haunted Houses* which, by the way, contained a very short piece about my beloved Mary , but I never forgot about vanishing hitchhikers.

Once I began making my living writing about ghosts and creating tours of haunted locations, it was not long before Resurrection Mary became a favorite subject of mine. She found her way into many of my books and into many of the lectures that I gave at libraries, for private functions and conferences. And these were not just lectures about or even taking place in Illinois and Chicago. I talked about her all over the country.

Something that I discovered during my lectures and travels though, was that many people would tell me: "Oh, I've heard that one already." They would then tell me that they had their own vanishing hitchhiker stories about beautiful young girls who hitched a ride along a deserted highway and then mysteriously vanished from the automobile that picked them up. Each tale was similar, but not quite the same, as the story of Mary. I would listen with interest to the tales but then would explain that Resurrection Mary is not just "a vanishing hitchhiker story," hers is "*the* vanishing hitchhiker story." She is the phantom who has inspired countless other legends and boasts one of the rare stories that did not take place on some forgotten highway somewhere, at some distant time, vanishing from the company of some nameless driver who was "a friend of a friend of mine's cousin." The story of Resurrection Mary occurs with real dates, real people, along a real highway, and is one of the only ghosts in my experience who has left physical evidence of her presence behind.

The story of Resurrection Mary is not some piece of "urban folklore." To the people who have encountered her, she is very real. She is not as elusive as she once seemed either - I know her identity, although it's much more complicated than we ever would have dreamed.

The legend of "Resurrection Mary" was born on August 10, 1976.

Around 10:30 p.m., a driver was passing by the front gates of Resurrection Cemetery in Justice, Illinois. As he traveled along Archer Avenue, he happened to glance over and see a girl standing on the other side of the gates. He said that when he saw her, she was wearing a light-colored dress and was grasping the iron bars of the gate. The driver was considerate enough to stop down the street at the Justice police station and alert them to the fact that someone had been accidentally locked in the cemetery at closing time. A patrolman named Pat Homa responded to the call but when he arrived at the cemetery gates, he couldn't find anyone there. He called out with his loudspeaker and looked for her with his spotlight, but there was no one to be seen. He finally got out of his patrol car and walked up to the gates for one last look. As far as he could tell, the cemetery was dark and deserted and there was no sign of any girl.

But his inspection of the gates, where the girl had been seen standing, did reveal something unusual. What he saw there chilled him to the bone. He found that two of the bronze bars in the gate had been blackened, burned and --- well, pulverized. It looked as though someone had taken two of the green-colored bars in his or her hands and had somehow squashed and twisted them. Within the marks was what looked to be skin texture and handprints that had been seared into the metal with incredible heat. The temperature, which must have been intense, blackened and burned the bars at just about the spot where a small woman's hands would have been.

The police officer didn't keep the story to himself. In fact, the story of the handprints made the newspapers and curiosity-seekers came from all over the area to see them. In an effort to discourage the crowds, cemetery officials attempted to remove the marks with a blowtorch, making them look even worse. Finally, they cut the bars out of the gate and installed a wire fence until the two bars could be straightened or replaced.

And while the furor over the mysterious handprints eventually died down, the cemetery always emphatically denied the supernatural version of what had happened to the bars. In fact, in 1992, they offered an alternate explanation. Officials claimed that a truck backed into the gates while doing sewer work at the cemetery and that grounds workers tried to fix the bars by heating them with a blowtorch and bending them. The imprint in the metal, they said, was from a workman trying to push them together again. While this explanation was quite convenient, it did not explain why the marks of small fingers were clearly visible in the metal or why the bronze never reverted back to its green, oxidized state.

As mentioned, the bars were removed to discourage onlookers but taking them out actually had the opposite effect. Soon, people began asking what the cemetery had to hide. The events allegedly embarrassed local officials, so they demanded that the bars be put back into place. Once they were returned to the gate, they were straightened and left alone so that the blackened area would oxidize to match the other bars. Unfortunately, though, the scorched areas continued to defy nature and the twisted spots where the handprints had been impressed remained obvious until the late 1990s, when the bars were finally removed permanently. At great expense, Resurrection Cemetery replaced the entire front gates and the notorious bars vanished for good.

But by then, it was too late - a legend was on its way to being born.

The incident in 1976 may not have been the first encounter with what the newspapers would soon call "Resurrection Mary," but it would become the first widely reported one. Soon after, the number of "Mary sightings" began to increase. People from many different walks of life, from cab drivers to clergy claimed they picked her up and gave her rides. They encountered her in local nightspots and saw her vanish from the passenger seats of their automobiles.

Around this time, Mary was said to have shown up at least twice at a nightclub called Harlow's, which was located at 8058 South Cicero Avenue, almost directly east of Resurrection Cemetery. Bob Main was the night manager at Harlow's at the time and he is perhaps the only person to ever encounter Resurrection Mary on two different occasions. He saw her on a Friday night that spring and then saw her again about two weeks later on a Saturday.

He described her: "She was about 24 to 30 years-old, five foot eight or nine, slender with yellow-blond hair to the shoulders that she wore in these big spooly curls coming down from a high forehead. She was really pale, like she powdered her face and her body. She had on this old dress that was yellowed, like a wedding dress left in the sun. She sat right next to the dance floor and she wouldn't talk to anyone. She danced all by herself, this pirouette-type dance. People were saying, "who is this bizarre chick?"

When Main and some of the other staff members tried to talk to the young woman to make sure that she was okay, the woman only shook her head. Main said she "seemed to look right through you."

Bob had no idea who the woman might have been, and while he doesn't dismiss the idea that it could have been some sort of prank, or just a person who was mentally disturbed, he did add something rather disconcerting to the story: "The strangest thing was, even though we carded everyone who came in there - --- I worked the door and there were waitresses and bartenders and people there --- nobody, either night, ever saw her come in and never saw her leave."

He added that he never would have assumed the woman was "Resurrection Mary" until he read a newspaper article about her a few years later. After that, it was the only explanation that really made sense.

Other types of accounts began to surface around this same time and now, Mary was being reported running out into the middle of Archer Avenue and being struck by passing cars. These reports, although unknown to most of those who submitted them, hearkened back to the middle 1930s - a fact that would later become apparent.

In these new accounts, though, drivers began to report a young woman with brown hair, wearing a light-colored dress, who ran out in the front of their automobiles. Sometimes, the girl would vanish just before colliding with the car and at other times, they would feel the impact and see her crumple and fall to the road as if seriously injured. When the motorist stopped and went to help the girl, she would either disappear before their eyes or no sign of her body would be found.

On August 12, 1976, Cook County Sheriff's officers investigated an emergency call about an apparent hit and run victim near the intersection of 76th Street and Roberts Road. The officers found a young female motorist in tears at the scene and they asked her about the body that she had allegedly discovered by the side of the road. She pointed to a wet grassy area and the policemen could plainly see a depression in the grass that matched the shape of a human body. The girl said that just as the police car approached the scene, the body on the side of the road vanished.

In May 1978, a young couple was driving north on Archer Avenue when a girl suddenly darted into the road in front of their car. The driver swerved to avoid her but knew when he hit the brakes that it was too late. As they braced for impact, the car passed right through the girl. She then turned and ran into Resurrection Cemetery, melting right past the bars in the gate. Another man was on his way to work in the early morning hours and spotted the body of a young girl lying directly in front of the cemetery gates. He stopped his truck and got out, quickly discovering that the woman was apparently badly injured, but still alive. He jumped into his truck and sped to the nearby police station, where he summoned an ambulance and then hurried back to the cemetery. When he got there, he found that the woman was gone. However, the outline of a body was still visible on the dew-covered pavement.

In October 1979, two women were driving past Resurrection Cemetery when a girl in a light-colored dress ran out in front of their car. The driver slammed on the brakes, sure that she was going to hit the woman, but there was no impact. Neither of the women could explain where the apparition had disappeared to.

They had seen the young girl clearly and described her as having brown, curly hair.

Just a few minutes after midnight, in the early morning hours of Friday, January 12, 1979, a taxicab driver had an unsettling experience with "Resurrection Mary." It would be this encounter that would finally reveal the mystery of Mary to the world.

It was a cold winter's night and at the time the driver picked up his unusual passenger, a major blizzard was just hours away from hitting Chicago's southwest side. As he traveled along Archer Avenue, rain and sleet pelted the windshield. The driver reached over to crank the heater up one more notch. He thought, *It's the kind of night that makes your bones ache.*

He was returning to the city after dropping off a fare in Palos Hills. His route took him past the Old Willow Shopping Center, located at the intersection of Archer Avenue and Willow Springs Road. As he passed the collection of stores at the shopping center, a pale figure, blurry through the wet and icy glass of the window, appeared along the road. The driver craned his neck and saw a woman standing there. He later recalled: "She was a looker. A blond. I didn't have any ideas or like that. She was young enough to be my daughter."

The young woman was strangely dressed for such a cold and wet night. She was wearing only a thin white cocktail dress. She never stuck out her thumb or gestured for the cab to stop. She just stood there, looking at the cab, but the driver pulled over and stopped anyway. The girl stumbled as she walked toward him and he rolled down the window to speak to her. She was beautiful, the driver saw, despite her disheveled appearance. Her blond hair was damp from the weather and plastered to her forehead.

He invited her into the cab and she opened the rear passenger door and slid into the seat. The cabbie looked over at her and asked her what was wrong. Had she had car trouble or something? The girl didn't answer, so he asked her where she wanted to go and offered her a free ride. It was the least that he could do in that weather, he told her.

The girl simply replied that he should keep driving north on Archer Avenue, so the cabbie put the car into gear and pulled back onto the road. He noticed that the young woman was shivering so he turned up the heater again. He commented on the weather, making conversation, but she didn't answer him at first. She stared at out the window in such a vacant way that he wondered if she might be drunk. Finally, she answered him, although her voice wavered and she sounded almost fearful. The driver was unsure if her whispered words were directed to him or if she was speaking to herself. She murmured: "The snow came early this year." After that, she was silent again.

The cabbie agreed with her and attempted to make some more small talk but he soon realized the lovely young girl was not interested in conversation. He said: "Her mind was a million miles away."

Finally, the girl spoke, but when she did, she shouted at him. She ordered him to pull over to the side of the road. She needed to get out. The startled driver jerked the steering wheel to the right and stopped in an open area in front of two large, metal gates. He looked across the road, searching for a house or a business where his strange passenger might need to go. He knew there was nothing on the right. She couldn't get out there; it was a cemetery.

He looked back at the girl to tell her that she shouldn't get out and he realized that she was gone. The backseat of the car was empty. "Vanished!" he later said. "And that car door never opened. May the good Lord strike me dead, it never opened."

The beautiful young girl had simply disappeared.

At the time of this encounter, the driver an ordinary 52-year-old working guy who was a father, a veteran, a church-goer and a Little League coach had no idea that he had just had a brush with the region's most enigmatic ghost. He wouldn't find out until a friend put him in touch with a newspaper columnist, who began looking into the story for himself. And with the publication of the story, all of Chicago and beyond was introduced to "Resurrection Mary."

The newspaper reporter began delving into the story and found that, despite the spate of recent sightings, the story of Mary was nothing new. In fact, people all over the southwest suburbs of Chicago were very familiar with it; it was a story that had been told since the 1930s.

According to the legend, Mary's story began at the Oh Henry Ballroom, a rambling, Tudor-style building at 8900 Archer Avenue that was a popular place for swing and big-band dancing during the middle 1930s. In those days, the ballroom was located on a secluded stretch of Archer Avenue in unincorporated Willow Springs, a town with a "wide open" reputation for booze, gambling and prostitution. Young people from all over Chicago's southwest side came to the Oh Henry Ballroom for music and dancing and owner John Verderbar was known for booking the hottest bands in the area and the biggest acts that traveled around the country.

The story goes that Mary came to the Oh Henry one night with a boyfriend and they spent the evening dancing and drinking. At some point, they got into an argument and Mary stormed out of the place. Even though it was a cold winter's night, she decided that she would rather face a cold walk home than spend another minute with her obnoxious boyfriend. She left the ballroom and started walking up Archer Avenue. She had not gotten very far when she was struck and killed by a passing automobile. The driver fled the scene and Mary was left there to die.

Her grieving parents buried her in Resurrection Cemetery, wearing her favorite party dress and her dancing shoes. Since that time, her spirit has been seen along Archer Avenue, perhaps trying to return to her grave after one last night among the living. Motorists started picking up a young woman on Archer Avenue, who offered them vague directions to take her home, who would then vanish from the automobile at the gates to Resurrection Cemetery.

Or so the story went.

Needless to say, the rumors led the reporter to the Oh Henry Ballroom, which had since been renamed the Willowbrook. He discovered that the cab driver had picked up the young girl just a few blocks from the Willowbrook on Archer Avenue. Was this merely a coincidence? The reporter didn't think so, especially based on the strange occurrences connected to Mary that had taken place at the Willowbrook Ballroom over the years.

The site of the ballroom in Willow Springs, right on Archer Avenue, started as a beer hall that was operated by the Verderbar family in 1920. In 1929, the original structure burned down and was replaced by an elaborate ballroom. They called it the Oh Henry but the name was later changed to the Willowbrook. Starting in the 1930s, the ballroom gained a reputation as one of the best dance clubs in Illinois and attracted customers from all over the area. The Oh Henry, and later, the Willowbrook, developed a strong following and today, it is one of the last of the old-time ballrooms in Chicago. Times and musical tastes may have changed, but a visit to the Willowbrook is like taking a trip back in time. The old dance floor, the tables, the cocktail bar and even the restrooms are just as they were back in the days when Mary danced here. It's a place where the big band sound can still be heard and is a time capsule of another era. I always like to say that it's impossible to truly comprehend the legend of Resurrection Mary without at least one visit to the Willowbrook Ballroom. I have walked on this dance floor when the ballroom was empty and when it was filled with party-goers, dancing to the sounds of a swing band. At moments like those, it's not hard to imagine how customers and staff members have encountered Mary here over the years.

Since the 1930s, Mary has been encountered numerous times on the dance floor by customers and employees alike. Commonly, reports tell of an attractive young woman in a white party dress who is seen from the opposite side of the ballroom. Occasionally, she is dancing and at other times, she is just standing at the edge of the floor, watching people with a slight smile on her face. At times, she vanishes without warning and on other occasions, she disappears whenever someone tries to approach her.

But in the early 1980s, few were going to the Willowbrook Ballroom to seek out Mary - that was still to come. There were still a flurry of sightings that had yet to occur. This time period proved to be one of the last truly prolific periods for Mary encounters.

On August 14, 1980, a Brookfield man named Nick Muros was driving north on Archer Avenue from the Holy Cross Hellenic Church, where he had been working until after midnight, cleaning up from the church's annual picnic. Although tired, Muros maintained that he was completely alert as he drove along the dark stretch of Archer Avenue, adjacent to Resurrection Cemetery. He said that when he reached the main gates, he noticed an object in the road, just out of the view of his headlights. As he got closer, somewhere about halfway between the gates and the large mausoleum that sits alongside the road, his lights illuminated the object and he realized that it was a girl in a white dress.

Muros recalled after the encounter: "She walked right up to the end of the road. Then she just walked right into the middle of my lane. I could see her clearly, she was walking very slowly and I took my foot off the pedal and the car began to slow."

Nick guessed that he was driving at about thirty-five miles per hour when he saw the figure and estimated that she was probably in his line of sight for about ten seconds, possibly more. She moved across in front of his car and then stopped in the median of the road. She made an odd sight as she stood there. Nick said: "She had her palms kind of turned up and I don't think she was wearing any shoes. At first I thought it was a kid, pulling a prank. But it was so dark and so desolate with nobody else on the road. She just walked right out there in the middle, a short-haired blond girl, with this flowing white dress, her hands outstretched like that. It was creepy."

Muros said that he knew nothing about the story of Resurrection Mary until he started talking to people after his unnerving encounter. At that time, she was still not widely known. He didn't know the particulars of her story but he became convinced that he had encountered a ghost.

As he passed by her, she turned away and simply disappeared. She walked right out of sight. He later said in an interview: "I've never been one to say I saw a ghost, but it was a warm night, a full moon. I had my windows down and I could see her profile, and it was a young, blond-haired girl."

During the last weekend of August 1980, Mary was seen by dozens of people, including the Deacon of the Greek Orthodox Church on Archer Avenue. Many of the witnesses contacted the Justice Police Department about their sightings. Squad cars were dispatched and although the police could not explain the mass sightings of a young woman who was not present when they arrived, they did find the witnesses themselves. Many of them flagged down the officers to tell them what they had just seen.

On September 5, a young man was driving on Archer Avenue after leaving a softball game. As he passed the Red Barrel Restaurant, he spotted a young woman in a white dress standing on the side of the road. He stopped the car and asked if she needed a ride. She accepted, and then asked him to take her down Archer. He tried to draw her into conversation, even joking that she looked like "Resurrection Mary," but she was not interested in talking. He tried several times to get her to stop for a drink, but she never replied. He was driving past the cemetery, never having stopped or even slowed down, when he looked over and saw that the girl was gone. She had simply vanished.

On September 7, Claire Lopez Rudnicki was traveling with her boyfriend, Mark, and another couple along Archer Avenue when they saw a girl walking along the side of the road outside of Resurrection Cemetery. According to the four witnesses, the girl was wearing a white dress but there was something very peculiar about her. She seemed to give off a sort of glow, as if a fluorescent light was shining from under her dress - or from her skin. The young woman walked along very slowly and Claire later recalled that she was terrified when she saw her. As they passed by on the roadway, she could feel her stomach clench with fear. Her boyfriend, however, wanted to turn around and drive past the woman again.

As they drove slowly alongside where the girl was walking, Mark leaned over and tried to get a close look at her. He really wanted to see her face so he could tell others what she looked like. He was stunned when he saw that the girl had no face. There was just emptiness, a black void, where her face should have been. The group quickly turned the car around and went back to take another look at her but the young woman was gone. She had simply vanished, even though there was no place that she could have gone.

On October 23, two couples who were driving on Archer Avenue spotted what appeared to be a woman in a light-colored dress just outside of the gates of Resurrection Cemetery. According to their account, she was walking quickly from the edge of the road, directly toward the gates. It was late at night, just a little before midnight, and the cemetery was definitely not open. One of the women in the car later stated that the girl just seemed to sort of appear in the middle of the roadway and then walk briskly toward the gates. She could not be sure that the woman had not come from the other side of the street, but she didn't think that she had. When the car reached the entryway in front of the gates, there was no one there. The mysterious young woman had vanished.

On November 6, two young men were driving south on Archer Avenue toward Willow Springs to visit some friends. It was early in the evening, around

7:30 p.m., and they had both recently gotten off work. As they passed Roberts Road, just north of Resurrection Cemetery, they saw a girl in a white dress appear from the edge of the road. There were a number of trees and bushes on the side of the cemetery, but they didn't think that she had come out of the woods. If she had, she would have needed to scale a chain-link fence before she could get to the roadway and the witnesses were sure that they would have seen this, even on the darkened street.

The young woman lurched forward quickly, as if she had started to run or had stumbled, and the driver slammed on the brakes. Convinced they were going to hit the girl, who had now run out into the middle of the road, they braced for the impact. Strangely, it never came. The young man in the passenger's seat said that he closed his eyes just before he expected the car to hit the girl and when he opened them, she wasn't there.

He asked his friend what had happened, had they hit the girl? His friend, shaken and out of breath, could barely reply: "We never hit her. She just wasn't there anymore. I never saw anything like it. She just disappeared."

The last Mary sighting for 1980 occurred just before Christmas. Two men saw a woman dancing in the middle of Archer, just east of Harlem Avenue, and they immediately knew that there was something odd going on. They watched the girl dance past them, even though other people who were around never seemed to notice that she was there. As strangely as she had come, the girl simply disappeared. Later that evening, they described the girl and the strange incident to the father of one of the young men. Neither of the boys was familiar with the story of Resurrection Mary but the older man was and he was convinced they had encountered the legendary phantom. He found out that, one week before the boys encountered her, Mary had been seen dancing outside the fence of Resurrection Cemetery.

During the weekend May 22, 1983, at least five different people saw Mary on Archer Avenue, near the Willowbrook Ballroom. One of them, a bartender at Johnny's Route 83, was traveling home after work on Friday night actually, early Saturday morning when she spotted a woman in a white dress. She was passing by Fairmont Hills Cemetery, just a little south of the ballroom, when she saw the woman dancing on the side of the road. There was really nothing too unusual about it, she later said, it was as if this young girl was just lost in her own world, listening to music that only she could hear. But what would a young woman be doing out on such a lonely stretch of road so late at night? The bartender drove past the girl and then turned around for another look. In the matter of seconds that it took her to turn her head, the girl in the white dress had vanished.

Another sighting that occurred that weekend took place closer to the ballroom. At that time, there was a bar located directly across the street, which was open until the early morning hours. According to a bar customer named Bill Hanning, he was leaving the place just after midnight on Saturday when he saw a girl in a white dress on the other side of Archer Avenue. He saw her hurry across the street from the Willowbrook and then start walking north up Archer Avenue. Wondering what a young girl would be doing walking by herself so late at night, Bill recalled that he walked to the edge of the parking lot and leaned out to watch her walk away. He remembered: "I had just watched her run across the street but in the few seconds that it took me to walk from my motorcycle to the edge of the road and look after her, she was gone. The side of the road was empty."

Bill was not familiar with the story of Resurrection Mary at that time but was sure that he had experienced something strange. He later heard about the stories when he mentioned the encounter to some friends. Many years later, he would recount this incident to me after hearing me speak about Mary at a local library. He vividly remembered the date of the sighting and was surprised when I told him that he was not the only one to see Mary around the Willowbrook Ballroom that weekend.

The next possible sighting occurred on an early Sunday morning in October 1983. Nancy Buck, a staff member at the Willowbrook Ballroom, had just gotten off work at about 1:30 a.m. and she and two co-workers walked out into the parking lot that adjoined the dance hall. They spotted a young, "strangely dressed" woman, who appeared to be in her early 20s, with blond hair, walking north along Archer Avenue. Whoever the woman was, she simply vanished without a trace.

Was this Resurrection Mary or simply some young woman out for the night around Halloween? None of the Willowbrook staff members could say for sure but this was not the first time that employees had experienced a similar incident. Two years before, also in mid-October, two of the waitresses at the ballroom saw a strange woman walking north on Archer Avenue. In that situation, the woman was dressed all in white and disappeared while the women were watching her. Staff members admitted that they had been on the lookout for the ghost ever since --- but had never really expected to see her.

And soon after, by the middle 1980s, the sightings began to fade. The stories were suddenly less frequent than they had once been and Mary was no longer being seen in the bars and dance halls along Archer Avenue. She no longer danced by the side of the road or ran out in front of passing cars. Yes, there were still encounters with a mysterious figure into the 1990s, and even today, but authentic encounters with the spirit are now few and far between.

Strangely, this is not the first time that Mary has disappeared from our consciousness. It happened before in the 1940s and she did not return again until the 1970s.

Based on the research that I've done over the years, I believe the first reports of Resurrection Mary came from the late spring of 1934. It was at this time that motorists on Archer Avenue, passing in front of Resurrection Cemetery, began telling of a young woman who would appear on the roadway, as if trying to hitch a ride. On some occasions, she became frantic as cars passed her by. Motorists told of a woman running toward them across the road, trying to climb onto the running boards of their automobiles and sometimes, even trying to climb into the open back windows. They all described her in the same way, wearing a light-colored dress and having curly, brown hair that reached to her shoulders.

What made matters worse is that many of the people in these automobiles, who were residents of Chicago's southwest side, actually recognized this young woman. Her name was Mary Bregovy and some of these motorists were her friends. They laughed with her, drank with her and often danced with her at their favorite spot, the Oh Henry Ballroom. Of course, that had been in the past because when they began seeing Mary trying to flag them down on Archer Avenue she had been dead for several weeks.

Of course, Mary Bregovy is not the only young woman who has been named as the identity of "Resurrection Mary" over the years. Even though most of the "Mary encounters" that I had collected were believable, they were also confusing and often contradictory. In one case, Mary would be a beautiful blond and in another, she would be a pretty, curly-haired brunette. Assuming that Mary was not a client at some otherworldly beauty salon, what was going on here? Could some of these people be mistaken? Was it really Mary they were encountering or some other ghost entirely?

The more that I researched the history of the case, the more convinced that I became that these motorists and witnesses really were encountering Resurrection Mary. The problem was that "Resurrection Mary" was actually more than one ghost. I have come to believe that the legend of Resurrection Mary has been created from two very different young women.

Over the years, there have been many who have searched for the earthly counterpart of Resurrection Mary and a number of candidates have emerged. Some are more likely than others. One of the options is Mary Duranski, who was killed in an auto accident in 1934. Another is a 12-year-old girl named Anna Norkus, who died in another tragic accident in 1936. That same year marked the date of another accident that some believe spawned Resurrection Mary. In this case, a farm truck collided with an automobile and three of the four passengers in the sedan were killed. One of the victims, a young woman, may have become

Resurrection Mary. Others believe Mary can be traced to an incident near Resurrection Cemetery that occurred in the 1940s. In this case, a young Polish girl had taken her father's car to meet her boyfriend in the early morning hours. She died in an accident and was buried in the nearby cemetery. Most believe this to be little more than a neighborhood cautionary tale told by protective parents, but it certainly adds another element to the legend.

It's possible that any one of these young women could still haunt Archer Avenue and may have contributed to the Resurrection Mary legend. However, I believe there that the majority of the sightings that have occurred can be connected to two young women who, ironically, lived only a few blocks away from one another in life.

You could say they have become "sisters" in death....

Mary Bregovy was twenty-one years old in March 1934. She had been born on April 7, 1912 and attended St. Michael's Grammar School, a short distance from her home. She lived in a small home at 4611 South Damen Avenue, which was in the Back of the Yards neighborhood of Bridgeport. She was of Polish descent and was employed at a local factory, where she worked hard to help support her mother, father and two younger brothers, Steve and Joseph, during the early days of the Great Depression.

Friends would later remember her as an extremely fun-loving girl who loved to go to parties and go out dancing, especially to the Oh Henry Ballroom, which was her favorite place. Her friend LaVern Rutkowski, who grew up with Mary and lived just two houses away from her, recalled in a 1984 interview: "She was personality plus. She always had a smile and you never saw her unhappy."

Mrs. Rutkowski, or "Vern" as she was commonly known, spent Mary's final day with her on March 10, 1934. The two of them spent a lot of time together and years later, Vern would vividly recall going out with Mary to dance halls all over the southwest side. Ironically, Mary's parents had forbidden her to go out on the night of March 10 and Mary might have listened to them if she and Vern had not met a couple of young men earlier that day. These two men, who are believed to have been John Reiker and John Thoel, were in the car that night when Mary was killed.

Mary and Vern spent that Saturday afternoon shopping at 47th Street and Ashland Avenue and it was in one of the stores located at the busy intersection that they met the two boys. After getting into their car to go for a ride, Vern took an instant dislike to them. She said: "They looked like wild boys and for some reason I just didn't like them." Vern was frightened that they drove recklessly, turning corners on two wheels and speeding down narrow streets. Finally, she demanded to be let out of the car a few blocks from home. She asked Mary if she planned to go out with the young men that night and Mary said that she did. Vern urged her to reconsider, not only because she didn't like the boys but also because Mary's parents had already told her that she couldn't fo out that night. Mary shrugged off her friend's warnings, saying: "You never like anyone I introduce you to."

Vern stood watching on the street corner as Mary and the young men roared away in the car. It was the last time that she would see her friend alive.

No one knows how Mary Bregovy spent the rest of the day but a few clues have emerged from family members over the years. The wife of Mary's younger brother, Steve, reported in 1985 that she had received a letter from a friend of Mary's years before that stated Mary planned to attend a novena at church before she went out dancing that night. The Bregovys were devout Catholics and this would not have been out of the ordinary for Mary to do. She also said that she believed Mary had been going to the Oh Henry Ballroom that night.

But did she ever arrive there? No one knows for sure but tradition holds that Mary and her new friends, who now included a young woman named Virginia Rozanski, did go dancing at the Oh Henry that night. After the ballroom closed, they drove into the city, where most of the clubs stayed open much later. In the early morning hours, they were leaving downtown, traveling along Wacker Drive, likely headed for Archer Avenue, which would take Mary home to Bridgeport, when the accident occurred. One has to wonder if alcohol, combined with the reckless driving described by Vern Rutkowski, combined to cause the crash.

A short piece in the March 11 edition of the *Chicago Tribune* described the accident:

Girl Killed in Crash

Miss Marie Bregovy, 21 years old, of 4611 South Damen Avenue, was killed last night when the automobile in which she was riding cracked up at Lake Street and Wacker Drive. John Reiker, 23, of 15 North Knight Street, Park Ridge, suffered a possible skull fracture and is in the county hospital. John Thoel, 25, 5216 Loomis Street, driver of the car, and Miss Virginia Rozanski, 22, of 4849 South Lincoln Street, were shaken up and scratched. The scene of the accident is known to police as a danger spot. Thoel told police he did not see the "L" substructure.

The accident occurred along Wacker Drive, just as it curves to the south and away from the Chicago River. At the point where Wacker crosses Lake Street, there is a large, metal support for the elevated tracks overhead. If a driver was coming along Wacker too quickly, it could be easy to not make a complete turn and collide with the support column, which is almost in a straight line around the curve. This is apparently what happened to John Thoel that night.

When the automobile collided with the metal column, Mary was thrown through the windshield and instantly killed. Her body was badly cut up by the glass. Before her funeral, the undertaker had to sew up a gash that extended all of the way across the front of her throat and up to her right ear. Tragically, Mary was not even supposed to be sitting in the front seat when the accident occurred. Her parents would later learn that she had switched places with Virginia Rozanski because Virginia didn't like John Thoel, who she had been sitting next to in the passenger's seat. She had asked Mary to sit in front with Thoel and Mary had agreed. Unfortunately, her good-natured personality would turn out to be fatal for her.

Vern Rutkowski accompanied Mary's mother and her brother, Joseph, to the morgue to identify the body. Mary was taken to the Satala Funeral Home, located just a couple of blocks from the Bregovy home, to be prepared for burial. The owner at the time, John Satala, easily remembered Mary. In 1985, he recalled: "She was a hell of a nice girl. Very pretty. She was buried in an orchid dress. I remember having to sew up the side of her face."

Mary was buried in Resurrection Cemetery and this is where some of the confusion about her story comes along. According to records, Mary was buried in Section MM, Site 9819. There was a Mary Bregovy buried here, but it was not the young woman who was killed in March 1934. A search for this gravesite revealed that the Mary Bregovy laid to rest here was a thirty-four-year-old woman who was born in 1888 and died in 1922. This is a different Mary Bregovy altogether. Family members of Mary Bregovy said that Mary was actually buried in a term grave and never moved. After World War II, when space was needed for more burial sites at Resurrection Cemetery, some of the term graves were moved but others, like Mary's, were simply covered over. For this reason, according to Mrs. Steve Bregovy, the location of Mary's grave is unknown - but she would not rest in peace.

In fact, the stories of Mary Bregovy's ghost began a very short time after her death. In April 1934, a caretaker at Resurrection Cemetery telephoned funeral home director John Satala and told him that he had seen the barefooted ghost of a young girl walking around the cemetery. She was a lovely girl with light brown hair and she was wearing a pale, orchid-colored dress. The caretaker was positive that the ghost was the woman that Satala had recently buried. Satala later said that he recognized the description of the girl as Mary Bregovy.

Soon after, other stories began to circulate, claiming that motorists on Archer Avenue in front of Resurrection Cemetery were encountering a frantic woman who tried to hitch a ride with them. These Archer Avenue sightings also included reports from people who actually recognized the ghost as Mary Bregovy.

I'm convinced that these reports were the beginning of the Resurrection Mary legend. These were the first stories of a young woman hitching rides on Archer Avenue and thanks to the destination of many of these motorists, combined with the fact that the Oh Henry Ballroom was Mary's favorite dance spot, the story began to grow. I believe that many of the reports of a ghostly woman being seen around Resurrection Cemetery can be traced to Mary Bregovy --- the "original Resurrection Mary."

But Mary Bregovy does not haunt this stretch of Archer Avenue alone...

Mary Bregovy may have started the legend of Resurrection Mary but she was not the only phantom haunting Archer Avenue and the area around it. As readers have likely realized, the stories of a "beautiful blond" don't physically match Miss Bregovy, who was certainly pretty, but definitely not a blond. She had naturally curly, brown hair, which means that she is not the same spirit who was so frequently being picked up by motorists and spotted on the side of the road.

However, thanks to a letter that I received in 2005 and the interviews that followed it , I believe that I may just have the identity of the second woman who has contributed to the legend of Resurrection Mary, who also may be the same woman encountered by a young man at the Liberty Grove & Hall in 1939.

Aside from the harried motorists who encountered Mary along Archer Avenue in the 1930s, there were those who came face to face with her under other conditions. One of these people was a young man named Jerry Palus. His experience with Mary took place in 1939 but would leave such an impression that he would never forget it until his death in 1992. Palus remained an unshakable witness and appeared on a number of television shows to discuss his night with Resurrection Mary. Regardless, he had little to gain from his story and no reason to lie. He never doubted the fact that he spent an evening with a ghost.

Palus met the young girl, who he described as a very attractive blond, at the Liberty Grove & Hall, a music and dancing venue that was near 47th Street and Mozart in the Brighton Park neighborhood. As it happens, this dance hall, which was a "jumping spot" on the city's southwest side for many years, was located not far from both of the homes of the women that I believe have created the "Resurrection Mary" legend. However, because of his description of the girl as an "attractive blond," I'm reasonably sure that I know who Jerry Palus met that night.

That night at the Liberty Grove & Hall, Jerry asked the girl to dance. He had been watching her for some time that evening, although he admitted in later interviews that he never saw her come into the place. She spent a couple of hours sitting by herself, since she didn't seem to know anyone, and Jerry finally gathered the courage to take her out onto the dance floor. The girl accepted his invitation and they spent several hours together. Strangely, though, she seemed a little distant and Palus also noticed that her skin was very cold, almost icy to the touch. When he later kissed her, he found her lips were also cold and clammy.

At the end of the evening, the young woman asked Jerry for a ride home. He readily agreed to give her a lift. When they got to his automobile, she explained that she lived on South Damen Avenue but that she wanted to take a ride down Archer Avenue first. Jerry shrugged and told her that he would be happy to take her wherever she wanted. By this time, he was infatuated with the girl and likely wanted to extend the night for as long as he could. He knew that it would be quite some distance out of the way to drive down Archer Avenue but he didn't mind, so he put his car into gear and drove off.

To reach Archer Avenue from the Liberty Grove & Hall, Jerry only had to travel west on 47th Street. Once he made it to the old roadway, they traveled southwest to Summit and then on to Justice. It was a dark, dimly lit road in those days but Jerry was somewhat familiar with the area, so he just followed the course of the road, heading eventually, he thought, towards Willow Springs.

But as they approached the gates to Resurrection Cemetery the girl asked him to pull over. She had to get out here, she told him. Jerry was confused, unable to understand why she would want to get out at such a spot, but he pulled the car to the side of the road anyway. He agreed that he would let her out, but only if she allowed him to walk her to wherever she was going. There was a row of houses to Jerry's right, about a block off Archer Avenue, and he assumed that she was going to one of them. He wanted to be sure that she made it there safely.

The beautiful young girl refused to allow this, though. She turned in her seat and faced Palus. She spoke softly: "This is where I have to get out, but where I'm going, you can't follow."

Jerry was bewildered by this statement, but before he could respond, the girl got out of the car and ran not in the direction of the houses but across Archer Avenue and toward the gates of Resurrection Cemetery. She vanished before she reached them -- right before Jerry's eyes. That was the moment when he knew that he had danced with a specter.

Determined to find out what was going on, Palus visited the address the girl had given him on the following day. The woman who answered the door told him that he couldn't possibly have been with her daughter the night before because her daughter had been dead for years. However, Palus was able to correctly identify the girl from a family portrait in the other room.

Needless to say, Jerry was stunned by this revelation but apparently, the address and identity of the woman were forgotten over the years. Some time later, when Palus was contacted again about his story when the passage of time had renewed interest in the elusive ghost he was unable to remember where he had gone on the day after his encounter. Despite this memory lapse, Palus' story remains one of the most credible of all of the Resurrection Mary encounters.

So, who was the blond woman that Jerry Palus danced with that night? I believe that she was a young woman named Mary Miskowski, a name that is a familiar one to Resurrection Mary buffs. There have been numerous brief mentions of her in ghostly literature, listing her as a possible candidate for the identity of the legendary ghost. Little has been known about her except for the fact that she was killed in October 1930 by a hit and run driver. She was allegedly crossing the street while on her way to a Halloween costume party.

In July 2005, I received a vague letter from a woman who promised me information about Resurrection Mary, claiming that the real-life counterpart of Mary had once been her mother's babysitter when she was a child. If I was interested, I could call her and get more information. Her mother was still alive and would be happy to speak with me about it.

I read the letter with interest but with a lot of skepticism too. This was not the first time that I received a letter of this sort but, out of curiosity, I decided to give the woman a call. She gave me a few details of the story and then gave me the telephone number of her mother, who was eighty-five years old, and urged me to contact her. The next afternoon, I called the number that she gave me and was soon speaking with Mrs. Martha Litak, who grew up on South Damen Avenue on Chicago's Southwest Side. I told her why I was calling and asked her what she could tell me about the story of Resurrection Mary.

Her answer surprised me. She laughed and said, "Resurrection Mary was my babysitter!"

According to Mrs. Litak, Mary Miskowski had lived down the street from her family when she was a child. Mary's house was located at 4924 South Damen Avenue interestingly, just three blocks away from Mary Bregovy, so it seems possible these two women could have known one another and she often watched neighborhood children to earn extra money. Mrs. Litak was not sure if Mary had a regular job or not. She lived with her parents but she was old enough to be out of school.

Martha did remember Mary very well: "She was a very pretty girl. She had light blond hair with just a little bit of curl to it. It was cut short, just a little below her ears. All of the boys in the neighborhood were in love with her. I do remember that she liked to go on dates but I don't recall that she had any one boyfriend in particular."

Martha remembered that her cousins told her that Mary loved to go out dancing, including to the Oh Henry Ballroom, which had opened in 1921. Her favorite place, though, was the Liberty Grove & Hall, which was located about twelve blocks from her home. I've since come to believe that Mary Miskowski was the ghost that Jerry Palus encountered at the dance hall that night. Mary certainly matched the description that Palus and many others have given over the years later gave of the young woman that he met and who vanished from his car in front of Resurrection Cemetery.

But this was not the only thing that convinced me.

Martha told me that she had spoken with her younger brother, Frank, after her daughter told her that I might get in touch. She had asked him if he could remember anything about their old babysitter, Mary Miskowski. Frank was only seven years old at the time Mary died but he did recall what she looked like. In fact, he remembered her very well because Frank believed that he saw Mary once night about ten years after she died! He was a young man at the time, out driving his first car on Archer Avenue. As he was driving north on the road, he saw a woman standing on the side of the road. He slowed down to take a look at her and as he did, the woman turned in his direction. He was stunned when he saw her face - it was his dead babysitter, Mary Miskowski! Frank slammed on his brakes and slid over to the side of the road. He looked frantically backward, but the woman was gone. In a matter of seconds, she had simply vanished. Frank was so shaken by the encounter that he didn't drive that particular stretch of Archer Avenue again for years.

According to newspaper accounts, like Martha Litak, Mary Miskowski had been killed by a hit and run driver in October 1930. A car had struck her as she was crossing 47th Street and had sped away. Whoever the driver was, he was never caught. Martha surmised that perhaps this incident was how the story got started about Resurrection Mary being run over by a car and left for dead on Archer Avenue. With the Oh Henry Ballroom, and later the Willowbrook, being so closely tied to the legend, she was not surprised that the accident had been moved to a location that was closer to the dance hall. Mrs. Litak also confirmed that Mary had been on her way to a costume party that night. She had been dressed as a bride, wearing her mother's old wedding dress. Martha didn't know what Mary had been buried in, but she did believe that perhaps the white dress that so many people reported Resurrection Mary wearing could have been this dress from the early 1900s.

Mrs. Litak further connected Mary Miskowski to the legend by adding that she had been buried in Resurrection Cemetery. I have been unable to confirm this but Martha and Frank were both sure this was the case. They told me that she had been buried in a term grave just like Mary Bregovy but she did not know the ultimate location of the site.

If any of this is accurate, it may explain the Resurrection Mary encounters that don't match the description and behavior of Mary Bregovy. Could the presence of Mary Miskowski explain the sightings of a pretty, blond phantom who hangs out in dance halls and vanishes from cars? And could she be the ghost who is seen running across the road in front of the cemetery where she is buried, perhaps re-enacting her final moments over and over again as she is stuck by a passing automobile?

I think it's possible, perhaps even likely. It's a fascinating and compelling story --- compelling enough that it prompted my theory that Resurrection Mary is not just one ghost, but two, or maybe even more.

But why did the stories of Resurrection Mary fade in the 1940s, only to be revived with such intensity in the 1970s? It was three decades after the stories waned that Resurrection Cemetery began undergoing major renovations, including the movement of the term graves that had been in place for so many years. Some of the graves were moved to other locations, while others, according to the relatives of some who had loved ones buried in the cemetery, were reportedly bulldozed under the earth. It's believed that this disturbance may have been what caused the frequency of sightings to increase so drastically in the 1970s. But once the work was finished, the sightings began to peter out again, just as then had done years before.

So, who is Mary and does she really exist?

I believe that she does and I also believe that we know the identities of at least two of the women who have created her enduring legend. But there are many other theories that also exist. Mary Bregovy and Mary Miskowski may be just two of the candidates for Resurrection Mary, and there may be many more.

Does she really exist? Many still remain doubtful about her, but I have found that their skepticism doesn't really seem to matter. Whether these people believe in her or not, people saw and in some cases are still seeing Mary walking along Archer Avenue at night. Motorists still stopped to pick up a forlorn young woman who seemed inadequately dressed on cold winter nights, when encounters seemed to be the most prevalent. Even today, curiosity-seekers still come to see the gates where the twisted and burned bars were once located and some even roam the graveyard, hoping to stumble across the place where Mary's body was laid to rest.

We still don't know for sure who she really was but that has not stopped the stories and even songs about her. She remains an enigma and her legend lives on, not content to vanish, as Mary does when she reaches the gates to Resurrection Cemetery. You see, our individual belief, or disbelief, does not really matter. Mary lives on anyway --- a mysterious, elusive and romantic spirit of the American night.

BIBLIOGRAPHY

Bruce, H. Addington - *Historic Ghosts and Ghost Hunters*, 1908
Anson, Jay - *The Amityville Horror*, 1977
Asbury, Herbert - *The French Quarter*, 1936
Aykroyd, Peter - *A History of Ghosts*, 2009
Birnes, William & Joel Martin - *The Haunting of America*, 2009
Blum, Deborah - *Ghost Hunters*, 2006
Brandon, Ruth - *The Spiritualists*, 1983
Brown, Slater - *The Heyday of Spiritualism*, 1970
Chambers, Paul - *Paranormal People*, 1998
Christopher, Milbourne & Maurine - *Illustrated History of Magic*, 1976
Clarke, Robert -- *Spirits & Spirit Worlds*, 1975
Coates, James - *Photographing the Invisible*, 1921
Crowe, Catherine - *The Night Side of Nature*, 1854
Darkis, Fred R., Jr. - "Madame Lalaurie of New Orleans", *Louisiana History*, Fall 1982
deLavigne, Jeanne - *Ghost Stories of Old New Orleans*, 1946
Doyle, Sir Arthur Conan - *Edge of the Unknown*, 1930
------------------------------ - *History of Spiritualism*, 1926
Evans, Henry Ridgely - *The Spirit World Unmasked*, 1902
Guiley, Rosemary Ellen - *Encyclopedia of Ghosts and Spirits*, 2000
Haining, Peter - *Ghosts: The Illustrated History*, 1987
Hall, Trevor - *The Medium and the Scientist*, 1984
--------------- - *The Spiritualists*, 1962
Horowitz, Mitch - *Occult America*, 2009

Houdini, Harry - *A Magician Among the Spirits*; 1924
Jackson, Jr., Herbert G. - *The Spirit Rappers*; 1972
Jolly, Martyn - *Faces of the Living Dead;* 2006
Kaplan, Dr. Stephen & Roxanne Salch Kaplan - *The Amityville Horror Conspiracy*; 1995
Love, Victoria Cosner and Lorelei Shannon - *Mad Madame Lalaurie*; 2011
Lynott, Douglas B. - The Real Amityville Horror; 2001
Maskelyne, John Nevil - *Modern Spiritualism;* 1876
McHargue, Georgess - *Facts, Frauds and Phantasms*; 1972
Melechi, Antonio - *Servants of the Supernatural;* 2008
Miller, R. DeWitt - *Forgotten Mysteries*; 1947
Moore, L. - *In Search of White Crows*; 1977
Mulholland, John - *Beware Familiar Spirits*; 1938
Northrop, Suzane - *The Séance*; 1944
Pearsall, Ronald - *The Table Rappers*; 1972
Permutt, Cyril - *Photographing the Spirit World*; 1983
Picknett, Lynn - *Flights of Fancy*; 1987
Price, Harry - *Confessions of a Ghost Hunter*; 1936
---------------- - *End of Borley Rectory*; 1946
---------------- - *Haunting at Cashen's Gap*; 1936
---------------- - *Poltergeist over England*; 1945
---------------- - *Search for Truth*; 1942
---------------- - *The Most Haunted House in England*; 1940
Rawcliffe, D.H. - *The Psychology of the Occult*; 1952
Reader's Digest Books - *Into the Unknown*; 1981
Saxon, Lyle and Robert Tallant and Edward Dreyer - *Gumbo Ya-Ya*; 1945
Slaughter, April - *Reaching Beyond the Veil*; 2013
Somerlott, Robert - *Here, Mr. Splitfoot*; 1971
Stashower, Daniel - *Teller of Tales: Life of Sir Arthur Conan Doyle*; 1999
Stein, Gordon - *The Sorcerer of Kings*; 1993
Steinour, Harold - *Exploring the Unseen World;* 1959
Stevens, E. Winchester - *The Watseka Wonder*; 1879
Tabori, Paul - *Harry Price: Biography of a Ghost Hunter*; 1950
Taylor, Troy - *And Hell Followed with It* & Rene Kruse ; 2011
---------------- - *The Devil Came to St. Louis*; 2006
---------------- - *Ghost Hunter's Guidebook*; 2010
---------------- - *Ghosts by Gaslight*; 2007
---------------- - *Haunted Illinois*; 2008
---------------- - *Haunted New Orleans*; 2010
---------------- - *The Haunted President;* 2009

--------------- - *Haunting of America*, 2010
--------------- - *Hell Hath No Fury: Legacy of Evil*, 2012
--------------- - *The Possessed*, 2007
--------------- - *Resurrection Mary*, 2006
Von Schrenck Notzing, Baron - *Phenomena of Materialization* 1923 English Edition
Walker, Mark - *Ghost Masters*, 1991
Weisberg, Barbara - *Talking to the Dead*, 2004
Wicker, Christine - *Lily Dale*, 2003

Personal Interviews & Correspondence

Special Thanks to:
Jill Hand - Editor
April Slaughter - Cover Design & Advice

The Family:
Rene Kruse
Rachael Horath
Elyse & Thomas Reihner
Bethany & Jim McKenzie
Orrin Taylor
Haven & Helayna Taylor

John Winterbauer
Ginger Collins Justus
Misty Taylor
Hannah Gray
Lisa Taylor Horton   & Lux

"I don't suppose you have to believe in ghosts to know that we are all haunted, all of us, by things we can see and feel and guess at, and many more things that we can't."
— Beth Gutcheon

ABOUT THE AUTHOR: TROY TAYLOR

Troy Taylor is an occultist, crime buff, supernatural historian and the author of more than 100 books on ghosts, hauntings, history, crime and the unexplained in America. He is also the founder of the American Hauntings Tour company. When not traveling to the far-flung reaches of the country in search of the unusual, Troy resides part-time in Decatur, Illinois.

See Troy's other titles at: **www.whitechapelpress.com**

www.ingramcontent.com/pod-product-compliance
Lightning Source LLC
Chambersburg PA
CBHW070958160426
43193CB00012B/1827